The Novels of
NADINE
GORDIMER

The Novels of

NADINE GORDIMER

History from the Inside

Stephen Clingman

Second Edition
The University of Massachusetts Press
Amherst

Library of Congress Cataloging-in-Publication Data

Clingman, Stephen.

    The novels of Nadine Gordimer : history from the inside / Stephen
Clingman. — 2nd ed.

      p. cm.

    Includes bibliographical references and index.

    ISBN 0–87023–802–7 (pbk. : alk. paper)

    1. Gordimer, Nadine—Criticism and interpretation. 2. South
Africa in literature. 3. Literature and history. 4. History in
literature. I. Title.

PR9369.3.G6Z62   1992

823–dc20   92–4691

                                                    CIP

British Library Cataloguing in Publication data are available.

To my parents

It is easier to write a history of matter than of consciousness.

Fredric Jameson, *Marxism and Form*

Contents

A pilot study for this book appeared as 'History from the inside: the novels of Nadine Gordimer', *Journal of Southern African Studies*, vol. 7, no. 2 (April 1981), pp. 165–93. A version of Chapter 2 appeared as 'Multi-racialism, or *A World of Strangers*', *Salmagundi*, no. 62 (Winter 1984), pp. 32–61. Part of Chapter 7 first appeared as 'Writing in a fractured society: the case of Nadine Gordimer', in L. White and T. Couzens (eds.), *Literature and Society in South Africa* (London: Longman, 1984), pp. 161–74. My thanks to Peter Warwick of Longman for permission to use this material.

Prologue

That truth is not all the truth
My Son's Story

Looking back on a book published six years ago can induce a strange sense of parallax: things are true and not true at the same time. Or, is it because one is seeing them at different times that the nature of their respective truths appears different, though these truths may overlap? A changing present affects our view of the past, and there is always the temptation to go back and change, make everything 'fit'. Yet, the temptation offers its own self-contradictory awareness: that the quest for finality can never be fulfilled. Perhaps the deeper truth lies in the sense of parallax itself.

That is one reason why, except for the addition of this new Prologue, nothing has been altered in the book, even though, on occasion, there may be things that I feel could be textured in different ways or changed. The fact is that this book was written from a specific time and setting with a particularly unified vision, and it may be wiser to allow that to come through. Indeed, it seems appropriate that a study that explores Gordimer's historical consciousness should speak so definitely from its own moment. What the text says reflects on its own awareness as much as on the object of its reflections: this is a hermeneutic principle now embodied in my book two ways, and of course it applies to this Prologue as well.

At the same time there are compelling contexts for a new edition. There is the fact that in October 1991 Nadine Gordimer was awarded the Nobel Prize for Literature. This was undoubtedly a moment for joyous celebration. Gordimer is the first South African, the third African, and the first woman in twenty-five years to win the prize. The award seemed due recognition for the sustained quality of her work over nearly half a century, for the rigour and prophetic nature of her vision, the authority of her presence as a writer, and the formal and technical mastery of her writing. Coming as it did with the apparent ending of apartheid, it was another kind of vindication: of the triumph of art over oppression, of the ethics of writing in the context of evil, of baring the truths of the present and imagining alternative futures. Pleasure at the announcement, therefore, was instantaneous and virtually universal.

In making the award, the Nobel committee recognized, in its own due and reasonable time, what many already knew. For years Gordimer's work has attracted an ever-increasing body of admirers, readers who value her writing for its artistry and its extraordinary insight into the inner life of South Africa. With these readers in mind, plans for a new edition of this book, incorporating a new Prologue, had been under way for some time before the award was announced.

The reasons are straightforward. First, since 1986, there have been extraordinary changes in the South African historical setting, and the country has reached a critical new stage. Second, during these years Gordimer has written two novels – *A Sport of Nature* and *My Son's Story* – that have both anticipated these changes and responded to them, indicating significant developments in her fiction. Third, partly as a consequence of both of these changes, my own perspectives have shifted, as it now becomes possible to see the world of Gordimer's fiction in the altering light of these transformations.

There is a final reason for a reconsideration: that, while enjoying this double moment of the apparent fall of apartheid and the acclamation of Gordimer's fiction, we should not be overwhelmed by a sense of triumph. We have not, to paraphrase the view currently being touted in some quarters, reached the end of history, neither in the global context nor in South Africa. Indeed, the profound transformations of the last few years, in the Soviet Union and Eastern Europe, together with those in South Africa, should be enough of a clue that history may take unpredictable turns and that there is no reason to believe we may now ease off for all eternity into some metaphorical neutral gear. Similarly, Nadine Gordimer has expressed some surprise that anyone should think the ending of apartheid will mean there is nothing left to write about in South Africa.[1] There is, and will be, much to write about, but it will take on different forms, different shapes. Some of those shapes are already

1 'The Future Is Another Country', conversation with Stephen Clingman, *Transition* 56, n.s. vol. 2, no. 2 (1992), pp. 132–50

apparent in Gordimer's two most recent novels: sufficient reason for addressing them here. It would, in fact, be extraordinarily demeaning to Gordimer's fiction to believe that since apartheid is over there is no urgency in what it says.

So if this is an 'update', it is of a particular kind. The original body of the work will remain unchanged, for the reasons given above. Yet the idea is to focus in this Prologue on Gordimer's recent writing in order to suggest where it stands now. In this way we shall be able as well to think about South African history, as it seems now to be poised on the cusp between an apartheid and a post-apartheid world, and about South African literature and culture in this setting. In this sense a new Prologue carries its own 'inner history' as it both explores and embodies the parallax I mentioned: examining Gordimer's new novels on the basis of past patterns and insights, but also allowing new positions and perspectives to alter our sense of those patterns. The idea is to set this Prologue in dialogue – a term that will take on increased significance in what follows – with the remainder of the book. Having 'closed' my study some years ago, it seems right now to 'open' it up again to reconsideration, and perhaps indicate that the sense of closure itself is illusory.

This kind of Prologue must necessarily be written as an 'afterword'. Reading it first might cast the rest of the book in an intriguing light, as if looking back on a view of the past from yet a new observation point in the present. At the same time, some of the points in this discussion will only take on their full significance in the light of issues and symbolic fields explored in the original study. For that reason I would suggest that, if it makes sense and appears worthwhile, readers either postpone the remainder of the Prologue until they have finished the book, or else return to look at it again afterwards so that they can, in their own way, both complete and open up its narrative.

Presents and Futures

Perhaps we should think of presents and futures, since this will be central to everything that follows.

In October 1989, as a group of African National Congress leaders headed by Walter Sisulu was freed from prison in South Africa, a process began in reality that had been prophesied in *The Conserva-*

tionist, envisioned apocalyptically in *July's People,* and announced with jubilation in *A Sport of Nature.* In February 1990 the seal seemed set on that process, as Nelson Mandela was released from prison and the ANC and South Africa's other previously illegal organizations were unbanned. South Africa had begun to enter the future that had been heralded and dreamed of for so long, a future that would mean the end of apartheid. The jubilation seemed to carry with it the release of generations of pent-up political emotion. It was like being born into a new world.

And yet, no sooner had this world been entered than it began to seem a perhaps more complex place than expected. The immediate past would not disappear overnight. The legacies of apartheid – political, economic, cultural, the disastrous states of education and housing – these could not and would not be transformed by one heady moment of magic. Perhaps apartheid would in some sense be reinvented, if not in legalistic terms then in other social and economic forms. And what of the politics of nationalism and ethnicity, now resurrected not only on the far right of the white political spectrum – as dangerously as might be expected – but also by Gatsha Buthelezi's Inkatha movement? The whites-only referendum on reform of March 1992 indicated how narrow a line South Africa was walking. But even before these issues had time to sink in with any force, an amorphous feeling had entered into the heady moment itself. 'Somewhere between November 1989 and February 1990,' writes Nicholas Visser, 'South Africa's future changed.'[2]

There are ways of specifying what he means. Before that moment – and infusing the everyday world of oppression, resistance, survival – at a level of symbolic and allegorical imagining, 'the future' had become an almost tangible presence in South Africa. For those on the right, revolution would bring total disaster, the end of the world; on the left, the moment of victory would be climactic, leaving a permanent afterglow as South Africa transcended into a mythic world of liberation. The textures of this imagining were apocalyptic and final: this was a moment one did not need to or could not think beyond. Indeed, the future became such a dominating presence in the South African imagination that it left a profound imprint on South African fiction. Gordimer, J. M. Coetzee, Mongane

2 Nicholas Visser, 'The Politics of Future Projection in South African Fiction', MLA paper 1990, forthcoming in *Bucknell Review,* vol. 37, no. 1 (Spring 1993).

Serote, and others – albeit in different ways – set their work in the revolutionary moment, or else were drawn to address it in other forms.[3] Yet on 'the day after', so to speak, what became apparent was that South Africa was in the land not of one 'future' but of *many possible futures*. How they worked out, what was to come of and be done in them, these were the essence of new problems and new kinds of awareness. Questions of the future suddenly devolved from the allegoric to the realistic level as time became visible in a new perspective. Just as the moment of transformation had not arrived 'complete' and had a prehistory of 'interregnum' leading up to it, so too might that interregnum continue afterwards. Instead of the realm of myth, this was the land of reality, and it was a reality both unknown and strangely familiar.

And yet, is it entirely true to say that South African fiction had not in some form anticipated and addressed this 'other world'? Coetzee's *Life & Times of Michael K* suggested strongly that the discourses of 'oppression' and 'liberation' were mutually interdependent and that a third way had to be found out of both of them. Gordimer's work has always been tied much more urgently than Coetzee's to the idea of political obligation and responsibility; it has also been deeply compelled, as I suggest in Chapter 7, by the imagined presence and demands of the future. Yet I would say that within the apparently idealized and allegorical summoning of the future in *A Sport of Nature* and the very politicality of *My Son's Story* there are other kinds of stories being told, and internal divisions within the novels that are of the greatest significance for the shape of a post-apartheid politics and culture. It is these that I want to follow up.

This study in its original form placed great emphasis on internal 'splits' in Gordimer's novels and indicated how crucial they were for a sense of her historical consciousness. What I want to do here is take up again that idea of division, and show how it suggests a next stage in the 'inner history' of her fiction. In doing this, I shall use only the broadest of strokes, suggesting rather than analyzing exhaustively where that history may be found. We need to look at those areas where theme emerges from the deep structures of the novels, where certain themes dictate certain structures. In the case of *A Sport of*

---

3 See Stephen Clingman, 'Revolution and Reality: South African Fiction in the 1980s', in Martin Trump (ed.), *Rendering Things Visible: Essays on South African Literary Culture* (Johannesburg: Ravan Press, 1990), pp. 41–60.

Nature this means thinking about 'bodily histories', and in *My Son's Story* about questions of transition, liminality, 'in-betweenness', built into the novel itself.

A Sport of Nature

In *A Sport of Nature* the dialectical pattern of Gordimer's novels continues. At the end of *July's People* Maureen reaches a harmony of body and mind as she 'runs with all the suppressed trust of a lifetime'. Yet her running at the end is surrounded by a mood of ambiguity: is she running from or towards? The apocalyptic moment brings with it an anxiety of crossing to the future. In *A Sport of Nature* that harmony of body and mind returns, indeed is complete, in Hillela; but the anxiety drops away: living in bodily fulfilment in the present, hers is a positive compulsion towards the world that is to come.

There is no need to begin elsewhere than with the obvious: we must consider the figure of Hillela, because all presentiments of the novel's historical consciousness will at the least be found here. The essential point regarding Hillela is that she is presented, throughout *A Sport of Nature,* as the 'organic body' – organic in that body and mind are in total harmony and seem to be uncomplicated extensions of one another.[4] Indeed, if anything, in Hillela's case consciousness appears to come from the body, and not the other way round. As her cousin Sasha and others begin to understand, she has a 'bodily intelligence', and there seems almost to be a philosophy of the body embedded in her. Like her mother before her, Hillela might say in both pre- and post-Cartesian fashion, 'I'm all over my body.'[5] It seems to be this that takes her beyond imposed limitations or frameworks, just as the body in its essence always moves just beyond the edges or categories of thought.

This is accentuated in the novel by Hillela's deeply sexualized identity in the world. As critics have noted with varying degrees of

4 For a more extensive analysis of *A Sport of Nature,* on which this account draws, see Stephen Clingman, '*A Sport of Nature* and the Boundaries of Fiction', in Bruce King (ed.), *The Later Fiction of Nadine Gordimer* (London: Macmillan, 1992).
5 Nadine Gordimer, *A Sport of Nature* (London: Cape; New York: Knopf; Cape Town: David Philip, 1987), p. 62. All further page references, to the Cape edition, are given in the text.

amazement, Hillela seems to give the term 'sexual politics' whole new dimensions of meaning. And it is fundamentally a sexualized drive that engenders her almost unconscious compulsion to transgression, as she crosses one boundary after another, escaping the world of apartheid in all its blatant and more subtle manifestations, and entering, in a precise sense, an unlimited world and identity. This is the basic pattern that underlies all her movements and attachments, from her first, casual relationship with a 'coloured' boy at school in Rhodesia, to her expulsion from her aunts' houses in Johannesburg, to her life in Tanzania and then West Africa with the French ambassador and his wife, to her marriage and commitment to Whaila, to her travels in Eastern Europe, America, and then, finally, back to Africa and her second husband, the General. The climactic scene of the novel, the celebration of South Africa's liberation, is written as a sexualized moment, and on one level the analogy is clear: sexuality is an unlimiting bodily drive beyond categories, analogous to the political drive to liberation.

That Gordimer is interested in the organic body is indicated both by contrast and by equation in the novel. Her cousin Sasha, whose real name is Alexander, bears his nickname as his identity, like a character from a nineteenth-century Russian novel. More to the point, like many of the disaffected youthful male figures of prerevolutionary Russian fiction, Sasha for much of the novel is the archetypal 'useless man' – a figure deeply aware of oppression and injustice, but also, agonizingly, of his own impotence and irrelevance. For the most part he exists in a world of paralyzed 'mentality', in which his consciousness of his own irony feeds off and circles on itself endlessly (compounded in his case by psychological complications in relation to his mother). Where Hillela is bodily and light, Sasha is self-conscious and grave, susceptible to threatening intimations from both without and within: after the two have made love, it is he who wakes up to the sound of a flapping window in the house. As this suggests, for Sasha boundaries mark areas of containment, vulnerability, or threat. He ends up in 'solitary confinement' in prison, subject to 'sensory deprivation' (almost impossible to imagine as a state of being for Hillela). The letters he writes, both outside and inside prison, are either never sent or never delivered, never crossing the space, so to speak, from one world to another.[6] It is true

6   For a Lacanian analysis of this, see Linda Weinhouse, 'The Deconstruction of

that Sasha engages with many of the ethical and philosophical concerns of the novel, and in that sense is a figure of real pathos; but it is
also true that he cannot go where Hillela can – not into the future
with her bodily instinct.

Hillela's first husband, Whaila, however, is represented in vividly
physical terms, 'pure hardness against the dissolving light' (p. 164).
Though he does not lack interiority, even this has a hardened and
brilliant physicality to it, with his 'spirit resistant and brain bright as
obsidian' (p. 236). Clearly, physicality is fundamental to resistance
against oppression, and part of the logic of the body in the novel
emerges in Whaila. He also, in this phase when resistance has been
transformed into an accumulating momentum towards liberation,
understands that the physicality of an armed struggle is inescapable – though some of the most agonized discussions between him
and Hillela have to do with issues of violence. Whaila dies by violence in the novel, gunned down by agents of the apartheid regime
in Lusaka: the price of bodily politics is clear. Yet it is because of an
almost physical loyalty that Hillela's commitment deepens and continues. When Whaila was alive, she would inspect the minutiae of his
body with wonder and love. Now, in the wake of his death, the path
that opens up to her, partly through chance, partly through trauma,
and partly through the necessity of her nature, is to ethicize her
own inner politics by transforming them in social terms. This she
does through her continuing commitment to Whaila's body, and the
world that it stood for, after he has been killed.

How do these associations fit together, and why should the 'organic body' be at the centre of Gordimer's preoccupations? If we
think back to her previous novels we see that each of her characters
has searched for this kind of unity with varying degrees of success,
and that always it is involved with a larger political context. Helen
Shaw, in *The Lying Days,* struggles to achieve it in the world of a
newly enforced apartheid. Toby Hood, in *A World of Strangers,*
catches glimpses in relation to the vibrant world of the black townships. For Jessie Stilwell, in *Occasion for Loving,* the possibility of
organic wholeness implodes with the collapse of a liberal framework. Liz Van Den Sandt (*The Late Bourgeois World*), Rosa Burger
(*Burger's Daughter*), and Maureen Smales (*July's People*) are three

Victory: Gordimer's *A Sport of Nature*', *Research in African Literatures,* vol. 21, no. 2
(Summer 1990), pp. 91–100.

female figures who find climactic moments of organic unity in crises of political decision – though the implications for each are different, marked by their different historical moments. For Bray, in *A Guest of Honour,* organic unity is cut off by death, while Mehring, who desires it most desperately in *The Conservationist,* could not be further from it in his own complicity as a bastion of apartheid. In *A Sport of Nature,* however, it is fully achieved and present in Hillela from beginning to end.

Some of the symbolic reasons for this may be evident. Conceptually, insofar as Hillela represents an evolutionary principle – as the genetic 'sport of nature' holding the key to the future – this must be registered primarily in the body, and then, as a consequence, in terms of consciousness, for this is our basic measure of evolution: a new state of body and mind. But that begs the question of why she needs to be a 'sport of nature' in the first place. As the novel intimates, where apartheid has divided according to the body, only the whole body can be a sign of reintegration: 'Skin and hair. It has mattered more than anything else in the world' (p. 206). There is no understanding the full enormity of apartheid like that which is impacted in the body. In this sense it is through her own body that Hillela is identified with the black world, not only in her love for and marriage with Whaila, but also in his violent death. As she is hit by the refrigerator door, Hillela feels the impact of the bullet even in the instant that she is saved. But she loses the second child in her womb, Whaila's death a living bodily shock inside her being. It is then as his living partner that she comes to reclaim a liberated South Africa at the end of the novel.

Insofar as the organic body establishes its own, inner, imperative teleology of liberation, the white body – at last in Gordimer's fiction – realizes a form of political necessity corresponding to that of blacks in South Africa. From that point of view there is a major turn in *A Sport of Nature.* In *The Conservationist* it was the improperly buried black body that returned at the end of the novel to claim the land. In *A Sport of Nature* the white figure is at last one with that body, returning in a sense to claim it with and for him. (It is perhaps no accident that it is a female figure, for the earlier novel showed how the hierarchies of apartheid were inseparable from Mehring's definition of sexual supremism.) If this marks out new possibilities in the South Africa of the 1980s, then it also occurs against the backdrop of a symbolic field already established in Gordimer's fiction. In contrast to *The Conservationist*, Hillela is one with the repressed black world; the subjective analogue of this is the redeemed identity, the unrepressed unconscious whose subjective reality can only be the organic body. Indeed, Hillela is Gordimer's first central character not to be subject to a 'return of the repressed', because she is identical with it.

And this allows other splits in Gordimer's fiction to be resolved – for instance, between nature and history, and between a 'white' and an 'African' identity.[7] In that light, the organic body becomes a sign of oneness with the African continent, the ultimate scene of Hillela's ranging operations. Unlike Bray in *A Guest of Honour*, Hillela is able to achieve an identification with Africa and *live:* clearly a more optimistic moment has arrived. From all these points of view Gordimer is extending a specific symbolic logic she has developed in her novels. And here it has allowed her to register an ontological claim: that in its non-recognition of imposed limitations, the organic body identifies with a revolutionary drive.

A Sport of Nature has given critics a good deal of trouble. Is the ending of the novel merely a sign of wish fulfilment, tacked on in contravention of the guidelines of both aesthetic taste and political realism? Is Hillela's progress, as she moves from man to man, and from one level of power to the next, an index of her sexual liberation, or of Gordimer's own submission to encompassing patriarchal rules? What, in fact, are the rules for reading this novel, which seems to shift so unashamedly from realism to political fantasy?[8] This reading shows that we have to understand the novel in the light of previous patterns in Gordimer's fiction. It also suggests that looking to the novel for forms of realism or any other expected representations is misguided. For instance, outside of her fiction, Gordimer has frequently disclaimed any primary commitment to feminism. And, though issues of gender obviously enter into the novel, this is not her primary concern in *A Sport of Nature*, for all her preoccupation with Hillela's sexuality. For specific symbolic and historical reasons Gordimer has been drawn to the code of the body, and it is this code she is exploring in the novel – which in a sense establishes the mixed and complex genre in which the book has been written.

7 See Chapter 7 for a fuller discussion.
8 See Diane Johnson, 'Living Legends', *New York Review of Books*, 16 July 1987, p. 9.

Prologue

It is a code explicated in part by Sasha's understanding. When he hears that Hillela has married Whaila, Sasha knows that this is not some cheap attempt to overcome the barriers of apartheid through sex or transcendent love, but in a letter to his mother he identifies the fundamental drive of the organic body:

> Reformers are . . . totally rational, but the dynamic of real change is always utopian . . . Instinct is utopian. Emotion is utopian. But reformers can't imagine *any other way.* They want to adapt what is . . . Don't you see? It's all got to come down, mother. Without utopia – the idea of utopia – there's a failure of the imagination.

(pp. 217–18)

In exploring the code of Hillela's (r)evolutionary body, Gordimer has imagined the utopian drive. And in doing so, she extends its allegories in unexpected directions. For in her utopian guise Hillela represents not only the 'organic body' but in a sense the 'resurrected body' as well. There are in fact allusions to resurrection dotted throughout the novel, and nowhere more significantly than in the case of Hillela herself. To be precise: allegorically, Hillela proceeds from parthenogenesis (her 'unknown' parents), to life as the organic body, through death (Whaila's, which she feels as her own) and resurrection (her resuscitated afterlife alone and with the General) to political Paradise – a liberated South Africa. In many respects Hillela can be seen as the incarnation of a transcendental archetype: when she marries the General she is thirty-three years old, the age of Christ at his death and resurrection. Yet it is not a spiritual paradise she offers – 'utopia' or 'no place' in the usual sense – but a secular, politicized version of wholeness, completeness, liberation.

Imagining the political drive towards utopia: it is a defining aspect of the historical consciousness of the novel. On one level we might say that it corresponds to the rising climacteric of the 1980s in South Africa, which was characterized by a sustained, bodily drive towards revolution. In the townships, in the streets, in the unions and mass organizations, in the innumerable 'bodies' and groups that proliferated (Sasha writes that South Africa had become a country of acronyms), there was a real sense of a physical resistance to power, and for some whites in Gordimer's position it meant a renewed form of participation. In the same way that the organic body does not recognize imposed limitations, this drive was in its most undiluted form, in Sasha's words, 'to overthrow the State' (p. 365) – to transform radically the entire framework of everything that existed. It was in some sense a quest for utopia, and it led, by the turn of the decade, to the situation we have already mentioned: the unbanning of the ANC and other organizations, and the vision of the end of apartheid.

And yet: in encoding this dynamic in the innermost structures of her novel, Gordimer also registers a degree of doubt or division in relation to it. For if the organic body is not subject to conventional limitation, then it is also not primarily an ethical principle; indeed, it can be fundamentally ambiguous. Towards the beginning of the work Sasha and Hillela are reading *The Brothers Karamazov*, which in the legend of the Grand Inquisitor contains one of literature's most profound dialogues between pure, utopian virtue on the one hand and the realities of worldly politics on the other. In Dostoevsky's novel the figure of Christ is the ultimate 'organic body': though he says not a word, the luminosity of his presence speaks intimately and overwhelmingly of a higher truth to the Inquisitor. Yet the essence of the Inquisitor's response is that worldly authority – precisely because it has an ultimate 'good' in mind – must make do with worldly ethics and practices; that it must enter into contract with what the General in *A Sport of Nature* calls 'the currencies of power' (p. 356).

And there is a sustained dialogue in *A Sport of Nature* on the question of power and its transactions – registered chiefly through the figure of the General who gains relatively virtuous ends for his country through compromised and mercenary means. The General is militaristic, macho, and dynastic; his view of power is that 'you get there with guns and you stay there with money' (p. 310). Even his name, Reuel ('Rue', 'Rule', 'Royal', and, in Hebrew, 'friend of God') sounds like an ironic commentary suggesting an ambiguous pathway to paradise. He jokingly refers to the presidency he has regained (after having lost it to betrayal the first time) as 'the Second Empire': this is a form of bodily resurrection, to be sure, but it is a Bonapartist reversion nonetheless. Certainly the General has learned from the disasters of utopian socialism in Africa, and the economy he resuscitates is 'mixed'; but there is no doubt that his political ethics, too, are 'mixed'.

Even Hillela's organic body is in that sense not the same as that of Dostoevsky's Christ. Indeed, from one point of view her sexuality becomes the very emblem of worldly ambiguity: even as she transgresses boundaries Hillela always negotiates and comes to terms with the realities of power, both political and patriarchal. This is the sine qua non of her advancement in the world: at some level, it is clear, Gordimer has accepted 'political mortality' – the historical nature, so to speak, of the 'fallen' and not transcendent body, and embedded it in her novel. The drive may be utopian, the novel seems to suggest, but you have to work in and through the real world.

And yet the ironies begin to accumulate to the point where they became an insistent presence. The phrase that everyone uses of Hillela – 'trust her' – allows of variable tones, ranging from acceptance of her essential integrity to an ironic perception of her ability to look after herself and get ahead. Hillela's child, Nomo – named for Winnie Mandela – goes to Bedales and becomes a fashion model. When the moment of freedom finally arrives, it is Hillela's cousin Clive – who had by no means been alien to the advantages of apartheid while they existed – who has been invited to serve on a Ministry of Agriculture Commission under the new regime. (With an eye ever on profit he has also provided, with the assistance of Afrikaner and Indian capital, the liberation T-shirts the jubilant crowd is wearing.)[9] Even Sasha, when he is imprisoned in South Africa, accepts that the General, in his country, must also have political prisoners. Indeed, there is a direct link between Hillela in the State House in Reuel's country and Sasha, who in prison is a 'guest of the State' in South Africa. There can be no utopian content, it appears, without worldly form. The State – politics – is inextricably bound up with power, and all are infected by its reality.

What are we to make of this? Clearly, in the South African setting of the 1980s Gordimer has undertaken a profound meditation on the imperatives and ambiguities of power, even as that power was beginning to be achieved. And there is a wider context as well. In her essay of 1981, 'Living in the Interregnum', Gordimer had seen not only South Africa but also the larger globe adrift in a stage of transitional and indeterminate meanings. The old truths of the left appeared suspect; the rapaciousness of capitalism was unchecked. It was a time of rampant materialism and ideological confusion. The

9   For a good sense of the ironies in the novel, see Rowland Smith, 'Leisure, Law and Loathing: Matrons, Mistresses, Mothers in the Fiction of Nadine Gordimer and Jillian Becker', *World Literature Written in English,* vol. 28, no. 1 (1988), pp. 41–51. See also Richard Peck, 'What's a Poor White to Do? White South African Options in *A Sport of Nature*', *Ariel,* vol. 19, no. 4 (October 1988), pp. 75–93.

cynicisms of power in the West, in the East, and in the Third World meant that perhaps the only way to go forward was through an almost instinctive ethics of bodily intuition. In that essay Gordimer's plea was for a resurrection of the left on a new basis. In *A Sport of Nature* Karel tells Hillela (and the setting, by no accident, is Eastern Europe) that her search for 'somewhere to go is right at the centre of this century' (p. 259). In this light it is significant that, for all her realpolitik of the body, the one thing Hillela never loses is a sense of loyalty to her larger community, the social family she comes to believe in.

Yet – and accentuating now the ironic vision of the novel – there are at least two signs of division in its resolution that we should note. Sasha, who has indeed learned to make his way from the entrapments of mental confusion to physical resistance, is finally left in Holland, an outsider when the moment of liberation comes. From there the legacy of his mental and ethical struggle seems almost a reproach to Hillela's bodily fortune. But even Hillela, present for the climactic moment, is a visitor. This is in part a sign, to be expected by now in Gordimer's fiction, that Hillela does not 'own' the revolution, that it must be surrendered to the people in whose name it has taken place. And this is, finally, why she must play a secondary and supportive role in her life. Hillela's inside/outside status may also be a sign of the uneasy correlation, in *A Sport of Nature,* between the ideas of 'liberation' and 'nation'.

But everything in the novel leaves open the question: who will participate in utopia? The lives of Hillela and Sasha, not to mention Clive, indicate that this will not simply be a matter of race. Perhaps even more to the point: how, and in what forms, will the utopian movement enter into contract with the currencies of power? The complexity of Gordimer's novel, combining both hope and irony in exploring the code of the revolutionary body, suggests that after the climactic moment of liberation there will be some hard questions that need asking and answering. *A Sport of Nature* not only envisions a post-apartheid South Africa, but also postulates some of its deepest and innermost questions.

The Double Graph of History

Anticipation: a number of times in this study we saw Gordimer's work not only embody a response to the present, but somehow anticipate developments in the future which could only have been dimly discernible in the precise forms they appear. Fiction plumbs beneath the surface, and there explores levels of intimation that only later enter into general consciousness because they are for the present submerged in terms of consciousness as well. 'It's Mehring, down there' (*The Conservationist,* p. 265). Yes, in a sense it is: it is his own unconscious – political as well as personal – Gordimer's fiction makes him confront, and what he sees there is his future.

In a sense Mehring is always in dialogue with himself. But what emerges from this analysis of *A Sport of Nature* is how central dialogue is in general to Gordimer's fiction. Only on one level does this refer to conversations between, or even within, characters. On another it must refer to a dialogue within the text itself, which characters, it is true, may reveal. Or we might say that at some level this dialogue exists within the writer's mind, embedded in multiple ways in her fiction, rendering the poles of an inner debate. All this is in Bakhtin's definition of the term, and he identified it, to add to our echoes, in Dostoevsky; indeed, at the very beginning of his researches, he found it exemplified in the legend of the Grand Inquisitor.[10]

Once one sees this, it is extraordinary how 'dialogical' Gordimer's novels – and especially her later fiction – appears.[11] Hers may not be exactly Bakhtin's 'plurality of unmerged consciousnesses'; Gordimer's dialogues are usually constructed and in some sense resolved

10 See, in general, Mikhail Bakhtin, *Problems of Dostoevsky's Poetics,* ed. and trans. Caryl Emerson (Minneapolis: University of Minnesota Press, 1984). Bakhtin wrote on the legend of the Grand Inquisitor in the first version of this study, *Problems of Dostoevsky's Art* (1929); see Emerson's edn, Appendix I, p. 279. Other echoes may or may not be incidental: Dostoevsky writes on the 'eccentric' in the Preface to *The Brothers Karamazov* in much the same way that Gordimer might write (with suitable modifications for gender) of the 'sport of nature': 'For not only is an eccentric "not always" an isolated case and an exception, but, on the contrary, it happens sometimes that such a person . . . carries within himself the very heart of the whole, and the rest of the men of his epoch have for some reason been temporarily torn from it, as if by a gust of wind . . .' (quoted, Bakhtin, *Problems,* p. 150; in varying translations elsewhere).

11 In an analysis of *The Conservationist,* Brian Macaskill draws in part on Bakhtin to specify the novel's 'dialogic interruption': see his 'Interrupting the Hegemonic: Textual Critique and Mythological Recuperation from the White Margins of South African Writing', *Novel,* vol. 23, no. 2 (Winter 1990), p. 166. My own account suggests we should see this not only in textual terms, but also in relation to Mehring's – and the novel's – political and historical unconscious (see Chapters 5 and 7).

within a certain historical field or framework. But elsewhere Bakhtin's descriptions of Dostoevsky could be made for Gordimer: 'A word completely alien to any internal struggle is almost never found in Dostoevsky's heroes'.[12] Such a formulation would fit exactly the inner engagement of Maureen in the phase leading up to her political crisis, or Rosa Burger in the phase leading up to her political decision. As Rosa remarks, 'always one is addressed to someone' (in her case her father, Conrad, Katya) – and there has never been a dialogue in Gordimer's fiction quite like that between Rosa and Zwelinzima, over the telephone in the middle of the night, when what is 'outside' comes 'inside', and the encounter functions in both political and psychoanalytic terms at once. Or, Bakhtin writes of Dostoevsky: 'Where consciousness began, there dialogue began for him as well': only a similar kind of creative awareness on Gordimer's part could account for the agonizingly contradictory world of Will and Sonny in *My Son's Story* (though there too we shall see that this has an historical dimension). In *A Sport of Nature* we have seen there is an internal dialogue in the novel's very recognition of a revolutionary drive towards power. In this light, it appears, Gordimer has raised the configurations of her 'split position' to a higher historical level, finding a crucial division within the moment of liberation itself.

This development reveals an extraordinary pattern. In *My Son's Story* there is a scene at a political funeral – a 'cleansing of the graves' – which may have derived in part from Gordimer's own experience. In 1986, at the height of the State of Emergency, she – together with some other whites – joined the residents of Alexandra Township, facing armed police, at a similar ritual.[13] That episode ended peacefully (the one in the novel – like many others in South Africa at the time – does not). Yet it did indicate that Gordimer was, in a direct way, prepared to place herself on the boundary her mind and imagination had occupied and explored for some time. Over the next few years this development was accentuated. At a political trial in Pretoria, Gordimer, called as a witness for the Defence, declared that she regarded the leaders of the ANC as her own.[14] She was a

12   For the three quotations from Bakhtin in this paragraph, see, respectively, *Problems of Dostoevsky's Poetics,* pp. 26, 261, 40.

13   *Weekly Mail* (Johannesburg), 23–29 May 1986, p. 8. The whites who went into the township were responding to a 'call to whites' issued by the United Democratic Front.

14   This was in December 1989, towards the end of the marathon Delmas Trial (so-

founding member of the Congress of South African Writers – an organization loosely affiliated to the United Democratic Front and the Mass Democratic Movement, and one of the innumerable acronyms (COSAW) that Sasha might have had in mind just a few years later. And in 1990, after the African National Congress was unbanned, Gordimer became a member.

In so many ways, then, Gordimer was joining the political and cultural world from which she had previously been separated, even if she had been approaching that world for many years. In her personal life she was enacting those crossings figured for so long in her fiction. We can say that previously her fiction, interrogating the world of Gordimer's real life, had taken her into uncharted imaginative territory. Now, however, there was a paradox. For as she entered this other territory in reality, so once again her fiction began to ask questions, and what was registered was not arrival, but new departures. As we have seen in *A Sport of Nature,* even as the moment of liberation approached, Gordimer found a division within that moment itself.

We can use another image to say the same thing. Previously, what this book seemed to show was a rising historical curve as, in novel after novel, Gordimer's work became more politicized, more radical, more linked to the idea of a thorough transformation in South Africa. So there was a graph, the rising curve of a parabola of commitment and engagement. Now, however, we can see something else. For as the curve begins to reach its peak, so, almost in a mirror movement, there is an equal and opposite curve beginning to arc downwards, as what Gordimer's fiction questions is exactly the dynamic of political development. We no longer have a single graph of history, but a 'double graph'; the graph itself becomes 'dialogic'. One of the chapters in this book is entitled 'Deep History', but if there were to be a title for this Prologue – and perhaps retrospectively for Gordimer's fiction – this could be its name: 'The Double Graph of History'.

My Son's Story

With this in mind, our analysis of *My Son's Story* does not have to be detailed: we have a sense of what double patterns to anticipate. In

called because it had begun in Delmas, east of Johannesburg), of UDF leaders and other community activists.

this novel Gordimer returns not to the 'organic body' – though sexuality is at the core of a good deal of what occurs – but, in the lives of Sonny and Will, to the world of Gramsci's 'organic intellectual'; and what she finds there suggests all kinds of unexpected ambiguity.

We see it everywhere in the novel. At this point in Gordimer's fiction a cross-racial love affair is hardly of significance in itself as some kind of challenge to apartheid, though it does indicate the extent of deracialization in South Africa. But what that relationship precipitates here is, in a way, unprecedented: the combination of the political, the racial, and the Oedipal in the interlocking triangles of Sonny, Aila, and Will on the one hand, and of Sonny, Hannah, and Will on the other, is a psychological masterwork. We are in unusual domains of deception. Sonny's psychological alibi in these triangles becomes the exigencies of politics; so politics can also be a form of betrayal. At the same time, politics is built into the very psychology of Sonny's response, constructing and compounding his relationships in this way. Indeed, politics is sexualized in the novel: as almost all the characters discover, one can be 'seduced' in various ways by politics and politicized in ambivalent forms by love. Surrounding all, as we learn by the end, is the vulnerable and controlling voice of Will, speaking his envy, emulation, love, knowledge, and distaste in impossible emotional combinations. The themes and character exploration are almost classical, with a South African twist. We are in a world not simply of political heroism and glory, but one in which virtually any term is liable to incorporate aspects of its ironic opposite.

Quite obviously, in *My Son's Story* Gordimer is giving an unorthodox picture of the realities of political life in South Africa, even as they are played out within the liberation movement. But if we are wishing to translate this as an index of *historical consciousness,* rather than as just a topical keeping-up with history, we have to focus our attention elsewhere, on something that may also seem obvious about the novel, but with which all of this is linked. For the first time in one of Gordimer's novels (though not in her short stories) the central characters she depicts, as well as her narrator, are not white. On a superficial level it may appear that in choosing a 'coloured' family, Gordimer has established a new narrative identity for herself in her fiction, in a world transforming beyond apartheid. Yet issues of voice and representation are not solved so simply. Black characters have been in Gordimer's fiction before; and in any case, whose voice, we might ask (without expecting anything like a simple answer), is 'really' speaking any fictional narration? Perhaps then this is a *symbolic* choice of narrative identity, representing some identification on Gordimer's part with a new and developing world. That may be so, but we first have to determine in this context what definition of 'symbolic' we wish to use.

It is worth stating clearly the parameters of Gordimer's choice: she writes not about a white family, nor about a black family, but about a family that in some sense is neither and is both. In South Africa the term 'coloured', used to signify people of mixed race, has to some extent always been a 'non-category'. This is partly because it is not necessarily accepted by the people whom it has been meant to designate. But from the other side as well, the term has suffered from symbolic overload, taken as a condition of racial impurity and degeneracy, of 'mixture', 'in-betweenness', 'non-identity'. From that point of view it would have been easy for Gordimer to abuse this family as symbols — that is, to use them positively or negatively only as flattened out representations of fixed qualities. That is what Sarah Gertrude Millin did (negatively) earlier in the century, and that is even what Gordimer did in her first unpublished novel (see Chapter 1). But that is not what Gordimer does here. On the contrary, in her depiction of the complex lives of this family, her account can only be understood as something else: an implicit tribute. One cannot encounter a family whose inner being is so caught up in the competing pressures and contradictions of political and psychological imperatives without realizing how fallible, human, tragic, and (in minor key) triumphant they are. It is not because of what this family *represents* but because of what it *experiences* that it becomes symbolic in a more meaningful sense.

That is to say, we have to resist any suggestion that Gordimer's narrative choice is 'racially transitional': at a mid-way point, out of the white world but not yet in the black. That would imply that 'coloured' identity — *and* the lives of this family — are not real for her in their own terms. And yet, it is possible to say that Gordimer may have been drawn to this family because of the realities of historical *transition*. How does the mind work when it is writing fiction? What locales, settings, figurations, and situations begin to seem logical, necessary, imperative? We approach a different, more authentic definition of 'symbolic': what is even only dimly perceived consciously is represented in fiction through some displaced and condensed form of mediation. And we are talking, in Gordimer's novel, of a political and historical unconscious as well as the more obvious personal one. South Africa is in a state of transition; its condition, between present and future, is 'mixed'. Its realities are those of ambiguity and complexity as well as promise. Gordimer has been drawn to a family whose reality is both promise and complexity. What we can understand now only in the most superficial sense as a narrative 'choice' becomes symbolic at a deeper and more revelatory level, as the logic of Sonny, Aila, and Will's liminal situation and experience becomes clear.

At every level in the novel this family lives 'in-between' and in transition, and nothing about this is straightforward. Sonny, the schoolteacher whose loyalties are to Shakespeare, becomes the political activist – having marched with his students, as the novel puts it repeatedly, 'across the veld': into a new locale, no-man's land, new identification.[15] As a 'coloured' man, he throws in his lot with black South Africans, and he falls in love with a white woman. As activist he becomes 'Sonny' (his identity shifted yet further) the political orator, and even as he finds a new identity in politics, he feels it slide from under his feet in betrayal. Sonny, husband to Aila and father to Will, becomes 'Sonny', the lover of Hannah and something both less and more than father to Will. Aila, the meek and obedient wife, becomes the consummate underground agent for the liberation movement, her practised silence in relation to her husband the very medium of her new power, even as Sonny's patriarchal and political authority declines. And Will: Will becomes a writer, identity shifted yet again, back in the direction his father left behind, except that he is now an active cultural agent rather than its more passive recipient (though that too will have its ironies). After the bodily conceptions of *A Sport of Nature* it can be no accident that Gordimer has returned to a mode of characterization registering, in the main, *mentality*: a mode in itself concerned with in-betweenness, ambiguity, transition. It is then perhaps not only South Africa's transition to the future, but also the very flux of the present that is caught up in

15 Nadine Gordimer, *My Son's Story* (London: Bloomsbury; New York: Farrar, Straus & Giroux; Cape Town: David Philip; 1990; Harmondsworth: Penguin, 1991), pp. 26, 32, for instance. Further page references, to the Penguin edn, are given in the text.

this family, as they make their commitments with conviction, but also with imperfection and unforeseeable results. Underlying everything in this novel is the structure of a world shifting as you grasp it.

Doubleness, in this moment, is all, in nothing less than meaning itself. In the same way that Sonny becomes 'Sonny', Will remarks that when his father tells Aila he is going to political meetings he is really going to 'meetings' – with Hannah (p. 177). But then Sonny discovers that the commitment of his politics has become entwined with another form of 'politics' – of cabals manoeuvring for power, in which he himself is displaced. No surprise then, that almost everything in the novel revolves around betrayal; but even betrayals can work in two directions. It is not just that Sonny 'betrays' Aila for politics (and Hannah); Aila herself will 'betray' her husband in becoming involved in an even more extreme form of the political struggle than he is. As Sonny himself knows, betrayal can be a kind of 'love', risk a kind of safety, safety a total illusion. Even the narrative structure of the novel depends on a deceptive duality. Right up until the end there are two narratives: the first is a feigned third-person narrative of Sonny (and the others), by Will; the second is a first-person narrative, by Will, in feigned ignorance of the other one. So the total narrative is one of feigning, both positively and negatively. This may be an allegory of the realities of writing, but it is also one of uncertainty, transition, transformation, in which what one *knows* can scarcely be defined. What is the narrative of that future, the interregnum, in the making? 'I keep thinking of it as an interlude, something that will be over,' writes Will; 'but it's our life' (p. 176). To find the fictional in this novel is to find the level at which it veers beyond and below and above what it even knew it wanted to say. This is also to find its true 'inner history'.

In this there is an inflection and an echo from *A Sport of Nature*. There Karel told Hillela that her 'somewhere to go is right at the centre of this century.' In this novel the awareness of incipient revolt in Eastern Europe is a matter of particular anguish for Sonny. He is committed to his own political struggle; yet, will the final end of the revolution he believes in be another form of ossification and repression from which the people will yet again have to liberate themselves? How far will the bodily momentum towards freedom relate to the questions and ambiguities of the people caught up in it? In this regard Sonny's conversation with Hannah on the topic is again, in the deeper sense, a matter of inner dialogue for the novel itself.

Prologue

In particular, it emerges as a crisis of *language*. For Sonny's concern is that the language he speaks as acclaimed political orator is
an artificial and formulaic one, suitable and even necessary for public occasions but drained of the depth, ambiguity, and breath that
would give it a more adequate truth. Perhaps as his own *name* is
alienated and distanced (as the 'Sonny' of the political posters), so
too his language may come to have implicit quotation marks around
it, a quasi-language, real and not real at the same time. And there is
for the novel the critical issue that the language of liberation in
South Africa has also constituted the language of oppression in
Eastern Europe, which people there have been driven to revolt
against. Perhaps what Sonny and his comrades have looked to from
afar has not been socialism but 'socialism' – a vaunting simulacrum
related only parodically to its original meaning (though that original
meaning may in some other form, at some other time, be resuscitated). What kind of truth might one know, and in what language?
Sonny finds much of the political speech around him banal in relation to the literature that gave him meaning in his youth. And, 'That
truth is not all the truth,' writes Will of Sonny's own misreading of
his daughter Baby's decision to become a revolutionary as an (albeit
complex) matter of political emulation (p. 124). But is the political
reading – is political speech – adequate? In many ways, and at many
levels, this is a novel in dialogue with politics itself, even as it affirms
the necessity for Sonny's commitment.

From that point of view it is of the greatest significance that Will is
a writer, and the novel begins to chime with Gordimer's extended
consideration, in numerous essays over a number of years, on the
whole question of being a writer and of writing in South Africa. In
'Living in the Interregnum' she puts it this way: 'nothing I say here
will be as true as my fiction.'[16] In *My Son's Story* there is an implicit
theory of the writer which perhaps explains why that is. Here the
writer is the one who fills in the gaps and the silences, who fits
between the all-too-sayable and the never-said; one who certainly
must invent for his insights, but who gets into the synapses of the

16   In Nadine Gordimer, *The Essential Gesture: Writing, Politics and Places,* ed.
with an introduction by Stephen Clingman (London: Cape; New York: Knopf; Johan-
nesburg/Cape Town: Taurus/David Philip; 1988; Harmondsworth: Penguin, 1989),
p. 264.

political, the familial, and the psychological and (like Gordimer) sees just how they are connected. Here, in Will, is the one who cannot speak – who has no being – in any other way; whose speech, significantly, is *suppressed* into writing through the authoritative weight of his father's political life; but who has experienced and seen through the illusions of surface and is therefore willing to take this detour into depth because nothing else is satisfactory. The writer is the one who disguises himself and even 'betrays' the lives of those around him, but (as we have seen, betrayal can carry other kinds of loyalties) whose language is the truth of the questions he is prepared to ask.

We may even read Will allegorically. In his family as well as in society, the writer is at-the-fringe-of, but not at the centre. He is inseparably in the world of politics, history, and power, but he is also in that of aesthetics and other definitions of value. From that world he sets into dialogue the claims of politics and fiction, and it is one in which he is directly involved himself – in this case in his very being and almost beyond his own understanding. For the writer (Will) is the offspring of politics (Sonny), but he is *not identical with it* and must search for his own definitions of meaning in the world. And the hierarchy can work the other way. As the father may be a 'Sonny', so presumably the 'son' may be a kind of 'father'. Certainly, as author of his narrative, Will is the progenitor of his own form of vision, and as the relations of power between him and his father turn around, so in a sense does the hierarchy of their respective languages. 'You had a father, let your son say so,' writes Shakespeare in Sonnet 13, and Gordimer takes it as the epigraph of this novel. In the transition from the father to this South African Will – and it is a transition of sexual power, colour, culture, and everything else in the novel – Gordimer measures a shift in the claims of politics and fiction in a world approaching the afterlife of apartheid. The revolution is necessary and must be entered into, but the questions of writing have a primacy of their own.

In that sense Gordimer has returned to the origins of her own writing, but with an accentuation and a difference. Perhaps it is no accident that *My Son's Story* reminds us of *The Lying Days;* there it was a young white woman who, as the product of her experience, found that she had written a novel. That work was to some degree autobiographical, as Gordimer discovered in displaced form her own 'story'. Here the writer is male and 'coloured' – perhaps an acknowledgement that others will take up the development of a cultural tradition. There is the irony that, unlike Helen Shaw's, Will's novel is 'not for publication' (the title of one of Gordimer's earlier short stories, also on the background of an African leader), at least not in his own voice: perhaps some comment here on the propensity for censorship of one kind or another even within the revolutionary moment – or on the limits to which one can 'betray' one's family even as a writer. Or perhaps it is because the book relates more directly to the period of repression before 1990 than to the one that opened up after. But, for whatever reason, it also helps to clarify that what Will has discovered specifically is not a novel but *writing:* its allure, its claims, the (sometimes ambiguous) nature of its vision, and just what it contests.

For most of her career under apartheid, Gordimer contested the dominant nature of South African reality, and that contestation had a political significance. Now, however, there is a difference. In reinvestigating this question through Will, she comes to contest politics itself as a *form of representation.* We might ask what the significance of this is. Certainly it links up with the question of Eastern Europe: there, in the world of 'post-revolution' it was pre-eminently writers who had to work against the hegemony of totalizing forms of political representation and find their own meanings, questions, and ethics. Gordimer, whose interest in East European writers is intense, has brought that awareness into her novel. In the South African context we might put it the following way. In a world in which apartheid reigned supreme, to be opposed to it was by definition to adopt a certain form of politicality. But when that future has arrived – and in some sense the future has always arrived in the present – there will be various forms of contest as to what that politicality means, and any number of claims to represent it. The inner dialogue of Gordimer's novel, establishing the pathos of Sonny's tragedy and affirming the need for his politics even as these issues are raised, suggests that writing may be an authentic form of questioning political representations in the post-apartheid world.

It's 'My time that's coming with politics,' writes Will (p. 276). Even as we hear the youthful male arrogance in his voice, we can recognize that there is something in the claim, because in her own fiction Gordimer has doubled the very nature of his speech.

Prologue

Openings

In some respects what Gordimer does in *My Son's Story* may not appear to be so new. J. M. Coetzee, for instance, has for a long time questioned the hegemony of the political as a form of representation. Yet what is distinctive here is the duality of Gordimer's vision, affirming the political at the same time that she affirms the need to question it. The writer and critic Njabulo Ndebele has also for some years (along with Gordimer) insisted that South African literature refuse the surface identifications of political writing, and more truly resist apartheid by in-depth explorations of interiority.[17] And yet, at this crossroads are all kinds of transitions. In Coetzee's most recent novel, *Age of Iron,* he comes closer than ever to the urgencies of political consciousness even as he doubts its priority. Gordimer, whose work has always been politically involved, begins to raise her own questions more insistently in *My Son's Story.* The two begin to meet at the same place from their different directions, and there are 'double-graphs' across and within both their fictions.

It may seem ironic: just now, when success is at hand, when black South Africans are about to achieve what they have struggled for for so long, in both *A Sport of Nature* and *My Son's Story* Gordimer begins to raise doubts. From that point of view, a 'double-graph' may appear to be a form of betrayal. Yet we have seen in *My Son's Story* that an apparent betrayal may carry deeper loyalties. We should not forget that in her personal life Gordimer's commitment is as strong if not stronger than ever. And here we are able to see something else. In one sense, Gordimer is *not* doing anything different from what she has done before. 'Nothing I say here will be as true as my fiction': that statement will now keep resounding. If Gordimer's fiction was true before – if it had some political resonance – that was because it asked questions, relentlessly and in every direction. That was what generated her own particular drive towards the end of apartheid. But why stop now that the end of apartheid may be at hand? Rosa Burger certainly questioned the political, though her questioning took place ultimately within the frame of a need for commitment. It is just that her successor, Will, is able to see that writing itself is a

17 Njabulo Ndebele, 'Turkish Tales and Some Thoughts on South African Fiction', *Staffrider,* vol. 6, no. 1 (1984), pp. 24–5, 42–8.

form of commitment. Placed on the cusp between an apartheid and a post-apartheid culture, Gordimer's fiction reminds us that writing the narrative of the present and the coming future as 'double' will not only be historically realistic, but may be the surest way of safeguarding the gains that have been, and that need to be, made.

As apartheid comes to its end, the mood of South Africa has changed. Similarly, our view of Gordimer's place within and against these developments shifts. 'History may well end up being harsh to white South African novelists of the twentieth century': the perspective of the original Afterword to this book may be revised. Gordimer is firmly part of a developing non-racial culture in South Africa, and her life as a writer as well as her writing indicate in and of themselves the centrality of her significance. At the same time, more recent developments in her fiction suggest new perspectives on the earlier work, allowing us to read the older work into the new, the new into the old. With one eye on Bakhtin we can see now that it is not so much that Gordimer takes up increasingly radical commitments in her novels, but rather that she *interrogates* increasingly radical positions in the midst of historical change. It is less a linear development than an exploration of successive ideological fields which are, nonetheless, linked to the need for transformation in South Africa.

These and further revisions may be left to others or later reinvestigation. Yet, given these latest developments in Gordimer's novels, we may be in a more secure position to understand 'the essential gesture' of her fiction, the signature of her specific imprint. Like any double-graph it must come from a dual momentum, or in Gordimer's case a dual commitment: to the craft and philosophy of writing on the one hand, and to the *responsibilities* of writing on the other. So, to the configurations of Gordimer's 'split position' – measured earlier in historical, cultural, social, and psychological terms – we must add another sense of doubleness, within Gordimer's writing. Yet, this is a doubleness without division, though it may *reveal* division. This is what sets fiction in dialogue with politics; this is what set Gordimer's fiction in contraposition to apartheid; this is what has produced the 'inner history' of her novels. And it is a doubleness that might, in some of the forms elicited here, be emblematic of a move into a post-apartheid culture.

Preface

This book grew out of an abiding dual interest in literature and in history, and in the relationships between the two. But in effect the concern was single. For I was interested in history as it has been lived and experienced by people – how they see the world they live in, what sense they are able to make of it, what obligations they feel it casts upon them. Literature seemed a perfect medium for exploring these questions, for it is in fiction that individual and social narratives are given visible and public voice. The issues that prompted this study, then, have always been basic and simple ones. Yet as soon as one delves more deeply they become more complicated. One must consider fiction in its specificities; one must develop a sound knowledge of political and historical contexts; one must continually think of the relations between these and literature; one must be aware of the various currents, historical, social, cultural and ideological, in which fiction is borne along, and whose presence it reveals. There is a long and respected tradition of thought about such matters. This book is a modest attempt to think them through again in the practical context of South Africa over the past forty to fifty years.

From this point of view there is secreted here what might be called a philosophy of the extreme example. For the extreme example illuminates in clearly defined form patterns that may be only more vaguely discernible elsewhere. The area of focus of this book certainly fulfils this criterion. If one were looking for a society that has undergone historical experience of a most intense kind, there would be few to compete with South Africa. Also, in its combination of class, racial and cultural struggles, South Africa condenses many of the major problems facing the world at large today. And if one were searching for a writer whose literary being and career have been directly involved with these issues over an extended period of time, then Nadine Gordimer must be one of the primary candidates. So, a writer deeply bound up with history encounters extraordinary historical circumstances. In this situation we search for an historical consciousness and see what it can mean for fiction. As for the story that consciousness tells, that is also the subject, and narrative, of this book.

In substance the book began as a doctoral thesis, submitted at Oxford University in 1983, and there are many people to whom thanks and acknowledgements are due. My supervisor at Oxford, John Bayley, gave me endless help and encouragement, as well as the freedom to follow my own path in pursuing my topic; I could not have wished for a better mentor. Terry Eagleton established a forum in which I could think of many of the issues raised in this study, and ultimately examined my thesis; my other examiner, Professor Jaques Berthoud, was of the greatest help in encouraging me to have the thesis published. Stanley Trapido provided an invaluable environment at Oxford in which to think about South African history; this book would have been much poorer without his presence. There is also a small group of people whom I will always associate with this study, either for their direct assistance or, more importantly, for their intellectual and human companionship, and I should like to remember them here: Mark Schneider, James Simpson, Peter Taylor, João Pina-Cabral, Penny Smith and Neil Lazarus. Others who have helped in one way or another include Peter Delius, William Beinart, Colin Bundy, Baruch Hirson, Professor Shula Marks, Dr Phyllis Lewsen, Millie Levy, Lorraine Chaskalson, Professor Mike Savage, Professor Henry Louis Gates, Jr, Stephen Watson, Johnny Clegg and Nick Visser. Working with my editor, Jane Harris-Matthews, has been a happy, as well as beneficial, experience. I have also been lucky enough to be housed at two marvellous places over the past two years, where I have been able to see this book through. At Yale University the Directors and members of the Southern African Research Program gave me a wonderful opportunity to further this and other work. At the African Studies Institute of the University of the Witwatersrand I have had the very good fortune to be associated with Professors Charles van Onselen and Tim Couzens, who have not only been more than generous in enabling me to finish the book, but have been models of scholarly endeavour and professionalism.

Finally, there are two people to whom I owe especial debts of gratitude. Nadine Gordimer, finding herself in the perhaps uneasy position of being an object of academic study, has been enormously helpful in making available material and information. Her openness in considering her career has been remarkable, but I suspect it is part of the same set of virtues that underlie her writing. Getting to know her has been one of the rewards of these years. Without my wife Moira this book would never have been written. Her tolerance of my obsessions was exceeded only by an extraordinary depth of spirit, and a willingness to encourage me at every step of the way to make this work as good as I can make it.

In discussing South Africa one is unfortunately obliged to use its system of racial categorization, without affirming any of its implications. In most cases my usage will be self-explanatory, but one note on terminology is perhaps required. The so-called 'coloured' (or mixed-race) people of South Africa do not necessarily accept their categorization as a race; this is a strictly legislative and historical term. Therefore it will always appear in quotation marks.

Stephen Clingman
Johannesburg
September 1985

Introduction:
History from the Inside

I

In discussing the value of African novels as a certain kind of historical evidence, Nadine Gordimer draws an example from Russian literature:

> If you want to read the facts of the retreat from Moscow in 1812, you may read a history book; if you want to know what war is like and how people of a certain time and background dealt with it as their personal situation, you must read *War and Peace*.[1]

In her view, the novel can present history as historians cannot. Moreover, this presentation is not fictional in the sense of being 'untrue'. Rather, fiction deals with an area of activity usually inaccessible to the sciences of greater externality: the area in which historical process is registered as the subjective experience of individuals in society; fiction gives us 'history from the inside'. What we shall be doing, in part, is turning this view back upon Nadine Gordimer's own novels. For, through their acute and sustained observation of the society she inhabits, Gordimer's novels give us an extraordinary and unique insight into historical experience in the period in which she has been writing.

In her view of Tolstoy, however, Gordimer has ignored a question of some importance. As a matter of principle she has accepted the truth of his account of the events of 1812; this is perhaps due deference to his authority. Yet it is not just that novelists (even Tolstoy) may be fallible in their understanding of history. What Gordimer has not considered is that Tolstoy was himself an historical subject, moreover one who was viewing history across a gap of some forty or so years. In this regard his account can in no sense be entirely objective or neutral; at the least Gordimer has underestimated the degree to which it is influenced by the needs and assumptions of his time, not to mention any ideological framework or preoccupations

1

that may have modified his vision.[2] Gordimer, by contrast, views the history of her society – or at least parts of it – at much closer quarters. But this does not mean her work is any more 'complete' or objective than Tolstoy's. Indeed, she suffers from added disabilities. For Gordimer is caught up in the midst of the processes she is attempting to depict. At the same time as she engages with history she is moulded by the patterns and forces she must try to assess. As much as she is an observer of the life around her, she is still a social participant in what she observes. If hers is a 'history from the inside', that is to say, it is not only privileged but also confined by its 'inside' position.

From this point of view it seems that of more significance historically than the world that a novel presents are the self-revealing features of its presentation. This, as it were, is the primary material that a novel offers: not so much an historical world, but a certain *consciousness* of that world. This is what Tolstoy gives us in *War and Peace*, and this is what Gordimer gives us in her novels; and it is this consciousness of history that we shall therefore be following in her work. If there is a 'history from the inside' to be traced through fiction, it is to be located here. It is as if one were to add to Gordimer's remarks on Tolstoy that if you want to know what life was like to a writer interpreting historical events in *War and Peace*, you must understand the interpretation historically.

II

In its widest context Gordimer's writing must be considered within the field of African literature as a whole. Here we begin to see why her novels should have an 'historical consciousness' in the first place. One does not have to believe there was no history in Africa before the advent of European colonization to say that, if the continent has been involved in anything over the last few centuries, it has been history. The invasion of European merchants, administrators and settlers; political, economic and cultural imperialism and resistance; struggles for independence and liberation; the appearance of neo-colonialism: these are nothing if not the stuff of an essentially historical experience. Given this, it is no surprise that African literature has been intrinsically bound up with its historical circumstances. As Clive Wake sees it, the very genesis of modern African literature has been historical. For him it was the 'political and social revolution' in Africa in the late 1950s and during the 1960s that inspired the rise of African fiction.[3] And it is clear that the great flood of literary production that has been so notable in Africa since Chinua Achebe's *Things Fall Apart* has been contemporaneous with the movement towards independence in the various African countries and, since then, its aftermath. More significant than this, perhaps, is that the *consciousness* of this writing is historical. Not only has African literature been generated by an intense and dramatic historical experience, but it has turned back on that experience itself, taking it as its especial subject matter. Whether it be the impact of colonialism, wars of resistance and struggles for independence, or the problems arising since then, these have been the themes that have preoccupied African writing. Lewis Nkosi detects a specific genre within African fiction in which 'history' itself is the hero.[4] And for Chinua Achebe an historical approach is a matter of necessity for the African writer. In Africa, he declares, it is impossible to explore the human condition without 'a proper sense of history'.[5] This is because in Africa human cannot be separated from historical experience.

South Africa is of course a special case in Africa, but it nevertheless falls into the same overall context. In contrast to other territories, here there were two broad layers of settlement (Dutch and English) instead of the more usual one. In South Africa, following the discovery of diamonds and gold, industrialization and its attendant processes took off in the twentieth century to a degree unequalled elsewhere on the continent, profoundly rupturing the whole basis of society and its cultural forms. And here, within these deeply changed circumstances, independence and liberation still remain part of the indefinite future. But for all these special conditions – indeed, precisely because of them – South Africa over the past few hundred years has been in the deep throes of historical experience. There have been the original wars of conquest and resistance, internal class and nationalist conflicts between the settler polities, the oppression and exploitation of the colonized and later proletarianized masses, the modern elaboration of apartheid and, throughout, a moving record of resistance. To mention all this is to give only the broadest and crudest features of South African history. But there can be scarcely a locality in the country that has not seen its own version, in microcosm and complex detail, of the patterns appearing at a national level. In these circumstances it is axiomatic that whatever writing has taken place has, positively or negatively, consciously or unconsciously, deliberately or by accident, been involved in the wider processes of South African history. At one extreme this would apply to Sol Plaatje's great novel, *Mhudi*, which is deliberately filled to overflowing with history, of both a past and present kind.[6] But equally it would apply to the stillness of Pauline Smith's Karroo or the rural tragi-comedies of Herman Charles Bosman.

Within this overall setting some of the dominant patterns of South African literature may be set out. It is impossible to give a full survey here, but a brief account can still help situate Gordimer's fiction in relation to a larger field, and suggest something of the wider history standing behind her central preoccupations. The novel that undoubtedly initiates the modern period in white South African writing in English is Olive Schreiner's *The Story of an African Farm*; published just over a century ago, it adumbrates much of the fictional terrain that has dominated the literature since then.[7] This has not been accidental, for Schreiner's novel set out prototypically one of the fundamental problems confronting her culture and its heritage. In the preface to the second edition of the novel she sounds a crucial note for South African writing:

> Those brilliant phases and shapes which the imagination sees in far-off lands are not for him [the writer] to portray. Sadly he must squeeze the colour from his brush, and dip it into the grey pigments around him. He must paint what lies before him.[8]

This most obviously is a reproof to European readers expecting exoticism in writing from Africa. But it is also a statement of intent; the writer here is committing herself to engaging with her local world. It is a statement, in a sense, of 'settlement', since Schreiner has assumed a local identity for her work. Yet we shall see in Chapter 5 that there is another side to this, that in some respects *The Story of an African Farm* registers only its alienation from its African environment.

What Schreiner's work sets out, therefore, may be seen as a 'colonial' problematic; it is settled and alien at the same time. Much of white writing has been struggling with this issue since then, and at the widest level in Gordimer's work this same issue is taken up in her novels. We shall see that one of her abiding concerns is the relation of a European culture to Africa, and particularly South Africa. At its broadest her struggle as a novelist lies in progressing towards a new, integrated South African culture of the future. And, as we shall see, her sixth novel, *The Conservationist*, stands in many respects as a direct reply to *The Story of an African Farm*.

A second moment of importance in South African writing (for our purposes) occurs in the 1920s. There is no point in attempting to put a date to the origin of what whites in South Africa have traditionally liked to think of as 'the native question' – that is, the problem of what to do about the black majority. There is no doubt, however, that in the 1920s it was assuming a definite prominence. This was a time of massive proletarianization, unionization and industrial unrest, amongst both black and white workers. It was a time that saw an alliance between white workers and Afrikaner nationalists, resulting in the Nationalist–Labour Pact government of 1924. It was a time when, it might be argued, if the foundations of the modern apartheid state had already been laid, they were now at least being substantially filled in. As such it was a time when the question not so much of race, but of the *use* of race, came to the fore, as in the 'civilized labour' policy of that era whereby white workers were differentiated economically and socially from their black counterparts on the grounds of colour.[9] And in these circumstances, as David Rabkin has pointed out, two novels of race emerged in South Africa that were (ostensibly) diametrical opposites of one another: Sarah Gertrude Millin's *God's Step-Children*, and William Plomer's *Turbott Wolfe*.[10] Millin's work is perhaps South Africa's most famous racist novel, and for the most part Gordimer's fiction does not relate to it at all (although we shall see that in one of her early works there is an unexpected overlap). But it is Plomer's novel that, in general terms, sets up the theme to which Gordimer's work responds most strongly. In a celebrated moment in *Turbott Wolfe*, one of its characters, Mabel Van Der Horst, remarks on the 'native question':

> native question! What the hell is the native question? You take away the black man's country, and shirking the future consequences of your action you blindly affix a label to what you know (and fear) the black man is thinking of you – 'the native question'. Native question indeed! My good man, there is no native question. It isn't a question. It's an answer. I don't know whether people are wilfully blind, that they can't see what's coming. The white man's as dead as a doornail in this country.[11]

Since Mabel stated the answer in this passage, virtually no South African writer of note has been able to avoid the question; least of all, as we shall see, Nadine Gordimer. It is no accident that this passage

5

has formed one of her favourite – and most forceful – quotations.[12]

Plaatje was South Africa's first black novelist to write in English. The first 'coloured' novelist to do so was Peter Abrahams. Working at first from within the urban proletarian world of Johannesburg's black townships in the 1930s, at a certain point in his career Abrahams took up Marxist leanings. At an even more decisive point, however, it apparently came to Abrahams that what was more important than political orthodoxies was the essential goodness of human beings; this alone had the capacity truly to overcome social divisions.[13] Thereafter his novels again and again announce, both implicitly and explicitly, the need for human beings to connect with one another as equals; some critics now find this objectionable, as Abrahams's social view often seems occluded by sentimentality.[14] But this shift within his writing sets the scene for the next notable phase in South African literature, involving what can be seen as a crisis of ideology. For along with Abrahams's work came a set of novels relating to the social policy of segregation, or, as it became known after 1948, when the National Party took power, 'apartheid'. What these novels – like Abrahams's – explore is an ideology of liberal humanism as a response to what they conceive of as a straightforward problem of racism. If black and white can relate to one another as human beings, so the logic of these novels runs, then the problem of apartheid will, *ipso facto*, be solved. Central among these novels is Alan Paton's *Cry, the Beloved Country*, but other writers involved at this time are Dan Jacobson and, of course, Nadine Gordimer. Liberal humanism is the keynote of her first two novels and, in a different way, of her third; her work charts an inner history of this ideology in this time.

From the 1950s onwards Gordimer's work is by definition caught up in the major movements of South African literature. There was a flourish of black writing in that decade centred upon *Drum* magazine, and part of the general ethos of multi-racialism that dominated the social and political opposition to apartheid at the time. Gordimer's second novel, *A World of Strangers*, is directly involved in this ethos; and her third novel, *Occasion for Loving*, traces its demise in the early 1960s. At about the time *Occasion for Loving* was published there was a fleeting revolutionary moment in South Africa, involving sabotage on a fairly large scale, which was, however, very soon defeated. In its wake there appeared a spate of novels dealing with the political underground: C. J. Driver's *Elegy for a Revolutionary*, Jack Cope's *The Dawn Comes Twice*, Mary Benson's *At the Still Point*, Alex La Guma's *The Stone Country* and *In the Fog of the Seasons' End*. In the midst of these, if not in the forefront, was Nadine Gordimer's *The Late Bourgeois World*. In the 1970s the dominant movement, in both literary and political terms, was that of Black Consciousness; this movement infused the renaissance of black poetry in this time as well as a much larger political revival. In her novel *Burger's Daughter* Gordimer responds most deeply to the challenge of Black Consciousness — and the Soweto Revolt of 1976 to which it led. In the late 1970s and early 1980s, as black writers such as Mongane Serote, Mbulelo Mzamane, Sipho Sepamla and Miriam Tlali turned the moment of 1976 itself into 'hero', white writers such as J. M. Coetzee and Karel Schoeman appeared to be writing allegories of a revolutionary future. In her latest novel, *July's People*, Nadine Gordimer turns towards this future.

These are then the broad preoccupations of Gordimer's work and some of the successive historical layers embedded in her writing. Clearly her novels have a wide resonance for South African literature both in the period in which she has been active and, in many respects, for the periods before and to come. Yet if all South African writers are to varying degrees 'engaged' with history either deliberately or by necessity, there is surely no other South African writer who has engaged with it so directly as Nadine Gordimer, and whose work has so sharply defined and attuned a 'sense of history'. How does this historical sense operate in her fiction, and what are we likely to learn from it?

III

A number of different features are useful for characterizing Gordimer's fiction in terms of an historical consciousness. The first and most obvious has already been suggested: the degree to which her novels maintain an extraordinarily close observation of the world in which she lives. This observation ranges from matters of minor detail, such as the language people use and their habits of dress and behaviour, to broader social and political themes, such as the rise and demise of the movement of multi-racialism in the 1950s, to major historical events, such as the accession to power of the

National Party in 1948, or the Soweto Revolt of 1976. In this observation Gordimer's eye is fixed resolutely on the present – its realities, its codes, its implications – and this is then a first level at which it is liable to relay to us a 'history from the inside': what this history looks like to as close an observer as Gordimer.

Close observation is, in this sense, a precondition of Gordimer's historical consciousness. And its appearance in so sustained a form is what makes Gordimer's novels such a perfect vehicle for our exploration of South African history in the period in which she has been writing. Yet considered simply on its own it is doubtful whether such observation would give us a 'consciousness' of history in any significant sense, that is, in any sense in which history gains *meaning* for fiction. A further feature of Gordimer's writing then becomes of basic importance: that the *perspective* she characteristically employs in her work is social and historical in nature. The key to this perspective is that social and private life are seen as integrally related; the Marxist critic Georg Lukács gave it its classic definition in his exposition of what he called 'true great realism'. For Lukács, following Aristotle as well as Marx, man had to be seen preeminently as a *zōon politikon* – a social or political being. Individual life was by no means metaphysically given and beyond the workings of history, nor could there be anything like a 'human condition' that was universally essentially the same. Instead, private life had to be seen as a social and historical construct only.[15] As restated in his definition of 'critical realism', seen from this perspective the 'ontological being' of characters 'cannot be distinguished from their social and historical environment'.[16] This seems a fair encapsulation of the perspective of most of Gordimer's writing. There are changes within it to be sure; we shall see that its implications are tested again and again, while in Gordimer's first novel, *The Lying Days*, the central character, Helen Shaw, partially escapes the limits of her social framework. But what this perspective in general implies for Gordimer's writing is that it persistently approaches the domain in which social and historical forces gain significance for private existence, a domain in which her novels surely specialize. And here an historical consciousness itself begins to develop, as the novels develop their sense of what history implies for individuals, and for a broader society at large.

Through the succession of Gordimer's novels there is then a dialectical interplay, in which the exploration of history and

8

character, of external and internal worlds, becomes entirely indivisible. Related to this is a further feature of her work: the degree to which her characters may be thought of as typical. The concept of 'type' has fallen into general disrepute in the twentieth century, especially where it appears in a Zhdanovite socialist-realist form, in which 'typical' figures are meant to sum up, by their mere presence, significant forces in history. In some respects it is none other than Lukács who is responsible for this degenerate conception, with his abiding concern that character should be wholly integrated with external reality. In others, however, he has indicated that the degraded version was never his intention, and overall it seems that he has still given us the best account of typicality that there is. Thus, for Lukács, 'types' are not to be confused with stereotypes, nor with the average, nor the eccentric, but should rather be seen as highly individualized characters who engage in their fullest potential with the social and historical circumstances of their situation. In this way they come to represent the fullest exploration *of* that situation, while retaining their individuality as characters.[17] Gordimer has warned against writers setting out deliberately to create types (as the result, she says, is liable to be bloodless); but she does allow that typicality may be a product of characterization.[18] And, in Lukács's sense, it does seem clear that all of Gordimer's central characters should be conceived of as types, though again there is some variation. Thus her characters are neither simple transplants of actually living persons, nor are they merely abstract fictional constructs. They are figures who, in general drawn from Gordimer's observation of life at large, both condense broader social and historical patterns and, in their individuality, engage with them in intense and extreme form. They are characters who fully become 'subjects' of history, and in turn explore it as far as their capacities and situation will allow. It is then in dealing with the subjectivity of these characters that Gordimer has, over the period in which she has been writing, also explored a much larger, and changing, world.

On these questions of perspective and typicality, it is perhaps significant that during her career Gordimer has been drawn to the work of Lukács. He is the prototypical historical critic; she, increasingly, has had to think of her own work and that of others in historical terms.[19] So, after a certain stage, her comments on other writers begin to show a Lukácsian cast. Of Sarah Gertrude Millin she writes that 'like the great Balzac before her' she gave away 'the big lie

in her society and herself';[20] in *The Black Interpreters* she characterizes the best of African literature as following a pattern of 'critical
realism'.[21] Given this correspondence, it might appear that Gordimer
is following Lukács not only in her literary criticism, but also, in
some way, in her writing. But it is evident, on the contrary, that when
Gordimer turned to Lukács she did so primarily because he was the
theorist of her own preoccupations. In fact Gordimer began to read
Lukács only in 1968,[22] but by at least three years earlier we find her
giving a perfect statement of the 'realist' perspective:

> whites among themselves are shaped by their peculiar position, just as
> black people are by theirs. I write about their private selves; often, even
> in the most private situations, they are what they are because their lives
> are regulated and their mores formed by the political situation. You see,
> in South Africa, society *is* the political situation. To paraphrase, one
> might say (too often), politics is character in SA.[23]

It is clear then that the realist perspective – and the implications for
characterization and typification that it entails – have, for Gordimer,
grown directly out of the situation in which and of which she writes.
She herself has said that it was not an awareness of the problems of
her country, or a political consciousness as such, that set her writing;
on the contrary, it was learning to write that sent her 'falling through
the surface' of the South African way of life.[24] Here we see the
converse of that point: the degree to which writing in South Africa
has shaped the innermost forms of Gordimer's fiction. One theme of
this study will lie in detecting exactly this sort of formal structuring
in her work, and tracing both its significance and its transformations.

An issue that must arise in South Africa – and it arises very strongly
– concerns what one might call the *morality* of the writer. What
stand, that is to say, should the writer take in relation to apartheid?
Because of the sheer nature of oppression and exploitation that life
under apartheid involves this issue would seem to leave no room for
imprecision or neutrality. Yet Gordimer's initial positions on this
problem appear, to say the least, as paradoxical. Her pronounce-
ments on the morality of the writer – the term is in fact hers – read as
if they might well have come from an aestheticist manifesto. As far as
'commitment' is concerned, she declares that the writer's first and
foremost obligation must be only to the craft of writing itself. To this
end she cites – as well she might – Proust:

> the artist must at all times follow his instinct, which makes art the most
> real thing, the most austere school in life and the last true judgement.[25]

Encountering positions put forward by Sartre she maintains that the temptation to place writing at the service of a social or political cause is always a betrayal.[26] Elsewhere she indicates that the only affiliation she is prepared to tolerate – indeed, it appears, to insist upon – is 'the writer's freedom to write or not write about whatever aspect of the life around him he chooses'.[27]

This all sounds very surprising in the South African context; it also seems surprising in the light of Gordimer's often stated and demonstrated personal antipathy to apartheid. But in this matter for her there is clearly to be a distinction between personal feelings and the vocation of being a writer. We might question how this could be the case; how, for instance, is one to separate one's beliefs and emotions as an individual from one's preoccupations and tendencies as a writer? How is one to separate out social ideologies and codes of reference from one's 'personal' view? Despite this, Gordimer maintains her primary fidelity; fiction is to be the servant of one good only – truth – and nothing should be allowed to stand in its way. In this she draws inspiration from yet another writer, Turgenev. For Turgenev also wrote in turbulent times, in pre-revolutionary Russia; he too was subject to moral and political pressures. But when criticized by sections of the Russian left for his unflattering portrait of the would-be revolutionary, Bazarov, in *Fathers and Sons*, his reply, as Gordimer quotes it, was a straightforward one: that in the given case 'life happened to be like that'.[28] For her this then becomes something of a creed; her task in every given case will be to describe life 'as it happens to be'. This does not mean her writing will be politically reactionary; indeed, as far as she is concerned, no political cause worth supporting has anything to fear from the truth. But it does mean that the taking up of prior political positions is liable to mar the truthful aspect of fiction. It is then partly *because* of the great political pressures existing in South Africa, and the temptation they offer of too easy or formulaic a response, that Gordimer is so intent on 'keeping her allegiance free'. Political questions will not be avoided in her writing; indeed we know the opposite is the case. It is simply that Gordimer will attempt to deal with them with the greatest honesty at her command. For her the obverse of a freedom to gaze on everything without fear or favour is clearly an obligation to do so.

This has definite implications for her fiction. For one thing, a corollary of this position for Gordimer is an implicit theory of what may be termed 'naïve realism'. This has less to do with any question of perspective than with what the fictional work is held to reveal. For Gordimer, in the work of the honest writer social truth simply 'appears':

> My novels are anti-apartheid, not because of my personal abhorrence of apartheid, but because the society that is the very stuff of my work *reveals itself* ... If you write honestly about life in South Africa, apartheid damns itself.[29]

After what we know of ideology, after Barthes's explosion of the fallacy of 'realism' in fiction,[30] we have reason to doubt this proposition. Social conclusions are not what simply emerge through the unmediating agency of the writer and her typewriter, and the appearance of ideology in successive and changing forms in Gordimer's fiction will be evidence enough that the writer cannot be wholly objective and neutral. At the same time, however, the position of naïve realism and the morality that infuses it are nevertheless of significance. To begin with they ensure that Gordimer's outlook, if not directly political, is, in one sense, 'historical'; her aim is to deliver the kind of fictional judgements whose vindication might be the verdict of history; one of her central objectives is to help *constitute* such verdicts, as the witness and chronicler of her time. Also, the 'naïve' aspect means that in each novel Gordimer has set out to investigate as honestly as she believes possible the implications of history for her world. This does not mean we have to trust her conclusions; as has been pointed out, to be honest is not necessarily to be correct, even to the extent that a wholly 'neutral' honesty is possible. But this procedure on Gordimer's part suggests that in her *consciousness* of history she has explored to the full the perceptions available to her of it; and we can then explore this. Moreover, this dedication on her part has a further relevance. For, committed to this position as she is, Gordimer is continually clarifying and reclarifying her thought. This keeps her novels always up to date with events and means she is always uncompromising in considering her own position in *relation* to these events. It also means that she is always modifying past positions in the light of whatever weaknesses her own reconsideration or the evidence of new developments implies. In other words, this makes Gordimer's historical consciousness a *developing* affair, a matter itself of historical process, which it is then up to us to trace and assess.

Gordimer's fiction is engaged with history in one final, and perhaps unexpected, way. For her novels are not just novels of observation, or of realism (in either sense seen so far), or of any of the other features just noted. In addition each of them ends with a vision, and it might properly be called an historical vision. It is a vision of the future, from the present, for the society and the characters with which it has dealt. The vision of each novel is not entirely separable from its observation; in part it is a product of its observation, in part it is towards the culmination of its vision that the observation of each novel tends. Also, the relationship between observation and vision is not always coherent; indeed, it is frequently contradictory (something that will be of great interest to us). But in terms of the complex totality made up by the two – observation infusing vision and vice versa – all of Gordimer's novels might be said to stand as social and historical hypotheses. They are fictional 'models', which, surveying both present and future, attempt to assess their implications for the world with which they come to grips. This totality may then be designated as embodying a specific historical consciousness, which is open to criticism to assess.

IV

At a certain point in her career Gordimer has realized that her fiction stands as an historical record. In the introduction to her selected short stories she writes that the chronological order of the chosen works is also, intrinsically, an historical one:

> The change in social attitudes unconsciously reflected in the stories represents both that of the people in my society – that is to say, history – and my apprehension of it; in the writing I am acting upon my society, and in the manner of my apprehension, all the time history is acting upon me.[31]

This is an important awareness; from this time on Gordimer is fully cognizant of the role fulfilled by her fiction. Yet rather than being a solution to the question of how history appears in her work, it seems instead to be the substance of all the questions we should be asking. Its key terms indicate large areas for investigation: 'unconsciously'; 'reflected'; 'society'; and perhaps the biggest abstraction of the lot, 'history'. What does each of these mean? How, and in what senses, is history 'unconsciously' reflected in Gordimer's work? Is it a case only of 'reflection'? What does one mean by 'society' in a country such as South Africa, and to which South African 'society' does Gordimer have access? Finally, what does a 'consciousness of history' itself imply for fiction? These questions are large ones, unlikely to be solved once and for all here. Yet ultimately they are the questions upon which our discussion must revolve, raising as they do issues of consciousness, ideology, social structure and historical development, and their relations to one another and to fiction. On these issues it would be as well to clear some preliminary ground, introduce some relevant concepts and pre-empt some possible misapprehensions.

The primary concept that we need to introduce – and not overestimate – is that of *limitation*. Our brief review of the various features of Gordimer's writing dealt with the 'subjective' aspects of its approach to the world, in terms of its methods, morality and vision. Another way of expressing this is to say that what we gained access to was the prospective *range* of Gordimer's historical consciousness in its view of the world. But there is another side to this; for an overall view we have to balance the subjective account by understanding the objective conditions that may affect and modulate, if not determine, Gordimer's approach. And in so far as we are dealing with a *consciousness* of history it will be clear that we must be able to measure not only its range, but its *limits*. For a consciousness of history is in one sense defined only by its boundaries; these give it its contours, perimeters and hence, for us, perceptible 'shape'. What then are the limits and limitations affecting Gordimer's writing? How are we to measure them, and what will they reveal? What part do they play in the shaping of an historical consciousness?

Let us begin again with textual matters. In so far as Gordimer's work is subject to limits of one kind or another, we may question her novels not only for what they say about their situation, but also for what they do *not* say. Each text may be examined for those areas towards which it gestures and appears to lead, but of which it cannot directly speak, or else must include only as the locus of an internal contradiction, because of some intervening limitation. This is one version of Pierre Macherey's concept of the 'not-said', and what it always reveals for him is a given text's ideological framework. This is because for him fiction is always a 'working on' ideology: provoked by it, and limited by it, the fictional text always displaces ideology through its formal operations. And it does so especially at those points that ideology is supposed to conceal, where it becomes contradictory or incoherent. Reading the text 'symptomatically' for its zones of silence or disjuncture, then, one determines the limits and contradictions of its ideology.[32] In Gordimer's work this kind of limitation appears to some extent. Though her novels are seldom neatly classifiable ideologically, and though ideology is sometimes a matter of positive statement in her work as much as it is of silence, this will form a significant area of our investigations. We shall be able to trace in Gordimer's novels a fairly dramatic ideological shift over the period in which she has been writing.

However, there are other kinds of limits that also apply to her work. First and foremost, Gordimer's novels are circumscribed by nothing less than their historical situation itself. As would be the case with any writer, there are necessarily always horizons to what is visible to Gordimer at any given time; partly this is because she is contained by the moment with which she engages. It is then primarily this historical limitation that her work will reveal at significant points of silence and contradiction. But there is also a further dimension of confinement to be taken into account, especially in a country such as South Africa, and this concerns the question of social limitation. For South Africa is an extraordinarily 'limited' society in a structural as well as a moral sense. It is impossible here to give a full account of South African social relations in their entirety, and any generalizations will have numerous exceptions. But the central feature applying to the world in which Gordimer lives is plain enough: that in South Africa there is a system of rigorous social division maintained and regulated by the apartheid state in the dual interests of white profit and white power. What constitutes this division at its most decisive level is that, in general terms, lines of class and race coincide; a politically oppressed black population is also, by and large, a dispossessed proletariat, moreover one maintained in that situation through the coercive powers of the state. Class and race are more or less defined in terms of one another; to be born black is not only to be deprived of the vote, but virtually to be committed to the role of worker, whether in industry, mining, or agriculture, at generally extortionate rates of pay. To be born white, on the contrary, is to enjoy a position of privilege, most obviously in terms of the vote but also socially and economically, even at the lower echelons of white society. Where exceptions occur (as for example

15

in an emerging black 'middle class') either the political or economic
function, but generally both, confines blacks to a subordinate role,
whites to a position of supremacy. From birth to death destiny is
divided; South Africa is separated down the class and colour line.

Reinforcing this is social apartheid. Laws exist to keep the races –
and classes – distinct, from the broadest of spheres to the most
intimate. In the former category the Group Areas Act prohibits
mixing in housing and living areas; in the latter the Immorality and
Mixed Marriages Acts have prohibited sexual relations and marriage
across the colour line for most of the period in which Gordimer has
been writing.[33] In education, racial separation and the gross
inequality of schools have meant not only that blacks have been
fitted pre-eminently for their positions as workers, but that culturally
separate worlds have been constructed for blacks and whites. It
is this that, as the *Oxford History of South Africa* points out,
constitutes Nadine Gordimer's 'world of strangers'.[34] All of this helps
define the general congruence of race and class; and this then most
decisively governs social mobility and access. In England a writer
such as George Orwell could go and live among the workers of
Wigan in the 1930s, and no legislation prevented him from staying
there for ever if he had wanted. In South Africa there is such
legislation, and it applies in every sphere of existence. Moreover, to
give the basic division between black and white is to note only the
most obvious aspect of social fracture in South Africa. In effect,
because of its peculiarly regulated and structured system, the South
African social formation is one riven in any number of different
directions – along the lines of class and colour, and various
sub-groupings within this, but also according to ethnicity and
gender.[35]

Living in South Africa in these terms may well be, as one
commentator has suggested, something like existing in a nightmare
world invented by 'a demented structuralist anthropologist'.[36] If this
is so in experiential terms, however, then analytically South Africa is
liable, ironically, to be a structuralist's dream. For if one is interested
in the relationship between consciousness and class, there is surely
no more class-ridden society than South Africa's, moreover one that
is fractured within its broad divisions into numerous fairly distinctive groups. In these circumstances, considering South African
literature, one might well expect that in any given instance a work of
fiction will be confined by, and to, its social point of origin. There is

even a ready-made literary theory that would seem to apply: Lucien Goldmann's account of 'genetic structuralism'. In his study of Pascal and Racine in *The Hidden God*, Goldmann argues that the great literary work condenses the world-vision of its class; there is a strict homology between the structure of the work, the structure of the world-vision it represents and the social structure from within which it emanates.[37] There is an especial temptation to use this model in relation to Nadine Gordimer. For in considering Pascal and Racine, Goldmann is also considering a *haute bourgeois* class that has been politically marginalized: the Jansenists of seventeenth-century Port-Royal. As a class characterization this would, in general terms, fit Nadine Gordimer's situation perfectly, and much of what Goldmann points out in relation to the Jansenist world-view – for instance, its 'tragic' vision and the prominence within it of paradox – is highly suggestive for Gordimer's fiction.

Yet, though the kind of social limit implied in Goldmann's approach is crucial, this is where it must not be overestimated. For although it is necessary to have a conception of social limitation in Gordimer's work, it is important to have no rigid presupposition of how it will apply in any given instance, nor a static conception of how it is effective over time. In fact a straightforward structural approach runs the risk of missing a good deal of what is going on. For one thing, Gordimer's marginality is itself an historical – and not simply structural – feature, changing in form and implication over the course of her writing career. Also, because her novels take up successive ideological positions they can be said to represent no one single 'class'. At different stages, indeed, the category of 'class' is both too large and too small to be adequate on its own for considering her work. In responding at certain times to an overall historical moment, which is after all general, Gordimer crosses both class and colour boundaries. At others, because of the ideological position she takes up, she occupies a small margin within her class situation. In short, historical process cannot be reduced to social structure, even – and perhaps especially – in South Africa.[38] If we have our eye on anything in particular in this study, it is process rather than structure. We shall see Gordimer pushing at limits, and sometimes crossing them, as well as being confined by them. At the end we shall return to some of the broader structural features of Gordimer's work, which perhaps obtain over the whole period in which she has been writing, in order to see what they can tell us about a 'deeper history' in her novels; but even here it will become apparent that their implications are by no means simple.

On this question of limitation, then, three levels apply: the historical, the social and the ideological; all will be under examination simultaneously in the analyses that follow. The notions of contradiction and silences within the text will be crucial, for this is largely where these limits will be revealed, and where the contours of Gordimer's historical consciousness will emerge. As to the wider significance Gordimer's novels may have, in terms of what or who they represent, this will always at the least be conjunctural: a combination of the overall historical moment with which she engages, her social situation and the ideological position she takes up. Such representativeness may range from the most general historically to the most defined socially and ideologically. It will be a matter of analysis in the case of each novel to determine what this representative aspect is.

V

In the light of the issues that have been raised, other methods and objectives of this study can be suggested fairly briefly. To begin with, it will be implicit here that Nadine Gordimer's work cannot be understood fully without seeing it in relation to its South African context. It is the stock response of critics and reviewers – both inside and outside South Africa – to insist that Gordimer's work is 'universal', that it could have been written 'anywhere'. In the guise of appreciation this is to deny what Gordimer herself discovers: the radical historicality of South African existence. Even those attuned in some sense to the politics of Gordimer's work are not sufficiently so; Gordimer is taken throughout as being simply a 'liberal' writer, without due attention to the shifts and complexities of her vision and its wider social resonance.[39] Elsewhere, thought-provoking interpretations suffer from inadequate knowledge of the facts of Gordimer's situation and their intricacies and nuances.[40] Gordimer's work could not have been written 'anywhere', and while there are many ways of approaching her fiction, these will never be complete unless its close relationship to South African history is taken into account.

It is then equally implicit here that 'valuable art comes into being not *despite* its historical limitations, but *by virtue* of them'.[41] It is not because Gordimer's fiction transcends its historical situation, but because it is significantly linked to it, that its value is created. Indeed, if there is a theory of value in evidence here, it is one of *use* value. There will be no attempt to decide how 'good' Gordimer's novels are according to some abstract literary or aesthetic criteria. Rather, Gordimer's work is valuable in so far as we are able to use it to explore South African history; this is the counterpart of our use of that history to understand her novels. Yet this does not mean there will be no attention to formal or aesthetic matters. On the contrary, Gordimer's novels are so valuable historically *because* they are so accomplished and developed as fiction. Thus, form will often be the key to consciousness, and it is where the novels are aesthetically richest that they are most useful for tracing out our history. For here they contribute something specific to that history; and if this means that they do so by delineating limits and contradictions, it does not make them any less valuable.

It should also now be clear why this study, while dwelling here and there on Gordimer's short stories, is focused more directly on her novels. It is not as if the short stories have no connection with larger social developments – on the contrary they do, as Gordimer's remarks in the introduction to her selected volume indicate. But there are some differences between the short story and the novel as forms, differences that make the latter far more significant for our purposes. To put it simply, the novel is both more intensive and more extensive historically than the short story could ever be; it is a question of degree, but one that approaches 'kind'. Gordimer's short stories, while often rooted in an identifiable social world, turn in general on human intricacies of a psychological or emotional nature, and this is the basis of the short story as a form. Also, because the stories are by definition shorter, and expressions of a more coherent moment of conception, they are more easily susceptible to what is normally called aesthetic 'perfection', a feature for which Gordimer's stories are rightly renowned. For us, however, this is a disability; we need the significant contradictions, silences and gaps revealed in the longer work. And the novels, due to the sheer expanse of their exploration in space and time, of necessity investigate their social and historical situation in greater depth and at greater length. Their project is more substantial historically, their need to make meaning of history more decisive. They are sustained meditations and examinations of what history involves for the world from which they emerge and with which they deal.

It is then largely through the novels that we shall be exploring our 'history from the inside'. This is not a 'literary history' in the conventional sense. One of the primary contexts within which Gordimer works is that of a specifically fictional tradition; this hands down to her the various modes, genres, operations and conventions of her work, the various ingredients of her novels. But what we are concerned to see here is what has been made of them in Gordimer's hands, and why, and especially what has been made of them in relation to her historical environment. Nor, on the other hand, is this a social history, though there will be some social history involved. What we are concerned with here is more specific than that; we shall be tracing a *textual* history, but one in which the notion of 'text' extends beyond the borders of fiction. We shall see how broader social and historical codes are embedded in Gordimer's novels; we shall see how her novels in turn illuminate those codes. We shall see historical developments as in part 'textual'; we shall see Gordimer's texts in historical terms.

Overall, then, the different aims of this study emerge as threefold: to understand the various aspects that go towards making up an 'historical consciousness'; to understand fiction as a narrative medium in which they are embedded; and finally, in following a developing consciousness of history in Nadine Gordimer's novels, to contribute, in some small part, towards a history of consciousness in South Africa.

1

Personal Exploration:
Early Work and *The Lying Days*

Our life in the mining town . . .

Nadine Gordimer, 'A South African childhood: allusions in a landscape'[1]

Before beginning with Gordimer's first published novel, *The Lying Days*, it is worthwhile 'placing' it in relation to the patterns of her earlier work in order to suggest some of the continuities and changes that it marked. Nadine Gordimer was born on 20 November 1923 in the small mining town of Springs on Johannesburg's East Rand. Her first literary attempt was a poem she wrote at the age of 9 as a school exercise. This was a eulogy on Paul Kruger, patriarchal President of the old South African Republic, and symbol for many South Africans of a proud Afrikaner nationalist heritage. We might remark on the fact that Gordimer's political consciousness at least was to change markedly over the years that followed, but she records that in composing the poem she was attracted as much by the rhythm of the words as by their meaning: a timely reminder that a consciousness of history in her work is always modulated through the determinations of form.[2]

Thereafter Gordimer's progress as a writer was steady and sure. An editorial note appended to a short story of hers on the children's page of the Johannesburg *Sunday Express* in 1938 reveals that for over a year (i.e. from the ages of 13 to 14) she had been producing work for the paper's young readership.[3] Her first publication in the adult world was a short story entitled 'Come again tomorrow', which appeared in *The Forum* when she was 15.[4] Of this story Gordimer remarked later that it was full of 'the respectable bourgeois sentiment one might expect',[5] but this is a little harsh. In fact the story shows a notable poise and sensitivity in dealing with the life of an old man who finds a lost human engagement through a financial crisis in his family. It evidently had some effect; after this Gordimer published regularly in local journals and magazines in South Africa, such as *The Forum, Trek, Common Sense, Vandag, Jewish Affairs* and *South African Opinion.*[6] These were not specifically literary magazines as such – indeed, there were really no such outlets for the young writer – but characteristically politico-cultural organs, many of which had been founded as organs of liberal opinion to counter a rising Afrikaner nationalism in South Africa in the 1930s and 1940s, and a wider world fascism at large. In this way, from the start, Gordimer's work fitted into the broader political and cultural history of her time, though here not only in terms of its content, but also because of where it appeared. Gordimer's only play was published in 1949,[7] the same year as her first volume of short stories, *Face to Face.*[8] Many of the stories included in the latter collection re-appeared in *The Soft Voice of the Serpent,* published in 1953,[9] the same year as *The Lying Days.*

A survey of Gordimer's short stories up to 1953 reveals some notable patterns. Most of them are not *politically* conscious as such; on the contrary their major concern lies in moments of psychological illumination, or in an exploration of the human condition *per se.* On the other hand they do provide a fictional point of entry into an intriguing social history, rooted as they are in the kind of world that formed Gordimer's early environment. Something represented quite well here, for example, though it disappears from her later fiction, is a significant focus on a poorer white class. In 'A commonplace story' we are presented with the daily – and it seems eternal – round of a small-town piano teacher, married to a fitter who works on the mines. Scarcely separable from her social situation in the story is Gordimer's strong imagining of the woman's internal life in its alarming depletion and vacancy. 'The battlefield at no. 29' presents another situation from this world: an Afrikaner nurse engaged in an obscure struggle for survival against her Scots mineworker husband and his mother (a struggle that in the end she loses). 'Sweet dreams selection' settles on the world of a Greek café owner and the ambiguity of his life – serving people whose culture he doesn't understand, and who certainly don't understand his. Indeed they seem set to use him as the explanation for, and the butt of, the threatened nature of their own lives.[10]

These stories, and others like them, represent microscopic observations to be sure, but they are social vignettes of remarkable precision. This was a skill, developed early on, that Gordimer never lost, which later led directly to the much vaster historical topics

22

tackled in her writing. As far as the particular focus on the poorer white world is concerned, in *The Lying Days* this is more muted, but is nevertheless still there as Helen Shaw drinks tea with Joel Aaron in Atherton's local tea-room, or as she observes Afrikaner assistants in shops.

More directly continued in the novel is a strong concentration on a local Jewish world. Nadine Gordimer herself came from a Jewish background; her father was an immigrant from Lithuania, while her mother was of English Jewish extraction.[11] Neither was particularly religious nor culturally integrated with the local Jewish community. Gordimer's mother, she tells us, was far more involved with the Scots Presbyterian women of Springs; and Gordimer herself went to a convent school. Nevertheless, she did have access to a local Jewish world, and one she found somewhat exotic as well as slightly alien. In telling the story of her childhood she relates how when visiting relatives in the Orange Free State she and her sister would be offered tea from a samovar and smoked duck flavoured with garlic for breakfast; this notwithstanding the fact that the young children of the immigrant family spoke Afrikaans and played with the Afrikaner children around them.[12] In *The Lying Days* Gordimer's depiction of the Aaron family is infused with this sense of richness and strangeness, whether it be in the kind of sweets offered to Helen there, or the talk that goes on around the Aaron table. There are other motifs overlapping from the short stories to the novel. Thus, both in the short stories and in the novel Gordimer is clearly drawn to the concession stores that were found on the mines, usually leased out to poorer Jews to sell goods to the black workers. In *The Lying Days* Helen Shaw's relationship with her parents is a difficult one, and also of interest in the early stories is then a distinct theme of betrayal, as children 'betray' parents in emerging from the economic and social world that the latter inhabit into new and developing environments. In 'The defeated' a daughter betrays her parents, who run a concession store. They have given the daughter everything they have; but when she marries well, and moves off to Johannesburg, she hardly ever comes to see them, and more or less forgets them.[13]

In this and other ways it is likely that Gordimer's early work responds to a period of social transition, as a world based economically on mining and culturally on colonial and immigrant formations gave way to a growing industrial economy and the more sophisticated social and cultural patterns to which it gave rise. In 'The defeated' it also pays attention to a characteristic manifestation of the white *nouveaux riches* of South Africa, whatever their origins: the way in which, lacking any other tradition, and needing to deny their own history, they conveniently tend to forget the past.

Some of Gordimer's early stories, however, are what one might call politically conscious in the more normal sense. Characteristically, these deal with the petty agonies of a troubled liberal conscience, as in her 'masters and servants' stories such as 'Ah, woe is me' and 'Monday is better than Sunday', which explore everyday exploitation within a domestic setting.[14] The limited focus does not mean, however, that these stories have no force. Given their time and place Gordimer was in a way treading new ground: 'Ah, woe is me' is in part a careful satire on the supposedly sensitive white 'madam' who, when the crunch comes, can afford to give no more than a few shillings and a bundle of old clothes to the daughter of the woman who used to work for her and who is now in desperate poverty and extremely ill. A few of the stories go further. 'The amateurs' explores both the inauthenticity of liberal 'good works' (in this case an amateur theatrical company playing in one of the black townships) as well as its alien cultural assumptions (the play produced is *The Importance of Being Earnest*, which hardly any in the audience can understand, and the evening descends into a farce of a different kind).[15] 'The train from Rhodesia' details the extraordinary meanness of white exploitation in Africa; here a black artist, selling his wares by the railway side, is beaten down to a ridiculous price for the wooden sculpture of a lion he has crafted. One of the white couple involved at least feels disgusted with herself, and again the question is at what price this already privileged class will count itself to be doing well; what, in a sense, it can really *afford*.[16] Another of Gordimer's earliest stories, 'Is there nowhere else we can meet?', is, as we shall see later, a remarkably concentrated anticipation of much that her future work would explore. An allegory on numerous levels at once, sexual, political and historical, it represents the inevitability of a future cataclysmic encounter in South Africa, as well as the ironies of its postponement in the present.[17]

Given this sort of development on Gordimer's part it is a matter of some surprise to come across one particular passage in an unfinished and unpublished novel, which she wrote early on in her career, dating from before 1946.[18] This was her first attempt at writing a novel, and the fragment shows the verve and spontaneity that perhaps characterize such first attempts. The setting of the piece repeats certain themes already mentioned. Once again there is a Jewish focus as the novel opens in the home of Sam Karanov, an immigrant Russian Jew and one-time concession store-keeper who has evidently explored some of the avenues open for success in a developing white capitalist economy; a brass plate on his office building reveals that Sam is now the wealthy director of 'KARANOV LTD, (SA)', incorporating 'SOUTH AFRICAN CONCESSION STORES, PTY LTD, EMPIRE BANTU STORES, "MINE BOY" & "EMPIRE" CLOTHING CO.' as well as a number of similar companies (pp. 26–7). In Gordimer's depiction of the Karanov household there is a certain amount of good-humoured observation of the Jewish–South African world, but if the fragment promises some social comedy, then there is also historic tragedy. For the work is set during the Second World War, and opens on the day that Sam learns, through the casual impersonality of a newspaper photograph and caption, of the death of his brother, and the latter's entire family, at the hands of the Germans in Poland. Such a coincidence (Sam coming across the photograph) may seem a little improbable, and the theme is not developed much further in the unfinished novel as it exists. But the juxtaposition of the Jewish concession store-keeper made good in South Africa with the Nazi holocaust in Europe seems to hold out some promise, in terms of the work's initial project, for the exploration of unusual historical overlaps and ironies.

In fact, as suggested already, there is only something of a surprise. The passage that provides it occurs a little way after the novel's opening, as Ruth Karanov (Sam's daughter, and evidently meant to be the novel's central character) is driving her father to work after he has received his dreadful news. The two traverse the city on a kind of condensed rake's progress from wealthier to successively poorer areas, passing through what Ruth calls 'the wonderful, young, thrusting, vivid town' (p. 23) until they get to its worst slums, where blacks and whites live together. The narrative voice comments:

> Here is the squalid, degenerate meeting-place of black and white blood; the common ground of commercial sex which is the only level upon which the ancient taboos are swept aside and the two bloods may meet. These are misbegotten people, thin, ugly, misbegotten children, living not because there was a place for them to fill, but because there was no place for them, because they were born of the misfits of both the black and the white races, of men without the sense of responsibility which is self-respect. (p. 25)

Here one might suspect some irony, seeing the novel has opened by giving a prime example of the larger, global effects of such racism. But in effect no irony is visible, and on the contrary the passage's keywords are a give-away. 'Degenerate'; 'bloods'; 'misbegotten'; 'misfits'; 'ancient taboos': this could easily be a quotation from Sarah Gertrude Millin's *God's Step-Children*, which, as noted already, with its racial obsessions sets up the standard in South African English fiction of a paranoid blood-consciousness.[19] Perhaps the young novelist *is* quoting Millin, in a sense; this may be what she feels a South African writer is obliged to say on such occasions. But the fact then remains that Gordimer found nothing objectionable in this recapitulation, and the ideological position it represents was one to which she was able to give assent.

We are used to Nadine Gordimer as the implacable opponent of apartheid, but the above extract on the contrary shows the degree to which, as a young writer, she could be held within the dominant patterns of white ideology in South Africa. At the same time it marks an extraordinary reference point – Gordimer's curiously unconscious low-water mark – by which to measure the remarkable series of changes undergone in her writing in the following period of over thirty-five years. It is also a suitable point to begin indicating how, since this passage was written in 1946, Gordimer has never let up on herself ideologically, how she has committed herself to a continuous process of self- and social scrutiny, clarifying, re-evaluating and, when necessary, rejecting her own ideas and values. To this extent she could not be more unlike Sarah Gertrude Millin. By the time of her second novel, *A World of Strangers*, what is 'young, thrusting and vivid' is the black world excluded by white Johannesburg.

Gordimer wrote a second unfinished and unpublished novel before *The Lying Days*, dating from about 1951.[20] If this merits any mention here at all, however, this is only because of its almost total obliviousness of the broader social and political issues at stake in South Africa. Instead, telling a tale of marriage, it gets caught up in a cloying world of bourgeois sophistication and ennui and never seems likely to get out. If the fragment suggests anything, it is only that there was nothing in any sense predetermined about Gordimer's becoming an historically conscious writer in the form in which we now know her. This was something produced as much as it was given, which has undergone a continuous transformation.

If Gordimer had not been born in South Africa, she might have been a very different kind of writer, and this is supported by the evidence of our survey of her early work. For its basic pattern is one of unsettlement, from the psychological focus of most of her short stories, to the critique of liberal postures in some of them, to the crude racism in her first attempted novel, to the social amnesia of her second. This, then, was the young writer finding her voice, exploring in a very personal way her own world and her literary capacities. And this is then also the perfect place to begin our discussion of *The Lying Days*. For *The Lying Days* is almost literally a novel of personal exploration, which grows towards finding its own 'voice'. It chronicles the moment in which a deeper historical consciousness is both discovered by Gordimer and then to some extent discarded. As such it marks a crucial transition as her fiction makes its first decisive, though ultimately incomplete, move towards its characteristic 'consciousness of history'. It stands as both a summation of what has gone before and a prelude to what is to come.

The fundamental historical concern of *The Lying Days* lies in its general encounter with its local environment (much like the 'allusions in a landscape' of Gordimer's article on her own past, it consists of a kind of continuing social geography). In general this is traced out in the novel in following the career of its central character and narrator, Helen Shaw, from the social strictures of a small Witwatersrand mining town, to a romantic interlude at the sea in Natal, to the experience of life, love and politics in the more hectic world of Johannesburg. As an intrinsic part of this encounter the novel undertakes a veritable wealth of social observation of the world with which it engages, and this is also the first level at which it tells a 'history from the inside'. The most arresting part of this observation concerns the Mine estate in the town of Atherton in which the young Helen grows up. To some degree it appears to be autobiographical; that is to say, this observation seems to have been drawn from the details of Gordimer's own early youth. The novel is after all autobiographical in form, and certain of the descriptions of Atherton are on occasion almost image for image the same as those of Gordimer's descriptions of Springs, where she grew up.[21] Yet Gordimer did not live on the mine estate in Springs, or 'The Property' as it was called; her father was a watchmaker and jeweller, and the Gordimers lived in the town. Furthermore, as Gordimer herself records it, there was a fairly strict demarcation between mining-folk and townspeople in Springs, and it was only through a close friendship with the daughter of a mining official that she came to know of the mining world at all.[22] What appears to be autobiographical in the most autobiographical of Gordimer's novels is therefore as much the product of close observation as it is of personal experience. It seems almost emblematic of Gordimer's method of writing in general that this should be the case.

An extraordinarily strict hierarchy governs the Mine estate on which the young Helen grows up; the novel details its written and unwritten codes. For the men, the pyramidal chain of command on the Mine is repeated in every aspect of their social and economic lives, down to the respective sizes of the houses to which they are assigned, and their access to private use of black workers as 'garden boys' to care for their lawns. For the women a ritualized and formalized pattern governs the cycle of their entire existence; after school they are expected to attend a secretarial course, work for six months, get married (preferably to Mine men), have children, go to tea parties and preside over the same pattern in the younger generation. Significantly, this world is shown as being part of the surviving remnants of an English colonialism. The colours the Mine women favour are 'the blues and pinks of English royalty',[23] while the whole of the parental generation still regards England as 'Home' (much as do the white settlers of Doris Lessing's Southern Rhodesia). When Helen brings home her lover, Paul Clark, her parents, not knowing she has been living in what they would call sin, view with favour a prospective marriage because Paul comes from Natal, which is in itself a guarantee of pure English blood and allegiance to England. If one married an Afrikaner, says Helen, the disappointment would never be swallowed. But interestingly for the English ideology that the novel portrays, the lowest rung on the social ladder is occupied by the Jews; if one went so far as to marry a Jew, Helen remarks, one would get the awe and sympathy with which people normally regard an aberration (p. 245). There is no mention of marriage with blacks. This, it seems, is totally outside the mental parameters not only of the Mine, but also of the novel itself. In this way *The Lying Days* reveals just how 'exclusive' white South African racism has been, in so far as it literally excludes blacks from its consciousness; but also it gives an indication of the degree to which 'racism' has existed within the white world itself.

Elsewhere the novel suggests the class stratification internal to the white world with which this racism is interlocked. The Mine itself is English-owned (its name is Anglo-Albion) and the English are characteristically in positions of command. Afrikaners work as their underlings, or else are assistants in English-owned shops. Lowest of all are the Jews who run the concession stores or, as Helen's mother puts it in a moment when the constraints of good manners are suddenly ruptured, 'live among all the dirt and the kaffirs' (p. 192). As an overall picture of the South African political economy, even at the time of the novel's writing, this account is not entirely to be trusted; it is a strictly small-town depiction that is given. But it is nevertheless of wider relevance. One of the primary motivating impulses of the Afrikaner political victory of 1948 was to overturn the social and economic dominance of the English in South Africa that the novel shows. From this point of view the novel illustrates the conditions providing that motivation.

Relations between black and white on the Mine are not detailed to any great degree, but one incident of note is the strike that Helen witnesses as a young girl (pp. 35–8). What is noteworthy about the strike, however, is its essential quietude and provincialism. In fact it is not quite a strike at all; the workers, objecting to the bad food they are given, lay siege to the Compound Manager's house one Sunday – not, after all, a working day. Nor is this siege particularly fiery; the miners sit around fairly amicably on the lawn outside the house, while inside there is yet another tea-party on the go, replete with a hostess handing round scones to the hastily gathered Mine officials, apologizing for the circumstances of the affair and blaming the flies on 'them' outside, because they always bring flies, apparently even to a strike. In the end the demonstration is resolved without fuss. The 'boys' agree to return to the Compound, while for his part the Compound Manager decides not to reduce their ration of 'kaffir beer' despite the fact, as the young Helen puts it (seeming to express the mood of the assembled whites), that the black miners had behaved 'very badly'. As the paternalistic pieties of the Mine world emerge unscathed it is evident that to some degree an extraordinary moral banality has sustained the practices of exploitation in South Africa.

Yet the docility of the workers themselves is remarkable, and here one might compare the strike, as it appears in the novel, with the most important strike that actually occurred in the period covered by *The Lying Days*, the African Mineworkers' strike of 1946. The difference could not be more dramatic, for the 1946 strike was the largest single stoppage in South African history up to that time, involving some 50,000 men, closing down nine mines and partially paralysing twelve others; it was also suppressed extremely brutally.[24] Interestingly, there is no mention of this strike at all in the novel, although the white miners' strike of 1922 – that extraordinary affair, fought under the slogan of 'Workers of the world fight and unite for a white South Africa!'[25] – is included. Of the latter Helen regrets that she had been born too late for its excitement and danger, but of the 1946 strike the novel knows nothing. Gordimer remarks that at the time of writing the novel she would scarcely have been aware of it.[26] In terms of her own political consciousness, Gordimer herself at this time was evidently still contained within the same framework in which the young Helen grows up, and which she tries to escape. But this again does not mean that the account of the strike in the novel need be dismissed. In her description of this tremor from the periphery Gordimer gives us a valuable insight into some of the daily realities of labour relations on the Witwatersrand in the 1930s and 1940s.

One of the most important areas of exploration in the novel concerns the experience of the non-conformist white growing up in this situation, especially in so far as it involves a consciousness of race. In an article of 1977 Gordimer detailed the problem precisely. In South Africa, she argued, the strictly historical development of race and class domination becomes ideologically 'naturalized' for most people, taking on the character of an immutable, eternal and, to all intents and purposes, God-given order.[27] Thus for most people growing up, and this includes blacks as well as whites, it becomes almost in the natural order of things that whites should rule and be wealthy and that blacks should be poor and be workers. But, she maintains, there is still the possibility of unravelling this myth-bound cocoon, and in doing so there is for the individual something like a rebirth – a birth into a 'second consciousness'.

This question of 'rebirth' forms a specific topic of *The Lying Days*, for one of Helen's deepest attempts is to attain a second level of awareness, in particular by transforming her attitude to blacks. It is interesting to see where she has to start from. At one point in the process Helen remarks that she suddenly understood that she had lived all her life among strangers, the Africans, whose very language to her had been like 'the barking of dogs or the cries of birds' (p. 186). Notably here Helen, in her 'naturalization' of the political order, had placed blacks *in the realm of nature itself*, evidently – in the large sense – to be exploited like any other natural resource. This question of the inversion of social and natural categories in South Africa is of continuing importance to Nadine Gordimer's work, as we shall see in *The Conservationist*. But if anything is revealed in *The Lying Days* it is the sheer difficulty of escaping the hold of an imprisoning consciousness, even for those who want to. Even the novel itself does not do it. Blacks hardly appear in their own right in *The Lying Days* at all, except as objects who create moral or human problems for whites; to this extent the novel reveals how far its own 'rebirth' is incomplete. And when Helen does try to break out of her ideological confinement by befriending Mary Seswayo, a black co-student at university, she ends only in failure, for ultimately she is unable to relate to Mary simply as a person. On the contrary, in her deliberate and over-conscious attempt to do so there is an implicit paternalistic overcompensation, a state of mind and morality that, Helen is forced to concede, is active within and not outside a framework of racial discrimination. This particular quest is left unresolved in *The Lying Days*, therefore, though in *A World of Strangers* it is taken up again. But here, because of this open resolution, the most telling representation of the dissident white experience lies in the novel's depiction of what Helen calls the 'slow corrosive guilt' (p. 211) plaguing her conscience, located in the gap between what she realizes ethically and what she is capable of practically. Helen claims this guilt appears in all white South Africans, but it is probably more true to say that it represents a characteristically white liberal feeling, our first indication that *The Lying Days* is in some sense a 'liberal' novel.

A related feature of white consciousness explored by the novel is its cultural alienation from its local environment. On this topic *The Lying Days* opens with a veritable *tour de force* as the young Helen, truantly straying down the road towards the Mine Compound, comes across the concession stores where goods are sold to the black workers (pp. 13–25). The contrast could not be more vivid; a young Scots girl dressed in a kilt, standing outside a concession store run by immigrant Jews, confronts the paraphernalia of an indigenous black culture drawn from all over southern Africa – its lions' tails, snake skins and colourful blankets. Helen discovers a life previously unimagined by her. Yet, significantly, half exhilarated, half scared by her daring and discovery, she runs back down the road to join her parents at the Mine tennis club, where all its members are dressed in uniform white, make uniform jokes and shut out entirely from their lives the colour and vitality of the world they are suppressing. Later in the novel Helen's friend, Joel Aaron, identifies this cultural alienation. Atherton, he remarks, is just a makeshift Europe or America, and has no South African identity at all:

> I think about it often. It comes up whenever I think of going away and coming back to Africa . . . I correct myself; not Africa, 129 Fourth Street, Atherton.
>
> (p. 147)

Interestingly, in the novel, both Joel and Helen *do* decide to leave South Africa, though ultimately Helen resolves to return. The decisions to leave are none the less significant in that both are in part occasioned by the alienation that Joel identifies. In Helen's case especially there is a more specific pressure moving her to leave, but at the general level a clear thematic point is being made: that the historical implication of the alienation of English culture in South Africa is a state of quasi-exile that more particular crises turn from a disposition into a reality. In his powerful short novel, *A Dance in the Sun*, published three years after *The Lying Days*, Dan Jacobson explores this same alienation.[28] And as far as Gordimer's writing is concerned, Michael Wade has shown that this theme of the 'European in Africa' is a recurrent and crucial feature of her work.[29]

A corollary of the novel's investigation of South African cultural identity is its exploration of the question of South African *literary* identity. Early on in the novel Helen remarks:

> I had never read a book in which I myself was recognizable; in which there was a 'girl' like Anna who did the housework and cooking and called the mother and father Missus and Baas.
>
> (p. 20)

In its own energetic insertion into its local environment this is a lack that *The Lying Days* – and all of Gordimer's fiction – is clearly designed to remedy. In this regard the moment in which the young Helen confronts the cultural mêlée of the concession store can be claimed for South African literature as the exact opposite of the alienation later identified by Joel Aaron. One of the novel's fundamental commitments, that is to say, lies in its acceptance of a South African identity for itself. In so far as Helen is both central character and narrator, the novel's exploration of her identity as South African is also the exploration of its own narrative identity, as it formally investigates the grounds of its production and existence. At base this commitment to a South African identity is also an historical commitment, for it marks an acceptance, by Gordimer and by the novel, of a local environment as an ultimate source and an ultimate destiny.

This is not a commitment to be underestimated; any broader social transformation for whites in South Africa must entail a moment of commitment such as this. But it is also not a commitment particular to this novel, or to the period within which it was written. If we think of Olive Schreiner's *The Story of an African Farm*, written some seventy years earlier, we find – albeit in more muted form – a sustained engagement with a local environment and, in theory at least, an acceptance of a South African identity.[30] But if we are concerned to uncover the more specific features of the historical consciousness of *The Lying Days*, then two aspects of the novel must be explored: first, its response to its immediate historical environment; and second, the attempt it makes to transcend history altogether.

The most important event that occurred in the period in which *The Lying Days* is set was the general election of 1948 in which the National Party, representing predominantly Afrikaner interests, came to power. The novel responds to this transition in strong terms. Remarking on the victory of what she calls the 'Fascist Nationalists', Helen Shaw notes its effect on the people around her:

> the moral climate of guilt and fear and oppression chilled through to the bone, almost as if the real climate of the elements had changed, the sun had turned away from South Africa, bringing about actual personality changes that affected even the most intimate conduct of their lives.
>
> (p. 256)[31]

This marks the crucial discovery for Gordimer of the integral relation between private and social destiny both in South Africa and therefore for her fiction, although it is a relation that the novel later tries to escape. But this response is important in other respects as well, for here the novel begins to identify itself with, but also to differentiate itself from within, broader movements of mood and feeling in the period from which it emerges. For Helen's appellation of 'fascist' is no mere matter of whimsy; on the contrary it was a term in widespread use at the time, and this for very good reasons.

The open affiliation of both leading and rank-and-file Nationalists to the German cause during the Second World War was well known, while some of the more extreme organizations associated with the rise of Afrikaner nationalism in the 1930s and 1940s, such as the Ossewa-Brandwag ('Ox-wagon Sentinel') and the New Order, had been explicit in their support for Nazi ideology and its characteristic forms of political practice. In the immediate aftermath of the war the National Party attempted to distance itself from such movements, but in the English-speaking mind no such easy distinction was possible. The National Party had itself barred Jews from membership during the war, while many who had been fascists or fascist sympathizers were now finding their way back into the Nationalist fold. Such memories and associations had a decisive impact on a broad spectrum of liberal and left opinion. Even the politically mild Torch Commando, formed by ex-servicemen in opposition to Nationalist manipulation of the constitution, felt that it was carrying on the struggle against a wider fascism that it had so recently fought.[32]

Reinforcing such memories was the political programme instituted by the Nationalists. In fact there are many reasons for considering that there was as much continuity as change between the pre-1948 United Party regime of Smuts and the Nationalist government of Malan that succeeded it, on both structural and ideological levels;[33] Helen Shaw herself says that the change she noted in the atmosphere around her was not sudden but seeping. Nevertheless, the victory of the Nationalists *did* make a difference, and of greatest force in this was its publicly voiced ideology of racial purity and white supremacy, legislated into political reality in many different forms. Thus, the early 1950s saw the first of the clumsy and protracted attempts to remove the Cape 'coloureds' from the common voters' roll;[34] it was primarily in response to this that the Torch Commando was mobilized. The Group Areas Act (1950) legislated for the forcible separation of different ethnic groups living in common or adjacent areas. The Native Laws Amendment Act (1952) reinforced and streamlined the regulation of black labour for white use in the urban areas. The ironically named Natives (Abolition of Passes and Co-ordination of Documents) Act (1952) standardized and extended the pass system. The Bantu Education Act (1953) brought all black education under state control – where, said its architect, future Prime Minister Verwoerd, it would be used to train its recipients to fill 'certain forms of labour' only.[35]

On a more intimate level there was the social projection of the

most obsessional aspects of Nationalist racism. Under th
lation Registration Act (1950), every South African had
registered as a member of one of the officially designated
groups. The Prohibition of Mixed Marriages Act (1949) made
marriage between members of different races illegal, while the
bizarrely named Immorality Act (1950) extended existing legislation by making sexual relations between whites and any 'non-whites'
illegal. *The Lying Days* details some of the humiliations involved in
this legislation, such as couples who may have lived together for
years being woken up in the middle of the night with police torches
shining in their eyes.

This legislation was enforced with a good deal of brutality – an
intrinsic component of the new Nationalist ethos. For this was the
period that saw the demise of the previous official ideology of
'trusteeship', under which whites were meant to act as guardians of
their supposedly 'uncivilized' black wards, and its replacement by a
less camouflaged position of *baasskap* (literally, 'boss-ship'), which
jettisoned the idea of guardianship completely in favour of the more
straightforward one of supremacy. The Afrikaans slogan under which
this took place was 'Die wit man bô en die kaffer op sy plek' ('The
white man on top and the kaffir in his place'), and its symbol was
the *sjambok*, on hide-whip. This must have been one of the few
occasions in history when a newly appointed Minister of Justice was
especially photographed with a cat-o'-nine-tails in his hand.[36] On a
political level the government indicated its determination to take
the initiative against its opposition with the Suppression of Communism Act (1950), in the face of which the Communist Party of
South Africa (CPSA) disbanded. However, the Act was used not only
against communists, but against many non- and ex-communists as
well. As a wide range of people were 'listed' as communists or
banned, it might have seemed as if a new era of total repression was
approaching. The new legislation invoked by the Nationalists and the
atmosphere that went with it can only have reinforced the logic of an
analogy with 'fascism' at this time.

If the analogy was correct, then South Africa indeed faced a grave
crisis, and this is where Helen's remark on the Nationalists is again of
wider importance. For its sense of cataclysm was the inevitable
correlate of its overall perception. For some South Africans, quite
simply, it must have seemed as if a world they knew was ending. For
the politically involved there was a definite urgency at this time.

Fighting Talk, the journal of the radical ex-servicemen's league, the Springbok Legion, reacted to the Suppression of Communism Act by predicting, 'without panic' (it claimed),

> the inevitable appearance of storm-troopers, imprisonment, 'suicides', religious persecutions, concentration camps, for Nazism is a process, an inexorable process.[37]

On Verwoerd's Bantu Education Act the Congress of Democrats (the white component of the Congress Alliance of the 1950s) remarked that this was a version of white culture that began 'at the school desk of white supremacy – "herrenvolkism" – and finds its end in the guards at the gates of Buchenwald, and the death factories of Maideneck'.[38] *The Lying Days* is not as strongly worded as this; the rhetorical comparison with Nazism was perhaps played for all it was worth at this time. But given the recent past, and the ideological associations of Nationalist racism, the logic of such a comparison was both compelling and dismaying. In its reaction to the 'Fascist Nationalists', Gordimer's novel absorbed the general feelings of its time, and its response was in accord with wider patterns.

But it would be a mistake to exaggerate the extent of this motivation in the novel, nor should the position of *The Lying Days* be too easily identified with the radical perspective of *Fighting Talk* or the Congress of Democrats. If anything is indicated here it is that a fairly unitary historical response can be dispersed across a wide ideological spectrum. For Gordimer's novel can in no sense be described as radical. For radicals in 1948 the world may have been difficult, but it was comparatively straightforward; in opposition to apartheid their commitment would have been to the immediate cause of black liberation. The deepest feelings of *The Lying Days*, however, are characteristically different, and in this it is responding not only to the Nationalist government but to the movement for black liberation itself, which, for special reasons, causes it an almost equal unease.

By the time the novel was being written, black assertion in South Africa was reaching a definite and climactic impetus. An important date in this development was the foundation in 1943 of the Congress Youth League of the African National Congress (ANC), which, within the parent body, was strongly nationalist minded in outlook and far more militant than the older generation of leaders had been.[39] But other factors too were involved. As industrialization and proletarianization increased both before and during the war, black workers themselves were becoming more demanding. It was a series of illegal strikes by black workers in the early 1940s that culminated in the African Mineworkers' strike of 1946. This in turn galvanized the leadership of the ANC, which, confronted after 1948 by the strict *baasskap* of the new regime, began to see its characteristic posture of supplication to white governments for participation in the ruling processes as essentially futile. In this context the leadership began to respond, as well as appeal, to a wider mass backing. During the 1946 strike the Natives' Representative Council had adjourned in protest, never to meet again. Now in 1949 the ANC's Programme of Action called for direct and universal representation in South Africa, and proposed as methods towards achieving this end the use of boycotts, civil disobedience and national stoppages of work. The immediate culmination of this ascendant phase was the Defiance Campaign of 1952–3 in which volunteers – mostly black, but also including Indians, 'coloureds' and a few whites – defied apartheid laws by wilful and systematic contravention. During this campaign it is claimed that the membership of the ANC rose to 100,000, its highest ever.[40]

The Lying Days was probably completed some time before the Defiance Campaign began. Yet from what has just been said it is clear that around the central moment of 1948 a dominant pattern had been formed in South Africa; this was the lining up of the two forces of Afrikaner and African nationalism, both decreasingly prepared to make compromises, for what may well have appeared to be both an imminent and ultimate historical showdown. And this in turn was the setting for a further important feature: the historical exclusion, because of its increasing irrelevance, of the middle ground in between. It is precisely this middle ground that *The Lying Days* occupies, and this exclusion underlies its characteristic response to 1948. This is first apparent in the novel through the figure of Helen's lover, Paul Clark.

Paul Clark works as a welfare officer in the Native Affairs Department, a state administrative institution that at that time regulated black life in South Africa in general. His job in the novel, however, is to deal with housing problems, and he is therefore not involved in the more oppressive features that work in that department entailed. And this is Paul's rationale for taking up his position in the first place; he feels it not only gives him access to a black world in a way open to few whites, but also allows him to be active practically in using the resources of an oppressive system to undermine it from within, or at least to ameliorate its worst effects. In this way he begins to live a strange double life, working for a department administering official state policy with regard to blacks on the one hand, and collaborating with friends of his in the ANC on the other. Under the Nationalist regime, however, Paul begins to be torn apart by the contradictions inherent in his position. Increasingly he comes to realize that the state charity he administers is part and parcel of a policy of systematic oppression. Equally important, his ANC friends, becoming more militant, begin to reject his collaboration, regarding Paul's position as intrinsically compromised. As for Paul, he becomes psychically divided, falling into bouts of cynicism and depression; there can be no escape for him within the circle of his structural entrapment. As Helen puts it: 'He cannot lose, and he cannot win. He scarcely knows anymore what to hope for' (p. 295).

Paul's love affair with Helen too begins to fail in direct proportion to his political anguish, and in its sustained investigation of this breakdown the novel explores very powerfully how broader political change can indeed affect 'the most intimate conduct' of people's lives. Between the forces of a white supremacist apartheid, with which he is objectively complicit, and a rising African nationalism, with which he sympathizes but in his complicity cannot join, Paul has experienced an historical exclusion.

In different ways the presentation of Paul Clark stands as an ideological marker for the novel. To begin with, through him it has explored the demise of a specific legitimating ideology: the ideology of 'trusteeship'. In effect this ideology has been the justification of Paul's position, that he is acting as some kind of paternalist 'guardian' of black welfare. Under the Nationalists, however, this ideology is displaced as its contradictions become bluntly apparent; in characterizing its downfall the novel has not only captured a central aspect of the history of its times, but has dramatized the implications of this change for individual life. On the other hand, this exploration reveals something about the ideological position of the novel itself. The point is made if we consider that never after this time would a character such as Paul have been of much interest to Nadine Gordimer. After this time the ideologies both of 'trusteeship' and *baasskap* would have been equally suspect to her as representing mere variations on a theme of white supremacy. In simply working for the Native Affairs Department a figure such as Paul would have clearly stated his affiliation. But in the degree to which Paul's case *is* of interest to the novel, its own ideological response is inseparable from the historical moment from which it proceeds. For at no other stage could the difference between 'trusteeship' and *baasskap* have been so important or comprised the basis of a real crisis of experience.

This feeling of historical exclusion is represented equally strongly in the case of Helen Shaw. Here, however, it is significantly different. For if Paul is in some sense still an *actor* in the world of 1948, then Helen is pre-eminently a *spectator*. This becomes most directly apparent in the novel's central symbolic incident. In accordance with its 1949 Programme of Action, one of the stay-at-homes organized by the ANC was called on May Day 1950, in protest at the Suppression of Communism Act. In fact there was much confusion and some bitterness over its organization,[41] but none the less the stay-at-home was one of the first tests of strength between the new government and the ANC. As the Commissioner of Police put it, expecting trouble, force would be met with force on that day.[42] In the novel Helen is made to witness something of what ensued; and what is revealed in this trial of strength is her own essential irrelevance.

On May Day, Paul is in one of the black townships, working with an ANC friend. Another (white) friend of his, Laurie, fearing for his safety, telephones Helen to find out where he is, and the two set out by car to find him. Travelling through the township, however, they are confronted by a riot, and this is where the incident becomes symbolic. Sealed in the immobilized car, Helen watches with meticulous yet horrified fascination the scene that unfolds before her, culminating in the shooting and killing by the police of a black rioter, who falls to the ground in front of her eyes. The encasement of the car symbolizes at once her privilege, security and alienation in the face of this 'force meeting force'. And, significantly, the traumatic memory of the rioter's death most deeply affects Helen in her later decision to leave South Africa; waiting in Durban to board ship the image of this death stays most strongly in her mind. Historically, therefore, the May Day riot acts as a kind of primal scene for the novel, and what it signifies is Helen's fundamental exclusion. In her closest approach to the realities of 1948, as spectator, she is also absent, precisely as spectator, and this basic alienation is acknowledged in her decision to leave. Certainly she also decides to leave because her love affair with Paul has failed; but in so far as political change has caused the breakdown between them, again the realities of 1948 stand behind her decision.

Ultimately Helen changes her mind, deciding that she will return to South Africa after all – after what is now to be only a holiday in Europe and not permanent exile. This marks a final acceptance by her and by the novel of a South African identity, and this is Helen's critical *rite de passage*. But to the extent that the pressures of 1948 have made a major contribution to the thematic tension that produces this resolution, it is clear that these pressures have been fundamental to the deepest movements and motivations of *The Lying Days*. Questions surrounding the transition of 1948 constitute the largest historical problem confronted by the novel. Finally, it may be suggested that all figurations of Helen in the novel as spectator – and they are numerous – are in part related to this feature of historical exclusion.

However, the novel's final concern is not with the events of 1948. Helen is made to go through them, and they have a major impact on her development, but all this must ultimately be seen in the light of the novel's wider interests as a whole. Structurally considered, *The Lying Days* is episodic in nature, and from this point of view the section dealing with the world of 1948, although vital, must be seen as only one among many, including Helen's childhood on the Mine, her holiday and sexual awakening in Natal, her continuing relationship with Joel Aaron, and her encounter with Mary Seswayo at university. In this context the novel's treatment of 1948 is only part of its wider social and historical engagement with a local South African environment, and its fashioning of a South African literary identity. But there is also in *The Lying Days* a diversification away from even these concerns towards more historically abstract areas. Thus Helen's remark on the 'Fascist Nationalists' is just one of innumerable observations in the novel, and this across a highly varied range covering matters such as the nature of love, the relationship between parents and children and – one of the more important themes in *The Lying Days* – the psychological dialectic generated by the antithetical attitudes of realism and idealism. In this way, like the majority of Gordimer's early short stories, the novel heads towards a far more conventional fictional concern with the 'human condition' as such. Moreover, this concern seems to be of greater final importance for the novel than its purely historical engagement. Here we must begin to consider what the novel does *not* approach historically as part of its historical consciousness. And here *what* the novel observes is of less importance than the terms of analysis governing its view. For these lead us not so much to the world observed by *The Lying Days*, but to the central features of the consciousness that is doing the observing.

There is in *The Lying Days* a structural absorption of all its concerns, both historical and non-historical, into an ultimately autonomous domain of private existence. In itself this is an attempt to transcend history. For at stake finally in Helen's career is not so much the importance of her observation, historical or otherwise, in itself, but the degree to which her *assimilation* of what she sees forms the character, constructs the personality and deepens the understanding of Helen alone. Even the death of the rioter on May Day, which is after all her most blunt confrontation with an outer reality, is abrogated in terms of its final significance to the more subjective war between realism and idealism being waged within her:

> even that real death, dropping on its victim before my eyes, seemed unreal to me because it was not my idea of death; even in the midst of a brutal reality, I was not involved, I remained lost, attached to the string of a vanished idea. I looked at Paul out of this lostness.
>
> (p. 328)

Moreover, it is precisely in the degree to which the rioter's death, distressing as it is, precipitates a deeper understanding, on Helen's part, of her own inner condition that the novel's teleology becomes apparent. For *The Lying Days* is in fact a fairly conventional *Bildungsroman* – a novel of education and learning. The emblem of its embodiment in this novel is that Helen is both central character and narrator, for in her case it is the accretion of subjective understanding through her experience as a character that converts directly into her knowledge as a narrator. Helen's transition is one from being into knowing. So we follow her path from one maturity of consciousness to the next until the novel itself is the outcome of her accumulated wisdom, and of the process of its accumulation. This process threads the episodic and otherwise picaresque nature of the narrative into a thematic unity. As far as its consciousness of history is concerned, however, little more need then be said to indicate that for *The Lying Days* the ultimate locus of historical development lies

41

in the inner life. This, indeed, as defined by Helen, is 'the real, the personal realm in which life is lived' (p. 330). And it is as a triumph of personal life that the novel's climax occurs:

> I was twenty-four and my hands were trembling with the strong satisfaction of having accepted disillusion as a beginning rather than an end: the last and most enduring illusion; the phoenix illusion that makes life always possible.

(p. 367)

The words come as Helen, waiting to leave for Europe, feels herself more than ever connected to South Africa; but in this, the novel's final satisfaction, a transfer from an outer to an inner dimension has clearly taken place. Helen's acceptance of an apparently eternal contradiction signifies that this is to be regarded as an achievement of maturity. And the future projected for her is one of unceasing advance and check between the poles of illusion and disillusion, realism and idealism: a history, that is, of consciousness, but of consciousness purely subjectively considered.

The novel's ethic supports this resolution. In general, in ethical terms *The Lying Days* is deeply socially aware. It would opt for a principle of love if it could to solve the problem of social division. 'It's integration, love is,' remarks one of the characters, and the pun is chosen advisedly, for the opposite of integration is of course segregation. But the novel is also instructed by its awareness that love cannot be decreed. Even in its most direct form, between Helen and Paul, love fails, while one of the stronger sub-plots of the novel concerns a latent but continuously suppressed love affair between Helen and Joel Aaron, which never comes to fruition. If loves does not last between individuals it cannot be expected to work socially. The principles of love, on the one hand, and realism, on the other, are therefore reconciled in the novel in a third term: that of 'acceptance'. 'Acceptance' is the ethical keyword of *The Lying Days*. Thus Joel, the novel's authoritative moral voice, tells Helen she must 'accept' her parents for what they are; in the end Helen comes to 'accept' Joel for what he is; finally, as we have seen, she joyfully 'accepts' the fundamental contradictions of life. In this respect the novel is typically humanist in form, not only tolerating paradox and contradiction, but actively coming to celebrate them.

If Helen could 'accept' Mary Seswayo as a human being this would constitute something of a triumph over apartheid. To this extent the novel's ethical principle is proposed as a method of social triumph.

On the other hand, in the instant that it becomes an overriding principle its political ambiguities become clear. What *The Lying Days* does not consider is that a thoroughgoing principle of 'acceptance' must ultimately fall subject to the governing terms of an apartheid environment; for this in the end decrees the social reality to be 'accepted'. In this light it is notable that the reason Joel and Helen finally become reconciled to the fact that their potential love has never been fulfilled is that both come to 'accept' what Helen, on virtually the last page of the novel, calls 'the unreasoning ties of the blood' (p. 366). This means that Joel is a Jew and Helen is a Christian, and that this has decisively obstructed their relationship. But in so far as the investigation of racial difference in the white world has served in the novel as prolegomenon for its exploration between black and white, an 'acceptance' of the 'unreasoning ties of the blood' sounds distinctly ominous. At this point Gordimer's terms of analysis revert back to those we found in her unfinished novel of 1946.

In its final affirmations, therefore, *The Lying Days* appears to fulfil Hegel's observation on the ultimate social complicity of the *Bildungsroman* or, as he calls it, the novel of apprenticeship in general:

> For the end of such apprenticeship consists in this, that the subject sows his wild oats, builds himself with his wishes and opinions into harmony with subsisting relationships and their rationality, enters the concatenation of the world, and acquires for himself an appropriate attitude to it.[43]

Historically considered the novel's ethic reveals its own self-contradiction: finally contained within an ideological framework that in other respects it tries genuinely to escape.

The overall patterns of historical consciousness in *The Lying Days* are then clear. As we have seen, the novel's widest engagement is with its South African environment, and in this it is particularly concerned to deal with questions of cultural and literary identity; most importantly, the novel stakes out a South African identity for itself. Within this, however, the focus of *The Lying Days* is almost entirely on a white world and white consciousness; blacks enter the picture only in so far as they impinge on the latter. The novel responds strongly to the immediate historical moment of 1948, and registers very deeply a feeling of exclusion between the forces of Afrikaner and African nationalism – a feeling that has characterized, in different ways, the political middle ground in South Africa ever since. Ideologically, it occupies a humanist position, and displays a largely liberal consciousness and conscience, though even within its own terms it suffers from basic contradictions, and has clearly not thought out a liberal ethic in anything like exhaustive fashion. Finally, the novel sites the ultimate locus of historical development within an inner, subjective realm; it is somehow fitting in this regard that the work in which Gordimer begins to find her distinctive literary 'voice' should formally declare itself to be one of 'personal exploration'.

In all these ways *The Lying Days* gives a precise image of the rise to consciousness of one version of South African liberalism. Finding its human concerns intrinsically involved in a broader social field, and following these where they lead, the novel nevertheless bears the marks of luxury in the final egocentricity of its form and the contradictions of its categories. Yet for Gordimer this historical and ideological position by no means ended there. Over the next three decades it was to change dramatically and radically. In *The Lying Days* Gordimer had found her sense of 'place'. What this was to mean, with increasing force from *A World of Strangers* onwards, was locking into the 'time' of her society.

2

Social Commitment:
A World of Strangers

Which new era would that be?[1]

The approach of *The Lying Days* to history is idiosyncratic. It engages with its social world only to withdraw, in its ultimate pursuits, to an essentially personal realm. It coincides with some of the major political moods of its time, but does so unevenly and only tangentially. However, in Nadine Gordimer's second novel, *A World of Strangers*, the personal focus of *The Lying Days* is fully socialized; moreover, the novel is absorbed directly into the dominant patterns of thought, mood and outlook of the moment from which it emerges. Conceiving of the problem of apartheid primarily at a social level, and attempting to solve it by social means, *A World of Strangers* falls within the discourse of a liberal humanism, and relates to the fullest flush of the last great moment of that ideology in South Africa. Gordimer's third novel, *Occasion for Loving*, is conceived within the same social field as *A World of Strangers*. But in the specific differences of their conclusions these two novels chart a remarkable inner history of liberal humanism in South Africa from the mid-1950s to the early 1960s, and of the shifts of consciousness that were its subjective experience.

The beginning of this inner history, as it appears in *A World of Strangers*, published in 1958,[2] relates primarily to the dominance of multi-racialism as the political philosophy of the movements opposed to apartheid in the 1950s and, especially in certain circles in Johannesburg, also as a social way of life. On a political level multi-racialism was firmly ensconced as the official ideology of the Congress Alliance. For it was the Congress Alliance which virtually constituted the opposition to apartheid in the 1950s, and the Alliance was *par excellence* a multi-racial movement under the banner of multi-racialism. Essentially, what the idea of 'multi-racialism' involved was the belief that a rampantly segregationist apartheid could be countered only and most effectively by a cross-racial or multi-racial front. The sources of this idea had been around for a long time in South Africa, but they received a certain emphasis at the end of the 1940s when the ANC and the South African Indian Congress (SAIC) came together in the wake of anti-Indian riots on the part of blacks in Natal.[3] The Defiance Campaign of 1952–3, which, as we saw in the previous chapter, in one respect marked the culmination of the phase initiated by the Programme of Action, also embodied a 'multi-racial' aspect. Alongside the far greater numbers of blacks who volunteered to defy the 'unjust laws' of apartheid appeared a smaller proportion of 'coloureds' and Indians, and also a few whites.[4]

Thereafter, multi-racialism became more securely entrenched, and there were a number of reasons why this should have been the case. As far as the ANC was concerned it was partly because it could not on its own sustain the momentum and militancy of the early 1950s that it began to work more closely with the other Congress movements. In part it was more simply because the endurance of the Nationalist regime indicated that a broader front against apartheid was necessary; in this regard one notes a distinct toning down of the African nationalist element of ANC rhetoric over the decade as its political alliances spread wider.[5] But also one may suppose that it was the sheer effect of apartheid as an ideology that provoked its opposite, multi-racialism, into being. For if apartheid demanded social division, claiming that the races could never combine, the Congress movement would demonstrably prove that they could and, furthermore, insist on total integration as its ultimate objective. (To this degree the Nationalist government and the Congresses perhaps represented opposite sides of the same ideological coin, in their common discourse of 'race'.) For the Congress movement, moreover, means were to be identified with ends; it was a multi-racial organization that would bring about a multi-racial society. Thus the ANC entered into a loose, but committed, association with the SAIC, the South African Coloured People's Organization (SACPO), the South African Congress of Democrats (SACOD, a white Congress body) and the South African Congress of Trade Unions (SACTU, the only multi-racial trades union federation at the time). This was the Congress Alliance, and it set the tone for the rest of the decade. It was a multi-racial movement whose political essence was multi-racialism.

There was dissent within the Alliance itself. In particular the Africanist segment of the ANC – later to secede as the Pan-Africanist Congress – followed a stronger nationalist line. Yet mainstream ANC and Alliance opinion detected in Africanism a national chauvinism potentially as dangerous as that of the Afrikaners, and in the 1950s Africanist claims were always countered with the rebuke that white racism could not be met with black racism. Multi-racialism, there-fore, was the credo, and in the mid-1950s attained something of the status of an orthodoxy.[6]

Key symbolic moments emphasized this elevation. Thus, when 20,000 (mainly black) women descended on Pretoria to demon-strate at the Union Buildings against the extension of the Pass Laws to include them, it was a conspicuously multi-racial contingent that carried their petitions to the door of the Prime Minister (who of course was not there to receive them).[7] The most important symbolic moment of all, however, was the Congress of the People, at which the Freedom Charter was propagated. For it was here that delegates of all races assembled from all over South Africa to put forward a charter proclaiming as first among its principles that 'South Africa belongs to all who live in her – Black and White.'[8]

As a symbol of an alternative society in South Africa the Freedom Charter has remained, to this day, unsurpassed. And at the time there was a deep dedication and optimism surrounding the Congress of the People, and indeed the Congress Alliance as a whole. Even when the state indicated its own intentions by arresting 156 Congress leaders in December 1956 on charges of high treason, largely arising from the Freedom Charter meeting, these feelings did not at once abate; on the contrary, in the early stages at least of a trial that was to drag on for four years, they were if anything strengthened and reinforced. As crowds stood outside the Drill Hall in Johannesburg (where the preparatory examination for the Treason Trial was taking place) with placards proclaiming 'We stand by our leaders', one of the proudest claims made on behalf of the defendants was that together they constituted a multi-racial body committed to multi-racialism. Counsel for the defence pointed out that the accused came 'from all races, but all of them hold one thing in common . . . and that is a belief in the brotherhood of man'.[9]

The Congress Alliance was not, on the surface at least, a liberal movement. In many respects, on the contrary, it was a radical movement, proposing significant changes in the economic, political and social structures of South Africa. Yet it is important to note (as historians of both the Liberal Party and African nationalism in South Africa have indicated) that the ideology of the Congress movement in the 1950s, and especially of the ANC leadership, derived in large part from the South African liberal tradition: hence its emphasis on non-violent struggle, its belief in parliamentary democracy and its affiliation to the principle of inter-racial co-operation itself.[10] Conversely Congress steadfastness in these regards provided a distinct point of hope for a more orthodox liberal consciousness in South Africa. In particular, a belief in 'the brotherhood of man' almost defined the purest motivations of liberalism. In the public domain this correspondence was by no means straightforward; indeed, relations between the Liberal Party and the Congress Alliance were strained in the mid-1950s. This was partly a legacy of the strong denunciation by the ANC of the Liberal Party at the time of its formation in 1953.[11] On the other hand the Liberal Party believed that the Alliance was under the sway of communists who had infiltrated the movement upon the disbandment of the CPSA (later in the decade it would resuscitate clandestinely as the SACP) and who were now concentrated especially in the Congress of Democrats.[12] And to many liberals it appeared as if the Freedom Charter displayed only an obvious socialist bent. But Janet Robertson has pointed out that in the crisis surrounding the Treason Trial, and possibly in the sudden heroic aura of the moment, many liberals were ashamed not to be counted as part of the multi-racial opposition, and therefore took to the movement with compensatory vigour.[13] Thus, during the Alexandra Bus Boycott, when black workers from the township of Alexandra refused to pay an increase in bus fares, it was for the most part liberals who assisted by giving them lifts into Johannesburg by car.

In relation to the Treason Trial itself, liberals helped administer the Treason Trial Defence Fund and, both to honour and entertain the Trialists, generated a heightened degree of social activity in their Johannesburg homes. For some Trialists at least this was an eye-opener. Chief Albert Lutuli, President-General of the ANC and one of the accused, wrote later that he found an unexpectedly free world of contact and encounter in the social life surrounding the Trial.[14] Nor was this social meeting ground without political importance; here black leaders could translate the implications of their introduction to sympathetic and sometimes seriously involved whites back into 'multi-racial' political terms; here liberal whites could at last meet and be impressed by the stature of black leaders whom they had previously known only as names.[15] The result was a growing *rapprochement* between the Congress Alliance and a broader liberal front. By the time *A World of Strangers* was published, Lutuli was able to state that the ANC was finding itself 'more and more in agreement with the Liberal Party'.[16] And in particular, there was a widening and strengthening of that specific discourse we are concerned with in relation to the novel: of a democratic and humanistic multi-racialism.

If for the politically engaged the Treason Trial produced an unexpectedly free world of encounter, then on another and more specifically social level it is clear that this world predated the Trial. Important as the general political environment was for *A World of Strangers*, it seems to have been its social setting that informed it most directly. Looking back on the 1950s Lewis Nkosi called them a 'fabulous decade', a time when for one golden moment the normal social restraints of apartheid seemed blown to the winds.[17] In fact this liberation was confined to a select combination of classes; it was for the most part a black intellectual and cultural élite – typified by the journalists who worked on *Drum* magazine and *Golden City Post* – who, from their base in Sophiatown, penetrated the parties, living rooms and beds of a similar white élite in Johannesburg. Reporters, writers, critics and musicians – people such as Nkosi himself, Henry Nxumalo ('Mr Drum'), Ezekiel Mphahlele, Todd Matshikiza, Can Themba, Bloke Modisane and Nat Nakasa – took on the white world of Johannesburg with a determined abandon, and in part absorbed that world into their own. In this respect Sophiatown was itself a vital symbol of the 1950s: an ethnically mixed and vibrant 'black' township on the borders of Johannesburg, virtually part of Johannesburg itself.[18] In a number of ways this social world was related to the broader political moment of which it was a part. It was, most obviously, 'multi-racial'. Also, if politics were social in the 1950s, then this social world had its political overtones. Nkosi writes that Johannesburg life in those years had about it the air of a 'vast conspiracy against the state',[19] where every drink tippled in a white man's home evidently had the nature of a political triumph. Finally, this moment was related by mood; here optimism was translated into daring, dedicated resistance into heady rebellion.

All in all, this world was a kind of living social counterpart to that of political multi-racialism in the 1950s, and as such provided a crucial and immediate ground for the energies and visions of *A World of Strangers*. Moreover, a distinct cultural renaissance in these years, in part also defined by its multi-racial aspects, was contributing to this energy. For this was the time when 'township jazz' took on a sudden fascination for whites,[20] while the jazz-opera *King Kong* – which took Johannesburg by storm, and for which Todd Matshikiza scored the music – was itself intended to be a symbol of inter-racial collaboration, and the embodiment of a Euro-African cultural synthesis.[21]

A World of Strangers was generated out of this combination of circumstances – political, social and cultural. This was not just a matter of some magic fictional correspondence. Rather, the example of this particular novel gives us a rare opportunity to consider some of the more straightforward, but none the less exciting, ways in which an historical response is generated in fiction. For *A World of Strangers* reveals what is only more vaguely apparent in Gordimer's other work, or perhaps in other writing in general: that there is between the novel and the historical world to which it responds a fairly direct transitional and transformational medium – none other than the social history of the author herself, and the implicit social history of her text.

On a personal level, Gordimer had become immersed in the different aspects of Johannesburg life in the 1950s. She had become friendly with the members of the *Drum* set, first with Henry Nxumalo, then later with Can Themba, Todd Matshikiza, Bloke Modisane, Lewis Nkosi and Nat Nakasa.[22] With and through these people, she began to play a part in the cultural renaissance of Johannesburg in these years. Thus, she formed a writers' friendship with Ezekiel Mphahlele, who was also beginning his career in fiction at this time.[23] Politically, too, Gordimer was being drawn into a new world, albeit somewhat indirectly. Her black writer friends were themselves becoming politicized; Mphahlele was a regular contributor to *Fighting Talk*, and proposed the paragraph on culture at the Congress of the People.[24] They in turn politicized her. An important influence on Gordimer, both at this time and later, was an at first unsteady, but then increasingly firm and long-lasting, friendship that she began to form with Bettie du Toit, a banned Afrikaner trade unionist, and ex-member of the Communist Party. For both this was first and foremost a personal friendship, but for Gordimer there was no doubt a good deal of political education involved.[25]

As for the Treason Trial, Gordimer has remarked that to her it was 'a most important event'. When she was writing *A World of Strangers*, she has said, people who were in the Treason Trial were in her life. And it is of great interest to learn that at the same time as Chief Lutuli was enjoying the unexpectedly free world surrounding the Trial, he was, at least for a while, staying in Nadine Gordimer's house.[26] It was no doubt at this time that Gordimer wrote a short biographical piece on Lutuli for the *Treason Trial Bulletin*, which she later extended into a longer article.[27] In *A World of Strangers* we perhaps get a view of Lutuli as he was then in descriptions of older ANC leaders in their overcoats, with their nearly statuesque presence.

Much of the world of the 1950s is figured in the novel, most obviously in the many direct correspondences that seem to exist between the work and the life from which it emerged. On one level this is apparent in the novel's characterization. Upon the publication of *A World of Strangers* a Johannesburg newspaper report suggested that a 'popular party game' in the city just then was identifying who the novel's characters were.[28] The figure of Anna Louw, for instance, has more than a little to do with Bettie du Toit. Similarly Sam Mofokenzazi, the composer of the novel's jazz-opera, bears some relation to Todd Matshikiza, in real life the composer of *King Kong*, though Sam is far more grave a character than Matshikiza was. Steven Sitole in the novel lives in the House of Fame; in real life Can Themba called his home in Sophiatown the House of Truth. Perhaps the most celebrated correspondence is that of the central character himself, Toby Hood, who to some degree is probably based on Anthony Sampson, the editor of *Drum* from 1951 to 1955. Like Toby, Sampson was an Englishman who had come out to South Africa on a venture connected with publishing, and Gordimer had also become friendly with him. And if one is looking for parallels of this kind, then even certain incidents in the novel appear to relate quite closely to events that actually occurred. In his book on his years as editor of *Drum*, Sampson writes of a narrow escape during a police raid on a party at Can Themba's House of Truth in much the same terms as Toby, in the novel, describes his escape with Steven through a shebeen window during a similar raid.[29] He also writes of lavish lawn parties in the northern suburbs of Johannesburg much like those attended by Toby in the novel.[30] Even the heading of one of Sampson's chapters – 'Two Worlds' – is reminiscent of the title and general vision of Gordimer's novel. Numerous other echoes with *A World of Strangers*, of parties, police raids and shebeens, can be found in the writing of all the Sophiatown set.

The more one traces these correspondences, however, the more it becomes apparent that to appropriate the social history of the novel in this way, by pinning it down on a one-to-one basis, is to miss a large part of the point. For if the proliferation of parallels indicates anything it is that the social 'reference' of the novel in each case exceeds any single referent. If Gordimer's writing shows similarities with Sampson's, this is because they were dealing with the same realities. As far as characterization is concerned, whatever correspondences exist are for the most part only matters of external detail: hence Sam's similarity to, but important difference from, Todd Matshikiza. Also, it is only because the real-life figures who have been mentioned are famous that these correspondences surface in the first place. Lost in this method are the possibly numerous other people upon whom Gordimer's characters may have been 'modelled', or the degree to which they were not modelled on any particular person at all. And this is then really the issue. For Gordimer's characters are by no means simply 'based' on single real-life people. At most they are conglomerate figures, based on very many, and in this, as was suggested in the Introduction, their purpose is very different: to represent, as extreme condensations of more widely dispersed traits and possibilities, a feeling for the socially 'typical' – those ostensibly essential features that represent a whole mood and moment.

Thus Can Themba was not alone in naming his house so unusually; it was the habit of the Sophiatown set to call their homes the House of Commons, the House of Saints and so on.[31] More particularly, the character of Steven condenses for the novel the psychological patterns of a talented but frustrated intellectual élite in Sophiatown: their wit, bravado and resilience, but also their desperation and irony. The individual character, therefore, is not so much an allusion to any single real person, but more of a much larger social 'quotation' – a matter to which we shall return. And what is true of characterization in the novel is true in other areas as well: of its incidents, themes and moods. On a plane of typicality there is a continual recourse in *A World of Strangers* to the general patterns of the moment from which it emerges. At this level, the implicit social history of the text is far stronger than it would be by simple reference to single people or incidents. It is far less arbitrary, far more socially inclusive, far more historically substantial.

As in *The Lying Days*, then, in its observation of its environment the novel first reveals its 'sense of history'. So we find a good deal of description of the black world of Johannesburg – of the street life of Alexandra Township, of the parties and shebeens of Sophiatown. Though all of this displays the immediacy of first-hand observation, none of the writing is as direct and intimately vivid as accounts of this world by black writers themselves.[32] On the other side of the social divide, the novel's descriptions of a more purely white domain are for the most part confined to the world of the High House, that extraordinarily luxurious social enclave in the northern suburbs of Johannesburg into which Toby is drawn soon after his arrival in South Africa. Here we see, again at the level of typicality, what the novel conceives to be the representative traits of white South African civilization: its vulgar wealth, its cultural alienation and banality, its aggressive 'heartiness' and not least (as in the hunt at the end of the novel) its internal brutalization and latent murderousness. On a more general level the novel observes a very deep embarrassment on the part of many white South Africans:

> an unexpressed desire to dissociate themselves from their milieu, a wish to make it clear that they were not taken in, even by themselves.
>
> (p. 64)

By far the most powerful observation in the novel concerns the domain that defined the world of the 1950s as we have described it: the in-between area of contact in which black and white engaged. As such, the novel registers deeply the mood of discovery, for whites, of the black social world around them. In as much as Toby is an Englishman, Gordimer is able to pursue in this area the ambiguities of being a 'European in Africa' – which is, as we have already seen in *The Lying Days*, one of her most abiding concerns. Swimming for the first time off the coast of Africa, Toby feels the icicles of his European-ness melt. On the other hand, fascinatedly watching the organic movement of black dancers at a party of Steven's, he registers for his own part only the absence of the same capacity in himself. He understands for the first time, as he puts it, 'the fear, the sense of loss there can be under a white skin' (p. 122). The possible converse, it appears, of a moment of white 'Négritude' is ironically one of self-denigration.[33]

As far as the assumptions of the 1950s are concerned, the novel offers a corrective to the sometimes unabashed glee that attended its inter-racial socializing. For example, Toby remarks on the pitfalls of a white liberalism in which it became 'an inevitable fashion' to mix with blacks, or even to have a 'pet African' whose name one could drop in company (pp. 160–1). Some of the more glaring incongruities of this behaviour are well documented in the novel. At one inter-racial party the white hostess feels so relieved at the way in which she has been 'accepted' by her guests that she remarks to Sam and Steven, 'I'm going to see if our black brothers in the kitchen can't rustle up some tinned soup for us' (p. 164).[34] Elsewhere the novel notes the real difficulties of living in this frontier zone. Anna Louw's marriage to an Indian has been broken up by the pressures of apartheid, and she lives in a much harder world than the liberals. Yet for all that the novel shows a deep admiration for her courage and clarity, and her unceasing attempt ever to widen this zone and make it more genuinely habitable.

Again, however, in passing from the novel's observation to the *terms* in which that observation is conducted we approach a second level of the novel's consciousness of history: the self-revealing aspects of its presentation. In contrast to *The Lying Days*, private life for the characters of *A World of Strangers* is allowed no final autonomy either within or beyond the social world. Indeed, the entire impetus behind the novel is to prove that private destiny is inconceivable beyond its social integration. This it shows specifically by putting private destiny to the test, and it does so through none other than its central character and narrator, Toby Hood. For Toby is determined to lead a private life. Rejecting what he considers to be the moral voyeurism of his own socially conscious family, he comes to South Africa dedicated only to neutrality and strict non-involvement. In this way he indulges in a kind of amoral voyeurism, merely observing the world in which he finds himself. Chiefly he sees the massive social divide of Johannesburg, separating black and white into the 'world of strangers'. But he himself does nothing about it. In this way he is able to drift between the different zones of Johannesburg, from the lavish and exclusively white sphere of the High House to the Sophiatown shebeens, with an attitude of total indifference and detachment. He is able to conduct a fairly anaesthetic love affair with one of the High House circle, Cecil Rowe (echoes of Cecil Rhodes?), without ever telling her that his best friends in

Johannesburg are black men. To do so, he knows, would be to lose her, and this he is not prepared to do. Toby's quest for personal enjoyment overrules any qualms of conscience.

Toby has a counterpart in the black world in this quest: his best friend Steven Sitole. Whereas Toby has never really had any social commitment, however, Steven has jettisoned his. Having experienced, as a black man, only bitter frustration in all quarters, Steven instead finds solace in reckless living, in a personal refusal to be beaten, in a personal refusal to care. He is 'Sick of feeling half a man. I don't want to be bothered with black men's troubles' (p. 96).

It is the whole thematic force of the novel that to be disconnected in this way is both illusory and culpable. This is first evident in relation to Toby, where, by means of various narrative ironies, the hypocrisy of his position is made plain. But the point is most forcefully shown through the life, and death, of Steven. For while Toby is off on a hunting trip with his High House cronies Steven himself is killed like a hunted animal, in a car crash after a police raid on a club. To the policeman who reports his death to Toby, Steven is still nothing more than a 'kaffir', his social identity fixed in this way by others, if never by him.[35] Moreover, his death brings home inescapable truths to Toby. For Toby realizes that in their common egocentrism and social indifference, he and Steven had been of one nature; as he puts it, 'he was me, and I was him' (p. 240). In South African conditions, however, this common identity had never been, and could never be fully celebrated. Most tellingly, in a moment of sudden dread Toby understands that it is precisely his attitude of self-centred indifference that has helped constitute the social divide of the 'world of strangers' in the first place, and that to this extent he has himself been complicit in the general cause of Steven's death. The only moral rehabilitation appropriate to Toby then lies in a new social commitment. Specifically, it is a commitment measured in another friendship that he now takes up, this time with Sam Mofokenzazi. This friendship has none of the easy spark of Toby's relationship with Steven; that seems to belong to a previous era. But it is a friendship that is more sober, and more considered, and full of a deep new dedication. The start of this friendship marks the climax of the novel.

Any assessment of the novel's historical consciousness must to a large degree revolve upon the precise significance of this ending. It is of some value, therefore, to indicate firstly what this climax does not represent.

The social commitment arrived at in Toby's friendship is by no means a form of socialism. Socialism is in fact proffered as a possibility in *A World of Strangers*, but mainly so that it can be deliberately undercut. The only socialist character in the novel, Anna Louw, never represents any real historical option for Toby, though as has been said her courage is admired. More to the point, she herself appears to have found any systematic form of socialism to be a dead end. Of her membership of the Communist Party the novel is prepared to say nothing except that after a visit to the Soviet Union she had left the Party 'in revulsion' (p. 173), a fairly summary narrative dismissal. Sam Mofokenzazi, on the other hand, is consistently described in the novel as a 'decent bourgeois'. His home, remarks Toby, looks like a Chelsea flat 'done over' by a young couple. In addition, his strongly felt political ambition is for *all* his people to become decent bourgeoisie; it is this, remarks Toby, that his mind is always quietly revolving upon. If this conjures up images of a South African 'Uncle Tom-ism', however, then it is an accusation levelled by the novel itself, but only in order to draw its sting. Thus Sam is frequently depicted in the novel as a 'Black Sambo' character. But as Toby in the end remarks with new respect, the smile Sam habitually offers in superficial servility is also 'the smile of a tiger' (p. 252).

The novel tends to favour a bourgeois—liberal response, therefore, but this with a very special emphasis. For, all in all, the reason Anna's socialist position is discounted, and Sam's class peculiarity drawn, is only to accentuate all the more unmistakably the real nature of the solidarity between himself and Toby at the end of the novel. And this is nothing more or less than an intense personal commitment to one another and to one another's destinies. In effect, the friendship of Sam and Toby is meant to transcend all ideology. Behind this commitment is packed the symbolic weight of the novel as it closes. At the Johannesburg railway station, where Toby is about to leave on a business trip for Cape Town, he and Sam clasp arms triumphantly, invulnerable to the suspicious but not entirely malicious gaze of a young white policeman. Toby, also, has promised to be godfather to Sam's baby when it is born. The child represents the fertility of the future in a truly integrated society based on respect and human commitment; likewise it represents a cultural synthesis. In the triumph of Toby and Sam the 'only connect' of E. M. Forster's *Howards End* seems to be a reality; the 'No, not yet . . . No not there' of his *A Passage to India* apparently inoperable.

In the South African context, however, when a novel attempts to transcend ideology, one may suppose that it is most of all being ideological. In this connection it is worth comparing *A World of Strangers* with *The Lying Days*, for both changes and continuities are registered. Thus, *A World of Strangers* is far more rooted in society and the whole idea of sociality than *The Lying Days* ever was. In contrast to the inner history of the previous novel, virtually seven-eighths of *A World of Strangers* is devoted to social observation as a narrative activity distinct in itself. Furthermore, in so far as there is a personal history in *A World of Strangers* – that of Toby – it takes on significance only to the extent that it is reintegrated with society at the end, and emerges in social action. Whereas Helen's apotheosis at the end of *The Lying Days* resides in her transformation from character to narrator, it is interesting that Toby proceeds in the opposite direction, as he is delivered from his position as narrator into a future, active life as a character in his commitment to Sam.

On the other hand, if some of the features of *The Lying Days* have been superseded, others have been retained. If *A World of Strangers* marks the socialization of the personal ethic of the earlier work, its form of social commitment is none the less still a *personal* one, based on the same humanistic assumptions found in *The Lying Days*. Importantly, a transcendentalism remains; Sam and Toby are able to transcend social barriers through a purely human and interpersonal relationship. To this extent their triumph is a triumph of consciousness, just as Helen's was in the earlier novel.

This leads to an obvious criticism of *A World of Strangers*: that the terms of its resolution show only a naïve and idealistic attempt to cope with the massive social problems it has been set up to solve. In so far as the major part of the novel unflinchingly depicts only the extraordinary division of South African society, a doctrine of inter-personal commitment, designed to bridge the gap, appears to be hopelessly simplistic. In the discrepancy between its observation and its resolution the novel reveals itself to be only profoundly self-contradictory. Moreover, this criticism can then be extended. For if these doctrines of humanist commitment and inter-racial transcendence are taken as being fundamental cornerstones of South African liberal ideology in the 1950s – which, indeed, they were –

then Gordimer's novel can be used to demonstrate a wider historical contradiction, within South African liberalism itself.[36]

In a study of this kind it is always tempting to seize on an internal contradiction in the text. This, after all, reveals the boundaries of vision or consciousness. It is an added bonus if such a contradiction appears to reveal broader truths concerning the historical environment of which the novel is a part. And no doubt there *is* some form of contradiction in *A World of Strangers*, which we must try to assess. To attempt to seize on it too soon, however, would seem to be a mistake. For in different ways, both inside and outside the novel, the question of contradiction is by no means as uncomplicated as it might at first appear. In accepting too easily the notion of a simple 'internal contradiction' we not only miss what is really going on in the novel, but other mistakes are induced: first, of underestimating the true historical richness of the novel; and second, of then misjudging the broader social movements of which it was a part. It is best to resubmit this question to further, closer scrutiny.

To begin with, if there is an internal contradiction in *A World of Strangers*, it is by no means a straightforward one; nor are the novel's affirmations to be dismissed as merely misguided and naïve. If on the one hand the novel is concerned to differentiate itself from a socialist conviction, then on the other it is clearly designed to *counter* the faults of a naïve liberal humanism. We may remember the sharp critique that Toby levels at fashionable liberal socializing. More significantly, the allegation of an internal contradiction in the novel can be stood on its head. Seen from another point of view, it might be stated with equal force that the ending of the novel is offered not so much in *defiance* of its observation, but rather in clear-eyed and exact *recognition* of it. This in fact is one of the express thematic functions fulfilled by the simultaneous use of Toby during the course of the novel as both central character and narrator. For if through his observation as narrator Toby has established the sheer magnitude of the social problem that has to be solved, this is so that in his final commitment as a character he can by no means underestimate that problem. Indeed it might be said that one of the major reasons why Toby has been made to undertake his lengthy social observation in the first place is to establish his authenticity in this regard. Moreover, the quality of Toby's commitment is increased in proportion to the depth of his understanding; and in a very direct way he has had to ingest the full meaning of the 'world of strangers' through the death of his friend Steven Sitole – a death for which he feels a personal responsibility. The novel's resolution, therefore – and here we may properly speak of its resolution in distinction to its ending – is derived in specific acknowledgement, and not denial, of the weight of its observation.

In this connection there is a weakening element in the triumph of the novel's ending that must also be taken into account. At the station Sam is sceptical of the depth of Toby's commitment (Toby has so far given him no reason to trust it). Virtually his last words to Toby are offered, as Toby puts it, in a spirit of advance forgiveness: 'Who knows? Who knows with you people, Toby, man?' (p. 254). Sam's reservation is overruled as the two clasp arms immediately afterwards, but the challenge has in effect been thrown down, and a crucial ambivalence registered. Sam's move from the general ('you people') to the particular ('Toby, man') is in keeping with the novel's personal view of social commitment, and also with an ideology of individualism, but then the fact of the matter remains that the onus of fulfilment still rests on Toby as an individual. He is going away on a trip; his faith can be proved only in the keeping of his promise, not in its making. In this way the ending of the novel keeps a wary eye on the implications of its observation, for it is precisely this observation, combined with Toby's previous intransigence, that thrusts his intention into contingency. In this way, too, the 'grammar' of the symbolic triumph is itself transformed, edging from the present tense into the future, from the indicative mood into the subjunctive. Toby *might* keep his promise, he might not. But if he does it will only be because he has understood the great difficulties he faces.

All in all, there is as much emphasis in the novel's resolution on commitment, onus and responsibility as there is on Sam's and Toby's achievements. Forster's 'No, not yet . . . No, not there' is reconstituted at a higher and more demanding level; and the novel's resolution, apparently so closed, is importantly left open. The ending of the novel represents less a naïve 'happily ever after' than the restrained vision, say, of a *Middlemarch*, in which there is scope for a limited social optimism, but solely on the grounds of a steadfast personal conviction. It is only in recognition of the odds against it that the symbolic arm-clasp of *A World of Strangers* takes on any meaning.

If the novel represents a liberal humanism, therefore, it does so in a suitably strengthened, disillusioned and self-probationary form. In outlining quite clearly the sheer difficulty of its project the novel virtually invites the allegation of its own self-contradiction, but in this respect its procedure may paradoxically be seen as a *recuperation* of liberalism. The novel subjects itself to an immanent critique, thereby only to immunize itself against obvious weaknesses. But in so far as its affirmation is more considered by this degree, its general significance for the ideology it represents becomes that much more important. This significance now becomes apparent. For through this very process of recuperation the novel represents some of the deeper and perhaps more crucial historical assumptions of South African liberalism, which underlie its vision of inter-personal communion. Moreover, here we have an excellent opportunity to consider how an ideological and historical response in the novel is first and foremost a *fictional* response; for in the broadest of its strategies as fiction – most of all at the level of form, least of all at the level of content – *A World of Strangers* composes its deepest historical codes.

Formally considered, *A World of Strangers* must be seen as a work of what Roland Barthes would have called 'classical realism'. Its fundamental motivation is to undertake a reading of social reality in apparently as objective a manner as possible.[37] Hence, in part, its sustained proximity to the actual social world of the 1950s. But this function is also expressly heightened in the novel. This is the formal rationale lying behind having its narrative 'eyes' belong to an outsider, an Englishman who is also, for the major part of the novel, determined to be socially neutral. In this way, bothered by no preconceptions or scruples – and even, one supposes, on account of a cultural disposition to detachment – it is suggested within the text that Toby's observation is the epitome of disinterested objectivity.

At the first inter-racial party in Johannesburg that Toby attends, this is precisely registered. He surveys the people around him:

> But if you are a stranger, recognising no one, drawn into no private context of friendship, there is a time, at the beginning of the evening, when you see the composition of the party as the armchair strategist sees the battle: steadily, formally and whole.
>
> (p. 79)

If one substitutes the word 'society' for 'party' in this passage one gets the strongest possible statement of a version of 'classical realism': that the social world can be seen 'steadily, formally and whole', and moreover can be represented in this way. It is hard not to feel that the impetus to objectivity behind this formulation is a significant component of much of what Gordimer has written; but at any rate, what it does in this novel, placed in the hands of Toby as narrator, is signal within the text a kind of structural guarantee as to the objectivity of his view of the world around him.

If the veracity of his social reading is implied in this way, then for the novel this is not to be regarded as an activity sufficient in itself; nor is it gratuitous. For if Toby feels omnisciently detached at the beginning of his arrival in Johannesburg, this is not exactly the way he feels at the end; he is transformed from an 'armchair strategist' into one who enters the fray. As far as his reading of society is concerned, only to the extent that this results in Toby's commitment at the end does its full significance become evident. For there is a distinct 'logic' to this result; it is precisely because he absorbs the implications of what he has been observing all along that Toby realizes the absolute necessity of his own personal engagement, and the impossibility of a pure detachment. This is where the novel reveals the assumptions on which it is based, or which it may even appear to be designed to demonstrate. For to the degree that, up to the point of his 'conversion', Toby has proved a wholly intractable case, the novel has shown that even the most recalcitrant of individuals is morally and socially educable. And in so far as the observation that has produced this result has been formally codified as unimpeachably neutral, the novel has shown that the most objective of eyes will naturally and inevitably draw humanist conclusions from the facts of social evidence.

There is a distinct *moral positivism* secreted in the text, therefore, along with a specific view both of 'rationality' and of human nature; the individual, in full possession and exercise of all his faculties, must through reason, and its counterpart, human identification, become socially engaged and produce a better society. *This* is the real recuperation of liberalism in the novel. For if the novel, soberly enough, has not been able to guarantee a humanist social order overnight, then it has at least been able to secure the grounds of its potential future production, through education, rationality and its inevitable result, morality. Similarly South African liberalism could on no account prophesy the imminent and total evaporation of all apartheid's barriers; but through education and the dissemination of knowledge, through rationality and its result – morality – it certainly believed that it could.[38] Moreover, in this way we understand a further typical liberal assumption represented in the friendship between Sam and Toby. At the end of the novel the two represent, precisely, a 'moral class', transcending all economic and social distinctions. The idea of this kind of 'moral class' has possibly been the essential historical hope of South African liberalism.[39]

But before branding *A World of Strangers* as simply a 'liberal' novel, even in its strengthened form, it is worth considering that its ideological and historical codes, as they have just been elicited, are by no means limited to the actual movement of liberalism in the 1950s. To some degree, as well, they incorporate positions represented by the Congress Alliance. From one point of view this should be no surprise, for it has already been pointed out that in many respects the Alliance in the 1950s fell within a liberal tradition. But this in turn suggests the widespread prevalence of these codes at this time. For example, in the 1950s the Congress movement represented a 'moral class'. Whatever political needs determined that a broad opposition to apartheid was required, and whatever differences were registered between the separate Congress organizations, this was nevertheless the implication embedded in their combination as an Alliance: that together they represented a moral transcendence of racial and economic differences, and a determination to make them of no account. To some degree, as well, there was a moral positivism in Congress assumptions. Not only was there a deep belief in the stature and force of morality in itself – hence, in part, Congress dedication to non-violent resistance – but to a significant extent in the 1950s the Alliance was prepared to rest its case on the intrinsic justice of its cause. It was a justice that, it was felt, no rational being in possession of the evidence could deny. At one level much of the Congress programme was geared to presenting this evidence; indeed, it was presented precisely as *argument*. Thus, the Defiance Campaign demonstrated the indignities of apartheid as much as it was an attempt to jam the gaols. The gathering of the women in Pretoria and the Congress of the People, both events high in symbolic value, were also presented as a kind of social testimony: of the dedication, dignity and vitality of an alternative South Africa. To this degree the very make-up of the Alliance was evidence of the moral superiority of multi-racialism to racialism, and of the fact that the different races could combine.[40]

In approaching the Alliance at this level, one ignores the daily political realities facing it, the struggles waged within and outside it. But at the level at which it presented itself as a 'code', this was the code it represented; and this is the code we find in *A World of Strangers*. If we consider this question less as a matter of 'form' and more as a matter of 'content', a further intriguing correspondence arises. We have seen how in the novel Sam is consistently portrayed as a 'decent bourgeois'. It is of some interest to find, therefore, that at the same time as the Congress Alliance was calling for the nationalization of the banks and mines in the Freedom Charter, at least one leading spokesman of the ANC was publicly welcoming the prospect of a 'prosperous non-European bourgeois class', which this nationalization would help to create.[41]

Simply to call *A World of Strangers* a straightforward liberal novel, therefore, is to miss a large part of its importance. In its own way the novel illuminates the unity in the diversity of the 1950s as well as the diversity of that unity. It suggests the common 'codes' that underlay the different social and political manifestations of this time as well as their widespread dispersal. In its ideological resonances it indicates that a study of this kind should not always look for a single historical 'meaning' in a text. And at this point a prevailing myth concerning Nadine Gordimer can be scotched at its apparently most illustrative moment: the myth that she is plainly and simply a 'liberal' writer. In responding within a complex historical moment, her novel has reproduced that complexity.

So *A World of Strangers* turns out to be a surprising novel. On the face of it a work of straightforward realism with a simple liberal 'message', we have seen already that the novel is, historically, far richer. In this regard it is worth paying further attention to aspects of the novel's form. For there are some subtler features of its historical consciousness, revealed through its form, which remain to be assessed; and these in turn clarify in particular and vital ways the novel's broader historical significance. To call *A World of Strangers* a work of classical realism and merely to leave it at that is not by itself adequate. For Roland Barthes, realism is not only a matter of a characteristic field of social investigation – which for him is secondary – but primarily one of *mode* or 'representation'. Realism, that is to say, represents the world 'realistically' or naturalistically, as if the novel were a transparent window on the world, as if its own signifying procedures entailed no distortion.[42] Moreover, for Barthes, this implies the essential social complicity of realism as a mode, for all it does is reinforce, without question, a prestructured way of seeing the world, of representing it for society. And in so far as it is the given social world that realism characteristically investigates, all the habits, patterns and assumptions of a society are thereby mirrored back to it with an effectively perfect complacency. *A World of Strangers*, however, gives us cause to question this monolithic view, and especially the ahistorical vision informing it. For the novel reveals, in some of its modal digressions, that a work of realism is not always likely to be a homogeneous form. Also, it shows that a work of realism may have a specific historical significance, which is not always one of simple social reinforcement. In its time and place a realist novel may well offer a social challenge as much as an endorsement, while the degree to which it does reinforce society is not likely to consist of a wholly unfractured affirmation. Finally, further consideration of *A World of Strangers* as a work of realism allows us to assess more fully its own historical significance. In this respect the innermost depths of its form will return us to an outer history.

E. M. Forster has already been mentioned in this chapter, and this should be no surprise. It is not just that Gordimer has acknowledged Forster to be a long-lasting influence on her literary consciousness,[43] but Forster is *par excellence* the novelist of the 'world of strangers', whether this be between England and Italy, England and India, or within England itself. Early on in *A World of Strangers* it is explicitly signalled that the question of mode – or as Toby more generally refers to it, 'genre' – is to become a topic in itself in the novel, and this specifically in relation to Forster. On an Italian boat on his way to Africa, Toby considers how inappropriate Forsterian romance, especially of the kind found in his Italian novels, would be for the harsh realities of Africa. What follows is something of a continuing 'generic' debate with Forster in the novel. For *A World of Strangers* is designed to work out an historically suitable form for itself; we have already noted the rigorous self-probationary strategies that ensure that its response is suitably 'realistic'. This fundamental commitment for the novel, however, is a paradoxical one. For if realism on the Barthesian model is essentially complicit with the structure of the reality it represents, then in various ways it becomes evident that *A World of Strangers* is more concerned to *contest* a given social reality. This occurs both in the act of its realism and also where the novel indulges in various 'non-realist' modes.

Even where Toby's observation is purely representational, his position is the classic expression of a fictional manoeuvre of social challenge: the outsider, suddenly introduced into the world of the familiar, embarrasses and defamiliarizes it by seeing it through unfamiliar eyes. From this point of view the more *realistically* he describes it, the more embarrassing it becomes. (This is surely a paradoxical version of the virtue that the Russian formalists accorded to 'defamiliarization', who in other respects were constitutionally opposed to 'realism'.) But Toby's observation is not all purely representational. When describing the High House he sometimes drops into the use of an essentially political grotesque, as when he vividly remarks on the enlarged hearts lying concealed beneath the silk shirts and cravats that the High House habitués wear. Here realism is purposively extended to challenge the veneer of South African reality. Elsewhere the grotesque fuses with a symbolic mode, as when Toby gives a symptomatic and symbolic reading of a mining landscape on Johannesburg's East Rand; uncovering its false naturalism, he interprets the cyanide mine dumps masquerading as hills as direct emanations from the subconscious of the culture that has produced them.

Perhaps most important is where the symbolic mode occurs on its own. Thus the hunt at the end of the novel takes place in an entirely symbolic world, the blighted landscape familiar to medieval romance. Moreover, it is a landscape in which the deepest truths emerge about the High House hunters and the white South African world they represent. Waking suddenly from sleep in the middle of his first night in camp, Toby hears a fearful sound surrounding the hunters: 'Rolling out over the stillness there came a yowl from the entrails of desolation, the echo of a pack of nightmares' (p. 227). The sound is simultaneously internal and external. Symbolically the hunters' aggression against both nature and society (in this case the black servants who accompany them on the hunt) is linked to an internal repression and fear that can only barely be suppressed through violence. In this instance one of the hunters is so disturbed that he feels obliged to shoot wildly straight past Toby's ear in order to try to silence the 'nightmare'.

Clearly there is a realm of the subconscious, apprehended in *A World of Strangers* through a symbolic mode, that deeply threatens the everyday realities of South Africa. This, as we shall see, is a theme – and method – that Gordimer takes up very strongly in her sixth novel, *The Conservationist*. More directly in this novel, however, it is through his experience in this landscape that Toby makes what is fundamentally a symbolic connection, linking his own activity, in hunting with the High House pack, with the death, like a hunted animal, of Steven. This *symbolic* understanding leads him at last to absorb the implications of his observation, and challenge the reality he has accepted for so long.

The overall 'realism' of *A World of Strangers*, then, is not as unambiguous as it might at first appear. Gordimer has learned as much from Forster as she criticizes. It is not just that Sam and Toby's symbolic arm-clasp at the end of the novel can be seen as a subtly transformed Forsterian 'good moment'. More to the point, in Forster's Italian and Indian novels it is invariably a rampant symbolic mode that undermines the prosaic world of the realistic English. But if, in both its realism and its non-realism, *A World of Strangers* has managed to contest the social representation of apartheid, there are nevertheless two important features of this challenge that must still be assessed. First, it is clear from the use of the symbolic landscape in general, but especially from the 'nightmare' quotation just given, that contained in the novel's anti-realist challenge is an implicit organicism. This is not at base Lukács's organicism, which he defines as the integral relation between private and social destiny, but a third term has been added as well: nature. The symbolic landscape reveals that a social offence is also an offence against nature, which is also an offence against human nature: hence the nightmare, in which external and internal natures are conjoined. In a slightly different sense than the one to which we are accustomed, therefore, in the instant that the novel forgoes its realism, it produces a kind of 'naturalism' in which the realm of nature is held to infuse the workings of human existence. This naturalism, moreover, is also a romanticism, for it posits an essential unity between man, society and nature. It is a romanticism not of marked importance for *A World of Strangers*, which is more wholly a socially based novel. But it does introduce a theme of recurrent importance for Gordimer's novels in general. In *The Conservationist*, as we shall see, the romantic vision reaches a particular climax as a force of nature comes into its own as a distinct historical power on behalf of society's oppressed. Here the novel's romanticism is linked with an historical optimism; through his symbolic experience Toby becomes socially engaged, and his 'good moment' with Sam has more than a touch of romanticism about it. This conjunction of optimism and romanticism, especially in its 'naturalist' form, will be of major importance for a final assessment of Gordimer's novels.

The second significant feature relating to the novel's social challenge is perhaps an unexpected one. In a paradoxical way the novel's diversification into a symbolic, 'non-realist' mode may also be seen as something of, precisely a *recovery* of, realism. Though definitely 'magical' ground from one point of view, from another the symbolic landscape may also be seen as a domain that *reinforces* empiricism — in this case Toby's observation. For the symbolic realm is one of deep social and psychological truths and profound moral essences, all of which not only underpin the novel's moral positivism but constitute the medium of its most striking revelations. In this regard we need only repeat that through his sudden symbolic understanding Toby most deeply ingests the true reality of the world around him, and his own place in it. But the novel's realism is recovered in another sense as well. In a straightforward way, after his symbolic experience Toby is delivered back into the 'real' world — one aspect of his transformation from narrator back into character. After his romantic good moment with Sam he heads off into the harsh realities of apartheid to prove, or disprove, his faith. As we have seen, only in the 'real' world can his commitment be made good, by sheer virtue of the definition of commitment that the novel is at pains to produce.

This, however, leads us towards a major point regarding the novel's historical consciousness. Anna Louw is described in the novel as a 'frontier' character, and in many ways *A World of Strangers* appears to imitate her position. Like Anna, its most significant area of activity lies in the in-between zone of black-and-white encounter. Further, like Anna, the novel has been concerned to bridge the gap between the two worlds without any illusions or favour. In these ways it might be said that the novel attempts to be a 'frontier text'. If this is so, however, there is a negative side to its status as well. For through our discussion of its modal complexity, its symbolism and final return to realism, it becomes evident that, in terms of the world it represents, although the novel has travelled to the frontier of an existing conception of reality, it has not finally crossed any borders. And though it has deeply challenged a given structure of reality from within, ultimately the framework of that reality has in effect remained unexchanged. Perhaps, ironically, it has been strengthened, just as Toby returns from the symbolic to the 'real' world with a strengthened commitment to engage with it.

This is exactly the point at which the novel's inner form returns us to an outer history, and here on the broadest of scales. For it may accurately be said of the opposition movements as a whole in the 1950s that they explored to the full the frontiers of an existing reality without ultimately crossing any boundaries. At stake, finally, in the 1950s was reform within a given structure of South African reality, and not its entire replacement. In certain respects, as we have seen, the Congress Alliance did represent a radical challenge to the status quo; hence its call for a universal franchise and for nationalization of the banks and mines. But in the governing *terms* of its challenge it was on the whole not suggesting social revolution. What the Alliance on the contrary desired was the *improvement* of subsisting reality and, in a sense, its perfection, as its characteristic rhetoric indicated. Thus, what the Congresses usually demanded was the 'extension' of freedom, the 'sharing' of power and 'partnership' within the social system as it stood.[44] The primary objective of the Congress movement in the 1950s, and especially of the ANC, was

> the winning of political and civil rights within the basic framework of South Africa's existing parliamentary democracy. The Freedom Charter . . . catalogued these goals in detail.[45]

As much as it was contesting the interpretation of South African reality, therefore, the Alliance was reinforcing the framework within which it made its challenge.

Even Congress methods in the 1950s suggested this ambiguity. Although the limits of licensed action were explored by the movements, these were never entirely transgressed. Congress employed passive resistance and civil disobedience, and also the stay-at-home. But its disobedience was, precisely, 'civil' – still recognizably within the governing terms of the existing civil state. And its resistance was still insistently 'passive' – a matter of peaceful demonstration rather than outright confrontation. Much of this was due to practical and political exigency; there wasn't much else that Congress could do. Also, different methods did not, yet, seem to be necessary. But in terms of the reality it was challenging, there was still a definite sense in which the Alliance was 'staying at home'. Only when the kind of opposition that it represented was driven beyond the framework of existing reality in the early 1960s, by being outlawed and forced underground, did its objectives become explicitly different. For now the historical stakes were entirely transformed; at issue after this time was no longer reform, but revolution.

In Nadine Gordimer's work, as we shall see, it is *The Conservationist* that most powerfully registers this change and stands in many ways as a crucial antithesis to *A World of Strangers*. But here we have seen an extraordinary correspondence between the inner 'skeleton' of *A World of Strangers* and the far larger history of which it is a part.

In numerous ways, then, it has become evident how deeply *A World of Strangers* is implicated in the historical moment of its production. We have seen how its roots are in the energies of this moment, and how there is a continual return in the novel to its social environment. Also we have seen how remarkably the assumptions and visions of this period are embedded in the novel, in both its content and its form, and how the novel in turn illuminates these. Most importantly, the basic unity of this moment has become apparent, even in its diversity. *A World of Strangers* has embodied this unity in its deepest codes and in its methods of representing social reality; in doing so it has incorporated both a more orthodox liberalism as well as positions represented by the Congress Alliance. But this very unity must lead to a final reassessment of an issue central both to the novel and to the moment in which it arose: the question of 'contradiction' in relation to *A World of Strangers*.

For the problem of contradiction has clearly not been eliminated from the novel. As we have seen, a putative internal contradiction has been resolved within the text, resulting in its strengthened form of social commitment. But there is a sense in which this resolution might still be held to be contradictory; precisely *what* sense must now be determined. Albeit in a strengthened form, the novel ultimately rests its moral and historical vision on the assumption that personal and human commitment not only can transcend the vast social antagonisms it has described, but can, alone, be historically transformative; it has presented a self-probationary 'logic' to suggest that such a commitment is both rational and natural. This particular optimism, disillusioned though it is in the novel, was to be belied dramatically in the years immediately following the writing of *A World of Strangers*. As we shall see in the chapters that follow, through both legislative and political onslaught and the hidden strengths of apartheid, the world of the 1950s was soon to be wholly destroyed. Evidently some form of contradiction was involved. If it was not a contradiction internal to the codes the novel represents, perhaps fault should be found with the entire way in which it understands the problem it has to face. Conceiving of apartheid as purely a social question, it attempts, in the strongest form available, to solve it by social means. But if the 1960s, as a decade, were to demonstrate anything, it was that apartheid was as much a matter of sheer political power and systematic economic exploitation as it was of racial discrimination; these facts have clearly not been absorbed into the novel's social paradigm.

From a philosophical or theoretical point of view this fault might be seen as an idealism. Perceiving apartheid as a problem of consciousness, a triumph of consciousness is offered to overcome inaccurately analysed material relations. Moreover, if this is a fault for the novel, then it is also a fault for the entire moment of which it is a part; for we have seen the solidarity of conceptions, assumptions and visions of the opposition movement as a whole in the 1950s. This, it might be said, is the real weakness of *A World of Strangers*, and of the moment from which it proceeds.

But if the very *unity* of this moment in turn demonstrates anything it is the invalidity of any philosophical or theoretical accusation, except at the shallowest of levels. For, in so far as a whole social moment was involved in this conceptual 'fault', it is crucial not to judge it ahistorically. If, as Nadine Gordimer wrote some twenty years later, the 'only connect' of the 1950s proved to be a fragile bond,[46] this was not simply because of some intrinsic naïveté. An allegation of such naïveté implies that it could have been detected very easily – and not just by a few, but by many. The degree to which the 1950s were unified in mood, assumptions and vision, across a whole social and political spectrum, argues to the contrary.

Rather, if there is a contradiction in relation to *A World of Strangers*, it can be nothing more or less than an *historical* contradiction, since in the 1950s the visions of that decade had not yet been disproved. Equally important, the whole discourse within which these visions were constructed had not yet been proved obsolete. Only the historical developments of the 1960s contradicted these visions and this discourse in showing that moral classes solely considered had no real political ground on which to stand; that reason could elaborate the workings of apartheid as well as work to end it; and that a free association of 'multi-racial equals' was impossible where the material conditions of equality did not exist. Gordimer's novel remains a most poignant record of this historical contradiction. The 1950s, then, were truly a 'fabulous decade', never before anticipated, never to be repeated, at least not in the same form. It is something of an irony that the gesture of universalism, both moral and racial, that underlies *A World of Strangers*, and that underlay the movement of which it was a part, should have arisen so strongly in such an historically unique, and historically specific, moment.

There is a sense in which the novel knows this. For there is more than a touch of nostalgia in its celebration of the world of the 1950s. When Steven dies it is as if an age of innocence has passed. Toby's friendship with Sam may be full of resolve and dedication, but on one level it exists only in mourning for Steven. A transition is suggested here, which is perhaps marked in the novel in no less a place than the name of the central character himself. We have seen how *A World of Strangers* attempts to be a frontier text. In Sophiatown the street marking the frontier between the black township and the white world of Johannesburg was called Toby Street, after the son of the township's original owner.[47] Toby Hood therefore lives in a state of Toby-hood in the novel, or perhaps to-be-hood.

By the time *A World of Strangers* was being written the destruction of Sophiatown had already begun, on government orders under the Group Areas Act. And the street where the demolitions began was none other than Toby Street.[48]

3

Social Failure:
Occasion for Loving

... white men, few, guilty, and unloved, in a continent of black men.[1]

Occasion for Loving, published in 1963,[2] brings to completion an important dialectical movement in Nadine Gordimer's first three novels, albeit one that ends with a negative conclusion. *The Lying Days* initiated this movement in embodying the beliefs and assumptions of a personal humanism. In *A World of Strangers* this humanism was socialized. In *Occasion for Loving*, however, this movement as a whole ends with the realization of social failure, and of the failure of humanism in general, whether in its personal or social forms. In this it becomes evident that each of Gordimer's novels acts in part as a critique of the former, that each takes up its position as a more developed appraisal of the one that precedes it. Thus the positive aspects of this dialectical pattern – which by no means ends here – are taken up later, in Gordimer's next two works, *The Late Bourgeois World* and *A Guest of Honour*. At the same time *Occasion for Loving* once again makes it clear that none of these shifts can be separated from the specific historical environment that engenders it. For in investigating the failure of social humanism, the dominant ideology of opposition to apartheid in the 1950s, the novel also responds very closely to the historical realities of the early 1960s. Its characteristic mood is elegiac, as the last vestiges of one kind of social optimism disappeared at the end of the decade. Yet clarified through its confrontations *Occasion for Loving* stands on the verge of new realizations, just as was the case in the external world.

There were a number of crucial developments between the mid-1950s and the early 1960s that have a direct bearing on the responses of *Occasion for Loving*. To begin with, the status of multi-racialism as the dominant ideology of the broad opposition to apartheid was now far less assured than it had been earlier. Although this ideology had been challenged from as far back as the formation

72

of the Congress Youth League of the ANC in 1943, that challenge had always been contained within the parent body. Now the secession of the Africanist segment of the ANC, and the subsequent founding of the Pan-Africanist Congress (PAC) in April 1959, publicly placed the assumptions of multi-racialism in question.[3] For the PAC was strongly opposed to multi-racialism – what it called 'racialism multiplied'; indeed this was the primary reason for the secession in the first place. As far as the PAC was concerned, oppression in South Africa was plainly and simply a *national* oppression, an oppression of the black indigenous majority by a white settler minority. Therefore resistance, in its view, should also be a national resistance, by Africans, for themselves, against the white oppressors. In this the PAC was especially suspicious of the make-up of the Congress Alliance; it felt that the white Congress of Democrats – which it believed was a communist front – was dominating the ANC, and had hijacked the national struggle for its own ends. The PAC denied strongly that it was itself racist, that it had merely inverted the racism of white supremacy. On the contrary its commitment, it maintained, was to non-racialism and to Africa. Thus any individual, of whatever colour, who owed his allegiance to Africa could in theory be considered an African.[4]

Partly for this reason, but chiefly because of its anti-communist stand, the PAC was popular with some white liberals.[5] None the less the PAC line represented a major challenge to multi-racialist assumptions in South Africa in general, and to the 'common brotherhood' assumptions of liberalism. *Occasion for Loving* responds very strongly to this challenge or, rather, to those realities that gave the PAC argument such force.[6] But interestingly, rather than offering any rebuke, the novel acknowledges a basic legitimacy to these claims. 'What's the good of us to him?' says the novel's central white character, Jessie Stilwell, when a love affair with a young Englishwoman has proved disastrous for its central black character, Gideon Shibalo; 'What's the good of our friendship or her love?' (p. 272). Gideon's fate at the end of the novel makes it clear that his trust of apparently well-intentioned whites has been severely misplaced. As the rhetoric of the Black Consciousness movement of the 1970s would have had it, the novel shows that as a black man he is definitely 'on his own'.

This is a remarkable turnabout, considering the affirmations Gordimer had so recently made in *A World of Strangers*. Yet the truth of the matter is that *Occasion for Loving* came to life in a world entirely unrecognizable from that of the earlier work, and a series of dramatic political events and more deep-seated social changes at the end of the 1950s and beginning of the 1960s meant that the assumptions of the previous decade could no longer remain unquestioned. The PAC had linked itself to the movement of Pan-Africanism in Africa in general – hence, in part, its name as an organization – and certainly it received some of its impetus from the continent-wide campaigns for, and then achievements of, independence throughout Africa as the 1950s ended.[7] By the time Africa entered its *annus mirabilis* of independence in 1960, there was a rising tide of expectancy in South Africa as well that liberation would not be far off. The 1958 All-African Peoples' Conference in Accra had declared that no part of Africa would be free until the whole continent was, and set 1963 as the deadline for total liberation. With only slightly differing degrees of conviction both the PAC and the ANC aligned themselves with the resolutions of the Accra Conference.[8]

Yet, if freedom was expected soon in South Africa, such feelings suffered a sudden and tragic reversal in the early months of the new decade. On 21 March 1960 at Sharpeville (one of the black townships of Vereeniging, near Johannesburg) 67 PAC anti-pass demonstrators were killed in police shooting, and 186 were wounded. 'Sharpeville', as it simply came to be known, more than any other single event marked the transition from one world to another. The Sharpeville massacre was followed on 30 March by the declaration of a State of Emergency, and widespread arrests took place throughout the country. In Cape Town, after mass demonstrations and a sustained strike at the townships of Langa and Nyanga, a young man called Philip Kgosana led a march of 30,000 people into the heart of the city, and could well have held South Africa's Parliamentary capital to ransom.[9] On 8 April both the ANC and the PAC were declared illegal organizations and driven underground. In October of the following year an organization called the National Committee for Liberation (later the African Resistance Movement) began a campaign of sabotage against state installations. And on 16 December 1961 *Umkhonto we Sizwe* ('The Spear of the Nation'), the newly formed armed offshoot of the ANC, began its own campaign of sabotage.

The transition from peaceful resistance to violent confrontation had been made. In these circumstances the old assumptions of the 1950s, of an essentially moral struggle, and of a peaceful inter-racial solidarity, no longer appeared to have much validity. As South Africa, ironically, gained its 'independence' from Britain and became a Republic, political realities were clarified as they had never been before.

By 1960 Nadine Gordimer had numerous friends who were in the ANC, and she remembers well the momentous effects of Sharpeville both for her and for the social and political group towards which she was gravitating. To her this was 'an incredible time when . . . almost everyone I knew was in jail, or fleeing'.[10] She felt a sudden solitude that was the exact reverse of her introduction into the social and political world of the 1950s. But at the social level, in fact, that isolation had already begun to take place some time before its dramatic political appearance. For state repression was by no means limited to events of such immediate impact as Sharpeville; piece by piece as well the social framework that had provided so crucial a context for the vision of *A World of Strangers* was being dismantled. And it was mainly due to developments at this level that *Occasion for Loving*, like the previous novel, owed its chief thematic inspiration. (Interestingly for a work begun before, but completed after, Sharpeville, there is no mention of the latter in the text.)

Referring directly to the liberal socializing that had characterized the 1950s, the 'architect' of apartheid, Verwoerd, had declared he would use an 'iron hand' to stamp out this subversion of state policy;[11] evidently he was being as good as his word. Sophiatown, by this time, was already destroyed. After the bulldozers moved in, flattening its houses and shacks, its inhabitants were removed to the township of Meadowlands, and the all-white suburb of Triomf ('Triumph') was erected in its place. In general the inter-racial world of Johannesburg found itself increasingly scrutinized and undermined, as legislation continued unabated to separate the races in various social fields. Thus the Native Laws Amendment Act and the Group Areas Amendment Act, both of 1957, were expressly designed to cut off multi-racial contact in white areas in the spheres of religion, education, health, recreation and entertainment; even the joint partaking of refreshment was outlawed.

Cultural oppression was an intrinsic part of this attack. The writers associated with *Drum*, who had been so crucial to Gordimer's introduction to the world of the 1950s, found themselves in one way

75

or another being driven into exile. By the mid-1960s Can Themba, Nat Nakasa, Lewis Nkosi, Todd Matshikiza and Ezekiel Mphahlele had all left; ultimately their work was banned in South Africa, while some of them, such as Nakasa and Themba, met untimely and tragic deaths.[12] Black musicians who had come to the fore during the 1950s renaissance were also being methodically ousted from the limelight.[13] The world of the 1950s was shrinking, its boundaries dramatically drawing in. The gathering isolation this implied for Gordimer, when linked to the disappearance of a multi-racial political environment, was of major importance for the overall historical awareness of *Occasion for Loving*.

There was a new mood at the end of the decade. In contrast to the optimism and rebelliousness of the mid-1950s, there was now an increasing seriousness, an awareness perhaps that an era was drawing to a close. In her own life Gordimer registered this change. In an article of 1959 entitled 'Where do whites fit in?' she wondered whether there would after all be a place for whites in an independent black Africa. There is a 'nationalism of the heart' brought about by shared suffering, she wrote. Whites had had no part in this suffering and therefore could not hope to share in the bonds it created; she could read this in the behaviour of her African friends. Judging from the article, Gordimer was tempted at this time by the idea of leaving South Africa.[14]

In a wider sphere, the spirit of the 'fabulous decade' was departing. Lewis Nkosi, who gave the period its name, characterized also its end, in particular by referring to the fate of its mixed love affairs, which had perhaps embodied the essence of its bravado and revelry. These affairs now became, in his words, simply 'nightmares of worry and effort to have some privacy':

> English or European girls who had no clear conception of the legal restraints and the risk such affairs entailed, arrived in the country, made impossible demands, assuming, for the most commendable reasons, that if you liked one another that was all that counted.[15]

But that was not all that counted, and elsewhere Nkosi gave an example of the kind of tragedy that could ensue – an example that takes us directly to the major concerns of *Occasion for Loving*. In his introduction to a selection of Can Themba's writings, Nkosi remarks:

> The only time I've seen Can Themba's nerve nearly snap was when he was in love with a beautiful young Englishwoman at a time when she was about to leave the country. He himself was trapped – and it seemed

forever – in the land of apartheid. At that time I had a glimpse into someone's suffering, and I don't care to see it again. Nadine Gordimer's novel, *Occasion for Loving*, may or may not be based on that period in Can Themba's life, but it offers a striking parallel.[16]

It is likely that *Occasion for Loving* is based to some degree on Can Themba's experience. But as in her other work Gordimer is concerned not simply to repeat a real story in and for itself; rather she uses the original example to investigate at a level of typicality the changed social and historical realities of the moment from which it emanates. In doing so *Occasion for Loving* becomes linked, sometimes in ways of which it is not quite aware, with general currents of consciousness in the period in which it was produced. Indeed it becomes the evidence of those currents.

In terms of its observation of the world around it, *Occasion for Loving* pays close attention to its historical context, from its broadest to its most intimate patterns. In 1959 there was much anguish in liberal circles over the Extension of Universities Bill, which was being promulgated to exclude blacks from white universities and send them off to various 'tribal' colleges. In *Occasion for Loving* Tom Stilwell, Jessie's husband, is an academic. The novel opens with his engagement in a campaign to oppose the Bill. Elsewhere, the novel presents political discussion in the black world, revolving upon the relative merits of the ANC and the PAC; there is also talk of the All-African Conference in Accra, while Kgosana's march on Cape Town is mentioned. Paradoxically, for a novel whose central concern is a love affair, *Occasion for Loving* reveals a consciousness that is far more politically aware, strictly speaking, than either of Gordimer's previous works; and this is undoubtedly due to the effects of political developments in South Africa and Africa at large. When Tom Stilwell goes to a meeting to discuss the Universities Bill, a black man tells him he can 'fight [the government] over this business' if he wants:

> but don't think that anything you do really matters. Some of you make laws, and some of you try to change them. And you don't ask us.
> (pp. 64–5)

This is some distance from the general image of blacks presented in *The Lying Days*, or even *A World of Strangers*; a crucial change of tone has been registered.

Significantly, too, Gordimer reveals that her conception of the nature of South African history has changed. Though her previous novels had, to differing degrees, included a black component in their overall focus, history there had dominantly been conceived of as white history. Here, however, Gordimer acknowledges for the first time that the ultimate current of history in South Africa – past, present and future – is black, and not white: that the latter is a subset of the former. Gordimer had been travelling in Africa since the mid-1950s, and this may well have had an influence on her perception of the direction in which the continent was heading. In 1954 she visited Egypt in the week that Nasser deposed Neguib; in 1959 she returned to find European Cairo sequestrated, a sustained air of 'national confidence' (which had nothing to do, she insisted, with official protestations, but concerned the inner assurance of ordinary individuals amongst their own people) and the Aswan Dam in construction.[17] In 1960 she visited the Belgian Congo at the time when it was about to gain its independence. 'Africa,' she wrote then, 'however troubled it may be, has never been more interesting than it is in this decade; it may never be so interesting again.'[18] Her account of the Congo at this time is full of a tremendous excitement, both politically and in environmental terms.[19]

This wider perspective, then, may have led to the reversal of previously unquestioned liberal and colonial ideologies in her work. Thus Tom Stilwell is not just an academic in the novel, but also an African historian setting out to write a history of the African subcontinent, including the history of colonialism, from the black point of view – which is also, as far as he is concerned, the 'historical point of view' (p. 15). Elsewhere, though, Gordimer reveals that the terms of her new historical consciousness are not entirely unambivalent. Jessie, the character who is the focal bearer of the novel's investigations, considers the pending African revolution in slightly mystical and, effectively, ironic terms. To her it is a 'new kind of magic', belonging

> to those who held in themselves for this one generation the dignity of the poor about to inherit their earth and the worldliness of those who had been the masters.
>
> (p. 269)

Retrospectively this may appear prescient, especially given the later advent of neo-colonialism in Africa, which Gordimer depicts so precisely in *A Guest of Honour*; but here, at this time and in this vague form, it simply seems too tired and 'knowing' a formula.

It is an index of the impact of events and the new atmosphere at the end of the 1950s that the most vivid observations in *Occasion for Loving* concern intensifications and extremities of mood, as changes in external life were matched by internal developments. In the black world, when Gideon is discussing with his friend Sol the relative positions of the ANC and the PAC, he explicates his idea of what he calls 'guerrilla politics':

> So why should I, or anyone else with an eye on the real objective, the only thing that counts, stick with any crowd if I see that some other crowd is getting something done? What does another name and another slogan mean to me? I've got no ambitions to climb up a party ladder, Sol. I just want to see the blacks stand up on their hind legs, that's all. I don't care if they give the thumbs-up [the ANC sign] or bow three times to the moon. The chaps in the street have got the right idea, man.
>
> (p. 131)

In general Gideon's mood is one of near extremity, of frustration and simmering bitterness, and his experience in the course of the novel brings this mood to a point where his alternatives appear to be either explosive anger or despair. Tragically, despair turns out to be Gideon's lot, and in this resolution a further crucial feeling of the novel becomes evident: that for blacks only political commitment and involvement can save them from destruction.

Gideon's life is made the testing ground of this particular conviction, for the fundamental choice lying before him is between the apparent freedom of love and of his art on the one hand, and the dedication of political engagement on the other. But interestingly – being the kind of writer she is, it is an issue close to Gordimer's heart – when Gideon's passport application is refused, effectively barring him from taking up an art scholarship in Italy, it appears that for him politics must have priority over art. Callie Stow, one of the novel's white characters, tells Gideon that his treatment has proved that only politics can mean anything to blacks: 'You don't need philosophy; you've got necessity ... You've got politics, that's all' (pp. 121–2). And when Gideon surrenders his political involvement with the ANC for the love of a white Englishwoman, he ends by being almost destroyed.

These are powerful themes in the novel, and evidently they are meant to apply not only to Gideon. As far as the work itself is concerned, as we shall see, Gordimer finds the world of art circumscribed by political realities in the context of the early 1960s.

In many ways *Occasion for Loving* marks a point of transition for Gordimer, away from a traditional, humanist conception of art, towards more politicized, post-humanist forms.

Gordimer also observes white moods in *Occasion for Loving*, and here the fundamental point seems to be that whereas blacks don't need philosophy because they've got necessity, whites, short of all necessity, turn to philosophy. But it is an abstract philosophizing they turn to, solipsistic and cut off from reality, enclosed within its own world on the margins of South African history. The dominant moods for whites are feelings of alienation, solitude, irrelevance, apathy and also, in their own way, frustration. However, these observed moods have so much to do with the feelings that have generated the novel – they are as much emanations of its consciousness as products of its perception – that it is best now to turn towards a fuller assessment of that consciousness.

The major features of the novel's consciousness of history first emerge through the love affair that forms the central thread of its plot: a love affair between the black artist, Gideon Shibalo, and a white Englishwoman, Ann Davis, who has arrived with her South African husband, Boaz, to stay with the Stilwells in Johannesburg. The very choice of this subject matter has an immediate importance in the context of South African literature. Love and sexual relations across the colour line have proved an obsessive concern in South African fiction, though in different ways, from Plomer, to Millin, to Paton and beyond.[20] Nadine Gordimer's own comment on the way it had usually been treated up to the 1960s is straightforward:

> The cat is out of the bag, indeed, for the nation and the novel. Is that all? Is that the stuff of sin? Is that the stuff of tragedy? And if it is, at what a curious disadvantage must it put us with the peoples of other nations, whose writers are concerned with man's survival and the meaning of his life on earth.[21]

Significantly, in Gordimer's own treatment of the subject, the love affair between Ann and Gideon is, in itself, completely normalized. It works within no framework of sin or abnormality, as it does in Millin or even Paton,[22] nor in terms of any 'speciality', as it does in Plomer. Rather, the novel makes a distinct attempt to see the love affair simply for what it is. This may reflect the degree to which such relationships had become less charged with symbolic significance in the Johannesburg of the late 1950s, revolving more, as Nkosi suggests, upon matters of plain practicality. At any rate, Gordimer is able to describe in simple detail the layout of the two bodies of Gideon and Ann after making love, down to the fly that settles indifferently on either. The illusory beast of 'sex across the colour line' is tamed and demystified by being named with dispassion, and also with beauty.

Yet if Gordimer is able to transcend sin, she is by no means able to transcend tragedy. Instead of approaching any universal 'meaning of life on earth', all she is able to find in the love affair is the radical historicality of South African existence. This is a highly conscious and contemplated finding in the novel, for there are deeper motivations at work in this investigation than simply the question of love in and for itself. On the contrary, in so far as the central focus of the novel concerns a love affair between a black man and a white woman, it may be said that Gordimer is testing again the assumptions that underlay the vision of *A World of Strangers*. Moreover, she is testing them at their heart; for a love affair across the colour line is a far greater trial of the potential of humanism than an inter-racial friendship; it exists at a higher level, as it were.

If this is so, however, then Gordimer finds her earlier assumptions wanting at the very core. This love affair fails, and fails inevitably, and the reason why it fails is even more important than the fact that it does so. The point can best be made by contrast. Gordimer was not alone in treating the theme of love across the colour line in the 1950s and 1960s. Peter Abrahams had already done so in *The Path of Thunder*; Dan Jacobson did so in *The Evidence of Love*; and it formed a central focus in Richard Rive's novel, *Emergency*.[23] In these works too the various pairs of star-crossed lovers either suffer or seem likely to suffer the wrath of an apartheid society. But what distinguishes these novels from Gordimer's is that in each case there is still a sense in which the lovers are *strengthened* rather than broken by their challenge. Jacobson's couple returns from overseas unbowed to face the legislative sanctions of apartheid; Rive's pair remain dedicated to one another as their political world begins to descend into chaos in the Cape Town events of 1960; Abrahams's are not so lucky – they are killed – but at least they die fighting *together*, in armed battle against an affronted and marauding white world. There is in these novels still a sense of triumph, therefore; the lovers become all the more heroic and dedicated for their trials, and their love itself is untainted. In Gordimer's novel, however, the love affair ultimately fails from the *inside*. No external sanctions are finally required to destroy Ann and Gideon's relationship; on the contrary these sanctions have become internalized. Into the matrix of her own personality Ann absorbs the obsessions and fears of the society she once flouted. Having fled into the countryside once with Gideon, the two make plans to leave the country altogether. But Ann cannot cope with the implications of loving a black man. In panic she suddenly leaves with her husband instead, while Gideon is left to the wreckage of his life.

There is an implicit criticism here of the outsider who arrives in South Africa with no understanding of its human complications and of the responsibilities that should ensue. But purely within the local context as well, the failure of the love affair involves major discoveries. Gordimer's vision, that is to say, has far more threatening implications than simply realizing that a private love affair has public difficulties. Here those very difficulties are private; no external sanctions are needed to break up the relationship between Ann and Gideon because the repressions of apartheid have become psychologically inscribed. In this regard it is the *prestructuring* effects of apartheid that count. These effects, as Jessie realizes, place Gideon in the position of a passive object, either as the beneficiary of white goodwill or as its victim; and it is these that have left privileged channels of irresponsibility and escape open to Ann. Apartheid penetrates to the most intimate of human relationships, and the last word on this in the novel is crucial:

> even between lovers they had seen blackness count, the personal return inevitably to the social, the private to the political . . . So long as the law remained unchanged, nothing could bring integrity to human relationships.
>
> (p. 279)

The humanist autonomy that was able to triumph paradoxically in a 'world of strangers' is found to be unavailable and obsolete, deeply ironically, in an 'occasion for loving'.

This discovery is a shattering one for a liberal humanism to make. In so far as liberal humanism is rooted in a belief in the incorruptibility and infinite social premise of authentic human relationships, in a contrary realization such as this the ground of its existence is swept away. Here authenticity is already prevented by politics, and social relations promise only to circumscribe the innermost recesses of human life. *Occasion for Loving* therefore marks a critical point of recognition for the ideology it is now seen to challenge, and the courage that prompted this change on Gordimer's part should not be underestimated. All her past positions and visions — her belief in triumphs of consciousness and the illimitable potential of human engagement — are involved in this relationship between Gideon and Ann; and this has proved distinctly vulnerable. At this point, too, Gordimer sheds certain received conventions of belief in the genre of the humanist novel in general. In responding to her local social reality with uncompromising rigour she has contributed something specifically if dismayingly South African to the view of personal relationships in fiction. And in the South African context itself her contribution is significant. Not only has she taken the visions of Abrahams, Jacobson and Rive a critical step further, but even more importantly Alan Paton's *Cry, the Beloved Country* has had something of a final reply. It is not just a question, as expressed in that novel, of whether, when the whites have turned to loving, the blacks will have turned to hating.[24] It is rather that in South African conditions an occasion for loving simply does not arise; or cannot arise simply, without other, prior changes.

What does Gordimer's treatment of the love affair imply for the historical perspective she characteristically employs? This, it will be remembered, is the perspective that links private development to social reality; it is, in general, one of the most intimate registers of the historical consciousness of each of Gordimer's novels, embodying as it does a view of the degree to which life is socially determined, how far private freedom is possible and the scope there is for social engagement. It is already clear from the two previous works that there is room for shifts in emphasis in this perspective. In *The Lying Days* private life encountered social reality, but ultimately retained an aspect of transcendence; in *A World of Strangers* the two realms were brought into much greater parity, but a transcendent aspect was none the less preserved. In *Occasion for Loving*, however, the swing has gone completely the other way. Here external reality becomes entirely dominant in its control of private life. Indeed, in places the novel gives an extraordinary and bitterly ironical insight into the way in which the power of apartheid affects even the most basic of human passions. Thus, even in his jealousy, Ann's husband, Boaz, is unable to intervene in the affair between his wife and Gideon — and thereby possibly prevent a major tragedy — solely because Gideon is black, and inbred patterns of guilt and consequent overcompensation have the effect of reducing Boaz to paralysis.

Gordimer has entered a powerful phase of historical realism in the more usual sense. There are absolutely no illusions here as to the extent to which historical reality sets the horizon of existence in South Africa. This is also evidently a highly pessimistic phase for her, and so an interesting corollary to these features is that Gordimer has dropped the organic link between humankind and nature that characterized the optimism of *A World of Strangers*. Nature itself is subject to social structures in *Occasion for Loving*; Jessie remarks that there is no corner of the country (and she means its natural environment) that is innocent of the realities of apartheid (p. 259); and there is plainly no triumph of 'natural morality' in this novel. Further assumptions of the 1950s are being shed, therefore, and *Occasion for Loving* is profoundly moved to disillusion. But it is possible to get closer to the sources of this disillusion than simply noting the failure of the love affair. Here a second major area of the novel's thematic investigation provides the illumination.

At a symbolic and generalized level the failure of the love affair also marks the collapse of the immediate prospects of inter-racial social commitment, simply considered. Yet where aspirations are blocked in the present there is a natural tendency to turn to thoughts of the future, to conceptions of process and development – in short, to historicize desire. On a higher plane of investigation this is a temptation that *Occasion for Loving* courts and then, with impressive honesty, drops. We have already seen that the novel shows a greater consciousness of history as such than either of Gordimer's previous works; there is an awareness of political currents in both South Africa and Africa at large, and numerous discussions on the African past, present and future. Yet in its more general thematic concerns as well the novel shows Gordimer to be in transition towards a consciousness that is decidedly more historical in form – though the categories in which this is expressed are, as we shall come to understand, still significantly reticent.

Chiefly this new consciousness is expressed in terms of a thematic polarity between the principles of 'being' and 'becoming'. Ann Davis, for example, is an embodiment of the principle of 'being'. Tom Stilwell sums her up at the end of the novel by saying she had only one reason ever for doing anything, 'that she was alive' (p. 281), and this seems fair comment. Initially this existential abandon is her virtue. She doesn't love Gideon *across* the colour line, or *despite* the colour line; she simply loves him. But in the end it is her commitment to her own personal freedom alone that results in her betrayal of Gideon. She has absolutely no sense of any long-term commitment to an evolving joint destiny with him that would at once be personal and social. She has no sense of 'becoming'.

This polarity is explored with much greater depth and feeling in the case of Jessie. In many respects Jessie is the negative image of Ann. Whereas Ann's existential freedom is for most of the novel a matter of exuberance and gaiety, Jessie becomes engaged in a negative dialogue with her own existence; she feels cast adrift in the vacuum of her own being. Whereas Ann has no sense that she should have any continuity in her life, it is because Jessie feels cut off from personal development that she feels trapped in the stasis of an eternal present. For Jessie is a woman without a past. There is a strong suggestion in the novel that she has, throughout her life, been denied knowledge of the true identity of her father. As a young girl she was withdrawn from school on the false pretext of a congenital heart ailment and kept at home by her mother in a kind of emotional servitude.[25] Married straight after school, soon widowed with a young son and then remarried, Jessie has never felt in touch either with external reality or with her own existence. She feels cut off from her identity *as* continuity, and hers is a crisis of 'becoming': 'I was; I am: there were not two different tenses, but two different people' (p. 23).

Married to Tom, she attempts to convert disability into a virtue, convinced there is some key to authentic existential being that will unlock the doors of meaning in her life. Yet, just as in Ann's case, this preference also involves a social betrayal. So when Ann and Gideon come seeking her aid at the seaside house where she is holidaying – a house that, uninhabited on any continuous basis, is usually as empty as her private existence – Jessie strongly resents the intrusion and the claim on her responsibility. Because she is confronted with social reality for the first time, in the needs of these two lovers in flight, however, and because she now has the opportunity for action as well as observation, Jessie is drawn out of her solitude. She becomes committed to Ann and Gideon and to the cause of their love, and at last is released from the self-oppression of being, into the connection of social engagement and the awareness of personal 'becoming':

> She was beginning to slip into the mainstream, she was beginning to feel the substance was no longer something she must dam up for herself. Passion would not leave the world grey when it went out for her;

struggle, love, the urge to grasp and shape living went on through the agency of others, too; Gideon and Ann held part of it; Morgan [her son] was coming up to have his share relinquished to him, and even the small girls were not far off.

(p. 274)

At this stage Jessie has reached something of an objective in the novel, finding personal serenity and a broader social meaning simultaneously. She has come to terms with time and the positive as well as negative processes that can be realized through it.

The category of 'becoming' underlying her discovery has its own wider interest. For one thing it easily links the spheres of personal, social and historical development, and in many cases in *Occasion for Loving* discussion within one domain functions as an analogue for the others. One of the more fascinating of these linkages concerns Jessie's relationship with her mother. As a young girl, the reason Jessie's mother had kept her out of school was for the psychological equivalent of an economic 'extraction' – in this case the extraction of emotional support from Jessie in her mother's own struggle against her husband. The method of this extraction was 'underdevelopment'; in keeping Jessie at home her mother was preventing her rise to maturity in the outside world. The ideology supporting this was an eternalized kind of 'trusteeship' (or, perhaps, maternalism) under which the 'ward' would never grow up. The myth supporting this ideology employed a false essentialism and fake metaphysic: the lie that Jessie had a congenital 'heart ailment' and was by nature unfit to take charge of her own life history in the real world. And this oppressive regime evidently relied on and cultivated the goodness of the oppressed not to rebel; that Jessie says she accepted a 'dwarf's status in the world of men and women' (p. 67) says it all. In all these respects the structures that obtained between Jessie and her mother can be seen as exactly those of colonial and neo-colonial practices throughout the world, particularly of oppression as it has been implemented historically in South Africa.

Yet there is still something to be said about the categories of 'being' and 'becoming' that carry this analogy. They are scarcely those of what one might call concrete historical thought. Rather they are categories of Aristotelian philosophy and medieval scholasticism, and more recently of some modern forms of existentialism. Moreover, the major focus of the novel, in so far as it uses these categories, is located primarily within a *personal* sphere, and the historical analogy is strictly dependent on this investigation. There is a sense, therefore, in which, although 'becoming' is affirmed in the novel, this is still done primarily through an exploration of 'being' – of the conditions of personal existence. There is an existential framework that governs the novel's very investigation of 'becoming'. This may reflect the fact that Gordimer is in transition from one conceptual level to another, in which case 'becoming' is midway between 'being' and a more substantial conceptualization of historical engagement. Also Gordimer has said that at the time of writing *Occasion for Loving* she was involved in what was potentially the only phase of religious belief in her life, and that she was reading modern religious and existential writing.[26] But it may be suggested that one of the major reasons that *Occasion for Loving* is still held within a framework of being (and perhaps, even, that Gordimer was herself) is because of the extraordinary realities confronting both novel and novelist at the turn of the decade, which prevented any possibility of real historical 'becoming'.

For the novel's investigation of historical reality by no means ends with the failure of the love affair and all that that connotes. Rather this investigation is translated to a higher and, ultimately, far more crucial plane. Again Jessie is the bearer of its discoveries. We have seen that towards the end of the novel she has discovered a new social commitment, as well as the secret of 'becoming'; and when Gideon and Ann's love affair is destroyed, it is she who realizes the futility of humanism, circumscribed as it is by the realities of apartheid. All in all Jessie at this stage is in as high a state of consciousness as she can possibly go, as far as the novel is concerned. But there is still a fatal discrepancy between her awareness and her possibilities, which *Occasion for Loving* examines with uncompromising honesty. By the time Ann leaves Gideon, Jessie has come to feel really close to the latter; she believes she understands his position and that she is, in a sense, of one common consciousness with him. Yet when she sees Gideon at a party some time later, he is in drunken despair, and at first does not recognize her:

> She spoke to him again, and his gaze recognized something, though perhaps it was not her. He mumbled, 'White bitch – get away.'
> (p. 288)

The remark is a slap in the face, and once again for this novel it is proved that there can be no triumphs of consciousness in South

Africa, no victory of personal relationships. But something far more important is proved as well. When Gideon looks at Jessie he does not see her as an individual. He may be seeing Ann, but what he certainly sees is a white bitch. One white is substitutable for another, and the point is that relations between Gideon and Jessie have become totally impersonal: not just on a personal level, but historically impersonal. There is an antagonism between the two that transcends individuality and must be worked out at the social level before other relations can resume. What the two characters feel, in a sense, is the burden of their typicality rather than their individuality. And for Jessie the significance is that even in realizing the futility of humanism she has no historical base on which to join Gideon, desperate as she is to do so. Impersonal reality surrounds personal desire like a moat. For Jessie now, to be anti-social is a failure, but to be socially engaged seems impossible.

For the first time one of Gordimer's novels ends in a paralysing irony. For the first time also one of her novels expresses the intense alienation of a dissenting but incapacitated white consciousness. Now, too, this consciousness first enters that area of solitary marginality that, in Gordimer's work, has surrounded it in varying degrees of intensity ever since. Much of this can be attributed to the extraordinary force with which historical events struck at the end of the 1950s. Separated from the body of opposition that had disappeared both socially and politically, this paralysis and irony is the most powerful inner illumination of the destruction of the common assumptions of the previous decade. And ideologically, the most significant thing about the novel is then a question of absence. For if the failure of the love affair marks the end of liberal humanism, Gordimer has been unable to put anything else in its place. Where the power of personality stops and impersonal necessity takes over, she is at the border of the historical conception that her earlier humanist terms can sustain, and she lacks adequate terms to effect a transition. Equally significantly, the tension thus deadlocked is diverted into unspecific, explosive terms. By the end of the novel Jessie considers she might in time help someone in 'blowing up a power station' (p. 279) – a reference, perhaps, to the campaigns of sabotage that had already begun. But if she does so it is evident that she will turn to this formlessly, and primarily out of sheer frustration. It is possible that the impasse in liberal consciousness expressed here has some relevance for the sabotage of the early 1960s, especially in its 'disillusioned liberal' form.[27] At any rate, *Occasion for Loving* represents a moment of profound transition as a dominant oppositional philosophy broke under the strains of its own assumptions, and as it was about to take up the next.

In this way *Occasion for Loving* brings to a close the inner history of liberal humanism in the 1950s and early 1960s that began in *A World of Strangers*. We have seen in these two novels the full development of some of its deepest codes, and also their later demise. Not the least valuable aspect of these novels is the 'history of mood' they give of their time – its optimism, uncertainties and final dismay. In terms of her own writing, in *Occasion for Loving* Gordimer has exhausted humanism as a discourse. All the hopes of humanism are centred in Jessie, and what she records is their futility in the face of apartheid. *Occasion for Loving* marks the decisive end, for Gordimer, of an exploration of subjectivity in and for itself. Rarely has she dealt with subjectivity so deeply, and often tenderly, as she does in the case of Jessie; but Gordimer is bidding farewell to this as a mode. Subjectivity has proved subject to political realities, and *Occasion for Loving* stands on the verge of Gordimer's future post-humanist forms. It also stands as a distinct moment of transition for the South African liberal novel in general.

Occasion for Loving is caught, then, between the categories of 'being' and 'becoming'. Not yet able to encompass an adequate conception of 'becoming', it is thrust back by historical reality into an ironical investigation of 'being'. Surrounded by an impersonal history it is trapped within the boundaries of personalism. Yet at the end of the novel it is clear that impersonalism is the only way out – only an impersonal commitment can tackle an impersonal history. At one point in the novel Jessie admires the clarifying effects of the sea and its processes, what she calls 'the physical honesty of salt water and abrasive sand' (p. 201). It is something like this physical honesty that *Occasion for Loving* goes through, and this abrasion that it has endured. For it is an historical impersonalism, clarified both through and of its vision in this novel, that is taken up in *The Late Bourgeois World* and *A Guest of Honour*, and indeed in all of Gordimer's future work. In this respect *Occasion for Loving* is a novel of profound historical sea-change.

4

The Short and the Long Term: *The Late Bourgeois World* and *A Guest of Honour*

What shall I do here?
What time is this for a woman?[1]

. . . a road glimpsed there![2]

I

Occasion for Loving ends with the contemplation of irony and the fact of social failure. Both *The Late Bourgeois World* and *A Guest of Honour* attempt to find new ways of understanding the political world and the demands it makes on the individual. In particular both are concerned to discover new and legitimate terms in which historical engagement can be undertaken, since the liberal humanist impulse of Gordimer's first three novels has now been so thoroughly quelled. For both this now means that they begin to take history as such as their field of investigation rather than simply the social environment of the first three novels; they are attempts to decode its patterns, discern the obligations it casts on the individual and fashion new grounds for a subjective response. Yet their findings are by no means the same. Continuing the pattern of the first three works, even in this new exploration there is something of an internal dialectic. For in various ways *The Late Bourgeois World* and *A Guest of Honour* are inverse images of one another. Respectively they are the shortest and the longest of Gordimer's novels. The one is most intensely South African, the other most generally African. The one, in a moment of desperation, abandons ideological principle; the other, enduring despair, rediscovers it very powerfully.

These inverse patterns proceed directly from the two successive moments from which the novels emerge, and which were in their

90

own way the reverse of one another. *The Late Bourgeois World*, a work of great compression, takes its impulse from the highly compressed world of political upheaval in the first half of the decade; *A Guest of Honour* was written in a period when that upheaval had been stilled, apparently for the foreseeable future. The two novels respond to the different needs of these two moments, proposing methods and visions appropriate for their times. Respectively *The Late Bourgeois World* and *A Guest of Honour* concern the short and the long term.

II
The Late Bourgeois World

If *Occasion for Loving* represents a moment when a philosophy of liberal humanism broke under the strains of its own assumptions, and before it could take up the next, then Nadine Gordimer herself was prevented from taking up any next, simple set of historical terms by the speed of actual events. At the end of the previous novel Jessie considers she may help someone to blow up a power station; and in the early years of the new decade, sabotage, as a tactic, was indeed tried. But by the time Gordimer's new novel, *The Late Bourgeois World*, was written this attempt had been ruthlessly crushed, and the work itself can properly be understood only in the context of this aftermath.

The Late Bourgeois World, published in 1966,[3] has a *double* entry into experience, corresponding to a dramatic twofold movement in South African history in this time. At the risk of some recapitulation this movement should be outlined in some detail for the full force of its effects to be understood. Its first part, as we have already seen, consisted of an intensification of political resistance at the turn of the decade and its transition from a peaceful to a violent phase, both by accident and as a matter of policy. This intensification began as early as 1957, when uprisings occurred in certain country areas of South Africa; in Zeerust, Sekhukhuneland and, by 1960, Pondoland, a black rural population rose up in revolt, primarily against the government's Bantu Authorities policy, and in the latter region at least this seemed to gain the form of a highly motivated and organized political resistance.[4] But it was events in the urban centres that were to prove of primary importance. In this connection Sharpeville has already

91

been discussed, as well as events in the Cape, at Langa, Nyanga and Cape Town. The response of the government has also been noted; a State of Emergency was declared, with widespread arrests taking place; both the ANC and the PAC were outlawed.

This series of events in turn led to a crucial transition for the opposition political movements. Peaceful methods had been the orthodoxy of the 1950s. Sharpeville itself had been intended as a peaceful demonstration.[5] This approach had been met with repression and violence; and far from making any concessions to the intensity of black feeling in South Africa, the state had on the contrary banned its representative organizations. Verwoerd's promise that in defending apartheid the government would be 'as unyielding as walls of granite'[6] was an accurate one, and for the opposition movements old methods and objectives appeared to have outlived their day. With the ANC and the PAC now driven underground, the logic of the situation indicated an historic shift: that the movements themselves take up methods of violence, and adopt a more explicitly revolutionary stance.

In this context *Umkhonto we Sizwe* ('Spear of the Nation') – a body related to, but not officially part of, the ANC – began a campaign of sabotage on 16 December 1961.[7] *Poqo* (meaning 'alone' or 'pure'), a movement aligned in mood and temper with the PAC but probably less so in terms of any formal organization, began to gather momentum in the Eastern and Western Cape, at its most threatening carrying out random attacks against groups of whites.[8] An altogether different body initiated the changed circumstances, however. In October 1961 an organization called the National Committee for Liberation, later the African Resistance Movement (ARM), began its own extended campaign of sabotage. The ARM was a diverse grouping, mostly white, and ranging in its ideological composition from fringe-liberal to Trotskyist. It was politically committed but badly organized and directed; but the ARM sparked off the immediate concerns of *The Late Bourgeois World*.

Retrospectively, given what happened, the transition to violent struggle may seem to have been inadequately prepared and premature. At the time, however, there can be no doubt that the shift was part of a new proto-revolutionary ethos, which was altering perspectives. In part the tone for this new ethos had been set by no less a figure than British premier Harold Macmillan, who on the last stage of a tour of Africa had declared at a joint sitting of both Houses of the

South African Parliament that the country would have to accommodate itself to the 'wind of change' that was sweeping through the
continent.[9] His speech had a tremendously unsettling impact on
white perceptions;[10] and, as independence in Africa continued to
gather momentum – with 1963 still the set 'deadline' for total
liberation – it may well have seemed that South Africa's moment, too,
had come.

Other developments confirmed feelings that things were on the
move. After the Sharpeville massacre money was pouring out of
the country as investors shifted or withdrew their capital.[11] During
the State of Emergency there was even a brief but heady moment for
blacks when the Pass Laws were temporarily suspended, first in the
Cape Town area only, but later also nationwide.[12] The day after the
ANC and PAC were banned, in front of a crowd of 30,000 people
celebrating fifty years of the Union of South Africa at Johannesburg's
Union Exposition, a white farmer from the Northern Transvaal
attempted to assassinate Prime Minister Verwoerd.[13] Whatever
immediate assumptions may have been that this was a political act,
later evidence put it that the farmer was mentally unbalanced, and
had been 'apparently deranged by the crisis'.[14] For those in power
this was surely as ominous a reason for an assassination as any other,
and the attempt, which failed only narrowly, stands as something of a
symbol of the degree to which the known mental and political South
African world was threatening to become radically destabilized. On
all sides South Africa was about to enter into a previously unchartered era. It was in this context that the first explosions of the
revolutionary movements were heard, and the echo of the blasts for
some may have sounded the approaching death of apartheid.

In the event there was nothing like this effect. Indeed, if the
transition to violent resistance was the first stage of the double
movement of the 1960s, then the second consisted of the way in
which it was crushed with unexpected brutality and expedition by
the power of the South African state. This outcome had been
signalled early on when, in Pondoland, armoured cars had been sent
in against people armed with sticks. In a wider context, too, the
political movements were very soon disabled. Within two years of
the first bomb blasts the leadership of the ANC was substantially
weakened. After his personal disappearance underground (which
included a tour of East and North Africa) Nelson Mandela, the head
of *Umkhonto we Sizwe*, was captured in August 1962. Virtually

the entire *Umkhonto* core that remained was taken in a police raid on its headquarters at Rivonia, near Johannesburg, in 1963. In the famous Rivonia Trial of a year later almost all, including Mandela, were sentenced to life imprisonment.[15]

For its part the ARM was also thoroughly broken by the police, its most memorable legacy being one of confusion as a bomb planted at Johannesburg's railway station killed a woman and injured two others.[16] *Poqo* was smashed by mass arrests, largely brought on by the carelessness of the new PAC leadership.[17] Finally, the underground Communist Party was infiltrated and badly crippled, its Central Committee chairman, Bram Fischer, being captured after an extraordinary ten and a half months at large, in disguise and on the run from the police; the rest of the Party was hobbled in a number of trials in the middle years of the decade. In contrast to the sustained activity of the period immediately following Sharpeville, it was effectively all over by the year *The Late Bourgeois World* was published. Whereas in the first six months alone of 1964 there were 203 cases of sabotage, in 1965 as a whole there was none.[18]

Repression, moreover, was enabled across the board. In the political sphere powers of detention without trial were first introduced, and then dramatically increased, the time limit being raised from 12 days in 1962 to 90 days in 1963 to 180 days in 1965.[19] Detention in these circumstances usually meant solitary confinement, and there were widespread allegations of torture; as the decade progressed a number of detainees died.[20] As far as the state was concerned, where prosecution was impossible or a waste of time, individuals were banned on an uprecedented scale, 531 serving banning orders by 1966.[21] Cultural repression accompanied the political. Legislation providing for detention without trial simultaneously listed writers whose work could not be quoted or distributed,[22] while the Publications and Entertainments Act, promulgated in 1963, allowed for the banning of everything from scenes depicting 'night life' and 'physical poses' to matter 'prejudicial to the safety of the state'. These years, too, saw the effective crippling of oppositional journals such as *New Age*, *Spark* and *Fighting Talk*, either by direct banning or else by banning of their writers and staff as individuals.[23] Indeed the tactic of banning conjoined the political, social, and cultural worlds, enclosing them all in what Hilda Bernstein has, in her memoirs of the period, aptly called a 'net of silence'.[24]

Compared to the peaceful movements of the previous decade, the early 1960s were a time of profound change in which the historical realities of South Africa suddenly and unmistakably became apparent. Equally, the way these years were contained and sealed off by the power of the state gives them a special character. Distinct from the years on either side, this was the period of open violence, of the false start of the South African revolution and the outright victory of the counter-revolution. *The Late Bourgeois World* emerges from this specific experience. The novel exists in a stunned world, down on the ground after having been knocked off its feet. It is a post-war novel attempting to find ways to restart the war.

Nadine Gordimer was affected by these developments in the first half of the decade. We have seen in relation to *Occasion for Loving* how the destruction of the world of the 1950s caused an isolation in her life that was also reflected in her work. As a proto-revolutionary movement first arose and then was crushed, and as the social and cultural attrition of further exile and banning increased, it must be assumed that earlier feelings of frustration and alienation, for her, as for others, could only have intensified. In other ways, however, in contrast to the tendency to withdrawal evident in *Occasion for Loving*, it appears that in the years leading up to *The Late Bourgeois World* Gordimer was again becoming involved in the political world surrounding her. In part this was something she could not avoid, as she herself had now been directly affected by the new ethos of repression (although in a relatively minor way) when *A World of Strangers* was banned in the paperback edition in 1962.[25] But then, to a degree disproportionate to this comparatively small disprivilege, Gordimer began to take up an attack against the cultural and political onslaught. Indeed, the cultural onslaught may well have had the effect of politicizing her in her own right; as she put it, as a writer she was now a member of a 'victimized group'.[26] The year 1963 then sees the beginning of an extended campaign on Gordimer's part, which has lasted up to the present day, against the censorship system.[27]

In her articles and speeches against censorship Gordimer was concerned to show the way in which cultural and political repression were interlocked. Thus she pointed out in 1963 that all the books by South African writers that had been banned had suffered that fate 'for a political reason'.[28] Yet there were signs, too, that her political consciousness, as such, was being roused. In 1966 she wrote two articles on the arrest and trial of Bram Fischer, in which her admiration for his integrity and commitment became clear (this particular interest, as we shall see, was to resurface thirteen years later in *Burger's Daughter*, in which Rosa Burger's father is modelled to some degree on Bram Fischer).[29]

One matter that came up at Fischer's preliminary hearing and especially interested Gordimer was the issue of channelling funds to the underground movements. For, according to Gordimer's account, a woman appeared as state witness against Fischer who said she had hired a deposit box in which sums of up to £1,500 were kept, presumably for the use of the Communist Party. Also she admitted to distributing money from the Defence and Aid Fund to political prisoners and their dependants (which was not illegal at the time, although it later became so).[30] From her report Gordimer was clearly intrigued by such activities, and a number of people were named or arraigned in connection with distributing funds in these years.[31] All this no doubt provides the background for one aspect of *The Late Bourgeois World*, in which Elizabeth's decision at the end concerns whether or not to channel money for the underground PAC.

But the central political interest of the period for Gordimer, as she recalls it, appears in the direct motivation of her novel itself:

> My short novel *The Late Bourgeois World* was an attempt to look into the specific character of the social climate that produced the wave of young white saboteurs in 1963–64.[32]

The reference to the 'young white saboteurs' indicates that Gordimer had in mind the ARM rather than *Umkhonto we Sizwe*; also the years 1963–4 were those when the ARM reached the peak of its activity, and when it was broken. It is perhaps significant, given her interest in Fischer, that Gordimer should have chosen this somewhat maverick group rather than the mainstream of the underground political resistance.[33] But one thing already is clear from her remark; of all her novels up to that date, *The Late Bourgeois World* was the one most explicitly linked to actual historical events. Not until 1976 and the world of *Burger's Daughter* would there once more be such a close and explicit linkage, and there the heritage concerned would be Fischer's rather than the ARM. Here, however, the ARM comes under the spotlight.

A substantial part of the novel is devoted to an examination of the revolutionary moment of the early 1960s, of its impulses and of its weaknesses. This is undertaken by the novel's narrator and central character, Elizabeth Van Den Sandt, on the day she hears of the death by suicide of her ex-husband, Max. For Max Van Den Sandt had himself been a 'young white saboteur' who upon his arrest had turned state witness, and Elizabeth's review of her relationship with him becomes inseparably a review, often with ruthless clarity, of his career as a revolutionary. Max's chief failure is that he is found to have been not revolutionary *enough*. With a greatly inflated image of his own role as historical saviour, and grossly overestimating the objective possibilities of the early 1960s, Max's conception of revolution had been naïve, idealistic and romantic in the extreme. (The fact that he had wished to write a treatise on African Socialism in the form of Platonic dialogues says – perhaps more than says – it all.)

Max's revolution had been an egocentric affair, for his deepest motivation had been a raging ambition for personal success. This had largely been a revolt *within* the terms of the bourgeois world, therefore, for his desire for personal glory is its characteristic feature, a direct and untransformed inheritance from the world he intended to overthrow. This constitutes the logic whereby Max literally turned 'witness' for the 'state' he ostensibly opposed. A symptom of the world that produced him – in this respect his parents are symbolically cast as pillars of the South African system – Max dies of the personality and historical situation he rejects but cannot transform.

An important question arises from this depiction. It has already been said that Max, as a character, has been drawn from the history of the ARM. The problem concerns exactly what sort of relationship this is. The figure of Max, it might be charged, is a travesty of the kind of commitment of some of those actually involved in the ARM. The problem is a special instance of the general one concerning the relation between fact and fiction, and the representative nature of the latter; it came up in a different form in *A World of Strangers*, and will recur more intensely in *Burger's Daughter*. But as is the case in both those novels, the issue can be resolved fairly easily. For in his historical dimension as a character Max has also been cast as a *type*, and, as we saw in *A World of Strangers*, a type does not necessarily bear a direct and complete relationship to actually living persons. An amalgam of characteristics, the typical figure corresponds to no single individual; an approximation of a movement in general, he or she is based upon a principle of significance, which selects the extreme embodiment and ignores the particular exception. At this level it appears that *The Late Bourgeois World* has hit some historical nails on the head. For the ARM *was* in many respects naïve, apart from being badly organized;[34] it was also an unstable movement, gathering its participants for all sorts of private reasons; and some of its members did turn state witness, in one case with complete abandon.[35]

The fact that Gordimer chose the ARM for the focus of her novel rather than any other underground movement again becomes significant. In terms of its general class and ideological composition, the ARM was much closer to Gordimer's own experience than *Umkhonto we Sizwe* or the Communist Party would have been. Growing out of liberalism (in the case of many of its members) and cut off for the most part from the black mass movements, as Gordimer was herself, the ARM would have provided a logical focal point for her in relation to her own historical and ideological development. But there is perhaps something more complex in evidence here. Just as Max typifies the ARM, there may be a sense in which the ARM itself typified, as an extreme embodiment, the overall revolutionary moment of which it was a part: its romance, dedication and fervour, but also its illusions and hidden desperation.

This does not mean that the saboteurs in the novel literally 'represent' *Umkhonto we Sizwe* as well as the ARM. But it does mean that they represent the general patterns of the moment in which both *Umkhonto* and the ARM participated. In writing about the ARM, then, Gordimer is writing about much larger events. It might be said that the writer has unconsciously been drawn to the underlying historical reality of the period she has experienced, and set it up at the level of the typical. At this point the logical progression of Gordimer's development and the far deeper historical insight coincide with remarkable congruence.

The use of typicality in *The Late Bourgeois World* brings up a related matter of some significance, although this does not so much concern Max as what he has to confront. It has been mentioned that the dominant features of white South African society are, in the novel, cast in the form of Max's parents, the Van Den Sandts. These two are figures at the extreme edge of typification and illustrate its potential disabilities as an historical mode if carried too far. Max's father is of English and Flemish descent; he is a Member of

Parliament; he has interests in mining and industry. Max's mother is of Afrikaner descent; her family has served at embassies all over Europe; her ties are with the land and with agriculture. Together, therefore, the two embody the dominant features of white South African society, politically, economically and culturally. Like equivalents of Conrad's Kurtz, all of European South Africa is in them.

In this regard the fact that the Van Den Sandts are United Party rather than Nationalist is immaterial; as Elizabeth remarks, they are 'united' only in the desire to see Afrikaners and English conjoined in common domination of the blacks. In their broadly incorporative role, however, it seems typification has passed into symbolism, and the essence of this symbolic representation of the South African structure is that it is monolithic. Here are none of the gradations, disjunctions, internal conflicts and mechanisms of the real political world with which one may come to grips in actual historical action – a feature that will change markedly in *A Guest of Honour*. But as such we could have no better introduction to the historical consciousness of *The Late Bourgeois World*. For in itself a method of symbolic contraction and abbreviation argues for a moment of intensity and compression standing behind the novel, in which there is neither time nor scope for a more exhaustive analysis. And as the substance of a vision it gives a particular feeling for the mood of this time, in the failed revolutionary moment: that the oppressive South African totality *was* monolithic and seemingly impregnable; that the possibility of practical politics had all but disappeared. *The Late Bourgeois World*, as we shall see, is designed specifically to deal with this problem. But in doing so, as will also become clear, it is obliged on one level to turn to symbolic means to overcome what it has conceived symbolically. In this respect conception and resolution are of a single symbolic piece, and this is then our first hint of the kind of intensity embodied in *The Late Bourgeois World*.

For all its focus on Max, *The Late Bourgeois World* emerges not so much from *within* the period of the ARM as after it had been destroyed. Accordingly, the work gives us an introduction *par excellence* into the realities of the post-revolutionary world of the 1960s. As usual in Gordimer's writing, the first level at which it does so is that of its social observation, but here, as in other of her texts, what is observed can scarcely be separated from the consciousness that is doing the observing. *The Late Bourgeois World* has been produced in an environment much changed from that of *A World of*

Strangers, or even *Occasion for Loving*. In contrast to the former novel, when Elizabeth characterizes the liberal socializing of the 1950s, she now describes its parties as simply occasions where 'white liberals' and 'black tarts and toughs' went for 'what each could get out of the other' (p. 85). Measuring what seems to be an immense distance between her own world and that of *Occasion for Loving*, she remarks flatly: 'I've had a black lover, years ago' (pp. 138–9). The black world is also observed in the novel, and the near desperate extremity of its condition evoked; on a coal delivery lorry black workers burn a fire in a blazing brazier to keep warm, uncaring of the proximity of the petrol tank; clinging precariously to a furniture van they don't 'care a damn' (p. 31). The reverse side of this extremity is a total disdain for whites; when one of the furniture delivery workers makes obscene gestures at a black woman, and Elizabeth smiles at him, he looks right through her as if she doesn't exist.

Overall, there is a crucial new tone in the novel, marking a new mood for the mid-1960s. It is one of combined rage, frustration and resignation, as when Elizabeth includes herself in a general indictment of the culture of which she is a part: 'Oh we bathed and perfumed and depilated white ladies, in whose wombs the sanctity of the white race is entombed!' (p. 38).

The Late Bourgeois World also marks a further stage for Gordimer in her disillusion with an ideology of liberal humanism. On more than one occasion Elizabeth remarks that a liberal humanist code, enjoining charity and kindness to dogs, in South Africa could at best produce only confusion. The only characters in the novel who embody a kind of humanism are the Van Den Sandts. In their case, however, it is clear that this is inseparable from an oppressive and exploitative paternalism. The ideology that had sustained Gordimer up to its crisis in *Occasion for Loving* here undergoes a further demise.

In the context of an historical aftermath it is not surprising that the central observations of *The Late Bourgeois World* concern patterns of white consciousness in the period of post-revolutionary silence. The central feature of this consciousness is that it exists in an absolutely reduced and divested world, a world of emotional and psychological fundamentalism. In this regard, if Max's suicide symbolizes the fact that the revolutionary period is over, then the telegram announcing it to Elizabeth is also something of a symbol; in the world that survives only the barest expression of essentials is appropriate. For this is a world in which emotion defers to fact, and fact refers only to itself. Learning of Max's death, Elizabeth feels nothing 'except that I believed it' (p. 14). It is a world in which all superfluities, even of consciousness, are hived off as being no longer valid. Even Elizabeth's love affair participates in this depletion; she says that she and her lover, Graham, have no private names, references, or love words: 'We use the standard vocabulary when necessary' (p. 53). Moreover, the historical logic behind this reduction is suggested. Elizabeth remarks that 'you can know too much for love' (p. 65).

This, unmistakably, is the death knell of liberal humanism, and it is significant that when Elizabeth begins to tell what she does know, it is a history of the 1950s and 1960s that she relates through her analysis of Max. For in these earlier phases, luxuries of consciousness – such as Max's romanticism – produced historical illusions. Now there are no illusions left. Only a state of absolute disillusion can guarantee any irreducible truth and guard against further false political estimations. And there is a factor of exhaustion involved; after the successive crises of the previous ten years, and the emotional intensity that filled them, Elizabeth survives now in a world drained of its energy to try again.

Elizabeth's disillusion includes an awareness of the vast irony governing her life. In this respect *The Late Bourgeois World* takes off where *Occasion for Loving* ends. Though the earlier novel ended in irony, the possibility of 'blowing up power stations' still remained. In Elizabeth's case, however, even this option is no longer available. Far from it; it is the failed revolutionary moment that itself constitutes her irony. Even more so than for Jessie, irony has now been driven further and deeper, into the very fact of consciousness itself. Elizabeth's awareness, even in its clarified form, is irrelevant. There is a vast disproportion between her extraordinary understanding of the world that she lives in on the one hand, and the degree of its public significance on the other. Basically it makes no difference what Elizabeth thinks – even the awareness of irony is in this sense ironical. As for her historical situation, she must simply concede that the objective conditions in which she might in any way have differentiated herself from the broad mass of white South Africans have by now wholly disappeared: 'I too have my package of pork fillets and my chair in the sun; you would not know me from the others' (p. 43).

The world has been levelled, and consciousness is irony. The attitude that meets this is reduced, fundamental. Three features in *The Late Bourgeois World* mark out its historical consciousness. This stunned world, in which only a startlingly clear disillusion survives to meet an all-encompassing irony, is the first of these three features.

This minimalist position is not finally acceptable for the novel, however. Paradoxically in a state of political closure, *The Late Bourgeois World* is on the contrary still concerned to revive the possibility of historical engagement. Thus Elizabeth tells her son, Bobo, that the reason Max's life was so disastrous was not directly because of politics, but because in general he wasn't equal to the demands he took upon himself. As she puts it to him in schoolboyish terms he can understand, it was like insisting on playing for the first team when one was only good enough for the third. What this proposition suggests, however, is that one *can* be good enough for the 'first team', so long as one knows one's own strength and the demands of the game. This position is different from that of *Occasion for Loving*, in which the potential for personal engagement was sealed off by objective reality. Here the idea of engagement is being recovered, though on condition that adequately objective terms are found to underpin it. This marks a significant advance for Gordimer. In *Occasion for Loving* she had reached the end of a discourse of personal relations; its inadequacy in the face of historical reality was there sufficiently demonstrated. Here, however, the principle of subjective agency is being reasserted, and on a higher level; there can be personal engagement if an impersonal enough analysis informs it. For Gordimer the crisis of personal relations comes to an end in *Occasion for Loving*; the tasks of objectivity begin in *The Late Bourgeois World*, carry on in *A Guest of Honour* and continue up to *Burger's Daughter* and *July's People* – and, no doubt, beyond.

The project of the novel is then to find adequately impersonal terms of action. As a first step in this direction it becomes clear that Elizabeth's reductionist position can by no means constitute these terms. For although her clarity is nothing if not impersonal, there is simply no action involved. In a sense Elizabeth has taken *refuge* in her objectivity; it is a kind of insurance against causes that fail. But in this purely preventive guise it cannot provide the basis for further political engagement. This first becomes evident indirectly in the novel, through Elizabeth's love affair with Graham.

As in virtually all of Gordimer's long fiction, the love affair in *The*

Late Bourgeois World functions as a central analogue for a world-historical posture in general. We have seen how Elizabeth's relationship participates in the divested world of the 1960s. But it is then also through this relationship that her failing in historical terms becomes clear. The incident in which this occurs is in some respects clumsily constructed, but for this reason the point comes across very strongly. Elizabeth and Graham are discussing what he, following a book he has read, calls 'the late bourgeois world', when suddenly he asks her 'how' she would say 'it is with us' (p. 112). He means the condition of the world, but for an instant Elizabeth takes him as referring to their relationship. At that point, for her, an essential failure between the two is revealed. Referring to Graham's question, she remarks:

> it was a quiet, impersonal demand, the tone of the judge exercising the prerogative of judicial ignorance, not the partisan one of the advocate cross-examining. There was what I can only describe as a power failure between us.
>
> (p. 113)

The judicial metaphor is a fitting one, for Graham himself is a lawyer. But his legality is clearly of the legalistic kind; for him there are no causes or passions, whether in the private or the public sphere; and the same, it becomes clear, is true of Elizabeth. She too has adopted a legalism – the legalism of being not wrong – and this is what her reductionism involves. But just as there is a 'power failure' between her and her lover, this is a posture of submission to power by one who seems resigned to never having any. There is a poverty in Elizabeth's defensive clarity, therefore, which is its essential passivity; it has rendered her life a subjective correlative of 'the late bourgeois world'.

Through this analogy a contrasting point is revealed. Any idea of the purity of truth is itself a deception; truth is always historically involved. Neutrality, no matter how profoundly motivated, in effect supports the status quo. On the contrary another kind of clarity is required, which has no illusions about its own innocence but takes on responsibility, commitment and 'advocacy'. Historical, as distinct from abstract, truth requires a principle of *partisanship*. Truth itself must be historically transformed.

This is the key to the novel's conception of historical validity, and to the code of action it is seeking. Such validity lies not in the distorted adoption of the terms of the bourgeois world, as in Max's

103

case, which produces only failure; nor in their absolute rejection, as in Elizabeth's own, which produces paralysis; but in their actual and material transformation. An ingenious working out of a principle of transformation occurs in the novel that shows how the terms of 'the late bourgeois world' can be entirely reconstituted through an altered historical usage. For as the novel ends, Elizabeth, having been approached by the underground PAC, is on the verge of deciding to use her senile grandmother's bank account, over which she can gain control, to channel money for the banned organization. On the one hand her plan is an outrageous attack on bourgeois morality; the idea that the private property of an incapable old woman can be so summarily annexed, in a way that would be entirely counter to her wishes if she had any, is something not to be countenanced under Graham's 'laws'. On the other hand, there is another kind of logic at work here. Elizabeth's grandmother is in any case cast as a kind of archetypal 'late *bourgeoise*' in an advanced state of decline; she has never done a day's work in her life, she is living on inherited money originally made in the mining industry at the time of Rhodes and Beit, and her cultural decay is parodically represented by the fact that she prefers artificial flowers to real ones.

But Elizabeth's planned action will successfully *transform* the morality underlying her grandmother's position, as well as the 'laws' maintaining it. Whereas bourgeois practice has historically used 'social thievery' for private gain, here Elizabeth turns its techniques against itself, appropriating the realm of personal privilege for social purposes. Her plan also involves a fundamental, and material, transformation of one of the basic institutions of the capitalist world: the private banking account, which is now to be an instrument of revolutionary politics. In this way white wealth, privilege and power are simultaneously transformed, as Elizabeth makes use of all of them in order only to undo them.

Even the personal terms of the bourgeois world are redefined. Elizabeth knows that Luke Fokase, the PAC man who has contacted her, will probably also make love to her. But this she is prepared to accept, because it is all he has to offer her, and in that case each will be giving what he or she has: an ancient, but also suitably historicized definition of love; and this also introduces to the two a new kind of equality. Finally, irony is transformed. In using her ironical powers of privilege ironically, Elizabeth beats irony at its own game and borders on the edge of a new world.

Here we should consider Elizabeth's position as a woman, in embodying this new historical vision. All along in the novel there has been a sense in which it is important that it is a woman who has carried its insights. From the start it is clear that Elizabeth is a person of exceptional intelligence; and it is intriguing that this should be counterposed to Max's adolescent and romantic impetuosity – indeed that Elizabeth should be the one to reveal it. A matter of sexual politics with specific reference to South Africa seems to be emerging. In a white-male-dominated culture, which has abrogated to itself a fiction of romantic bravado (consider Mehring in *The Conservationist*), it has very frequently been women (both black and white) who have been amongst the most courageous opponents of apartheid or, as in Gordimer's own case, the most uncompromising witnesses of its social effects.[36] More particularly, Gordimer seems to be working out a new female role in the novel, in which political and sexual hierarchies are simultaneously challenged. Elizabeth's intellectual supremacy is on one level evidence of this, while her new political awakening at the end is perceived in distinctly sexual terms; Elizabeth feels the thought of her grandmother's bank account grow 'like sexual tumescence' within her (p. 146).

A great change in Gordimer's writing is being marked here. In *The Lying Days* Helen Shaw first discovered sexuality as a joy in itself. In *Occasion for Loving* it became wholly subject to political power. Now, by contrast, sexuality is becoming politicized, as political engagement takes on a definite sexual quality. And with increasing force, as we shall see in *Burger's Daughter* and *July's People*, Gordimer's women become interlocked with politics, as politics transforms sexuality. [The writer who began with traditional 'female' concerns – such as those of love, parents and marriage – has, under the pressure of history, undergone significant change.]

In Elizabeth's code of transformation a dialectical model is involved. Having rejected the late bourgeois world, Elizabeth then re-engages with its material realities, and in doing so transforms them, transcending their previous limits. Similarly, there is an historical dialectic involved; Elizabeth's clarified world, negating the romanticism and idealism of the period that Max represents, but reassuming its objectives, discovers terms for historical action adequate to the conditions it faces. In a sense a self-fulfilling guarantee is involved, and Elizabeth's methodical doubt stands as insurance that there is to be no repetition of previous mistakes. We shall see shortly that the novel contradicts its own guarantee, but for the moment let us note that Gordimer's work is shifting from a social to what may more properly be described as an historical plane of action.

No longer is Gordimer prepared simply to describe the social world as it is given, as in *The Lying Days*; nor, as in *A World of Strangers*, to prescribe action within the framework of that world. Nor, as in *Occasion for Loving*, is the social world sealed off from the possibility of historical change. Here the social world that is given, even within its extraordinary enclosure, is the site of further change; the effects of previous failure provide the roots of a new dispensation. The idea of constructing an objective and impersonal code of action such as Elizabeth conceives is also fundamentally an historical one, for it rests on the principle that action must be based not only on the needs of the moment, but also on an accurate assessment of the forces governing that moment and its relation to the past and to a desired future. In this respect Elizabeth's choice is historic in a sense beyond that in which a decision to help an underground guerrilla movement is the stuff of which history is made. The form of Gordimer's literary consciousness is now more precisely historical rather than social.

Yet it still remains to determine the exact character of the historical consciousness of *The Late Bourgeois World*. Earlier it was said that there were three primary features of this consciousness, and that the first was the stunned mood of the aftermath of the failed 1960s revolution. At this stage, in the novel's resolution, it becomes possible to discern the remaining two features; these become apparent in the terms in which Elizabeth once again faces the prospect of action. The first concerns the likelihood that she will channel money to the PAC. If she does so, a radical utilitarianism will underlie the move. A subliminal theory of utility is already evident in Elizabeth's idea, expressed in relation to Luke, of simply 'giving what one has'; but in so far as she is aware that the PAC would in all probability construct what one of Max's African colleagues once called a 'black capitalist country' in South Africa (p. 75), immediate utility and function override all her other motives:

> Am I going into politics again, then? And if so, what kind? But I can't be bothered with this sort of thing, it's irrelevant.

(p. 159)

This attitude is again something that will change dramatically in *A Guest of Honour*, in which the question of 'what kind of politics' is a major thread of its investigations. Here, however, ideology has been entirely abandoned, and Elizabeth makes it clear why this is so. In the changed historical circumstances in which she finds herself the time for 'niggling scruples' (p. 121), as she puts it, is over. The government itself makes no distinction between the various revolutionary movements. And in conditions in which the state has such absolute control the imperative of revolution *per se* far outweighs the question of what kind of revolution it will be. At this point the novel is not so much affirming any support for the PAC as indicating that dabbling in ideological niceties is an inadmissible luxury.

This utilitarianism is part of the novel's historical realism, which as we have seen attempts to find a code of action appropriate to the conditions it faces. To this extent – in its uncompromising motivation – *The Late Bourgeois World* differentiates itself from some of the other 'revolutionary' fiction of the 1960s. In C. J. Driver's *Elegy for a Revolutionary* the hero ends by contemplating the vagaries of life within the charmed enclosure of an Oxford University library. Though the story the novel tells, also based on the ARM, is compelling enough, its ending reveals there is nothing except defeat and a kind of effete solitude for its author to foresee.[37] Jack Cope's *The Dawn Comes Twice*, though at times sustaining a lyric power, gives an entirely garbled account of revolutionary activity.[38]

Only in the fiction of Alex La Guma is the impulse of Gordimer's novel matched, and in some ways surpassed. In *The Stone Country* and *In the Fog of the Seasons' End*[39] La Guma explores in an unpretentious yet unremittingly realistic fashion the difficulties, strengths and triumphs of underground political activity. Where Gordimer finds the cold clarity of solitude La Guma manages to fashion an unusually humane vision of political struggle. But this is also undoubtedly because he has access to a community and a social strength (in the 'coloured' world of Cape Town) denied to Gordimer in her marginality. And this, in a way, is the point. For in Elizabeth's planned action something else besides realism is apparent. In her radical appeal to utility Elizabeth is clutching at straws, and, as she herself affirms, one straw is as good as another, so long as some action is taken. The stray chance of channelling money to an organization whose political integrity she suspects is taken as doing one's bit for the revolution. In Elizabeth's plan, that is to say, there is a strong element of desperation. She feels it imperative to do something; but there is nothing else she can do. This fact largely underlies her appeal to utility.

Such a feeling of desperation is reinforced in the third main feature of the novel's historical consciousness. In an entirely contradictory move Elizabeth's radical utilitarianism is conjoined with what can only be termed a massive romanticism; it is far more elaborate and intense than Max's kind, for example. At the end of the novel, having had her request from Luke, Elizabeth lies musing in bed, in moments of half-sleeping, half-waking, before dawn. The thoughts of her day are germinating in her mind, which is, as she puts it, perfectly clear. What follows is a lengthy rumination, but worth quoting from in order to see what is going on. Elizabeth compares her situation with that of the astronauts who happen to be circling the world at that very moment:

> Isn't it the same old yearning for immortality, akin to all our desires to transcend all kinds of human limits? The feeling that if you bring such a thing off you're approaching the transcension of our limits of life: our death ... They are alive, up there ... The very scene of operations is significant. We call the nothing above me 'the sky'; and that way it's become the roof of our environment, part of our terrestrial and finite being ... But we know that that 'nothing' ... is space. Twin of time, the phrase goes. I hear it in Graham's voice: together they represent, in the only conception we're capable of forming of it, infinity ... If that man over my head can get out of 'the sky' into space ... can he really be still mortal? If God is the principle of the eternal, isn't he near God, to-night? ... After all, religions teach that the kingdom of God, of the spirit, is not of this world ... Space is not of this world, either, and yet you can walk about alive in it, up there ... Is there anything surprising that there should be a deep connection in our subconscious between the eternity of God and the infinity of space? ... nearly all believe that there is some identity, at least, between religious myths and the evolutionary drive towards higher forms of life ... What's going on overhead is perhaps the spiritual expression of our age, and we don't recognise it ... Could any act of worship as we've known such things for two thousand years express more urgently a yearning for life beyond life – the yearning for God?

(pp. 154–6)

From one point of view, in terms of the novel's code of transformation, Elizabeth's lengthy analogy, though surprising, is justified, and indeed clarifies the logic of her intention. For both she and the astronauts are transcending the limits of their previous existence, they by venturing into space, she by advancing into an unchartered political zone in which the terms of the bourgeois world are to be overcome. Yet this comparison also begins to take off into the outer reaches. Elizabeth sees her transcendence, in which she and the astronauts are equally involved, as an expression of the same archetypal, mythic and religious quest to go beyond the known barriers of existence and approach, apparently, its source. The conquest of space is connected with a timeless yearning for immortality and with the desire to transcend every human limit, including death. All this is linked with God, subconscious mythic processes and a basic evolutionary drive. For Elizabeth the space venture is the human approximation of God and the mythical enaction of humanity. As her thoughts slip from the world overhead to her own intended plans (pp. 157–60), everything that applies to the astronauts in this doctrine of transcendence by implication applies to herself.

This is an extraordinary equation. If on one level political choice is granted a cosmic kind of stature, then on another it is being entirely absorbed into myth. Elizabeth's theory of transcendence threatens to transcend history altogether. Here other aspects of Gordimer's depiction are significant, for a symbolic realm has been entered in Elizabeth's musings. Allegories of birth, for example, abound. Elizabeth's mind is 'pregnant' with gestating thoughts after her 'proposal' from Luke, and its sexual overtones. She herself is in something akin to a foetal situation, half-waking in bed before dawn. Overhead there are the astronauts in their own womb-like 'capsule' in space, evidently being born into a new dimension of existence. The space-walker, actually launching himself into that dimension, is attached by an 'umbilical cord' to his capsule.

Circles, the mythic symbol of fulfilment and completion, surround Elizabeth. The twenty-four-hour day-in-her-life is approaching full turn, while in the silence of night the world is revolving, the astronauts orbiting above it. Elizabeth is at 'the still point of the turning world'; T. S. Eliot, who coined the phrase 'the mythical method', would recognize this intersection of time with the timeless. And the idea that subconscious but surfacing night-thoughts connect with archetypal realities is one most famously embodied by Joyce (of whom Eliot used the phrase) in both *Ulysses* and *Finnegans Wake*. Both in form and content the novel's historical realism is counterposed by a sudden and vast mythology. Gordimer is seeking security on strange and extraordinary heights.

All this enables a final assessment of the novel's consciousness of history. We have noted some of its different aspects: the fact that it is specifically an historical rather than a social consciousness, the fact that it has arisen in a moment of ironic post-revolutionary aftermath. But when it comes to characterizing the content of that consciousness, there remain the three primary features that have been discerned: the stunned psychological fundamentalism of the period of aftermath itself; the radical utilitarianism of Elizabeth's prospective action; and the mythic romanticism whereby it is legitimized. There is no resolution between these three features in the novel; its realism and romanticism especially remain in flat contradiction. It seems remarkable that, in the stunned and divested moment from which the novel arises and that it describes, such an overwhelming romanticism could appear. But at this point what the novel reveals unconsciously is far more significant than anything it approaches deliberately. For, both separately and together, these three features can be understood only as different aspects of the selfsame phenomenon: that *The Late Bourgeois World* represents an oppositional consciousness in a moment of anguish and crisis. Taken separately, this is what is connoted by the stunned world, as it is by Elizabeth's utilitarianism, as it is by her mythic romanticism. And together the same reality is represented, where a mind – and a novel – that will accept nothing but irreducible essentials, can seek security at such ephemeral and flamboyant heights; where any historical straw can be clutched at, and its legitimacy be found at the level of cosmically romantic myth.

It is true that by the time the novel ends Elizabeth has not actually taken her decision to channel money to the PAC, although it seems certain she will do so. If, however, she does *not*, it only makes a mockery of her own, and the novel's, entire development – thereby, if anything, increasing the sense of historical desperation in which both are caught. For or against, therefore, *The Late Bourgeois World* returns to the moment from which it has emerged, as the frenzy of its methods only heightens a sense of the silence from which it was generated. Once again we are given history from the inside as Gordimer's novel represents an extremity of consciousness to match the extremity of its time. Paradoxically, the novel becomes an extension of the period that it tries to supersede, proposing desperate short-term measures for an overwhelming and immediate crisis.

III

A Guest of Honour

At first sight it may seem inappropriate that Nadine Gordimer's fifth novel, *A Guest of Honour*, published in 1971,[40] should be included in a study of what has proved to be her specifically South African consciousness of history. Whereas the succession of her novels so far reveals an intensifying encounter with the particularities of South African existence, until the extreme concentration of *The Late Bourgeois World* is reached, *A Guest of Honour* is not even set in South Africa, and its concerns seem to be with African politics and an African consciousness in general. Yet if there is a paradox here it can be explained, and in this Gordimer herself gives us a clue.

Asked upon publication of her book whether there were any more African novels to come, she replied that to her they had 'all been African novels'.[41] If the South African novels are in some sense African – and we have seen a recurrent African dimension to Gordimer's South African consciousness – then there is a strong likelihood that the work explicitly set in Africa should also in some respects be South African. This expectation is borne out by a closer consideration of *A Guest of Honour*. It is not just that a work projected from a specific situation must in its very projection bear its imprint (which, going on the principles we have discovered so far, may now be taken for granted), but *A Guest of Honour* has in fact been set up to deal with problems of great relevance for the time and place from which it emerges. The novel that upon its publication Gordimer declared to be her 'favourite',[42] and which she later said 'means most to me',[43] has a great deal to do with her South African historical consciousness at the time when it was written.

As we saw in the previous chapter, Nadine Gordimer had been travelling in Africa at least since the mid-1950s.[44] Her travel writing, dating from this period and after, often shows her at her observational best, revealing not only an active, but a very perceptive interest in Africa in environmental, social and political terms. Her 1960 trip seems to have been an extraordinary one; not only did Gordimer visit the Belgian Congo, but she travelled up the Congo River from West to East Africa, crossing the Ruwenzori Mountains (the 'Mountains of the Moon') on the way. Gordimer's descriptions show all the sensuous receptiveness to the continent that has been a hallmark of her writing since she first described the bare veld of the compound and concession stores in *The Lying Days*.

In the Congo she comes across baobab trees ('those anthropomorphic, zōomorphic, geomorphic living forms') and holds their 'mammalian' vegetation, each weighing fully five pounds: 'There came to me, through my hand, all the queerness of the continent, in the strange feel of that heavy-hanging fruit.'[45] Later she describes going out on elephant back, 'sway[ing] regularly through the early-morning air', when she and the two cornacs she is with are surrounded by a herd of wild elephant. She fears some danger, but none arises:

> the wild elephants seemed unaware of the two who bore men on their backs, and the tame elephants showed no remembrance of the freedom from which they once came. I have often seen the wild animals of Africa from a car, or even on foot, in game reserves, but I have never expected or felt myself to be anything but an intruder among them. On elephant-back they accepted me as one of themselves; it was a kind of miraculous release from the natural pariahdom of man in the world of the beasts – an hour, for me, that early morning, which was the reverse of that hour at midnight on Christmas Eve when it is said that beasts can speak like men.[46]

This aspect of Africa is magical territory for Gordimer, her writing fully open to and revealing its allure. This sort of description – and there is much of it in *A Guest of Honour*, as Bray drives through the rural outreaches of Gala province, or goes swimming in a Central African lake – shows one of Gordimer's primary attachments to the continent, which is, strictly speaking, one of the senses. But here there is that other kind of attachment as well, as Gordimer writes of the (somewhat contradictory) message painted on one of the river barges in which she travelled: '*Vive le Roi M. Kasavubu et l'Indépendence*'.[47] In *A Guest of Honour* these two interests are reconciled; indeed they are found to be indivisible. Gordimer's passion for Africa as a continent becomes fused with a definition of what constitutes that affiliation politically.

During the 1960s Gordimer also spent a good deal of time in Central Africa, and later revealed that she had toyed with the idea of going to live in Zambia.[48] These travels were no doubt of some significance in forming the background to *A Guest of Honour*; we now learn that a certain amount of what happens in the novel appears to be based on Zambian history and society, although much of it evidently is not.[49] It would be a mistake to attempt to pin down too closely the exact country to which the novel might be meant to 'refer'. For the fictional 'country' of *A Guest of Honour* is, much like the characterization in *A World of Strangers*, constructed at a level of *generalization*. The developments depicted in the novel could have been derived from, and could relate to, any number of African countries since independence. The unspecified country of the novel, then, has been constructed at a level of the *typical*, as a country that condenses in extreme and concentrated fashion a much broader and more generalized historical experience. Gordimer is not interested in the social or historical particulars for their own sake, but for the far more widespread patterns of which they appear to be a symptom. On its own this is important; the reason this is so has much to do with Gordimer's South African circumstances at the time she was writing the novel.

As the mid-1960s turned into the late 1960s the period of silence in South Africa was, if anything, intensified. Not all political or resistance activity had ceased – there were a number of political trials at this time, which suggested some continuity[50] – but for the most part the underground organizations had been decisively crippled inside the country, while in exile they were primarily preoccupied with recuperation. All in all the repressive state had never had greater control, and it may well have seemed as if no change in this state of affairs was likely in the foreseeable future. In a wider context, soon to become so significant for South Africa, white Rhodesia was still in the first flush of exhilaration over its unilateral declaration of independence from Britain (although the first guerrilla incursions there had begun); Portuguese control of Angola and Mozambique, though under pressure, still seemed relatively secure. These were lean years for the inheritors of an earlier opposition politics in South Africa therefore. After the optimism and broad front of the 1950s there was now only an ironic fragmentation; and after the drama that even *The Late Bourgeois World* had constructed *ex nihilo* in the mid-1960s there was now an inescapable closure.

In such circumstances it is understandable that Gordimer should have turned away from South Africa in her fiction. If she was interested in reformulating problems and possibilities, there was a sense in which she had to do it on fresh ground.[51] And in terms of an immediate historical realism as well, if she was trying to foresee a future, there were strong reasons for doing it 'elsewhere'. In these respects, negatively considered, turning to an unspecified African

113

country in *A Guest of Honour* is paradoxically part of its South African response.

From a more positive viewpoint, the turn away from South Africa in the novel is also a return to profoundly South African issues, but at a higher level of consideration. To grasp this point properly we have to understand what the *method* of the novel's fictionality is about. For *A Guest of Honour* is a deeply meditational novel, one that arose in circumstances requiring its form of meditation. In the South Africa of the late 1960s a time of re-evaluation had arrived. The assumptions of the 1950s had been superseded in the transition to violence, but a proto-revolutionary movement had suffered a crushing defeat. Expectations of an imminent changeover of power, based on either liberal or more radical ideologies, had been indefinitely postponed. The methods of the past had proved vulnerable, the obligations of the future seemed uncertain. Now that the frenzy of the early 1960s had died down, circumstances required a thorough reappraisal: of the *legitimate* grounds and the *legitimate* expectations of any renewed historical commitment. To be at all adequate to the times this also required a more complete understanding of the objective conditions in which such a commitment was to be made. Such a re-examination had to be undertaken with disillusion and with clarity, and it had, in a sense, to be done *in principle*. For objective conditions had to be understood in principle if individual expectations and obligations were to be assessed. Because there could now be no guarantee of any kind of 'return' on a political or emotional investment, personal commitment also had to be made in principle, since the future had opened out into an indefinite long term.

This was the time when, in academic and political spheres, re-evaluations (largely theoretical in nature) were made of the South African political structure and its possible future, in an attempt to correct previous underestimations.[52] And such an impulse towards re-evaluation is partly what *A Guest of Honour*'s move into an unspecified African country is about. In this respect the frame of its 'fictionality' is an enabling procedure. It has been suggested that all of Gordimer's novels are in some sense social hypotheses: attempts, within a fictional domain, to formulate the structures and forces of social reality and their implications for personal life. Here, however, the hypothetical 'frame' is explicitly given, and the move sideways out of South Africa is also a shift to a higher plane of investigation.

The novel's method is not only meditational but it too is theoretical; it sets up an abstract model at a level of the typical where both social forces and subjective implications can be explored in something approaching (in the scientific sense) 'ideal' conditions. Here, moreover, the question of time is important. Relative to South Africa, *A Guest of Honour* is a 'post-apartheid' novel in that it is set in an unnamed African country that has just gained independence from colonial rule. In South African terms this was (and is) something that still had to take place, and to this degree the novel is set in the future. While from one point of view this provided a form of prophetic consolation in a South African moment of defeat – the idea that there *would* be a post-apartheid state – from another its function is different. For the novel shows that history does not stop with 'independence'; problems and commitments will continue. Its shift into the future, then, is also part of its move towards abstraction and generalization.

If the geographical shift to an unnamed country represents the novel's investigation *for all places*, its move into an unspecified future in a sense tests its hypotheses *for all time*. In these ways, transcending the immediacy and intensity of South African life (which in previous phases may have obscured any deeper or more durable understanding), Gordimer views her historical prospects theoretically and in principle; she does so for all places and all time. In the South Africa of the late 1960s nothing could have been more appropriate, for it was exactly this sort of encompassing reassessment that was required. In this way, too, what came out of the period would not only be negative. As far as Gordimer was concerned the South African hiatus gave her an opportunity, as well as a need, to explore her general situation in something approaching 'total' terms. This was no doubt one reason why *A Guest of Honour* was the novel that 'meant the most' to her.

The inclusive nature of the novel's approach is evident in Gordimer's exploration of its central character, Bray. In so far as Bray is a 'white African', Gordimer is, in this African novel, dealing again with one of her predominant South African concerns; the novel's generality does not exclude a definite local resonance. And there are some key correspondences between *A Guest of Honour* and South African conditions at the time when the novel was written. We shall see that as part of its 'post-apartheid' stance *A Guest of Honour* investigates with an extraordinary thoroughness the mechanisms of neo-colonialism in Africa – those social, political and economic patterns that came into being after independence and ironically kept Africa dependent. Much of this, ironical or not, was, as has been suggested, still a matter of the future in South African terms. In some respects, however, the neo-colonial focus of the novel seems to have had a decidedly domestic relevance in this period. For it was at this time that South Africa first took up something like a 'neo-colonial' posture towards the rest of Africa: the time of its first *détente* initiative, and of the special relationship with Malawi, when the South African police were in Rhodesia, and Prime Minister Vorster declared he would send troops anywhere in Africa, on request.[53]

There were perhaps even more important correspondences *within* the country. South Africa's attitude towards the rest of Africa was in a way only the external aspect of a more fundamental internal elaboration, itself expressed and enacted in geo-political, 'neo-colonial' terms. This was a time of ideological renewal for apartheid, in which 'multi-nationalism', 'homeland independence' and 'homeland citizenship' became the keywords. The shift was not simply ideological, or rather the ideology was not simply rhetorical; each of the features of the new model fulfilled a range of effects from the ethically imaginary to the economically and politically functional, as a consideration of its working parts – such as labour bureaux, influx control, removals, resettlements and 'homeland independence' itself – would show.[54]

As influx control together with removals and resettlement hived off surplus labour from the towns, as labour bureaux were set up to select only those considered suitable for contract work in urban areas, as the façade of 'homeland independence' attempted to lend all this a kind of international legitimacy as well as to dump the effects of these policies on so-called 'foreign governments', it seemed that South Africa was methodically being broken up into an interlocking system of classes and sub-classes, and dispersed and centralized élites, all in the fundamental interests of white profit and white power.[55] Except for the fact that it was happening *within* the country, this could also be seen as a classic case of neo-colonialism, in which the façade of political independence – ceded in this instance to the 'homelands' – concealed the reality of continued exploitation. But when it is considered precisely in these terms, the parallels between the South African case and the kind of social totality analysed in *A Guest of Honour* become apparent; for, as we shall see, it is exactly these kinds of relationships that the novel explores.

One cannot push the correspondence too far. As has been suggested, Gordimer's novel is concerned to investigate the general and not the particular case. On the other hand Gordimer was very much aware of South African developments at this time; for example, she wrote the foreword to Cosmas Desmond's book, *The Discarded People*, which catalogued very powerfully the human reality of (and grim strategy behind) the policy of resettlement.[56] In many respects the South African case was distinctive, given its peculiar political and historical dynamic. But in so far as it fitted into the wider model that the novel investigates, it is clear that, consciously or unconsciously, in *A Guest of Honour* Gordimer was exploring strongly South African themes simply by virtue of the larger social reality that drew her attention. This is one more reason to hold that the significant context of the work includes South Africa.

In this light, then, we should view the novel. The 'guest of honour' of its title is Colonel Evelyn James Bray, who returns to celebrate the independence of the Central African country in which he once served as colonial administrator. Bray had been no ordinary colonial official, however; for perceiving at a certain point the historical obsolescence of colonialism, and questioning radically the grounds of his own position, he had 'changed sides', becoming involved with Mweta and Shinza, the two leaders of the People's Independence Party (PIP), with whom he had formed the third member of an unofficial triumvirate, campaigning for independence. For his pains he had lost his job and been expelled from the country, but this is why he is now welcomed back with such honour. Mweta is to be the new country's first President; it seems all the old dreams have come true.

The sudden return of the outsider who is also an insider gives Gordimer a superb opportunity for engaging in social observation at a heightened level of clarity. In this respect the novel repeats in modified form the strategy used with such success in the case of Toby in *A World of Strangers*. Again we have a first level at which Gordimer's fiction reveals a consciousness of history, observing the world around it from the smallest to the broadest of details. At the lesser end of the spectrum Gordimer gives a depiction of the kind of expatriate white community she would have come across in her travels, for the most part in favour of independence, but still troubled by relative isolation and uncertainties for the future. By contrast, at a golden-plate presidential dinner, Bray overhears the distasteful and contemptuous tones of a cruder but more orthodox colonialism:

> Thank Christ it's gone off all right, eh, Greg? Jesus, but it's heavy going with these chaps. And one mammy I had to push round the floor – I'm telling you, I needed to go into low gear to get that arse on the move.
>
> (p. 196)

Elsewhere the novel observes with great acuity the futility of colonial education systems in Africa. Bray comes across a schoolmaster studying for Cambridge O-level exams, which he will most likely never pass, and where the very questions set – to describe a film seen, or a visit to a picture gallery – are entirely beyond the range of his cultural experience and alien to the needs of his social situation. The 'frame' of the novel's fictionality is not incompatible with a thoroughgoing realism, but sometimes the transactions between the two are complex. Bray sees a photograph at Shinza's:

> a football team group – Nkrumah, cross-eyed Fanon, mascot Selassie, Guevara, a face among others that was Shinza himself: a meeting of Afro-Asian countries in Cairo, the beginning of the Sixties. Shinza saw Bray looking and said, 'Rogue's gallery.'
>
> (p. 123)

Released by its fictionality, the novel has entered into the real historical life of Africa.

Bray becomes involved with education. Though his plan had been to remain in the country only for the duration of the independence celebrations (his wife has remained at home in England), Bray is, albeit reluctantly, co-opted into the service of the new state by Mweta, as a special educational adviser. The post is in a sense appropriate – Bray says the white man in Africa has had no image for himself other than as mentor – but soon he has to search for a new image and attempt to define new grounds for his role. For Bray finds himself confronted with a more advanced form of the same kind of dilemma he experienced as a colonial administrator; under Mweta he finds the country in the grip of a thoroughgoing neo-colonialism, and he is once again faced with the prospect of historical choice.

It is interesting to see how Bray had made his earlier decision:

> I understood perfectly what I was doing . . . when Shinza and Mweta started PIP it was something I believed in. The apparent contradiction between my position as a colonial civil servant and this belief wasn't really a contradiction at all, because to me it was the contradiction

inherent in the colonial system – the contradiction that was the live thing in it, dialectically speaking, its transcendent element, that would split it open by opposing it, and let the future out – the future of colonialism *was* its own overthrow and the emergence of Africans into their own responsibility. I simply anticipated the end of my job.

(pp. 246–7)

Bray's debt to Marx, out of Hegel, is obvious, and this is an important first pointer to the ideological framework within which the debate of *A Guest of Honour* is conducted. On the other hand, his account might seem fairly glib (whether the fault in rhetorical terms is Bray's or Gordimer's is unclear), and one of the successes of the novel lies in superseding simple, abstract formulae in finding again the struggle, and unevenness involved in 'contradiction'. The point about Bray's view here is that he says it no longer obtains. As he continues to insist in the novel, Mweta's country is no longer 'his place' (see, for example, p. 214); it is not for him to get involved. But one of the central discoveries of the novel is that in becoming politically involved, he does indeed make it 'his place'

Through Bray's eyes, then, as he travels around the country, or from his base in the northern province of Gala, the novel's account of neo-colonialism occurs. And here the highly sophisticated nature of its political analysis is revealed. No brief discussion can do justice to the novel's sustained powers of observation in this regard – the political, economic and social structures of the country are detailed with a sustained and remarkable clarity – but a few examples will have to suffice.

The country's economy revolves upon three metropolitan based concessionaire mining companies (avatars of Gordimer's early mining concession stores?). With independence they have 'African-ized' certain of their working strata – that is, promoted Africans into positions previously occupied only by whites – but the price of this is the continued extraction of a major share of their profits overseas. This is the basis of neo-colonialism; political independence is granted, economic domination continues. As Shinza, who has been shunted out of power by Mweta because of his opposition to such policies, puts it on any number of occasions:

We move up into the seats of the expatriate whites, and go on earning dividends for them when they go back 'home' to retire ... We're exporting our iron ore at their price and buying back their steel at their price. (p. 256)

In the fishing sector Mweta's minister renews a contract with the British–Belgian trawling company that transfers a percentage of stock to the government, but leaves the wages of the workers at the level of colonial times. What happens under such agreements is that class stratification within the 'independent' country is both constructed and reinforced; a local élite is created, usually with strong governmental links, but it exists only at the price of the relative oppression and exploitation of the mass of the people. Within this basic division there is regional differentiation. Thus Mweta dances to the tune of the international aid agencies in transferring a scheme for a new dam from the underdeveloped north, where it would be extremely valuable, to a more developed area where it can be shared with a similar neo-colonialist country.

Even within the regions the novel's analysis is acute. Not only are there primary class divisions, but a whole range of classes and sub-classes is observed. At the fish factory in Gala there is a complete spectrum of dispossession, from the most destitute, who are excluded from the local union, to the regular union members, to a labour élite who keep the union in line with the neo-colonialist policies of the government. At the iron-ore mine in Gala this form of collaboration is all too clearly apparent; when a strike threatens, PIP Youth Pioneers, in league with a union élite that also comprises the local Party officialdom, attack and beat up workers – meaning in this case that the state and foreign capital are in alliance against the workers through the ironic mediation of the Party. Elsewhere this alliance takes on even more chilling terms, as when Mweta concedes the use of a private police force to one of the mining companies. It is clear that this force will be used either by the company in the case of strikes, or by the state in the event of a political emergency. In the end it is in the context of exactly such an emergency, in which both strikes and political insurgency threaten, that Bray himself is killed, as an indirect result of the intervention of this company force. The novel's analysis of neo-colonialism is rounded off when, in this gathering breakdown, Mweta invites Britain, the old colonial power, to send troops to restore 'peace' and 'stability' to his country.

At this level the novel's observation has been inseparable from the terms in which it is conducted. *A Guest of Honour* has dissected the entire workings of a social and economic matrix of élites (expatriate, indigenous and labour) and exploited (labour and peasantry) as they play their roles in the mechanisms of neo-colonialism (metropolitan extraction, the unequal distribution of resources, regional under-development and so on). Setting up her fictional model in this way is of the greatest significance as far as Nadine Gordimer's historical consciousness is concerned. For the terms she has used in this novel are those of the most developed of radical debate at the time when the novel was being written. The perception and conceptualization of neo-colonialism was coming to the fore in the radical debate on Africa in this period; and in her analysis of classes and sub-classes Gordimer for the first and possibly most explicit time indicates her participation within a Marxist discourse. Gordimer was evidently looking to the radical theoreticians, and she has said that she was reading leading African political thinkers at this time, such as Nkrumah, Fanon and Cabral.[57]

A Guest of Honour is, therefore, sharply differentiated from her previous novels. In *A World of Strangers* the world was simply divided in two; the division was as much symbolic as analytic. Here the novel has been deeply concerned to account for the smallest details of political and social interaction, to understand their every gradation and intersection. This also distinguishes *A Guest of Honour* from *The Late Bourgeois World*, where Gordimer's political understanding was entirely monolithic and symbolic; here that novel's romanticism has been eliminated in the very *form* of this work. A straightforward emblem of this difference is that whereas in the previous novel Elizabeth's night-thoughts are about God, here the protagonist's meditations concern one of the most powerful of political thinkers within the African context, Frantz Fanon. Bray gets up in the middle of the night to check a reference in full:

> The people find out that the iniquitous fact of exploitation can wear a black face, or an Arab one; and they raise the cry of 'Treason!' But the cry is mistaken; and the mistake must be corrected. The treason is not national, it is social. The people must be taught to cry 'Stop thief!'
>
> (p. 292)[58]

Gordimer's dependence on such theory for her model of neo-colonialism ties her novel to a very specific era, but none the less a clear transition point has been reached. In transcending, in the tow of Fanon and others, a nationalist conception of colonial and post-colonial relations in Africa, the novelist has entered the domain of class analysis. In the South African context this is a conceptual revolution of the greatest significance, affecting the entire way in which one understands the realities of the country and proposes strategies for change. No longer is it simply 'national' or 'race' oppression one is talking about, but class relations become a basic element within the pattern.

The consequent ideological shift implicit in the novel's analysis becomes even more pronounced in that *A Guest of Honour* takes as the basis of its political position a socialist standpoint. Michael Wade has argued that the novel is essentially about European liberalism and its decline in African conditions, but his case underestimates what is going on within the work.[59] There is, as might by now be expected, Gordimer's customary review of past positions; thus when it is shown that 'kindness is ridiculous' in the colonial state (p. 88), this is because a paternalistic charitableness cannot remedy a situation in which the vast proportion of the country's wealth is being exported overseas. Gordimer also undertakes a most damning re-examination of her earlier belief in the priority of personal relations – the ideology that had sustained her without question in *A World of Strangers*. The power of personality is embodied in the novel by Mweta; his attraction for Bray is a personal one, and at the critical PIP congress in the capital, where he is challenged by Shinza on ideological grounds, he wins the day on the strength of his personality and his charisma alone. But in a crucial series of recognitions Bray comes to realize that the power of personality as such is not only inadequate to deal with vast social problems, but on the contrary is politically suspect. At its worst, as comes to pass in the case of Mweta, it produces a personality cult and a messianic myth, expressed in the idea that 'the leader' knows best and alone can save society; to the last many of Mweta's subjects continue to believe this. The novel shows what its culmination can be when Mweta makes a midnight radio speech, just as Hitler used to do, announcing a Preventive Detention Bill along South African lines.[60] So the creed of personal relations, which began as Gordimer's most sacred belief, has undergone a remarkable reversal by the time of *A Guest of Honour*.

If Mweta embodies the power of personality, Shinza's province is a 'power of ideology'. This in effect is the reason for the breakdown between him and Mweta in the first place. Shinza had been Mweta's mentor (considering what Bray says about whites in Africa as 'mentors', and the forces Mweta is now serving, the fact is more than a little ironic) but he has been cast out of power precisely because of his strict opposition to Mweta's policies on socialist grounds. Bray is at times uneasy in his relationship with Shinza, and there is none of the easy cameraderie that exists between himself and Mweta. In the public sphere Shinza is in many respects an awkward man. Yet in the gathering political crisis it is towards Shinza that Bray is drawn.

This development is intended to be seen in specifically ideological terms and it comes to a head at the Party Congress in the capital. Shinza is Secretary General of the United Trades Union Congress (UTUC), but under Mweta's auspices a move is afoot to make the post a presidential appointment. The question becomes the central issue of the Congress, and a power struggle between the two men ensues. In wider social terms, the two represent what are now opposed interests in the country: Mweta those of a neo-colonialist élite, Shinza those of the mass of the workers and peasantry. If Mweta gains control of UTUC the latter are exactly the forces he can neutralize. It is then at this Congress that Gordimer executes a sustained and remarkable narrative triumph, modulating drama and suspense, complex political contentions and characterization together as the struggle unfolds. Shinza's key speeches combine his impersonal approach with his ideological conviction:

> The People's Independence Party grew from bush villages and locations in white people's towns where villagers came to work. It grew from the workers' movements in the mines, where the mineworkers were also people from the bush ... If we were a classless people, we are now creating a dispossessed peasant proletariat of our own.
>
> (pp. 342–3)

> The trade unions saw then that the workers' greatest need was the country's need to struggle against colonialism and imperialism. The reason why now their Secretary-General should not be appointed over their heads is not because they think their role after independence is to be *less* involved at government level, but on the contrary, because it is to be *more* involved, because the workers' greatest need *now* is to ensure that the government continues the struggle against neo-colonialism and all that it means to the workers ... After independence, *trade unionism is the population's means of defence against foreign capital.*
>
> (pp. 361–2)

As Mweta's personal star rises higher at the Congress, it is Shinza's position that increasingly convinces Bray. Its implications become concrete and practical; he bargains for votes for Shinza, and later, as strikes and unrest bring the country towards breakdown, at Shinza's behest he agrees to go to Europe to find arms and support for the guerrilla struggle that is now evidently necessary. On his way to the capital to leave, Bray is himself killed in an ambush; but his commitment, in principle, could not have been more forcefully stated. It is all the more forceful because its price has been nothing less than his death.

The novel is unambiguous on this issue. Mweta's position is that the development of his country requires foreign capital, and it is part of the scrupulous objectivity of the novel that he is allowed to put his case as persuasively as possible. But *A Guest of Honour* makes it abundantly clear that neo-colonialist methods involve social betrayal. As for the proposed solution, this is stated most generally by Bray:

> We've always accepted what Sartre once wrote, that socialism is the movement of man in the process of recreating himself . . . Whatever the paroxysms of experiment along the way – whether it's Robespierre or Stalin or Mao Tse-tung or Castro – it's the only way there is to go, in the sense that every other way is a way back.
>
> (p. 380)

Again the formulation might be a little too pat. The 'experiments' of Stalin are perhaps not so easily acceptable. However, the novel has stated its ideological preference, and for Gordimer a turning point has been reached.

We shall see that for the novel a political framework is not ultimately seen as entirely adequate to cope with the complex nature of human existence; but in so far as it is, the framework that suits best for *A Guest of Honour* is one of socialism. Liberalism, which entered into crisis for Gordimer in *Occasion for Loving*, has here been replaced; and the question of ideological principle – abandoned in the desperate haste of *The Late Bourgeois World* – has been reasserted in a new form. This shift has taken place under the deep compulsions of the late 1960s, in which a rigorous re-evaluation of presuppositions was required. Under the pressure of historical developments, and through a process of unremitting social scrutiny and self-reflection, Nadine Gordimer has come to take up positions ever further leftwards. In its prospectus for the long term, *A Guest of Honour* has turned, politically, to socialism.

A related set of issues arises through the novel's political investigations: specifically questions of social and cultural identity. It is of the greatest importance in the novel that in Bray's political commitment lies his way of becoming a 'white African'. For, in his very individuality, Bray is also a massive historical 'type' (he is in the novel physically massive). He is the European whose legacy has placed him in Africa, but whose inclinations have placed him outside that legacy; on one level there could be no better statement of the fundamental problem with which Gordimer has all along been involved. In his status as a 'guest' Bray had refused to become politically engaged. As we have seen he continued to insist that Mweta's country was no longer his 'place'. But in his new commitment the problem is solved both practically and in principle; in becoming dedicated to the cause of the people, Bray is dedicated to Africa and he makes it his place in this dedication. To be sure he dies for his commitment – being a white African is evidently no guarantee of longevity – but this is also something of a self-fulfilling prophecy.

Earlier Bray had spoken of all the remarkable men of Africa who had ended up 'dead in a ditch' (p. 405). In his own death (it happens just next to a ditch) he becomes, if not identical to these men, then as close in identity as it is possible for someone in his situation to get. If his life is in part a struggle to claim Africa as his own, then at least in his death Africa has claimed *him*. Above and beyond the colour of his skin, therefore, Bray is in a sense a new 'everyman' in Africa, searching for new grounds of affiliation in new historical conditions. And in so far as he is a white man, it is through his social commitment that he has *won* his place. Political, social and cultural questions of identity are resolved for Bray inseparably from one another.

In an extraordinary way this resolution is repeated in the very *form* of the novel itself. To explore this matter further we should turn to Gordimer's other writing of this period, in particular to her work of criticism on African literature, *The Black Interpreters*. This study and *A Guest of Honour* were germinating at the same time, and the two are illuminating in terms of one another. Thus in *The Black Interpreters* Gordimer is concerned to leave room for herself as an African novelist. African writing, she declares, is

> writing done in any language by Africans themselves and by others of whatever skin colour who share with Africans the experience of having been shaped, mentally and spiritually, by Africa rather than anywhere else in the world.[61]

By this account Gordimer is an African writer; and, considering its preoccupations, *A Guest of Honour* is an African novel. But Gordimer goes further. There is a fundamental distinction between European and African writing, she asserts. In Europe, where the orthodox 'social novel' has become tired out, and where even the conventional exploration of psychology in fiction has become overdone, writers are turning to more bizarre forms, as they find themselves 'on the very edge of being'.[62] In particular, the experimental novel has been induced, where communication itself is now a problem to be explored. In Africa, on the contrary, she says, it is overwhelmingly *external* reality that has to be accounted for, and social problems that have to be solved; here the problem of communication is still 'the practical one of roads and telephone wires'.[63] This is then the deep historical logic whereby in African fiction content takes precedence over form, realism over experimentation, external reality over subjective introspection.

Gordimer may or may not be correct in the details of her argument. For example, her remarks on European literature are a fairly straightforward repetition of Lukács's tirade against the excesses of modernism (*The Black Interpreters* is heavily influenced by *The Meaning of Contemporary Realism*, which Gordimer had been reading at the time).[64] By and large her account of African literature seems nevertheless to be correct, and measured against this distinction *A Guest of Honour* is evidently designed to be an 'African' novel. In this regard we have seen how, within its fictional framework, its fundamental impulse is realistic, and how it has attempted to pin down the workings of social reality from the smallest to the largest of details; its basic concern has been to demystify politics and to assess their practical implications for subjective life. Further, in so far as Bray's development in the novel is so deeply bound up with social reality, *A Guest of Honour* is a novel in the best traditions of Lukács's 'critical realism', which Gordimer claims in *The Black Interpreters* represents the most important genre in African writing.[65]

A related point: one issue on which Gordimer chides African novelists in general concerns the question of ideology. In the African novel, she writes, there is a lack of ideological consciousness as such. African writers, she argues, have yet to present characters faced with 'the historical choice of political means' whereby a full social liberation may be achieved; there is no equivalent in African fiction of an ideology of African Socialism.[66] In her generalization Gordimer is not strictly correct – there were in fact African writers who had actively adopted a socialist position in their fiction;[67] but her remarks point once again to the preoccupations of her own work.

For the issues she mentions are those that most directly concern *A Guest of Honour*. Bray's whole development in the novel relates to 'the historical choice of political means'; and in its analysis of neo-colonialism and its affirmation of an African form of socialism, the novel has tended to represent an African Socialism.

The novel is African in its general consciousness, therefore, in its specific form of realism and in its socialism; these are sufficient reasons for suggesting that *A Guest of Honour* might well be considered as a work of 'African socialist realism'. Michael Wade makes the claim that the novel's specific contribution lies in the way it undermines the dominant liberal and 'meliorist' view of time in the European novel;[68] but after Joyce, Kafka *et al.* this is hardly likely to be necessary. On the contrary, this 'African socialist realism' is probably the novel's most important feature, marking a dedication that it makes politically and as a work of art simultaneously. It represents an achievement in the forefront of African literature at the time, and even now the novel is probably unparalleled in its specific fusion of complex political theory and discourse with more conventional narrative forms.

We might also consider *A Guest of Honour* in relation to the Western tradition of novels dealing with Africa. There is no need to go into any detail to see that a moment of significance has been reached. Here is a writer, in part an inheritor of that tradition, explicitly and deliberately stating her identity as an African rather than a European writer, and working out appropriate forms to embody that affiliation. *A Guest of Honour* brings to a culmination a matter of fundamental importance to Gordimer's work all along, ever since Helen Shaw in *The Lying Days* noted the lack of an African identity in her literary and cultural heritage; and a whole European line of writing has been inverted. Physically, Gordimer's novel is set in the 'heart' of the continent, but nothing could be further from the vision of *Heart of Darkness*. What is presented there as mystery is here resolved as political; the 'unspeakable horror' that Conrad projects on to Africa as its supposedly archetypal embodiment is here broken down into questions of historical struggle. Nor is anything 'unspeakable'. The impetus behind the novel has been to render the potentially mystifying unmysterious, by identifying, in a realistic form, the workings of a social condition. A novel such as V. S. Naipaul's *A Bend in the River* may in some respects repeat and reinforce a Conradian mumbo-jumbo (in so far as it involves the supposedly atavistic mysteries revealed by the dark continent), but Gordimer has set herself to work in the harder school of African political and social realities.

The novel's political commitment is not to be overestimated, however, nor is its 'socialist realism' to be conceived of in Zhdanovite terms. Here no implacable triumph of socialism is predicted. And ultimately the novel's perspective begins to open out into a dimension beyond the political. This by no means negates its political findings, but it does enclose them within a further frame of understanding. When Bray says that he has always believed what Sartre wrote, that socialism is the movement of man in the process of recreating himself, it is significant that this is an existentialized version of socialism that he gives. Once again in *A Guest of Honour* – not for the first time in Gordimer's novels – her work seems to be reaching towards a plane of existence and 'being', as a kind of eternal backdrop to social and political struggle. In one passage in the novel Gordimer presents an allegory of uncertainty and knowledge as Bray, secretly on his way to deliver a car for Shinza's use, pauses for a moment to reflect:

> He had the feeling that the area of uncertainty that surrounded him visually when he took off his glasses was the real circumstance in which he had lived his life; and his glasses were more than a means of correcting a physical shortcoming, they were his chosen way of rearranging the unknowable into a few outlines he had gone by.
>
> (p. 431)

Existence as such is unknowable. A clarifying lens is required for its organization into coherency. In political terms this lens for Bray must be socialism; but socialism does not account for the whole of existence. The novel's political commitment thus begins to be circumscribed by a wider dimension of comprehension, and here other recurrent features of Gordimer's writing once again come into operation, beginning to point out where it is likely to be found. A certain 'organicist' vision, for example, is revived, in which the human and the natural spheres are conjoined. This occurs most directly in the linkage between political engagement and sexuality, which in the figures of both Bray and Shinza are deliberately constructed in the novel as correlates. In Gala, Bray is having an affair with Rebecca Edwards, one of the more 'natural' of the country's white expatriates. His political revival is associated with a sexual revival – or, as he puts it, a 'last kick of the prostate' in late middle age. In old age Shinza has gone one step further in producing a son, and if he is uneasy in the public political arena, in his base in the outreaches of Gala province there is a certain rural and populist mystique that gathers round him; in the area of Shinza's settlement what look like buck feeding to Bray as he approaches in his car turn out to be women gathering sour wild fruit, who laugh and chatter as he passes by. Wade has pointed out that images of birth and rebirth multiply in the novel.[69] Elsewhere too, as we shall see, the novel's central symbols are drawn from nature.

There is something of a shift taking place in the novel, then. The ending of *A Guest of Honour* both embodies this shift and makes it clear why it should occur. Bray's death, coming some thirty pages or so before the end of a work of over five hundred pages, is the narrative equivalent of the apparently anarchic guerrilla action that kills him. In conditions of gathering crisis within the country, of endemic strikes and political resistance, Bray is on his way to the capital with Rebecca to leave on his mission for Shinza. A band of local people, seeing a white man in a car, take him for one of Mweta's mercenaries, or an organizer of the company police force. They ambush the car and beat him to death; Rebecca is left alive.

In terms of the novel's development, this death comes as a profound shock. Just as Bray has made his commitment, apparently coming to understand the real conditions of his life and the obligations these involve, he is killed off, it seems for his understanding. For readers this death is distressing and contrary to conventional expectations; the character whom they have come to know so intimately, whose consciousness has in a sense been their entire vision, is killed off seemingly callously, for no apparent moral or narrative reason. And he is killed off extremely ironically. In principle Bray is on the side of the men who beat him to death, while they kill a man on a mission to help their cause.

Even Bray's legacy appears to die into irony. In the pages of *Time* magazine he is billed as Mweta's 'trusted White Man Friday' (p. 488). Bray's immensely important private history and new commitment, on the verge of becoming public, remain unknown, indeed distorted. Mweta himself co-opts the memory of the man who opposed him; Bray's educational recommendations, salvaged from the wreckage of his car, are produced some time later by Mweta in the form of *The Bray Report*. The revolution to which Bray had committed himself fails as Mweta calls in British troops and Shinza flees. Rebecca escapes to Europe where she feels entirely alienated, alone and with an overwhelming sense of loss.

This reversal is an extremely powerful one, and no attempt can be made to argue it away. It has been put there deliberately and with purpose. Just what that purpose is becomes evident when one makes a distinction between this ending, which is ironical, and the novel's resolution, of which it forms a part. *A Guest of Honour* does not, as Wade seems to suggest, end by simply staring into the void at the end of the liberal European universe.[70] The irony in this novel has not been used to negate but, as in Joyce, that other great clarifier of exact positions, to locate. To begin with, it defines and guarantees the novel's realism; the white African may make his commitment, but he cannot expect either immediate success or even, necessarily, acknowledgement. One of the things he must be prepared to risk is nothing less than irony itself; his commitment must be made in principle, even though in practical terms it may in the end seem to prove useless. In this way the novel is not smashing all historical hopes, but it is smashing *romantic* historical hopes – once again the response of *The Late Bourgeois World* is reversed.

In the South African context, also, through Bray's death a traditional hierarchy has been reversed. The white who becomes politically engaged cannot expect glory or pre-eminence; he must be prepared to accept a secondary and supportive role, which may never necessarily be recognized or come to fruition. In this Gordimer anticipates the lessons of the mid- and late 1970s (to be registered more intensely in *Burger's Daughter*) some years before they became more generally evident.

On the other hand, the irony of the ending does not all work one way. Bray's life may be travestied in *Time* magazine, but even in its debased account something of the truth emerges: for example, that Mweta is, in Shinza's taunting words, a 'black watchman standing guard outside the white man's enterprise' (p. 488). Even though Bray's name and memory are co-opted by Mweta, none the less his work endures, to be implemented by the latter's regime as a blueprint for the country's education system. What is being elucidated here is a 'long perspective'; if there is to be a revolution, then it is going to take a long time. (And going on the history of Africa, or indeed South Africa, at the time when the novel was written, nothing could have been more realistic.) But this does not invalidate the necessity of that revolution, nor even the wastefulness of its arrival.

In one key passage Bray considers that wastefulness, the futile violence and bloodshed that take place in support of a cause not properly understood by most of its participants. He, too, is party to the waste and confusion; the means, as always, will be dubious. But, he decides:

> He had no others to offer with any hope of achieving the end, and as he accepted the necessity of the end, he had no choice.
>
> (p. 465)

The end is valid; the means, if unpleasant, are valid; but the new African must understand the historical odds. It is these that Bray's life has helped to estimate.

The 'long perspective' is presented definitively and finally on another level of the novel's action. This has to do with the dimension of existence or 'being' that has been mentioned. As in Bray's allegory of the glasses, for much of the novel 'existence' as such is the background to its development in time. Thus Bray lapses into a moment of timelessness and feels he can see all the way up the continent; in one instant out of time he even seems to foresee images of his own death, though he has no idea what they signify (pp. 201–2). In the moment of his decision to help Shinza, however, Bray significantly feels committed on both existential and historical levels at once. This is perhaps the most important passage in the book:

> His mind was calm. It was not that he had no doubts about what he was doing, going to do; it seemed to him he had come to understand that one could never hope to be free of doubt, of contradictions within, that this was the state in which one lived – the state of life itself – and no action could be free of it. There was no finality, while one lived, and when one died it would always be, in a sense, an interruption.
>
> (pp. 464–5)

This too is a self-fulfilling prophecy in the novel, for as Bray is killed his last thoughts are that he has been interrupted. But what this passage indicates is that this death is not to be seen as an 'end'; it is, precisely, an interruption. Life goes on. Rebecca survives. Even Bray's educational report survives. Most of all, history continues. This, in a way, is the 'long perspective', and Bray's 'honour' resides in the fact that he has willingly accepted its patterns and consciously contributed to its unfolding.

In various ways the novel comes to suggest that, if contradiction is the state of life, then the one thing that is guaranteed is change; change is literally in the nature of things. What the novel chronicles is, precisely, change, as contradiction after contradiction sorts itself out and is resolved until entering into some further contradiction. The novel's basic pattern is that of the cycle, as states of affairs invert, turn round, but also come round again in altered form. Bray's own life, in which he has successively opposed both colonialism and neo-colonialism (both times unsuccessfully in the short term, but in the former successfully in the long) is only the central emblem of this, which is then the novel's ultimate insurance. Mweta's regime may survive today, but in the long march of time it must surely be overthrown, just as colonialism was before it and the slave traders of Arab East Africa before that.

This, in principle, is the long perspective. Bray's cause will triumph even if he, personally, does not. In this way existence is itself historicized in the novel, as life comes to be the continual working out of successive oppositions. But in the instant this occurs for *A Guest of Honour* the reverse is also taking place; at a categorical level history is being absorbed into existence. For where contradiction is the state of *life*, it is also being contracted to *condition*. The processes of history are eternalized and made static, as the endless perpetuation and permutation of a formally permanent process. To come back to a term used in relation to *A World of Strangers*, history itself becomes *naturalized*, part of the endless cycles and patterns of nature. This is how Bray understands it:

> But human affairs didn't come to clear-cut conclusions, a line drawn and a total added up. They appeared to resolve, dissolve, while they were only reforming, coming together in another combination. Even when we are dead, what we did goes on making these new combinations (he saw clouds, saw molecules): that's true for private history as well as the other kind.
>
> (p. 385)

Given this understanding, it is also significant that the novel's central symbols are drawn from nature. These are the fig tree (a symbol perhaps of eternal fruitfulness and hope), under which Bray takes to sitting in his garden in Gala like some latter-day, if historically degraded, version of Buddha under his Tree of Enlightenment; and the slave tree, under which the Gala workers gather for their meetings (a symbol probably of eternal oppression – and resistance). These principles are in endless congress and conflict as the cycles of history revolve repeatedly upon them. They prefigure both eternal continuity and change. It is not surprising, then, that the novel's final view on this matter is presented in straightforward 'naturalist' terms. Walking in a park in London, Rebecca sees what she understands to be 'the callousness of the earth endlessly renewing itself' (p. 500). The phrase makes sense of all we have witnessed in the novel; it encapsulates realism, irony and hope. Irony and hope are exactly the novel's prospectus for the long term.

In entering the realm of nature Gordimer's vision once again transcends the purely historical. Yet this transcendentalism is nothing like the mythic manoeuvres of *The Late Bourgeois World*; in this respect *A Guest of Honour* is far more muted. The 'naturalist' vision is also by no means as powerful as it will be in *The Conservationist*. None the less, a note of historical and ideological withdrawal has been sounded. History has come to be identified with existence and with nature; and along with Bray's practical commitment is the degree to which he has made the gift of his life 'freely', as it were – for its own sake, and in principle, without regard to the likelihood of any substantial achievement or personal recognition. In this dedication existential reasons have become as important to him as political ones.

At this point, and in the light of all these features, we are able to make a final assessment of the novel's consciousness of history. We have seen how deeply *A Guest of Honour* is implicated in South African conditions in the late 1960s; it seems that the most notable features of its consciousness relate back to the needs of this time. Again, as in *The Late Bourgeois World*, what we find is a contradictory combination; but again, as in that novel, it points to the complex nature of a unitary historical moment. The radical commitment of *A Guest of Honour* is strong and unmistakable, as we have seen in its terms of analysis, in its form as a novel and in its political convictions. On the other hand the novel's long perspective, built firstly into its very project and then into its vision, suggests a contrasting realization: that in the stilled world of the late 1960s anything approaching hopes of real social transformation had to be indefinitely postponed. This may have been a matter of general significance within the country as a whole, but it is possible that there is a more specific registration marked out here: that the novel's eternalism, and the degree to which Bray's commitment is given 'freely', suggest the isolation of a radical white opposition in South Africa at this time – politically committed, but forced to recognize for both the present and the foreseeable future the invisibility of its measurable involvement.

A Guest of Honour has come down from the romantic heights of
The Late Bourgeois World. It has endured despair and attempted to
see beyond it. It has courted irony and developed a realistic vision of
history and personal engagement, adequate to the long term. But
in its very realism it has been forced to make a different kind of
withdrawal. The novel, set from a South African point of view in
the 'post-revolutionary' future, speaks profoundly for a revolution
indefinitely postponed in its present.

5

Prophecy and Subversion: *The Conservationist*

In Africa! A farm in Africa!
Nadine Gordimer, *The Conservationist*[1]

All that is buried is not dead.
Olive Schreiner, *The Story of an African Farm*[2]

. . . everything is ambiguous, here.
Nadine Gordimer, 'Africa emergent'[3]

I

If the primary colonial dispossession in South Africa, as elsewhere on the African continent, was that of land, then Olive Schreiner's *The Story of an African Farm* is the prototypical South African colonial novel. It is not as if Schreiner's work treats the question of land appropriation as a theme; far from it, it takes it entirely for granted, and this is exactly why it is a colonial novel. Apparently secure in its territorial possession, it ignores the history whereby that possession came about in favour of another kind of history: one of the human soul, which it then projects on to the surrounding African landscape as if the latter were an external correlative of the former. This solves the enigma of why a novel about human trials and tribulations should specifically be called the story of an *African* farm. And this is then the novel's colonial arrogance; Africa becomes (in more senses than one) subject, a mirror to the settler condition.

At the same time, this arrogance is undermined by the tale the novel has to tell, for it is one of suffering, endurance, mystery and the implacable indifference of nature. In the very substance of its subjective projection, an objective truth concerning the novel's relation to its environment seems to be emerging. For, moving as the work is on an existential plane, seen from another point of view it represents only the reverse side of an appropriating settler consciousness: the degree to which a fundamental alienation from the world it ostensibly possesses controverts its formal annexation. It is

135

an intrinsic part of the novel's colonial framework that this aspect of its alienation is never recognized for what it is, but is offered only as an intense vision of a universal condition.[4]

Across a gap of some ninety years it is in part to *The Story of an African Farm* that *The Conservationist* is addressed. Set on a farm in Africa, its primary allusion is implicit. Yet Gordimer's novel stands, especially when taken together with other tendencies within white fiction of the early 1970s, as part of the next great literary sign-posting, after Schreiner, in the history of a colonial consciousness in South Africa. For if Schreiner's work, drawing on an unspoken past, represents the uneasy settlement of a colonial order, then it is the dissolution of this order that Gordimer's work, telling a history of the future, prophesies. Crucially, the question of possession comes to the fore; here the African farm that Schreiner settled at once so assuredly and uncertainly returns to those from whom it was dispossessed in the first place; the material and mental hold of the European on Africa is loosened, as the land comes back to its people and they to it.

For its fullest significance, therefore, Gordimer's novel must be seen against the South African colonial backdrop as a whole. Across the nodal points of *The Story of an African Farm* and *The Conservationist* a history of settler consciousness in South Africa is written. The primary reason why this shift appeared in Gordimer's novel was because of the immediate realities to which it responded in the moment in which it was produced.

II

At the time of *A Guest of Honour* revolution in the southern and South African context seemed impossible to foresee. When *The Conservationist* appeared in 1974, however, the prospects appeared to have changed. The novel responds to this transition and, in its own way, reveals it. In its central character, Mehring, it captures two emphatic but opposed developments in southern and South African history at this time. On the one hand Mehring represents what Gordimer now perceived to be the virtually unitary nature of white historical destiny in this period, considered both regionally and domestically; indeed, that he is such a representative figure is in itself an important piece of analysis in the novel.

On a regional level this perception was accurate, as the fates of the white regimes of southern Africa became increasingly interlocked. As the liberation struggles gained momentum in Mozambique, Angola and Zimbabwe, it became ever clearer that the security of any one country in this bloc depended on that of the others. This, too, obviously included South Africa; if any of the other countries fell, the 'front-line' of territorial conflict would be brought right up to its own borders. In this context, opening the Rand Easter Show in Johannesburg, the Governor-General of Mozambique stressed there could be no slackening in vigilance along the frontiers of his own country and South Africa, while the South African Southern Cross Fund presented the Mozambican armed forces with R60,000 of medical supplies.[5]

Partly because of this, domestically as well white South Africa was becoming increasingly unified. This was the period when the country began to 'draw up into the laager' behind which it prepared to resist what it now began to conceive of as a total historical onslaught. Defence spending and military service were steadily increased, 'youth preparedness' was taught in schools, and an all-out attack was launched against the last remaining institutions of liberal opposition in the country: the National Union of South African Students (NUSAS), the South African Institute of Race Relations and the Christian Institute.[6] In political terms previous divisions between English and Afrikaans speakers seemed to be becoming of less and less account, while on more fundamental levels as well this unification was occurring. Since the Second World War an interpenetration of capital had occurred, between the different sectors of the economy and across the divide that had previously separated English and Afrikaner interests.[7]

Mehring's name sounds Afrikaans, though probably German in origin, but his speech is in English; it is partly the obsolescence of previous internal conflicts as absorbed in a new class alliance that he represents. At the same time the lines of transmission between capital and state had grown ever stronger, partly because an Afrikaner élite that penetrated the former had the serviceable ear of the latter,[8] and partly because the mechanisms of profit and power looked increasingly complementary.[9] As a 'prominent industrialist associated with the economic advancement of the country at the highest level' (p. 264), Mehring also represents this development. Moreover, in his international ventures, selling pig-iron to the

Japanese, Mehring represents an additional penetration in this period: of a unified national capital into the international market.[10]

Gordimer did not deliberately set out to capture these different phenomena as if according to some conscious programme; but in approaching South African reality these were the phenomena she captured. In his own person Mehring is a structural pillar of the South African political economy, recognizably South Africa's 'new man' of the early 1970s. In investigating him, Nadine Gordimer is also investigating the condition of the entire edifice that he supports.

This, however, is where the contrary movement becomes apparent, for Mehring also embodies a further major reality of this time: that the foundations of white South Africa's unitary destiny were, in their very cohesion, already beginning to crumble. Domestically the first signs of this appeared, appropriately enough, in the territory over which South Africa still exercised a mandate inherited as a last legacy from the colonial era: Namibia. For in Namibia in 1971–2 there occurred a massive strike against the system of contract labour, which virtually brought the region to a standstill;[11] moreover Namibia itself was now a country in dispute (South Africa's first disputed territory, as it were) at the United Nations and the International Court of Justice. The contract labour strike is explicitly mentioned in *The Conservationist*; and Mehring, whose origins are in Namibia, is shown in the novel as being profoundly agitated as the ground of his past already begins to slip from under his feet.

Following the Namibian stoppage a series of strikes ensued within South Africa itself, occurring for the most part in Natal in 1973–4.[12] At the same time the Black Consciousness movement was taking a strong hold amongst a black student intelligentsia, and this development in particular was creating the context for the great challenge to the state of the Soweto Revolt of 1976.[13] *The Conservationist* probably registers the impact of the Black Consciousness movement; and this new ethos of revived resistance, after the long silence of the mid-1960s, no doubt lies behind some of the political impetus of the novel.

But *The Conservationist* seems to have responded most deeply to developments at the regional level. It was here that it appeared the end of white supremacy in southern Africa was being foretold. In Zimbabwe guerrilla incursions were increasing in intensity and penetration, and by 1972 the first white farms were being attacked.[14] (In a country where land dispossession had been crucial historically, farms – perhaps significantly for Gordimer's novel – were key sites for battle.)

In Mozambique by 1974 white farmers were appealing to Frelimo for protection,[15] but this was in response to the event that, amongst all others in the decade, seemed to signal the promised end of colonialism in southern Africa as a whole: the army officers' coup in Portugal of 25 April 1974, which brought down the Caetano government and preceded the Portuguese withdrawal from Africa. After Guinea-Bissau, Mozambique was the next country to gain its independence from Portugal, and this became an event of tremendous symbolic significance for South Africa. For this was the first neighbouring country to gain its liberation through armed struggle; to whites it was the very incarnation of the threat of black revolution. To blacks, and especially to the Black Consciousness movement, it was an enormous inspiration. Freedom had been won through a long and dedicated battle; Mozambican independence seemed an omen for South African liberation. In this context the Black People's Convention (BPC) and the black students' organiz- ation, SASO, called for nationwide 'Viva Frelimo' rallies, the most celebrated of which occurred at Currie's Fountain in Durban.[16]

In relation to the *coup d'état* in Portugal, Basil Davidson has pointed out that it was a direct result of the colonial wars in Africa that the Portuguese could no longer sustain. He asks:

> when was the last occasion that a major constructive change in Africa had caused a major constructive change in Europe?[17]

The balance of history was demonstrably swinging. This was well understood by people as diverse as Ian Smith – who warned white South Africans not to criticize his country, for they would be 'next on the list' if white Rhodesia fell[18] – and Steve Biko, the principal leader of the Black Consciousness movement, who later expressed his certainty that since the Second World War Africa had experienced the death of white invincibility: 'The blacks in Africa now know that the whites will not be conquerors forever.'[19]

This, precisely, is the understanding of *The Conservationist*, and the substance of its vision. At the end of the novel a storm sweeping in, prophetically enough, from the Mozambique channel rises up to drive Mehring from the land. Mehring does not literally die at the end of *The Conservationist*; but he – and therefore all he represents – does die historically, as he surrenders the farm he has so desperately been trying to conserve. Published as it was in 1974, *The Conservationist* must have been completed before the Portuguese coup took place, and on no account could Gordimer have known about it or its effects in advance, except perhaps as a general inevitability. Still, the degree to which the coup confirmed the necessity that *The Conservationist* predicted, in the very year of its publication, indicates the tremendously strong 'sense of history' that infused Gordimer's novel.

Besides Mehring, there is another main character in *The Conservationist*, even if he is an unusual one. This is the figure of a black body, buried shallowly beneath the surface of Mehring's farm. Despite its condition – or perhaps because of it – the body becomes Mehring's central antagonist in the novel, and *The Conservationist* cannot properly be understood without understanding its role.

Bodies, characteristically black ones, either asleep or dead in the veld, have always been important in Nadine Gordimer's fiction, as Christopher Hope has suggested.[20] Moreover, one of Gordimer's short stories, 'Six feet of the country', written in the early 1950s,[21] serves as a significant precursor to *The Conservationist* in this regard. Briefly recounted, the story tells of a black Rhodesian who, travelling down to South Africa to look for work, contracts pneumonia from sleeping out along the way, and dies on the farm of a white couple near Johannesburg; they, similarly to Mehring, have opted out of the city to indulge themselves in the romance of rural life. The local black farmworking community wishes to bury the body, according to custom and with due respect, but a series of macabre confusions ensues. First the body, after a post-mortem, is buried without consent by the health authorities. Then, when the black workers collect £20 for an exhumation, the wrong body is returned sealed in a coffin. The deception is discovered only when the dead man's father, who has travelled down for the funeral, complains that the body is too heavy to be that of his son. The implication is plain: 'six feet of the country' cannot be granted to blacks, even in death. South Africa is a white man's country in which the basic dignities, in death as in life, are not to be afforded to blacks. As the dead man's father is fobbed off with an old suit, the story ends in a kind of liberal anguish, contemplating this fact. The ancient story of Hector, in which enmity is carried on beyond the grave, has been reworked in new and strange circumstances.

In 1974, however, the body returns to be buried. And it is even a

'Rhodesian' who buries it – the farmworker Witbooi ('White Boy'), otherwise known as 'Swart Gevaar' ('Black Peril'), who marks out the grave with stones as he would a white man's flower-bed.

In the difference between the story and the novel the distance of over twenty years is measured. For in *The Conservationist* it is the body that, paradoxically, triumphs, and Mehring who comes to be vanquished. The personal and social relationship between the two is clearly marked out. For its part the body is that of a man who has been murdered and dumped on Mehring's land probably while making his way to or from the black location on which the farm borders. Structurally considered there is a sense in which Mehring has had a hand in his fate. For in this location 50,000 black workers and (some of) their families are concentrated in inhuman conditions to serve the needs of white-owned industry: the industry that is the source of Mehring's wealth. Not only is Mehring directly responsible for their circumstances, but the peace and serenity he enjoys on his farm are dependent upon the institutionalized social violence that keeps the location politically subdued and quiet, and that in this case has resulted in the death of the man. It is the police who (in similar fashion to the health authorities in the short story) have given the body an improper burial, in order to save themselves the trouble of yet another murder investigation connected with the location.

Just as Mehring represents the white world in its entirety, therefore, so the body represents the black; it is a symbolic 'everyman' victim of the systematic oppression, exploitation and abuse afforded to blacks under apartheid. In this guise it also prefigures an eventual return. Increasingly haunting Mehring's thoughts with its significance, in the end the storm from Mozambique 'revives' the body, bringing it back to the surface to drive Mehring in terror and crisis from the farm, and to reclaim, in its representative capacity, the land. The implication, as clear here as it was in the short story, is that the body is claiming more than 'six feet of the country'. The novel's vision is one of historical transfer; prophetically, *The Conservationist* is situated at the point where white history ends and black history resumes. In this regard an explicit indication is not to be missed. Referring to the return of the body, almost the very last words of the novel, 'he had come back' (p. 267), are a direct paraphrase of the great rallying cry of the African National Congress in the 1950s: 'Afrika! Mayibuye!' ('Africa! May it come back!')[22]

141

Before considering the substance of this vision, it is valuable to examine the figure of Mehring more closely, since in Mehring, as has been suggested, the condition of white society in South Africa is condensed. The novel's observation here is intrinsically thematic; it is a sense of the white South African condition that appears in its assessment of Mehring. But if Mehring is presented as a structural pillar of the South African political economy, he is also, to use the phrase with which his liberal mistress describes the poet Roy Campbell, 'no ordinary S. A. fascist' (p. 249). Indeed, Mehring is far from being a stereotype, but on the contrary is a fully realized and individualized character. Thus Gordimer establishes a certain immediate sympathy for him in embodying his sensitivity for nature. Mehring is also intelligent both politically and morally, and his clear-sighted realism on occasion comes as a distinct relief when measured against the vacuous and sentimental posturings of his liberal ex-mistress and his son. It is Mehring who knows that there is no easy 'Peace, Happiness and Justice' to be achieved by 'pretty women and schoolboys' (p. 79), and it is Mehring who considers most deeply in the novel:

> What percentage of the world is starving? How long can we go on getting away scot free? . . . Soon, in this generation or the next, it must be our turn to starve and suffer.

> (pp. 46–7)

At this level, however, Mehring's intelligence and realism serve only to bolster the imperatives of his survival. For if there is no necessary guarantee of the perpetuation of his supremacy, then Mehring, the admirer of nature's *realpolitik*, knows that the law of the jungle prevails. In its more benign aspect this law takes on for him the form of an ideology of 'development', which is really one of imperialism, legitimizing the colonization of ever wider areas of profit and power according to an abstract notion of 'progress' whereby everyone, supposedly, benefits. So, in Mehring's view, the white man's development of South Africa – or, for that matter, the first world's development of the third world – means that blacks and other underprivileged at least have 'shoes on their feet', which is all that he thinks they really want.

This is one of the most traditional (and cynical) excuses within the ideological armoury of imperialism. And it is plain that when in a tight spot the negative extremes of Mehring's law of the jungle will surface. In a moment of psychological stress, he addresses his absent ex-mistress, following up his creed of physical expansion:

> The only way to shut you up is to establish the other, the only millennium, of the body, invade you with the easy paradise that truly knows no distinction of colour, creed and what-not – she's still talking, somewhere, but for me her mouth is stopped.
>
> (p. 160)

Her mouth is stopped, like that of the murdered man, lying face down in the earth in the third pasture. With metaphoric compression, the image here is also one of rape; concealed beneath Mehring's creed of development is a licence to kill, to invade.

In this way Mehring is fleshed out as a character. But if Gordimer has thereby avoided the reductions of stereotyping, then it also appears she has approached a typification of an important kind for the period with which the novel deals. The point is a difficult one to back up empirically, but this is perhaps one occasion where the strength of fiction is revealed, in its capacity to draw together themes of the widest social and historical importance. Mehring is no great racist; he represents primarily a capitalist sector in South Africa that has always been less obviously 'ideological' than the state, and for which a paraded ideology of apartheid has always in some sense been an embarrassment. But it is precisely in this guise that his representative importance should not be underestimated. For it was during this period that, on the part of the state as well, the older fetishizations of apartheid began to disappear, especially the more obsessive aspects of its racism. These were now displaced by a much more functional and technocratic approach, which – preserving the basic objectives of profit, domination and power – submerged the more obstructive aspects of a previous ideology. The degree to which racism constituted an end in itself therefore began to disappear; but it was precisely this post-ideological *lack* of constraint that made the apartheid system so dangerous, as it now exhibited a degree of cunning, intelligence and even imagination that had never existed in the era of a more straightforward *baasskap*. Also a new adventurism was emerging, as in South Africa's ill-fated invasion of Angola in 1975.

Certainly Mehring is the go-ahead new capitalist of the 1970s, sophisticated, urbane, cosmopolitan; but in him Gordimer appears to have captured a mood of wider political and ideological importance as well. Mehring has the energy and intelligence of a ruling class that means to continue its dominance; he has its realism, and therefore also its degree of pragmatism. But he also has, if needs be, its ruthlessness. In Mehring, Gordimer has condensed the ultimate resources, both material and mental, of a white South Africa about to enter the era of historical contest that the early 1970s, on a regional level, signalled. It is therefore all the more significant that he is, in the novel, prophetically overthrown.[23]

One aspect of Gordimer's condensation of all these resources in Mehring is the way he tends to *include* all white society in his condition. The internal stratification of the white world is delineated in the novel. Thus Mehring, the English-speaking urban industrial capitalist, is differentiated from his farming neighbours, the De Beers, on linguistic, cultural, social, economic and even political grounds; also he is differentiated from the police, whom he despises as the crass agents of a cruder version of white supremacy in its most undiluted form. But after speaking to the police on the telephone about the way they have dealt with the body, his snort of derision is nevertheless kept low, so that his black farm-manager, Jacobus, will not hear. White authority, as far as he is concerned, is evidently not to be brought into disrespect in front of blacks, no matter what he may think himself. This is what his liberal mistress, Antonia, calls his 'collusion'; and we have seen how in general the police are in fact the agents of the white industrialist himself. Of equal significance is that the accusation of collusion is turned powerfully back on Mehring's liberal mistress herself; it is Mehring's inclusion of *her* kind of opposition that, principally, extends the boundaries of a unitary white destiny.

If the white industrialist is in league with the police, the liberal is in league with the white industrialist. Indeed, *The Conservationist* contains Gordimer's most lacerating presentation of liberalism yet seen. Here a caveat must be entered, for this presentation is conducted in its entirety through the medium of Mehring's stream of consciousness – which, as we shall see, is by no means always to be trusted. On certain occasions, moreover, the liberal gives as good as she gets; it is she who foresees Mehring's future fate, and this is perhaps her final virtue. But otherwise Mehring in general sees right through her, and in the end an image of Antonia is built up that has a certain consistency and is far from flattering.

The essential features of Antonia's liberalism, as presented in the novel, are its artificiality and the fact that she is always, as Mehring puts it, 'promising what you can't give' (p. 136). The two aspects are counterparts. When Mehring purchases his farm, Antonia tells him to buy it and 'leave it as it is' (p. 43) – an artificialization in its very attempt at 'naturalness'. But when she is detained by the police, on account of her political flirtations, she decides to leave the country – just 'as it is' as well, as Mehring observes – while at the same time basking in the glory of having in some way proved herself. Her political noises are in this respect shown to be little more than the conventions of a certain social group, and her liberalism is the function of a definite surplus: Mehring's surplus. For liberalism, as shown here, is the flourish of conscience whose possibility is created materially and licensed morally within and by capitalist society, and the fact that Antonia is Mehring's 'mistress', with whom he enjoys a love-hate relationship, is no doubt meant to be symbolic in this regard. In the end liberalism is contained within the power of capitalist society, and is dependent upon it. When Antonia is first detained it is to Mehring, whose politics she otherwise despises, that she turns to obtain the services of his company lawyer for her defence; this is, ultimately, her own collusion. In being tied to Mehring she is also tied to the structures of oppression that in South Africa create his surplus.

It is likely that some part of Gordimer's own feelings on liberalism by this time lie behind the depiction of Antonia. Soon after *The Conservationist* was published – and it seems precisely with Antonia's sort of faults in mind – she took pains to distance herself from liberalism. 'I am a white South African radical,' she said in an interview with Michael Ratcliffe of *The Times*. 'Please don't call me a liberal.'[24] Gordimer's remarks in this interview (or at least her reported remarks, since there was some confusion) provoked an angry response from Alan Paton, author of *Cry, the Beloved Country* and ex-leader of the Liberal Party, who thought she had been deriding the Party itself and the memory of some of its finest members. The result was a celebrated clash between the two conducted within the pages of the Johannesburg *Sunday Times*.[25]

However, Gordimer's depiction of Antonia indicates that she was not attacking the Liberal Party as such, which had in any case been forced to disband by 1968,[26] nor what may be called the major tradition of South African liberalism. Rather Antonia is first cousin to that other line of liberalism that we first came across in *A World of Strangers*: the fashionable, posturing kind, wedded more to empty gestures and talk than to any significant practice. In some respects by the early 1970s this was the only tradition which remained; any stronger form of white opposition had by this time been successfully neutralized by the state – as had the Liberal Party itself. In Antonia, therefore, Gordimer is also measuring a general *malaise* within white political opposition in this time, broken down by more than a decade of attrition, and now to all intents and purposes contained within the collusory structures and discourse of white power. We have seen Gordimer's own growing disillusionment with liberalism since *Occasion for Loving*, and the socialist politics of *A Guest of Honour*. It was perhaps this now blatant collusory aspect that led her to declare herself with such force 'a radical'.

There was possibly another reason to see liberalism in this way; the point relates to the Black Consciousness movement. For, paradoxically for a movement addressing itself to the problem of white power, Black Consciousness reserved some of its deepest anger for white liberals, and the accusation it levelled at them was exactly that of collusion. As far as Black Consciousness was concerned white power was an essentially integral phenomenon. Thus, even those whites who claimed not to be part of white supremacy nevertheless lived in conditions of privilege, and drew their ideological assumptions from that position. This was particularly true, maintained Black Consciousness exponents, of white liberals. White liberals had consistently presented themselves as champions of the underdog, but this was precisely the problem; in speaking *for* blacks instead of *to* them white liberals had merely repeated the assumptions of white supremacy. The effects of this had been especially invidious, since in acting on behalf of blacks by proxy they had prevented blacks from acting for themselves. White liberals, so the argument generally ran, were people who eased their consciences while enjoying all the benefits of their situation. As Steve Biko put it, just like all other whites they could expect only 'the blanket condemnation that needs must come from the Black World'.[27]

By the early 1970s Gordimer was familiar with the arguments of Black Consciousness.[28] At at least one point in the novel Mehring seems to register its impact (albeit in degraded form) when he tells Antonia that the blacks wouldn't want her on their side any more, but would prefer her to be a 'white bitch' (p. 199). In her general depiction of white liberalism, then, it may be suggested that Gordimer was, at least to some degree, responding to the Black

Consciousness movement. At any rate her depiction confirms to some extent the observations of Black Consciousness at this time; there was an indisputable social reality to its arguments. And an awareness of the Black Consciousness position adds an additional layer of significance to that other phenomenon noted earlier – the degree to which the white world in the novel is seen as essentially unitary; for this was of course exactly how Black Consciousness saw it at the time.

In so far as Mehring represents the dominant features of white society in the period from which the novel emerges, in his relationship to his farm Gordimer is able to measure some of the deeper aspects of the ideology, culture and historical condition he represents. In symbolic terms the farm is an enormously important site for measuring the *ethic*, in the largest sense, of an individual or collective relationship with the environment of nature, man and beast.[29] But in the South African literary context – and this includes Schreiner – the farm has additional layers of importance. For one thing, it is a significant site of origin, since farms formed the very definition of the 'settled' aspect of an original white colonial expansion; and it was round and about agriculture and farming as a mode of production that the original struggles of land possession and dispossession took place. Also, in that the farm is an *indigenous* site, it represents *par excellence* a way of measuring a *cultural* relationship to the environment. In this respect 'cultural' signifies in two senses: as a productive site or site of cultivation (of which the farm is symbolically the essence), and as an intense point of focus for socio-cultural attitudes to the environment in general (how one sees the role of the farm, both ecologically and socially).

What, then, is the historical fertility of the culture that Mehring represents? What is the ethic of its relationship to the indigenous world in which it has settled?

The short answer to these questions in the novel is that, at least in the phase represented by Mehring, this relationship is a sham. For Mehring is not even an authentic 'farmer'; he is by no means dependent on the farm; nor is the farm fully productive. On the contrary, Mehring is an industrialist who runs the farm as a sideline. Originally bought as a place where he could enjoy sexual assignations with his mistress and entertain his friends, now it is kept for him to indulge his romantic feelings for nature and the imperious demands of his ego – and, in a bad year, recoup his losses as a tax rebate from the government. Here Mehring represents the ideo-logical inversions of his culture and his class. To him, his central concern is 'conservation'; he cannot bear to see his farm trammelled by the imprint of society. Yet, in this guise we see that he cares for nature at the expense of people – the people who actually work on his farm, or provide the labour for the industry he owns.

On a symbolic level Mehring is therefore guilty of the greatest cultural bad faith. Preserving the museum-piece of his false paradise, he refuses to make it fully productive in order to provide for all its inhabitants. The degree to which he embodies the ostensible virtue of conservation (which in other circumstances might be a real one) is the same degree to which he conserves the political and economic injustice that makes his devotion to nature possible. Mehring's privileged relationship with nature and his social and economic privilege are part of the selfsame political reality.

This categorical inversion of the social and the natural is of great significance for the South African context as a whole. In *The Lying Days* we saw how Helen Shaw had to break out of a 'naturalized' mythology that placed blacks in the realm of nature itself; in Mehring's case we see how cynically advanced that mythology could become. One need only consider how central the concept of a 'labour reservoir' is for denoting a fundamental reality of the South African economic structure: notwithstanding whatever tendencies there may be for the system to break down, that human labour is stored up in designated collection zones, just as natural water might be, for controlled release, under the pressure of regulated employ-ment and unemployment, into the white-owned economy.

In the location next to his land, Mehring's farm borders on just such a 'reservoir'. Evidently Gordimer is puncturing some of the major myths of South African ideology, and not the least of these is Mehring's romanticization of his relation to the land, a romanticiz-ation that has historically been a central component within the self-representations of white South African culture. Gordimer has shown it to be based on an emptiness. In Mehring's case, moreover, she demonstrates the degree to which this feeling is a sentimentaliz-ation of a more fundamental passion, which for him is one of *possession*. Mehring 'buys' the farm; it is frequently referred to as his 'property'. Yet as Antonia informs him, he has tried to buy what is not for sale, and his desperate attempt to obtain some form of natural communion through the very means of his social oppression is perhaps the final index of his cultural alienation, both from Africa and from its people.

In one episode in the novel this is precisely demonstrated by Gordimer. Alone in the third pasture on New Year's Eve at midnight, with only a bottle of whisky to keep him company, Mehring imagines that the farm-manager, Jacobus, is with him. On this particular night he feels closer than ever to the land, and his projected relationship with Jacobus, though retaining the hierarchy of master and servant, is enveloped in an aura of forgiveness, male cameraderie and mutual, universal understanding: 'We're going to finish the bottle, Jacobus, you and I, just this once' (p. 207).

Many things are revealed in this episode, not least the maudlin melancholy that is perhaps the reverse side of Mehring's 'frontier' type of bravado, the banality of Mehring's cultural quotations (he could be some cowboy weeping into his beer) and the need for absolution subconsciously concealed beneath the colonizing mind. But the most important fact about this scene is that it is just a fantasy; the encounter with Jacobus never takes place outside the internal world of Mehring's half-drunken reverie. Indeed there is more than a little comedy to the incident, and as a symbolic moment in which Mehring feels most 'at home' on his farm in both social and environmental terms, the episode is intimately revealing. Mehring's whole sense of cultural satisfaction is no more than a self-deceptive dream, a myth of belonging without substance. His culture in its supremacist form is as alien from the African environment as are the Spanish chestnut trees he tries to plant on his land. Gordimer has brought up for inspection what lay buried, unconsciously, beneath the surface of Schreiner's *The Story of an African Farm*. And in this way too she represents the reverse side of the 'European-in-Africa' theme presented in *A Guest of Honour*. There Bray won his 'natural' affiliation with Africa through his social affiliation; here it is shown that without the latter there can also be no former. Social oppression is the underlying basis of an irredeemable cultural alienation, from land and people alike.

We have seen in Gordimer's earlier novels that sexuality in her work is generally used as an analogue for political attitudes, or for a world-historical posture at large. This is once again the case in *The Conservationist*. Thus the aggression that Mehring is at least mentally prepared to entertain against Antonia stands as a parallel for the violence of the political system he supports, and that supports him. Furthermore, as Judie Newman has pointed out, sexuality functions as an analogue for Mehring's attitude to the land.[30] As with the land, as far as women are concerned Mehring finds a special gratification in possession: 'there's a special pleasure in having a woman you've paid' (p. 77), he tells Antonia. She calls this 'sexual fascism' (p. 102), and being the kind of character she is, she must be at least half right. In the sphere of sexuality, as with nature, Mehring's ultimate creed, as we have seen, is one of 'invasion'.

Yet if all this explores his brutality in general terms, then in his sexuality the other side of his condition is also investigated: its lack of anchorage, its loosening hold, its self-enclosed world of a gathering separation from reality. For in his very strength Mehring is already beginning to suffer from an historical *malaise*, and an extended depiction of this runs with gathering force through the course of the novel.

It becomes apparent in the episode in which Mehring casually and impersonally 'fingers' (any other description is euphemistic) a young Portuguese girl all night long on an aeroplane flight returning from Europe to Africa. Seen from one point of view this is the extreme of Mehring's sexual abuse. The girl herself is probably under age; in any case, hardly a word is spoken between the two for the length of their encounter. Mehring's hand is all the contact there is, while the girl herself is entirely passive (the image most tellingly used is that of a servile dog). At the same time, however, there is a peculiar kind of 'absence' for Mehring in which this all takes place. He feels detached, as if his hand has a life of its own, while he himself is not really involved. Nor is there any physical energy between the somnolent couple; both Mehring and the girl perform throughout like automatons. In terms of the spectrum of possible sexual relationships, theirs is surely the barest reduction. But it is precisely as such that the episode comes to represent the essential state of Mehring's historical condition.

The encounter happens 'nowhere', in 'an hour between the hour of Europe and the hour of Africa' (p. 129). This is Mehring's overall displacement. Far from synthesizing the worlds of Africa and Europe, on the contrary he exists between them, in an historical space or gap. The event is governed by other negatives as well; 'nothing is disclosed' by the infinite distances of the world outside the aeroplane (p. 126), and 'nothing is disclosed' of or between the two lovers either. Resting against the girl's thigh Mehring's hand clasps for a moment excitedly against 'nothing' (p. 129). We shall see that 'nothing' is a central pun in the novel, coming to refer both to Mehring's inner condition and to his coming inheritance, and this is symbolized in the episode. As Mehring's 'absence' and 'nothingness' indicate, he is the site of an imminent historical evacuation. And as his habitual habitations make clear – in this case the aeroplane, but equally the motor car, the hotel room and ultimately even the farm, which at best he visits only intermittently – he is the locus of an historical transition.

Mehring's inevitable destiny becomes the import of a message running increasingly threateningly through the narrative of *The Conservationist*. In a series of prophetic incidents his historical demise is continuously, proleptically embodied, right from the moment when he falls asleep in the third pasture (where the body is also buried) and then wakes in very great distress:

> For a moment he does not know where he is – or rather who he is; but the situation in which he finds himself, staring into the eye of the earth with earth at his mouth, is strongly familiar to him. It seems to be something already inhabited in imagination.
>
> (p. 41)

Perhaps Gordimer is paying tribute here to the prophetic power of fiction, for Mehring's future destiny (and therefore that of the world he represents) is something most definitely inhabited in the imagination of her novel.[31] And overall, the feeling of being akin to the body, or more precisely of being about to exchange places with it, is one that grows ever more menacingly for Mehring – until at the end, when Jacobus tells him the body has risen to the surface again, and he runs towards it to see, the narrative is explicit:

> Up on higher ground he hears himself crashing through [the mielies] as if he were coming towards himself, about to come face to face with . . . He stops dead.
>
> (p. 227)

Mehring is certainly due to 'stop dead' in *The Conservationist*, and everywhere the novel is full of this kind of innuendo and portent. Surrounded suddenly by a 'ragged army' of black women advancing on him with hoes (p. 182), he feels an uncontrollable – and it can only be historical – instant of panic. Another time, while tramping over his farm he is sucked down into the mud in the third pasture. It feels as if someone is pulling him down, and he feels exactly the same anguish.

151

A central aspect of this proleptic structure is that it comes to embody Mehring's future fate at a *generic* level, as a representative member of his *class*. Arriving early for work one morning after having spent a night on the farm, Mehring slips out of his office for a cup of coffee in a coffee-bar nearby. There he is confronted by a roomful of young women, any one of whom, he feels, could be his daughter – and Mehring is in fact greeted by the daughter of one of his financial associates, a man who is a wealthy director of a number of companies. Later he returns to his office to find that in the wake of 'yet another' business scandal (on these occasions the novel is insistently generic) the financier concerned has committed suicide by gassing himself in his car. Mehring, who felt he could have been the father of the man's daughter, takes the suicide personally; his very next thoughts, remembering how she had singled him out in the coffee-bar, are in this respect an acknowledgement: 'It's me' (p. 194). In this way a feeling is built up that there is some avenging nemesis being directed at Mehring as a member of his class, and his existence in the novel indeed consists of a series of close shaves from which his escape is on each occasion narrow. Thus, the threat of scandal (the ironic scourge of capitalist over-indulgence) hangs perpetually over Mehring's head, and the danger that his abuse of the Portuguese girl will be discovered is only the most obvious example. During the storm at the end of the novel, when a car is swept away and its occupant killed, Mehring knows full well that it could have been him, for it occurs on the road to the farm that he regularly uses.

To this extent the proleptic structure of the novel is also something of a subjunctive structure; it is continually *as if* all these things were happening to Mehring, as if *he* were the subject of some relentless class fate. And in the end it is as a culmination and encapsulation of all these portents that his fate is prophesied. Fleeing in mental disarray from the farm after the body has risen, Mehring picks up a female hitch-hiker – in this case a tawdry avatar of all the women he has dealt with so far – who leads him on with what seem to be blatant sexual intentions to a deserted mine-dump area. There Mehring finds himself watched by a man – whether a gangster associate of the woman's or a member of the police (the ironic agents of Mehring's own empire) he cannot be sure. But one thing is certain; the historical scandal of Mehring's existence has come home to roost, and this is then the site of his final and total breakdown. Mehring is not literally beaten up and killed amongst the cyanide mine-dust[32] (he has previously thought of cyanide as the classic method of suicide) but he does prefigure the death of his class. The man who enters the novel generically as 'the owner of the farm' (p. 9) exits as well as 'the farmer' (p. 266). Possibly he has sold the farm to 'the next white man' or 'the next buyer' (p. 260), but this does not matter at all. It is immaterial how many 'farmers' follow Mehring, or whether he, in some sense, still owns the farm. Prophetically he has lived out a class fate, which is to surrender the land to the black body, which in the end is the figure to claim it.

A further aspect of Mehring's condition is of interest, not only in itself, but also because of the *mode* in which Gordimer represents it. Here once again Lukács provides a point of departure for this study. In his sometimes outrageous tirade against modernism and its methods Lukács distinguishes as one of its essential techniques the use of the stream of consciousness, or interior monologue. Its use in modernism is dangerous, he asserts, because it tends to equate the world of subjectivity with objective reality. Thus in Joyce's *Ulysses* there is no objective authority to set against the internal musings of Bloom, which comprise much of the narrative, or other equally subjective narrative voices. The world of impressions becomes for the novel universal.[33] Lukács also maintains that modernism has endorsed Bergson's subjectivization of time, which undermines the foundations of objective historical time altogether. The logical end point of this for him is the *angst* and despair embodied by Kafka, which occurs precisely because the subjective world has grown out of all proportion. The present is taken for the eternal, external chronology comes to an end, and a world of virtual insanity becomes indistinguishable from reality.

Lukács's strictures on the decadence of modernism have in many respects rightly come under attack.[34] Nevertheless his remarks, when applied appropriately, can be useful for considering Mehring and illuminating basic aspects of his condition. For Mehring is, within a Lukácsian framework, recognizably a 'modernist character' (here we remember how closely Gordimer had absorbed Lukács's writings in the late 1960s). Thus, his whole narrative is relayed through his stream of consciousness and, equally important, within this domain there is no necessary distinction between subjective and objective reality. We have seen how Mehring is able to concoct an entire dramatized scene between himself and Jacobus that it later transpires has never taken place; an international telephone call with his wife is similarly invented. Perhaps the essential point regarding Mehring is that his entire world is lived in terms of either remembrance or reflection. Pre-eminently he is engaged in a kind of circular mental discourse, in which he addresses absent characters, or goes over the past, or very occasionally thinks about the future. In so far as this discourse comes to comprise the world of his narrative, all time and space have become internalized. On the one hand this represents the stamp of his ego on his environment – in a far advanced version of Schreiner's novel it becomes literally 'subject' to him. On the other hand, for Mehring *real* time seems to have stopped; very little actually *happens* to him in the novel outside the series of mental events that comprise his circular chronology, and those external events that do occur tend to foretell only his own demise. In this way time itself is 'spatialized'; a symbolic synchrony is set up that portends Mehring's destiny from the beginning, and in which his only significant development lies in accepting it at the end.

Mehring, in short, is in stasis. His history has come to a standstill. There is a severe disjunction between his sense of his own history and its reality. Like the aeroplane on which he engaged in his ludicrously reduced love affair, which gave 'the sensation of motionlessness' while in fact being 'the nest of extreme speed' (p. 130), Mehring's internal world gives him the impression of stability and security while he hurtles towards his historical fate. Or, the reverse is the case; while his interior monologue gives him the sensation of life and development, in fact his historical condition is 'motionless'. It is a measure of the power of Gordimer's novel that both, simultaneously, seem to be true.

Ultimately Mehring's circularity is resolved into a politically edged version of a Kafkan *angst*. Beginning as a condition of distress, which the novel defines as 'a compulsion ... to keep going over and over the same ground' (p. 97) (the ground, of course, that is the burial site of the body), Mehring ends in total mental breakdown in the face of his inevitable destiny. This breakdown is the counterpart and conclusion of the subjectivism that has sustained and undermined him all along.

Gordimer's depiction of Mehring had wider echoes within South African fiction in the 1970s. In J. M. Coetzee's novels as well his central characters were enclosed inside their own subjectivity, which was also a social and historical subjectivity, to the extent that there seemed no possible way out. The narrator of his *In The Heart of the Country*,[35] the decrepit spinster, Magda, in particular seems to be a correlative of Mehring, living within a self-enveloped nightmare world where fact and fantasy are barely distinguishable. She too represents the terminal *malaise* of a whole history and culture, and an essential alienation from the land and its people. Figures such as Magda and Mehring have led some commentators to discern a crisis of subjectivity in South African fiction in the 1970s, and in particular a crisis of the liberal view of the individual subject, with its assumptions of the (at least potential) coherency of the individual and the capacity for a personal transcendence of social conditions.[36]

There is probably something to this case, although in Gordimer's work we first saw this view of the individual being undermined as far back as *Occasion for Loving*; there was no sudden crisis of liberal subjectivity in South African writing a decade later. But the example of Mehring makes something else clear. It is not so important that there is a crisis of subjectivity in *The Conservationist*; far more important is *whose* crisis of subjectivity this is. Indeed (if we return to Lukács for a moment) Gordimer has by no means used the formal technique of the stream of consciousness to signify a *universal* crisis of subjectivity. Instead she has put the technique to powerful social and historical use; a specific *segment* of reality has been undermined – Mehring's segment, and the world he represents. This is certainly the significance of Coetzee's work as well, for what his novels trace is the demise of a certain kind of subjectivity, and the cultural and historical framework within which it is constituted. It is here that one thinks again of Schreiner, and the context of uneasy settlement that constituted the subjectivity of her characters, which here is being overturned. From this point of view the novels of the 1970s perhaps stand as advance signals of a fundamental historical change in South Africa; especially, as we shall see in Mehring's case, in terms of what the crisis of subjectivity signifies – the destabilization of a whole framework of reality and its eventual replacement.

This sense of replacement is embodied in *The Conservationist* in the black world. We must examine the novel's depiction of this world and its vision of historical transfer more closely, for these will add directly to our understanding of the range and limits of its historical consciousness. Just as Mehring's demise is prophesied throughout *The Conservationist*, so too the black world appears to be in a state of imminent return. Its hold on the land is in any case more secure than Mehring's; whereas he is absent from the farm for

much of its working life, it is the farmworkers, and especially the
farm-manager, Jacobus, who are in effective control. When Mehring
is cut off from the farm because the Mozambican storm has washed
away the road, Jacobus of necessity has to run the place as if he owns
it. In searching for a syringe to cure a cow of mastitis, in the way he
has seen a white vet do, he goes through Mehring's house as after a
death, sorting through his possessions. And (as part of the novel's
generic vision) during the storm it is indeed as if Mehring has died. A
car has been swept off the road and no one knows whose it was. In
running the farm while he is away the black workers take to it as if it is
naturally theirs. On a different occasion, on the night of the dance,
when Phineas's wife becomes a diviner, this natural relationship
comes to the fore. Without Mehring the black community enjoys an
organic relationship with the farm, and 'all', we are told, 'might have
been theirs' (p. 172). As the farmworkers bury the body at the end,
this possibility seems to have become a reality.

Yet significantly this vision is shown to be an impossibility on a
realistic plane. Although the black farmworkers may enjoy a moral
superiority over Mehring – in their communal ethic, their sharing of
work and food – nevertheless within the novel's realistic mode their
world lacks all resources of historical effect. There is no way in
which the depleted and poverty-stricken black farmworkers can
realistically take on Mehring's power – this is something *The
Conservationist* does not even entertain. Elsewhere, where the
black world is described, the only solidarity it displays is one of
irony. The Indians who own a store near Mehring's farm are in
breach of the Group Areas Act; this is a 'white' area, and they can be
evicted for illegal occupation. Having to find money to bribe officials
in consequence, they exploit the blacks who work for them. These
selfsame workers, because they have a place and jobs, and under
threat from those who do not, have willingly constructed a fence
around the Indians' compound where they live, in order to keep
other blacks out.

Within the black world, then, there is an effective political
economy of consciousness, a chain of exploitation whereby those
who are excluded from privilege are constrained to exclude others,
to maintain their radically unstable hold on possession, whether of
property, place, or employment, against the ever-present threat from
below. This is what Stanley Trapido has characterized as being 'the
desperate self-interest of the severely deprived',[37] surely one of the

most insidious effects of apartheid. And here Gordimer provides some of her most poignant observation in the novel, as when Dorcas's husband, lacking a few cents to pay his subscription to a Christmas Club, sees his whole year's investment disappear before his eyes. Here her evocation is powerful of the desperate condition of the hopeless, whose entire struggle is for the very minimum of dignity and the barest degrees of subsistence.

Given this sort of social and political realism, much of what we have discussed so far takes on an additional significance. Precisely because the novel's vision is recognized to be impossible within its realistic mode that vision is, as a consequence, displaced into various aspects of the novel's *form* – features of which have been touched on already. The fundamental strategy whereby this vision is embedded in the novel is through the hypostatization of formal procedures as actual historical forces.

On one level irony, which at base is a formal disposition within the text, becomes exactly such a force. In fact irony runs riot through *The Conservationist*. Mehring's relationship with the farm is fundamentally ironic; it is he, as a conservation-minded master, who is obliged to clean up after his 'servants', or fret about how they are treating the wildlife on the farm. In a novel in which ancestorship is so important it is also ironic that Mehring's son, Terry, as the offspring of the ultimate male chauvinist, is possibly homosexual; on this level alone Mehring's line might be unlikely to continue. Or, to take a different example, part of Mehring's cultural power, as Michael Wade has suggested, is expressed in the 'grids' of his daily habitation[38] – in particular the road network that carries him from office to farm to airport and back. Yet gradually this grid begins to exert an ironical power over Mehring, programming him on pre-selected paths over which he has less and less volitional control. Finally it is just such a road that leads him mindlessly to the cyanide mine-dumps, the site of his class 'suicide'. Needless to say this setting is also suitably ironic, since the gold mines have, historically, formed the basis of Mehring's industrial empire and perhaps represent his culture as a whole. Once again more than just Mehring's fate is prefigured in his breakdown.

Even language participates in the ironic structure of the novel, in particular the central pun, 'nothing'. When the body is first discovered, Jacobus says there is 'nothing for this man' (p. 16). On a realistic level this is correct; there is nothing for the black man and all he represents. Yet, through perpetual repetition, 'nothing', as in E. M. Forster's use of the word in *A Passage to India*, comes to refer to a 'something', not least of all in this case the body itself, Mehring's inner condition and his coming inheritance. So when in a kind of humble pride of possession Mehring sits in his fields and declares that he 'want[s] for nothing' (p. 159), his statement is enormously ironic. Puns in *The Conservationist* (as in Freudian theory) refer to a 'subconscious' level of the surface text, and at this level Mehring's future fate is present beneath his every slightest word. Everything he says is in this sense a pun, totally laced with irony. Mehring says he wants the farm for relaxation, but look at what he 'gives away': 'Time to let go, as the saying has it. It's agreed that's what a place like this is for' (p. 156).

The black body itself is a kind of incarnation of irony in the novel. The more Mehring attempts to repress its significance within his own mind (as we shall see) the more decisively it returns to haunt him. The political analogue of this is clear: the more relentlessly the black world in South Africa is oppressed, the more certain will be its eventual return. Part of the reason the body rises at the end is simply because of the power of irony in the novel.

On its own this ironic strategy might appear obtrusive and inadequate were it not linked (in a combination that becomes totally compelling) with the novel's other main formal elaboration, carried in its symbolic mode. We have already had some evidence of this mode, as Mehring's fate is symbolically foretold on numerous occasions. But most directly the novel's symbolism – once again in Gordimer's work – is one of nature, and it becomes intricately woven into the text. The novel's central motif is that of the egg, in relation to which everyone can be measured. For Mehring eggs are for conserving; for the black children on the farm they are 'naturally' for eating; Mehring's wife gets an artificial egg as a present from Terry; for the Indian son his 'egg' is the shape of a futile peace-sign. As these examples suggest, it is the black world that is most directly connected with nature in the novel; indeed there are elements of a barely submerged pastorale in *The Conservationist* in so far as it applies to the farmworkers. In this respect we have already noted the organic linkage built up between the black farmworkers and the farm; and when the body is reburied at the end, it is as if the black community has once again come into harmony with its natural environment, a harmony that is both backward looking, to a time before the white settler came, and forward looking, to a time when it may be regained. Primarily, it is none other than the body which represents this special relationship. First borne up gently by reeds, then crudely covered over with earth by the police, the body is like a child of nature whom the storm from Mozambique returns to life. In its eventual burial by the black community it is in every sense returned to its own.

Nature, as an hypostatized entity, becomes a power in its own right in the novel – *The Conservationist*'s ultimate historical power. All the visions of the novel come together within its ambit. In nature the power of irony ultimately resides, embodied in its fundamental law of balance and return. Thinking how rain will replenish what fire has razed, Mehring considers that for everything in nature there is the right antidote. He little knows how directly he will prove his own case, when the storm from Mozambique raises the body and symbolically sweeps him away. This is also the cleansing and re-plenishing rain that clears away Mehring's 'unnatural' violation – a violation that consisted in his treatment of people with less concern than he had for nature itself. For the cycle of Mehring's oppression, the novel suggests, there is an equal cycle of return; the storm stands for a dispassionate force of nature that turns on the arrogant with ironic certitude.

Apart from its satiric moments, therefore, as when Mehring communes with an absent Jacobus at midnight in the fields, *The Conservationist* might be considered as a comedy, for in the best of comic traditions it is essentially a tale of 'natural' rejuvenation that it tells. *A Guest of Honour* suppressed this vision in its sense of 'the callousness of the earth endlessly renewing itself'; this was entirely appropriate to its historical circumstances, although the natural cycle held out some long-term hope. In *The Conservationist*, however, the earlier ratio between 'callousness' and 'renewal' has been inverted. In the world of 1974 the comic implications of this formulation have been prophetically and triumphantly released. Moreover, Gordimer presents the power of nature in distinctly *political* terms in the novel. When Mehring visits his farm after the first rains of the season have occurred, he is amazed at the growth that has taken place, and the words he utters are 'Look how every-thing came back' (p. 245). This is exactly the same phrase Gordimer uses to describe the body when it is buried, the body that also, as we have seen, 'comes back'. 'Afrika! Mayibuye!' literally *occurs* in *The*

Conservationist. It is Africa, in the form of nature, that comes back, and nature, in the form of the storm, that does away with Mehring.

Given all this we are able to make a first major assessment of the historical consciousness of *The Conservationist.* Once again, we have seen a dramatic appeal in Gordimer's fiction to the power of nature; indeed it occurs here in its strongest form in all her novels. This is a feature of such recurrent importance in her work that its final significance must be left to later analysis, but the pattern of which it forms a part here can be identified. The vision of historical transfer foreclosed by the novel's realism is recovered and redeemed within its symbolic mode. Irony, the symbolism of portent, the appeal to nature: these have made good what realistically the novel recognizes to be impossible. There is a model elision in the novel that fuses its realism and symbolism and issues in the prophetic vision. The symbolic status of nature in particular constitutes a transcendentalism, as a force above and beyond the workings of history takes on historical power. But this should not simply be considered as an expression of narrative or visionary weakness. On the contrary, there are few more powerful – if indeed any other – modes of prophecy than symbolic suggestion linked to an idea of absolute certainty; in this respect *The Conservationist* participates in the oldest of visionary traditions.

Finally it is the relationship between the novel's realism and its symbolism that holds the key to a central aspect of its historical consciousness. For if the novel's prophecy expresses its historical certainty, that black history is once more to resume, then the manner in which it is produced in the work – formalistic, symbolic and transcendental – can, in the light of the novel's realism, signify only a radical uncertainty as to the actual process whereby it may be achieved. There is a gap between means and ends here, or between desire and reality, which the novel negotiates through a sustained virtuoso performance in symbolic and formal displacement; but the gap, or contradiction, is none the less revealed in that process. A number of things might be said about this. To some degree the contradiction revealed in *The Conservationist* perhaps represents the isolation of the white radical in South Africa, cut off from the locus of actual historical change – that same black world that the body represents – while not doubting that change will occur. But partly it represents a larger moment and mood in South Africa at the time of the novel's production.

Written before the Portuguese coup; written before the liberation of Mozambique, Angola and Zimbabwe; written before the Soweto Revolt of 1976, and indeed before the contest for South Africa became next on the southern African agenda: *The Conservationist* represents a moment when the eventual downfall of white supremacy – in general historical terms – seemed almost absurdly manifest, but the precise timing or means of its realization still remained unclear. In this respect we should not confine the significance of the novel's vision too narrowly within the boundaries of its ideological or class origins. There would have been few in South Africa in 1974 who could have overcome the novel's historical problem realistically; or on the other hand, it seems, escaped its certainty.

III

Through the musing of Mehring, then, and the novel's treatment of the black body, *The Conservationist* becomes powerfully linked with far larger movements in South African history. This fact has not always been clearly apparent. '*The Conservationist*,' writes Abdul R. JanMohamed, 'eschews history . . . This attempt to escape history . . . results in a highly subjective and ambiguous novel.'[39] What we have seen so far enables us to challenge this judgement. There is no contradiction between the 'subjectivity' of or in the novel and its broader, 'objective' historical significance; and the novel's 'ambiguity' has been a constitutive element of what it signifies. In terms of its vision and formal energy *The Conservationist* is probably the richest of Gordimer's novels, historically considered, to date; but precisely for that reason its full significance has not yet been exhausted. For there are further secrets to be elicited from the novel's subterranean operations. Once again Gordimer's work registers crucial realities relating to the moment from which it emerges, and once again it returns us to the deeper social and historical codes it embodies. In this regard three features remain to be discussed: the novel's thematic and textual use of Zulu myth; its treatment of Mehring's unconscious; and the question of 'textuality' in the novel. All of these areas are linked with one another, both structurally and by analogy, and all point to a central, major concern: the replacement of a framework of reality.

The use of Zulu myth in *The Conservationist* has been well

161

followed up by Judie Newman.[40] She has shown how Gordimer, drawing on her cited reading of *The Religious System of the Amazulu* (compiled by the Rev. Henry Callaway in the second half of the nineteenth century),[41] has populated her novel with motifs from Zulu mythology. For example, the bed of reeds that bears up the black body is a highly important site in Zulu myth, according to Callaway, for it marks the place where the first ancestor (*uNkulunkulu*; also the Zulu word for God) came into being. Indeed the word for reed (*uthlanga*; modern spelling, *uhlanga*) is also the word for ancestor; a reed 'breaks off' and produces new shoots. The notion of ancestry then is highly important to the novel; on the one hand the spirit of the dead body has apparently returned to the ancestors, but on the other we see it become again a symbolic progenitor as it returns to claim the land for its people (always the first action of an ancestor, according to Callaway). Elsewhere Phineas's wife, in becoming a diviner (*inyanga*), feels pain between her shoulders and sings and dances in reverie: precisely the symptoms described in Callaway's compilation.[42]

In this way, as Newman remarks, Zulu myth intrudes as a kind of sub-text into the main narrative, and it does so in another way as well. For Gordimer has used extracts from Callaway's work as a succession of epigraphs punctuating the narrative at intervals. Once again we may see this as a definition of the novel's modernism or even 'post-modernism'. Callaway's work is already a collage of separate accounts, collected over time, broken up, reorganized into themes and translated into English; and Gordimer extends the collage, taking out further extracts and putting her own novel into 'constellation', as Walter Benjamin would call it, with them. Also here, once again, Gordimer's novel perhaps takes on significance in relation to the Black Consciousness movement, for the movement strongly emphasized a return to black cultural roots and traditions.

Gordimer has once more put the formal strategy in her work to powerful historical use. For the extracts that she takes are always in *ironical* relation to the central narrative. At first, as Newman indicates, this is an irony in which the central narrative dominates. For example, the first epigraph opens on a theme of 'I pray for corn' (p. 39), but the narrative that follows tells why Mehring wants the farm, which is primarily as 'a place to bring a woman' (p. 47). Increasingly, however, as the novel progresses, the relations between sub-text and text are reversed, as the sub-text comes to prophesy or even control the direction of the main text. Thus, the second-last epigraph deals with a flood, and the last with the question of ancestry and an eternalized process of return. The correspondence of these textual prophecies to the main text is never wholly direct or complete; in the way that myths relate to everyday life they are suitably oblique and mysterious; or, as Callaway's book informs us, in the way that ancestors test out aspirant diviners, they demand a degree of inspired or licensed interpretation.

But the analogy at any rate is clear. Just as the body, buried beneath the surface of Mehring's farm, comes to control his destiny and reclaim the land, so the sub-text – or sub-version, we might call it – of Zulu myth comes to control and appropriate the surface narrative of Mehring's stream of consciousness, and take possession of the text as a whole. Callaway's own text, which on every page displays the genuine fascination, but also the complacent benignities, of a nineteenth-century clerical anthropology, has been used ironically to foretell the demise of its own partial legacy of cultural supremacism.

This 'sub-version' exists on another, highly suggestive level in the novel, in which the realities sustaining Mehring's conscious life are displaced by those that have been relegated to his unconscious. For a central theme of *The Conservationist* is that, just as the black body is buried shallowly beneath the surface of his farm, so is its significance buried shallowly beneath the surface of Mehring's conscious mind, in his unconscious.[43] Just as the body represents an oppressed black world in South Africa, so too it represents a site of psychic repression within Mehring's mind. It is not that Mehring is unaware of the significance of the body. Rather, it is because he *is* aware of it that he represses it, thereby avoiding any sense of his own complicity in the system that has caused such an horrendous violation. Yet this significance cannot be repressed entirely. Linking up with the novel's ironic structure, the more Mehring attempts to repress the body psychologically, the more threateningly it begins to haunt him, intruding ever more menacingly in unguarded moments into his consciousness.

There is another aspect to this. In some respects *The Conservationist* might well be called *The Conversationist*, for Mehring is, in a sense, a compulsive conversationist. Much of his stream of consciousness is indeed taken up in dialogue. Yet this dialogue, as we have seen, is almost entirely conducted inside his own mind, in a continuous, obsessive debate with absent characters. This does not apply only to Jacobus; we have seen how Mehring addresses his absent mistress, after she has fled the country; similarly he addresses his son, first absent in Namibia, then later in New York with his wife, whom he also 'speaks to' in this way. All these are addressed without name, simply as 'you', sometimes a matter of difficulty for the reader to identify. But (almost literally) the underlying absent character in the novel, and the ultimate 'you' for Mehring, is the black body. As part of his own repression it is a 'you' whom he seldom addresses directly,[44] but his entire address as an historical character is in part to this figure and what it represents, even in so far as it determines what he feels an overwhelming need to try to avoid. In the degree to which the body haunts him this address becomes ever more compulsive. Finally Mehring finds himself addressed. In the wake of the storm he confronts the body, now risen to the surface of his farm. Simultaneously its significance rises to the surface of his conscious mind, and this is then the meaning of Mehring's mental crisis. Signifying symbolically that he is to exchange places with the body 'down there', his subconscious repression has literally taken over his mind. Mehring flees in terror and breakdown from the farm, and succumbs to his fate, surrendering the land.

Apart from the political level with which it coincides perfectly, the coming back of the body signifies a 'return of the repressed' in a classic psychoanalytical sense; a site of psychic repression is bound to return to consciousness in threatening and subversive ways. This marks the spectacular *tour de force* of *The Conservationist*. For on any number of levels in the novel this tale of return is linked. On a structural level it is contained in the novel's irony; on a linguistic level it is contained in the puns we have seen; on a narrative level it is contained in the relations between sub-text and text; on a psychic level it concerns the relation between Mehring's conscious and unconscious; and on a political level it concerns the return of the black world represented by the body.

If we consider the return of the body a little further from a psychoanalytical point of view, then its *burial* at the end of the novel is also of relevance. In Freudian terms, to raise the repressed to consciousness is also to bury its threatening aspect properly, to lay it to rest, to peace. Here it is important that the black community that buries the body, but more particularly Phineas's wife – who throughout the novel has been hounded by obscure messages from the ancestors – is also, with the burial of the body, at peace. Evidently it is a theme of the novel that the political outrage that the unburied body represents is also a reproach in the black unconscious, which can be laid to rest only through political revolution.

These themes are fascinating in terms of what they imply about the relations between politics and the psyche. Moreover, we shall see later that the concepts of the 'return of the repressed' and 'address' may be of great significance in understanding some of the underlying compulsions and motivations of Nadine Gordimer's own work.[45] Here, however, let us just follow up the central thread of these questions. For if, for the black world, to raise the repressed to consciousness is to 'lay its ghost', so to speak, then as far as Mehring is concerned it is the repressed world that has laid claim to his consciousness itself. Mehring's mental world does not survive the return of the body, and this signifies the replacement of his framework of reality.

The theme is developed in the novel's 'textual' investigations. *The Conservationist* is highly intrigued by the whole concept of 'textuality' (its use of Zulu myth being only one aspect of a more general concern). Analogies of it abound in the novel. Thus, Mehring's 'fingering' of the girl on the aeroplane is cast in the form of a narrative, with his finger taking up the dialogue – which is only, in this case, like his stream of consciousness, 'a monologue' (p. 129). Elsewhere, even nature appears to have certain text-like qualities; as spring begins on the farm Mehring sees things come to life before his eyes 'as the syntax of a foreign language suddenly begins to yield meaning' (p. 133). The 'grid' along which he travels by road is in this sense also a cultural 'text' which has been superimposed upon the landscape. And in general Mehring's coherence as a character, in so far as he has enjoyed any for the length of the novel, is inseparable from the 'text' with which he has grasped reality – that combination of beliefs, certainties, prejudices and ideological and cultural myths that have constituted his conviction and security. It is this text that has enabled him to deride the arguments of Antonia, or feel assured in his treatment of Jacobus, or indeed feel in touch with and safe in his own identity. And Gordimer clearly finds this fascinating in the novel: the degree to which identity is constituted within and by a certain 'social text', the degree to which the appropriation of reality is indivisible from the social text through which it is mediated. It is then all the more significant that Mehring's text at the end of the novel slides entirely out of control. As he enters the whirligig of breakdown the circularities of his consciousness spiral ever faster; the very ciphers of his code become unstable as he becomes dislodged from the grid of his certainty into the abyss of a deranged agnosis.

Confronted by a green traffic light in his hectic flight from the farm, for a moment Mehring cannot remember what it means; at the mine dumps, seeing the man watching him and the woman, Mehring doesn't know whether he is a 'policeman' or 'thug' (the fact that the two are probably identical is part of the point here). Even Mehring's language means the opposite of what he intends. Thinking 'no' when the woman asks him for a lift (p. 252), he nevertheless lets her into his car; repeatedly saying 'No, no' (pp. 248–51) to his fate, he is irresistibly drawn towards it and succumbs. In this way Mehring's 'no' becomes the ultimate pun in the novel because, of course, it means 'yes'. Similarly, 'nothing' for the black body now comes to mean 'everything', while Mehring, who has 'everything', learns that it will come to 'nothing'. Like the narrator of Gordimer's appropriately titled short story, 'Africa emergent', Mehring discovers inescapably the foreboding truth that 'everything is ambiguous' where he lives.

From all points of view in the novel, then, Mehring's framework of reality has been displaced. Zulu myth has gained control of the narrative; Mehring's consciousness has been overturned by his unconscious; the text with which he grasps reality has come radically unstuck. The wider significance of this comeuppance is clear. From the perspective of those in power, who have imposed a 'social text' on their world, the replacement of a framework of reality is nothing less than a social insanity; it is the known world that for them disappears, and a 'world turned upside down' that replaces it. This is the significance of Mehring's mental crisis at the end. The text of his conscious world corresponds to a subsisting reality, which is inseparable from his social hegemony; his subconscious represents an alternative reality that he cannot finally keep down; it is, precisely, 'revolution' *The Conservationist* predicts.

Here we might compare *The Conservationist* with *A World of Strangers*, for in this conclusion there seems to be a major transition marked out, not only for Nadine Gordimer's own historical consciousness, but for South African historical reality itself. In different ways *A World of Strangers* and *The Conservationist* clarify between them a crucial – perhaps *the* crucial – historical shift in the entire period we are considering. We saw that *A World of Strangers* was primarily an urban-based novel conducted within a mode of classical realism. Although one of its basic motivations was to contest a dominant reading of reality, chiefly through symbolic disruptions, in the end this all took place only within a given realistic framework, a framework that was finally affirmed. This pattern, moreover, corresponded to the dominant codes of opposition to apartheid at the time when the novel was written; although the opposition movements called for an extension of rights to blacks and their incorporation into existing structures of political and economic power, the very thrust of this campaign implied an affirmation of those structures. While the Congress Alliance contested the interpretation of subsisting reality, and challenged it from within, ultimately it did not transgress any boundaries, and in effect affirmed the framework within which its challenge was conducted.

Merely to give this account is to suggest that *The Conservationist* – and what it represents – is almost the exact inversion of *A World of Strangers*. Whereas the earlier novel contained a rural intrusion within its predominantly urban setting, in the later work the rural setting of the farm in more senses that one 'contains' the man from the city. Moreover the respective fictional modes linked to these two sites are reversed in terms of their dominance. In *A World of Strangers* it was the 'natural' setting of the hunt where the novel's symbolic disruption primarily occurred, but in the end the insights gained here only fed into and reinforced the 'realistic' framework of Toby Hood's future social commitment. In *The Conservationist*, however, the opposite occurs; the power of the symbolic mode is fully unleashed as, linked to a force of nature, it overthrows the realistic framework of Mehring's industrial culture. This is the decisive difference between the two novels. Whereas *A World of Strangers* finally accepts a given framework of reality, it is an unspecified, but none the less distinctively alternative, reality that *The Conservationist* prophesies.

Here the wider significance of the novel is apparent in terms of the broader social and historical codes it embodies. By the time *The Conservationist* was written, at issue in the historical struggle for South Africa was no longer the *interpretation* of a given reality, or even the *improvement* of a given reality, but clearly the very basis and substance of social reality itself. It was no longer reform but revolution that was at stake. The movements of the 1950s had explored to the limits whatever scope there was for change within subsisting social structures; but it was nothing less than the exercise of power within those structures that indicated there was no scope for change and contrived the almost complete defeat of the movements. Now, even more than in the 1960s, it was evident that the very notion of change in itself implied the complete overturn of existing social reality. This at any rate was what seemed to be signified by regional developments in the 1970s as the white regimes of southern Africa came under increasing threat from the liberation movements.

From this point of view, at a symbolic level, there are some striking correspondences between Gordimer's novel and the South African movements of opposition in this time. Outlawed politically and expelled geographically, the liberation movements were for one thing literally *outside* an existing South African framework of reality. For another, like Gordimer's black body, they had been suppressed and gone 'underground'. But it was precisely from this position that they represented an *inverse* social reality; and it was this that (most alarmingly for white South Africans) threatened to 'come back' from below.[46] We cannot take Gordimer's symbols too literally as representing South Africa's underground movements; primarily what they represent are the *idea* and implications of revolution, which on one level are what the underground movements represented. But at this level there is a deep necessity to the code incorporated in the novel. Here what Gordimer's novel represents is what the underground movements also did, as both responded to what was signified by history: that at stake in South Africa by the 1970s was nothing less than the overthrow of an entire framework of reality. In *The Conservationist* this framework is prophetically overthrown, and it is for all these reasons that the novel is such an important fictional and historical signpost.

A final assessment of the novel's historical consciousness now becomes possible. The dominant impulse behind *The Conservationist* is symbolic. Symbolism has carried its vision, symbolism has been its dominant mode. Earlier it was suggested that this mode registers the *limits* of the novel's vision in the present – the way in which, though the prophecy it represents is certain, the exact means of its realization, or timing, still remains unclear. Here, however, we come to the complement of that assessment. For, though the novel cannot envision the process whereby an alternative reality is to come, it has at least registered that there is an alternative reality that is coming. The novel has in fact acted like a self-fulfilling prophecy; in itself as a text it has succeeded in destabilizing Mehring's social reality.

From this point of view the future has already entered into the novel's limitations in the present; the same symbolic mode that registered this limitation carries this destabilization. Moreover, *The Conservationist*'s own role in the context of South Africa in the mid-1970s should not be underestimated, for it is very deeply a threatening novel. Telling the tale of a body that returns, it has many of the attributes of a politicized ghost story; chilling, uncanny and (almost literally) blackly comic by turns, it holds out the prospect of an irrepressible 'ghost' about to 'come back' from the future. White South Africa is threatened on every page. For good historical reasons Gordimer's novel may not have been able to give any real substance to its prophecy. But in so many ways it has (much like the political movements of this time) subjected the present to its 'sub-version'.

6

The Subject of Revolution:
Burger's Daughter
and *July's People*

Wait for it: waiting for it.
Nadine Gordimer, 'A lion on the freeway'[1]

I

In *The Conservationist* there are no white characters whose task it is to respond positively to the prospect of revolution; it is part of the novel's prophetic release that this is not deemed to be necessary. However, in the two novels that followed, *Burger's Daughter* and *July's People*, Gordimer returned to the question that *The Conservationist* leaves out: whether whites can participate in the future it predicts. Yet she did so in very different circumstances. As independence came to Mozambique, Angola and, later, Zimbabwe, the prophecy of *The Conservationist* seemed to be fulfilled on a regional level; but in South Africa its price was made clear. The explosion of the Soweto Revolt of 1976 indicated just how tortuous the path of change was going to be, at the same time thrusting the position of dissident whites into radical ambiguity; the easy mood of celebration of just a few years earlier was dramatically displaced.

In *Burger's Daughter* and *July's People* Gordimer therefore comes down from the symbolic plane of *The Conservationist*, and what she attempts to do is assess whether there can be a role for whites in the context of Soweto and after, and what the practical implications of such a role might be. The two novels are in some ways very different; Rosa Burger, in *Burger's Daughter*, comes from an official and conspicuous political tradition; Maureen Smales, in *July's People*, is amongst the most ordinary of Gordimer's characters, politically considered. But the underlying themes of the two novels unite them, at the same time suggesting new developments in Nadine Gordimer's consciousness of history. Both are deeply concerned with the climactic historical moment that Gordimer's fiction increasingly seems to be 'waiting for': the moment of revolution in South Africa. And both of them deal with the subject of revolution by scrutinizing its effect on the 'subject': Rosa Burger in *Burger's Daughter* and Maureen Smales in *July's People*. Dealing with social transformation as it affects the individual is the primary way in which Gordimer's novels develop a consciousness of history. And it may be that the future that is written here, especially in *July's People*, is the ultimate subject of Gordimer's historical consciousness.

II
Burger's Daughter

It is, however, history as a sense of the past, that for the first time, enters Gordimer's work in her seventh novel, *Burger's Daughter*, published in 1979.[2] Also for the first time she concerns herself with an obviously recognizable public figure. This dual interest appears in the novel in its investigation of Lionel Burger, Rosa Burger's father. For, both positively and negatively, Rosa's career is measured out in the novel in relation to that of her father; and her father was a man with a significant, though fictional, personal history. Born an Afrikaner of staunch nationalist stock, Lionel Burger had 'betrayed' his people in becoming a member of the Communist Party of South Africa (CPSA – later SACP) in the late 1920s. Involved in the ideological swings of the Party at that time and in the decade following, and in the campaigns of the 1940s and 1950s, Burger had remained a member of its Central Committee when the Party dissolved itself in the face of the Suppression of Communism Act, and went underground. Captured in the mid-1960s and sentenced to imprisonment for life, he died in gaol in the early 1970s. His fictional career has therefore coincided with most of the major developments in the revolutionary opposition in South Africa in the twentieth century.

In most of these respects the character of Lionel Burger bears a strong resemblance to the real-life figure of Abram ('Bram') Fischer, one of the most prominent leaders within the SACP, upon whose personal history his career has evidently been based.[3] We have seen that in the mid-1960s Gordimer was very much interested in Fischer;

at the time of his arrest and trial she wrote two articles in which her admiration for his integrity and heroism are evident.[4] This interest comes to the fore again here. Certain details have been changed; Fischer joined the Party somewhat later than Lionel does in the novel, and Lionel Burger is cast as a doctor, whereas Bram Fischer himself was a lawyer. Other particulars, especially in so far as they concern the Fischer family, have been changed in the life of the Burgers, though sometimes only by rearrangement; for example, at one stage the Fischers took into their household a young black child, the niece of a servant; in the novel this is changed into the figure of Baasie/Zwelinzima, the son of a political colleague, whom the Burgers take in.[5]

But in the end it is not the details that matter. Primarily Gordimer has been concerned to capture the *spirit* a man like Fischer represented. In this way the Burger home, with its symbolic centrepiece, the swimming pool, represents in the novel the social warmth and historical optimism for which the Fischer household (along with its own swimming pool and 'open house' policy) was renowned. And in drawing in Lionel a charismatic figure – doctrinaire, but first and foremost full of what Rosa at the end of the novel considers to be his 'sublimity' – the figure of Fischer most of all appears.

The concept of typification should by now pose no problems for this study. In being concerned to capture the spirit rather than the details of Fischer's life, Gordimer has been after a specific typification: notwithstanding whatever faults the Burgers may exhibit, of the very best heritage there has been in the white revolutionary tradition. Nevertheless, in so far as Burger *is* based on Fischer, Gordimer has extended her usual practice of close observation in the present, into historical research of the past. Not only has she made direct use of basic political and historical texts (as we shall see) but she also undertook interviews with people connected with Fischer and his times.[6] So the figure of Burger acts as a bridge in the novel between fact and fiction, and past and present, as the methods of the novelist and a more orthodox historian coincide.

This does not mean that Gordimer's view of the past is somehow 'neutral'. We have seen the role that ideology has played in her fiction so far, and in *Burger's Daughter* it enters again, though ultimately by no means in anything like simple fashion. It first becomes apparent in the novel's view of the Communist Party, to which its response is to some extent mixed. Subtly, for example, a distinction is drawn between communist doctrine and communist performance. In contrast to the usual basis upon which such a distinction is made, however, the communist performance in South Africa is, if anything, seen to be superior to its doctrine. Where Rosa rehearses the 'litany' (her word) of Party dogma, the mood is frequently – though not stridently – ironical; on the other hand, it is demonstrated in the novel that the historical record of the SACP is a proud one.

In her own commentary on the novel Gordimer has suggested why a figure such as Lionel Burger should have joined the Communist Party. In the late 1920s when he did so, she has pointed out that there was no other political party in South Africa that incorporated blacks into its membership and leadership as equals, and envisioned them as such in the running of the country.[7] This is a fundamental good faith, the novel suggests, which the Communist Party kept up throughout its history. If this is so, then the basis of the novel's (and perhaps Gordimer's own) approval is clear. It is primarily a human and democratic approval; the Party's human record is affirmed, and its politics only at the 'non-ideological' level of performance. This is most definite in the figure of Burger; for where he, as representative of the revolutionary tradition, is shown in his most favourable light, it is because of his magnificent qualities as a human being: his warmth, generosity and dedication. In this regard the novel's respect for him is entirely unambiguous, and so in an important way – though it is by no means exaggerated – theory is separated from practice; the novel's reading of the past is selective. It is thus not entirely surprising that one of the only unfavourable reviews *Burger's Daughter* received appeared in the *African Communist*, official organ of the SACP.[8]

Although the character of Lionel Burger bears a significant resemblance to the real-life figure of Bram Fischer, Gordimer's novel is not about Lionel Burger himself, but about 'Burger's daughter', Rosa. In this respect there would be little point in attempting to trace any 'real-life' parallels between the book and Fischer's family, though parallels exist. To assume that these are what are finally important for the figure of Rosa, however, is to miss the central thrust of the novel's concerns. For in Rosa, more so than in the case of Lionel, Gordimer has given an even clearer example – perhaps the clearest in all her novels – of her practice of typification at work; a particular social

'space' has been carefully constructed for the imaginative exploration of the historical possibilities and necessities applying to a
certain kind of figure in a given situation. At this level Gordimer is
primarily concerned with the predicament facing the inheritor of
a revolutionary tradition in the context of South Africa in the
mid-1970s. Precisely because Lionel Burger is a recognizable type of
historical figure, this is what he enables Gordimer to explore most
imaginatively through Rosa. But for the same reason Rosa herself
does not depend on any correspondence with living persons; there
is a sliding scale of typification in the novel – from Burger, who
establishes the historical situation, to Rosa, through whom its
implications are examined. It is, finally, because Gordimer is
concerned with the deepest internalities of Rosa's existence on the
one hand, and the broadest of social and historical themes on the
other, that the figure of Rosa far transcends whatever documentary-
like parallels exist, which ultimately function only to set the basic
context of her struggle.

By an apparent paradox, considering its overall framework, one of
the major themes of *Burger's Daughter* concerns a challenge to the
whole idea of political or historical commitment. On one level this is
conducted through the novel's categories of analysis. Thus along
with Marx, who stands behind the text of *Burger's Daughter* as a kind
of symbolic analytical figurehead, are two others: Freud and, less so,
Christ.

On occasion Lionel Burger is compared to Christ, and it becomes
apparent that, if there is any meaning at all to a Christ-figure in South
Africa, it is likely to be found in a character such as Lionel Burger.
Also, the phrase that Rosa most frequently (and ironically) uses to
describe the Party members is that of 'the faithful', as if they belonged
to a religion. This kind of interest does not proceed much beyond the
realm of analogy in the novel, however, and is only of minor concern.

More important to *Burger's Daughter* is the figure of Freud.
A Freudian discourse is first represented in the vicarious, and
degraded, form of Conrad, the self-absorbed hippie with whom Rosa
takes up, and for whom the entire experience of the world can be
reduced to two words, 'sex' and 'death'. But at a deeper level, an
intriguing attempt is made in the novel to psychoanalyse political
commitment itself. In meeting Marisa Kgosana, activist wife of an
imprisoned African leader, Rosa recognizes just how much the
strictly political dedication of her family was mediated by the

sensuality and warmth that Marisa both embodies and represents, acting as an unconscious physical and emotional attraction for whites. Marisa is physically the promise of 'return', of reintegration, which is at once a subjective and objective issue in South Africa. As Rosa says, addressing Conrad in her mind, the Burger household was 'closer to reaching its kind of reality through your kind of reality than I understood' (p. 135).

But the novel's psychoanalytic politics go deeper than this. The basic organizing motif of the text is that of the family; we see Rosa not only in relation to her father, but also in relation to her surrogate mother, Katya, in France; and the relationship between Rosa and Conrad is presented in what are finally incestuous terms, as if they were brother and sister. The Communist Party itself is presented as if it were a 'family' (this was in fact the code name for the SACP when it was underground) but it is one in which Rosa is always regarded as a 'daughter'. *Burger's Daughter* might then be regarded as a *Bildungsroman* with a difference, in which Rosa is eventually expelled from the womb-like infantilization she is subjected to from so many sources into the mature acceptance of her own life history (which of necessity leads her into another kind of womb, the prison cell).

Judie Newman has shown that the most important 'family relationship' of the novel politically is also a psychological one – it is that between Rosa and Baasie, the black boy who had been her virtual brother. Brought into the Burger household as a child because of his own father's political involvement, he and Rosa had taken baths together, discovered the world together, slept together in the same bed. Yet this is a sibling relationship in which primary issues had remained unresolved. For it too had been an 'infantile' relationship, held forever in amber in Rosa's mind, as it were, due to the fact that Baasie had been removed from the Burger 'safe' environment when his father took him away. There are unresolved questions of sexual displacement, and there is a basic problem of projection; Baasie has remained a construct in Rosa's mind, and a childish construct at that, something of an eternal playmate or plaything. Drawing on psychological and cultural theories of colonialism, in particular Mannoni's *Prospero and Caliban*,[9] which Gordimer had been reading at the time, Newman then argues that this forms the basis of Rosa's political development. Whereas blacks had never been truly 'other' for her, by the end of the novel Rosa has reached the point where they are objects neither of mental

175

projection nor of displacement, but exist fully in their own right. This allows her own authentic political re-engagement.[10]

If this is so – and the argument is in many respects a fascinating and persuasive one – then much of the force of this exploration in the novel must derive from its own historical context in the second half of the 1970s. We shall see that the primary phenomenon to which *Burger's Daughter* responded in this period was the movement of Black Consciousness and its culmination, the Soweto Revolt. Yet as we saw in the previous chapter, the primary question Black Consciousness posed for whites who were politically involved was that of their authenticity. Despite their outward protestations, Black Consciousness proponents argued, at certain levels – most likely including subconscious levels – whites, no matter what their political persuasion, still participated in deep-rooted patterns of white supremacy.

In the late 1970s Gordimer showed herself much exercised by the question of 'white consciousness' as a response to Black Consciousness. This by no means had anything to do with a white racist response; on the contrary, as a term that was in currency at the time, especially among white students, in its very phrasing it accepted the point the Black Consciousness movement was making. It primarily denoted an attempt by whites to transcend the horizon of even an unwilling complicity in the patterns of supremacy by recognizing the real possibility of its existence, and thereby being able to construct an authentic alternative.[11] *Burger's Daughter* can be seen as a fictional way of working out the same problem. Thus, the only way in which the novel, and Rosa as a character, can avoid the accusation of even a subconscious participation in the supremacist syndrome is to internalize this accusation by first displaying it, then analysing and eradicating it. Moreover, *Burger's Daughter* does so in explicitly psychoanalytical terms, which in one respect indicates just how seriously it takes the problem with which it is dealing. The novel's explorations in this area have a certain autonomy and are of great interest in their own right. At the same time, seeing them in this wider context is to analyse the novel's own psychoanalysis, within an historical framework. In this view, the pressure applied by the challenge of Black Consciousness added force to the novel's researches into the unconscious of a white political response, making Rosa's development to some degree hinge on the eradication of deeply embedded subconscious patterns.

The idea of political commitment comes under even more direct challenge in *Burger's Daughter* in the figure of Rosa herself. For much of the course of the novel Rosa is in straightforward revolt against both her historical heritage and the demands of her current situation. After her father's death, rejecting what she regards as the oversimplifications of Communist Party ideology – and, more immediately, rejecting her father himself, who had made her deny her own individuality in favour of political needs – Rosa opts for what she has never had: the experience of a private life. Considering her own only past experience of love, she remembers how she subjected herself to her father's wishes by undertaking a pretended betrothal to a political prisoner in order to carry messages more easily back and forward from prison. Rosa is not scandalized by her past performance; as she says, in her family 'prostitutes' were regarded as victims of necessity while certain social orders lasted (p. 68). But what lay behind her pretence was an even deeper one, for in fact Rosa *really* loved this prisoner – something that out of exigency and sensitivity she never allowed anyone else to know, neither her parents nor her 'betrothed' himself.[12] There is no great sentimentalization of such issues in the novel, and part of their force is to indicate that in the South African political context sentimentality is an inadmissible luxury. Nevertheless, for Rosa herself it means that she has never explored a private existence. The need now to do this determines her to go to Europe, to leave the site of all these problems, the site of revolutionary struggle itself. In this her motivation is plain enough; the keyword Rosa uses to describe her reason for going is that of 'defection'. Quite simply Rosa Burger goes to Europe to learn how to 'defect' from her father and the historical legacy he has handed on to her.

Adding to her feelings in this matter is the sense that Lionel's ideology is ultimately inadequate to cope with the complexities of existence as such and, particularly for Rosa, the complexities of existence in South Africa. This becomes evident in two separate scenes in the novel where Rosa confronts the human condition in its barest and simultaneously almost abstract forms. The first occurs at lunch time in one of Johannesburg's city parks, where a hobo, sitting on one of the benches near Rosa, suddenly dies where he is, without ceremony, as it were, in public; this to Rosa seems to signify the blunt and blank realities of life – and death – which are beyond the scope of a purely political framework to comprehend.

The second scene occurs when Rosa is returning to Johannesburg from Soweto and she comes across what seems to her to be the very incarnation of cruelty and despair. She sees a black man, violent in drunken anger and tiredness, repeatedly whipping a donkey that can no longer pull the cart in which a woman and child sit starkly terrified.[13] Social and political conditions have conspired to produce this scene, but to Rosa what she is witnessing appears to be an existential essence and total or, as she puts it, the 'sum of suffering' (p. 210). She identifies it with all the suffering there has ever been, including that of her own country:

> the camps, concentration, labour, resettlement, the Siberias of snow or sun, the lives of Mandela, Sisulu, Mbeki, Kathrada, Kgosana, gull-picked on the Island, Lionel propped wasting to his skull between two warders, the deaths by questioning, bodies fallen from the height of John Vorster Square, deaths by dehydration, babies degutted by enteritis in 'places' of banishment, the lights beating all night on the faces of those in cells.
>
> (p. 208)

Precisely because the scene has such a vast significance, however, Rosa feels powerless to act to end it. Also, it appears that the only way she could intervene to stop the immediate cruelty at hand would be to exploit her position of white authority; in this case she will be yet one more white who evidently cares for animals more than she does for people. This need not necessarily be true; it is easy to think of action Rosa might take that would show her concern for the people involved as much as for the animal, and there is no reason why she should not use the power she has to help. But Rosa simply feels that things have got beyond her. Confounded by the implications of her situation she just does not know what role to play. Absorbing the fact of her own impotence, she recognizes that she no longer knows 'how to live in Lionel's country' (p. 210). This is another way of saying that she is defecting from politics in search of other ways of understanding and living out her life. The scene acts as a final spur to send her on her way to Europe.

The idea of social engagement is thus brought under severe test in the novel. Freud is posed strongly against Marx, existence is posed against history; and Rosa is moved to 'defect'. Looking back on Gordimer's other novels it is clear that this procedure of contestation is very much an intrinsic component of her work – ever since Helen, in *The Lying Days*, took her own decision to 'defect' from South Africa to Europe. (In this respect the donkey-whipping scene in *Burger's Daughter* functions in much the same way as the killing of the man in the May Day riots; both episodes indicate the central character's historical exclusion.) This theme of defection is present in the other novels as well. From a moral point of view Toby Hood in *A World of Strangers* is a defector from social responsibility for much of that novel; Jessie Stilwell opts for 'existence' at the price of politics in *Occasion for Loving*; for most of *The Late Bourgeois World* Elizabeth believes that social engagement is no longer possible; and Bray in *A Guest of Honour* is faced with a further option of 'defection' upon his return to his African country. For Gordimer, then, a 'sense of history' is itself a site of struggle; it is by no means easily given, but comes under challenge again and again.

In *Burger's Daughter*, as in the other novels, this contestation is itself only a part of the overall movement of the work. In Europe Rosa is on the point of finding the personal fulfilment she has never had. She falls in love, and is making plans to defect on a permanent basis. But precisely at this moment (for good historical reasons, as we shall see) she comes to understand that it is after all imperative for her to return to South Africa and take up the social engagement she had tried to avoid.

And so the overall pattern of *Burger's Daughter* takes on a dialectical form. In the first movement we have Rosa, together with her revolutionary inheritance; in the second she rejects this inheritance in favour of her personal life; in the third she re-unites with that inheritance, simultaneously finding her personal identity in becoming socially and historically committed. From one point of view this procedure of contestation can be seen as a method of self-probationary verification; only through having challenged the category of historical engagement to its utmost can there be any certainty as to its necessity when at last it is confirmed. It is the historical equivalent of a philosophical procedure of 'methodical doubt', which is in the end all that can verify what is doubted in the first place. Furthermore, this pattern of self-probation is recognizably present in all of Gordimer's novels; after the challenge against a social and historical destiny (even Mehring opts for a private seclusion on his farm) comes the confirmation of its final necessity. This pattern of challenge and probation must therefore be considered a major component of the way a 'consciousness of history' is tried and tested in Gordimer's work.

This phenomenon is also revealing from another point of view. It has been suggested before in this study that if Gordimer had not been a writer in South Africa she might have been a different kind of writer. From this standpoint what appears in her work as a procedure of verification looks more like one of renunciation. There are whole dimensions of existence and its understanding that Gordimer recognizes must be surrendered in favour of historical priorities. This can be seen as a direct consequence of living in South Africa, in which history must be seen, for better or for worse, as the category of comprehension that includes all others, and as the dimension of engagement that must take precedence.

In pursuing these themes so far we have dealt very little with the novel's treatment of the present – the area that, overall, appears to be of greatest concern for Nadine Gordimer's consciousness of history in general. The 'present' to which *Burger's Daughter* responded was one of momentous importance. On 16 June 1976 some 15,000 schoolchildren gathered at Orlando West Junior Secondary School in Soweto to protest against the enforced use of Afrikaans as a medium of instruction in certain subjects in black schools. The meeting began with peaceful intentions, but by the time it ended two children had been shot by the police.[14] They were the first of many to follow, for what came after this was one of the most climactic periods of modern South African history, as an unexpected phase of resistance burst with extraordinary intensity. It is impossible here to give a full and detailed account of what came to be known as the Soweto Revolt, since its ramifications were vast as well as geographically dispersed; nevertheless some of its central patterns can be delineated.[15] It was for one thing a sustained episode of cultural as much as political resistance; not only was there the issue of the use of Afrikaans (widely regarded by blacks as the language of their oppression) in schools, but feeding into the revolt as well as burgeoning from it was the Black Consciousness ethos, with its emphases on cultural revival and the assertion of black dignity and identity. It was also, pre-eminently, a revolt of children. For the schoolchildren consciously saw their assertion as being not only against the white state, but also against their parents whom they felt had been passive for too long. This was a revolt that started in schools, spread through schools and sometimes reached the universities, but in which the youth led, and their elders, if anything, followed.

For any (including the government) who thought that a children's eruption could be easily contained, the course of the revolt proved the opposite. Where children confronted the police they often seemed fearless, marching into police bullets. The path of the revolt also spread like wildfire, darting from place to place throughout the country, being quelled here, but then flaring up there, and then back again where it had begun. Scarcely an area of the country was not in some way touched by the Soweto Revolt. In some respects the youthful leadership of the insurrection was not equipped to deal with wider issues of political organization;[16] but also it showed great ingenuity. Thus the Soweto Students Representative Council (SSRC), which led the revolt in Soweto, had a rotating leadership. Partly this was due to necessity, as successive leaders were forced to flee or were taken into detention, but it was due to astuteness as well, since a revolving leadership was that much more difficult to pin down.[17] Nor was the revolt without its successes; it brought down the Urban Bantu Council in Soweto, and some local school-boards; there was a mass resignation of teachers; stay-aways of workers were organized (though there were other failures in relation to migrant workers); both in Cape Town and Johannesburg student marchers penetrated into the city centres.

The impact of the countrywide revolt as a whole is best measured in the fact that it took the full force of the police, with all the resources and laws at its disposal, a good deal more than a year to bring it to an end; indeed they were kept at full stretch for much of that time. When the revolt finally subsided towards the end of 1977 there had been a significant migration of black youth across the borders to join the ANC. On the other hand the toll paid during the uprising was a heavy one. Amongst those who died violently during its course was the Black Consciousness leader Steve Biko, kept naked and manacled in police custody.[18] And the numbers of dead were tragically far greater than this; official (and probably underestimated) counts put the figure at 575 – most of them schoolchildren shot by the police – with some 2,389 wounded.[19] Yet by the time it ended Soweto had become an historical landmark. The quiescence of the previous decade had ended, the tone for the decade to come had been set. The Soweto Revolt had earned a central place in the calendar of resistance in South Africa.

This was the context from which *Burger's Daughter* grew. How was it, how could it all be, transformed into a consciousness of history in Gordimer's fiction? Some of it was translated directly. One striking motif is that of the revolt of children against parents; this occurred in Soweto and this is what Rosa Burger goes through in relation to her father. An added dimension is the feeling in the novel that new forms of struggle are required for new circumstances, that the heritage of the fathers must be evaluated, modified and reformulated; again, this was the immediate import of Soweto. However, if this was the positive impact of the revolt on the novel, there was nevertheless another side. *Burger's Daughter* is inspired by its circumstances; but there is also a sense in which it was sidelined by them. We saw in relation to *The Conservationist* that in as much as the Black Consciousness movement constituted a threat to official white supremacy, it was equally a challenge to white liberalism; for it classed the paternalism it found there with white supremacy itself. But if Black Consciousness was the challenge in theory, then the Soweto Revolt was that challenge in practice. Moreover, it was a challenge not just to liberalism but also to white radicalism. Black children were being shot while white liberals and radicals could at most only look on in horror. Now mountains of words spoken in the past could only seem sickeningly shameful in view of the blood of children running in the streets. If anything seemed to demonstrate the irrelevance of white dissidents on the periphery of the democratic struggle, then that event was the Soweto Revolt.

Ever since the early 1960s Nadine Gordimer had occupied a narrowing margin within the domain of white society. Now that margin itself was qualitatively different; for the whites who occupied it were being rejected in theory and bypassed in fact by their only historical source of relevance, the oppressed black world itself.

Gordimer was deeply affected by these events in the second half of the 1970s. In a speech published in 1977 she said that though rationally she understood Black Consciousness, and even considered it necessary, as an experience she found it 'as wounding as anyone else'[20] (this marked a change from her calmer acceptance of it earlier in the decade). As to those whites who maintained a commitment to an eventual, and authentic, meeting ground of liberation, all they could do, she suggested, was make a 'Pascalian wager' on their commitment.[21] Elsewhere, her response to the events of 1976 was filled with a mood of outrage, horror and impotence. In the aftermath of Soweto she wrote:

We whites do not know how to deal with the fact of this death when

children, in full knowledge of what can happen to them, continue
to go out to meet it at the hands of the law, for which we are solely
responsible, whether we support white supremacy, or, opposing, have
failed to unseat it.[22]

Burger's Daughter is an attempt to deal with the practical and moral
implications of this massive psycho-historical problem. Generated
from this mood, it is a grave examination of what can remain of white
'action' when it has been so fundamentally called into question, and
in what terms such action can be revived.

Black Consciousness is central to this. Its challenge is implicit in
the novel's major themes, but it is represented explicitly as well.
It first enters directly at Fats Mxange's party where some of the
younger blacks reject the class analysis of South Africa offered by the
communist fellow-traveller Orde Greer. Their spokesman, Duma
Dhladhla, angrily dismisses him:

> *This* and *this* should happen and can't happen because of *that* and *that*.
> These theories don't fit us. We are not interested. You've been talking
> this shit before I was born.
>
> (p. 162)

In the novel it is Rosa who is made to confront Black Consciousness in a most direct way. In London, at a party given in honour of
some Frelimo representatives, she comes across Baasie, the little boy
who had once been like a brother to her. She thinks she recognizes
him at the party, but he refuses to acknowledge her. Later that night,
however, he does so, and with a vengeance. After Rosa has gone to
sleep he telephones her; what follows is one of the most powerful
and extraordinary scenes in Gordimer's fiction (see pp. 318–23). He
tells Rosa he is no longer her 'Baasie' – his real name, and the one
Rosa never knew, is Zwelinzima Vulindlela (Zwelinzima meaning
'suffering land'). And Rosa should set no sentimental store by his past
in the Burger household, for this too was not without its ambiguities.
For his part he now bitterly rejects the false brotherhood he had with
Rosa and the (almost literal) paternalism of Lionel, which both set
him aside from the rest of his people in privilege and, at the same
time, he feels, belittled him; the name he was given ('Baasie' – 'Little
Boss') says it all. Most of all he rejects the heritage of Lionel Burger
himself; there are hundreds of black men, including his own father,
who have also died in gaol, often more violently than Lionel (his own
father died of an improbable prison 'suicide'). But the black names
have been forgotten, their heroism remains untold; instead it is white

men, such as Lionel Burger, who get all the accolades and glory. 'Whatever you whites touch,' he tells Rosa, 'it's a takeover'; the Burgers, and Rosa in particular, are no different from any other whites. As Zwelinzima urges her to turn on the lights (she has been speaking to him in the dark) and she confronts the full import of what is happening, Rosa is literally sickened, finally vomiting up the remains of what she has consumed at the party in anguish, shame and anger.

The symbolic significance of this scene is a powerful one in the context of South Africa in the mid-1970s. Here the accusations of Black Consciousness are clearly hitting home. Actions taken with the best of intentions and out of genuine care are rejected as compromised and hypocritical. If a previous generation of whites devoted their best energies and talents to the liberation struggle, they should not expect any gratitude. The allegorical setting of the multi-racial 'family' gives a perfect and exact sense of earlier assumptions of inter-racial harmony and solidarity that were now being ripped apart, as well as the intimate violence aroused by the passions surrounding Black Consciousness.

As far as Rosa and Zwelinzima are concerned, there are also wider resonances. These two inheritors of a previous politics, who in principle are in favour of the same political objectives, are in a sense divided by the history uniting them. They are divided particularly by some of the undeniable insights of Black Consciousness, which Rosa seems merely to have proved in her 'defection' from the struggle. The result is a love-hate relationship between these two 'siblings' of the younger generation, which can be neither consummated nor set aside. In a far advanced form of the irony that contained Jessie and Gideon, Rosa and Zwelinzima face one another on opposite sides of a chasm that, at some level, both are desperate to cross. But in contrast to *Occasion for Loving* (and possibly because of the very effects Gordimer is describing) what emerges from the scene is as a result not entirely negative. For one thing, if Rosa sees Zwelinzima as 'other' by the end of the novel, it is because he, for all his vindictiveness, *forces* her to do exactly that here. Moreover, she, confronting this fact, is then propelled towards her own separateness and assertion. Black Consciousness forces a white reassessment, but also provokes a new dedication; absorbing the impact of all that her encounter with Zwelinzima signifies, the revolt of Rosa's body presages the revolution of her identity once again. The direct challenge that Zwelinzima has levelled determines Rosa to return to South Africa to renew the social commitment her father left off. Taking up physiotherapy work at Baragwanath Hospital in Soweto, she is overtaken by the events of 1976. In this context she once again becomes involved in some form of undisclosed work in the underground, is detained under Section 6 of the Terrorism Act, and finds herself in solitary confinement, much like her father before her.

In the decade after 1976 the movement of Black Consciousness subsided in both intensity and significance, especially in its political forms. At the same time, however, whatever emerged in the after-math of Soweto could never be free of some or other aspect of the Black Consciousness experience. And if one is looking for the classic condensation of what Black Consciousness *meant* at the apogee of its ideological authority, especially to sympathetic whites, then there is possibly no better place to find it than in the scene between Rosa and Zwelinzima. Yet the novel does not simply submit to the Black Consciousness onslaught in its own terms. It is significant that Rosa does again become 'Burger's daughter' at the end of the novel, accepting her family identity and linking up with her father's tradition. If the events of the novel's present, that is to say, have governed its 'remembrance of things past', then its research of that past has by no means been gratuitous. Rather it has scanned a previous history for a definite guideline in the present. Rosa does not become politically re-engaged at the end of the novel in exactly the same terms as her father – for her the fact of suffering is paramount rather than any question of ideology:

> I don't know the ideology.
> It's about suffering.
> How to end suffering.
>
> (p. 332)

But she is acting in the spirit of her father's tradition and reconnect-ing with his heritage. The novel has looked to the past in order to find the only source of inspiration that could be adequate to its present. There are many places it might have looked, but that it found it in Lionel Burger's heritage confirms that *Burger's Daughter* is, despite its ideological qualifications, truly, as Gordimer has said, her most radical novel yet.[23] Fusing the needs of the present with the traditions of the past there is a strong revolutionary alignment in the novel.

One of the ways this alignment enters is in aspects of the novel's form. This should be no surprise; form has consistently been a bearer of historical consciousness in Gordimer's other novels, and in *The Conservationist* was the key to its historical consciousness itself. In its own way *Burger's Daughter* embodies two kinds of formal operation less easily discernible in Gordimer's other writing, but both of which have wider resonances. The first is perhaps unexpected, and concerns form as a matter of *quotation*. *Burger's Daughter* is full of quotation.[24] The most obvious example of this is the pamphlet attributed to the Soweto Students Representative Council (SSRC), which appears in the novel on pp. 346–7. Considered solely within the text there is no way of telling whether the pamphlet is a reproduction of an actual one, or has merely been 'simulated' by Gordimer, but in fact this pamphlet did appear on the streets of Soweto during the Revolt, and has simply been inserted in full into the text.[25] This, in an explicit way, is quotation, and other instances of it abound in the novel. Thus, when Duma Dhladhla says black liberation cannot be divorced from Black Consciousness 'because we cannot be conscious of ourselves and at the same time remain slaves' (p. 164), he is quoting Steve Biko, who expressed the same sentiments in almost exactly the same words.[26] More distantly, as Orde Greer suggests (and as Biko himself acknowledges), Dhladhla is quoting Hegel. Similarly, when Lionel Burger, in his speech from the dock, talks of national liberation as being the primary objective of political struggle in South Africa, and the rest being a matter for the future to settle (p. 26), his words echo those actually spoken by Bram Fischer in his own trial before sentence was passed.[27]

Gordimer's chief written source for *Burger's Daughter*, however, seems to have been Joe Slovo's essay, 'South Africa – no middle road', first published, appropriately enough, in 1976.[28] This source is particularly interesting in that Joe Slovo has himself been a long-standing member of the SACP, and his essay was an historical review of South Africa from the point of view of tactics required in the revolutionary struggle; as such it has provided many of the most memorable encapsulations within the text of *Burger's Daughter*.[29] When Rosa Burger talks of the small group of white revolutionaries who are supposed to have solved the 'contradiction between black consciousness and class consciousness' (p. 126), the phrase comes directly from Slovo, although the context in which he writes it has been changed.[30] Similarly, when she talks of the sixth underground conference of the SACP in 1962, at which Party ideology was finally evolved in the form of the thesis that 'it is just as impossible to conceive of workers' power separated from national liberation as it is to conceive of true national liberation separated from the destruction of capitalism' (p. 126), this account comes verbatim from Slovo.[31]

In the novel's numerous quotations – of which these are only the most obvious, there is sometimes – as in the examples just cited – an oblique suggestion that there may be quotation involved. Elsewhere quotations are clearly marked, even though their source is seldom given; on yet other occasions quotations are not indicated in any way at all.[32] In one elaboration of the novel's quotational gymnastics, a statement by Marx, given in a footnote by Slovo, appears in unattributed quotation marks as a central sentiment in Lionel Burger's speech from the dock.[33] Elsewhere, Marx, Lenin and others are quoted regularly.

In this way a textual collage is built up in *Burger's Daughter*, cutting across temporal, geographical, political and ideological space. Once again in Gordimer's work, however, there is a distinct logic to her fictional procedures that goes beyond any pure formalism. Regarding the SSRC pamphlet, Gordimer has explained why it entered the novel as quotation. The document was a necessary part of the book as a whole, she maintained; she presented it as it was because her 'stylistic integrity as a writer' demanded it:

> I reproduced the document exactly as it was ... because I felt it expressed, more eloquently and honestly than any pamphlet I could have invented, the spirit of the young people who wrote it.[34]

There is a particular functionalism at work here. If the original document is good enough, there is no reason, for the sake of convention, to invent another one that looks exactly like it; and the same may be said, one supposes, of the phrases reproduced from Slovo's essay. This functionalism is also a method particularly suited to the revolutionary subject matter dealt with by the novel; spare and economic, it not only introduces the actual mood of the time (in the case of the SSRC pamphlet) but from the point of view of authorship it overrides the conventions of bourgeois property relations – in this sense 'ownership' of the documents or phrases used. The novel opts for use-value in preference to exchange-value; what is important is that the words are reproduced, and not the exchange of ownership rights denoted by the 'purchase' of textual attribution. Also, to put words into the mouths of the SSRC leaders would be to fall guilty of the sin of patronization; instead the novel lets them speak for themselves.

This is the most important function fulfilled by the quotations that Gordimer uses. They give voice to a certain social or historical presence, and this in its own authentic form. Thus, the Soweto students are represented in *Burger's Daughter* in their own voice; equally so is the historical analysis of Slovo. This is not to say that the novel, or Gordimer herself, necessarily approves of or confirms the import of the sentiments quoted. Sometimes they are put in an ironical context (although this is invariably muted); sometimes, as in the case of the pamphlet, presented with complete dispassion. But this always means that the reader is given a chance to make up his or her own mind. Whatever irony there may be apart, Gordimer has given SACP doctrine a chance to claim what respect it deserves by the force of its own arguments. By this method, furthermore, she has allowed her novel to act as a vehicle for presenting sentiments, documents and opinions that would otherwise be unavailable in South Africa – a function traditionally fulfilled by fiction in oppressive societies – and this is the final legitimacy for abstracting the quotations from her various sources. In this light Gordimer's novel has played an important role, especially in a country such as South Africa, where access to certain ideas and even to certain forms of thinking is so overwhelmingly constrained. In political terms, too, quotation in this form is not to be underestimated; there are few other ways that Joe Slovo, as an official inside the SACP, could have 'got into' South Africa.[35]

Although quotation is used in an emphatic form in *Burger's Daughter*, it enables us to recognize an aspect of Gordimer's fiction less marked in her other novels: that all of them, either explicitly or implicitly, employ a method of 'quotation'. In *A Guest of Honour* it is perhaps most obvious of all; Fanon is quoted directly, Shinza alludes to Cabral and Mweta to Senghor, Nkrumah is an underlying presence. At this level Gordimer's work reminds us of what she has always insisted, that her novels are also novels of ideas[36] (all of them, as we remember, are prefaced by epigraphs from Yeats, Thomas Mann, Turgenev, Gramsci and so on). Even in the text of *A World of Strangers* there is, in a different way, a form of quotation. When Steven Sitole says he is 'sick of feeling half a man', it is not necessarily as if Gordimer is reproducing someone's actual words. Rather, these words are representative of the sentiments that could well have been expressed (and sometimes possibly were) in the kind of situation Steven inhabits. In this sense quotation in Gordimer's work is *typification* at the level of verbal representation, and its essential function is to represent a social or historical voice in its most intense and resonant form. Conversely, as was suggested in that novel, typification may be thought of as a social 'quotation'; in this case the character, though concretized and individualized in his own 'voice', is also a generalized reference drawn from, and alluding to, broader social patterns.

A second formal aspect of *Burger's Daughter* invites examination; this can be approached obliquely by first considering the novel's reception in South Africa. When *Burger's Daughter* was first published there it was immediately embargoed, and then soon after banned. Some time after that it had what was at that stage the unique experience of being unbanned due to an appeal by the Director of Publications against the decision of his own Committee. All this is dealt with – and some of the reasons for this strange turnabout analysed – in a booklet that Gordimer later produced, along with the collaboration of some others, entitled *What Happened to 'Burger's Daughter'.*[37] Many reasons were given for the original banning, but all of them seemed to centre upon the chief one, which was, in the Committee's own words, that 'the authoress uses Rosa's story as a pad from which to launch a blistering and full scale attack on the Republic of South Africa'.[38] In its banal way the Committee was perhaps trying to be poetic in its suppression of Gordimer's novel.

This decision has been examined by Robert Green, who has demonstrated its essential absurdity (not difficult to do on the grounds of common sense, but Green has been more sophisticated).[39] His primary objections are set up on formal grounds; the Censorship Board, he maintains, made the fundamental critical error of identifying the politics of the author with the politics of her text. Over and above this, he argues, there is in fact no necessary politics of the text *at all* in *Burger's Daughter*; this can be shown by exploring its narrative structure. Thus, in contrast to *A Guest of Honour*, in which there is a single narrative voice, in *Burger's Daughter* Green shows there are five. In his ordering these are: (1) Rosa's internal narrative, which is by definition identical with her view of the world; (2) a sympathetic third-person narrative

189

that focuses on Rosa; (3) a third-person narrative in which Rosa is presented neutrally and dispassionately; (4) a narrative hostile to Rosa (usually that of a Security Police dossier); and (5) a narrative in which Rosa disappears altogether, as in the SSRC pamphlet. In the light of this compound structure Green argues it is impossible to claim that any one view of Rosa triumphs, or has priority in the text. Consequently, there can be no single 'point of view' in the novel, and Green believes he has shown

> the ineffectuality of any reading of *Burger's Daughter* that approaches it as a 'univocal' text, as a novel that simply expounds the author's own views. The plurality of narratives ensures instead that no single straightforward judgement on Rosa Burger is tenable. Only a novel of such stature can persuade the reader that Rosa's dilemma was at once massive and historically marginal; that her father's political devotion was both saintly and sterile.[40]

Effective as Green's argument is in showing the central narrative features of *Burger's Daughter*, however, it may reveal some mistakes in interpreting them. First, Green has possibly underestimated the number of narrative voices involved in the novel, or at least the degree to which they modulate through, or are interfused with, one another; sometimes this occurs within the course of a single sentence.[41] A second and more important point is that Green is, in a sense, hoist by his own formal petard; for there is no reason in principle why a multivocal text should be more 'objective' than a simple third-person narrative. Both alike are simply conventions, and (given certain technical skills) the one form may be as potentially manipulable as the other, or similarly employed in self-effacing exploration by the writer. Both, after all, are generally written by only one author; in this regard it seems likely that the differences in Gordimer's methods of narration are ones of degree rather than of kind. *A Guest of Honour*, despite its 'univocal' narration, is clearly intended to be as 'objective' as possible; nor can it, any more than *Burger's Daughter*, be regarded as a novel that 'simply expounds its author's own views'. As to the supposed social complicity of the realist text *à la* Barthes, that is another question, but even then, as we saw in the case of *A World of Strangers*, there are not likely to be any straightforward answers.

As far as *Burger's Daughter* is concerned, from another point of view Green's argument can, and must be turned on its head (though once again here he has provided the basis for further investigation).

For what Green sees as the construction of an indeterminacy in *Burger's Daughter* by means of a narrative plurality can, from a different angle, be seen as the construction of an *overdeterminacy* instead. The epigraph to *Burger's Daughter* comes from Lévi-Strauss: 'I am the place in which something has occurred.' As a statement what that epigraph connotes is inevitability, necessity and, primarily, the *objective* construction of identity. In this sense we have seen that Rosa Burger's identity has been objectively constructed. For most of her life, except in her revolt against her father, Rosa's private existence has been 'empty', responding only to objective political needs, and shaped by her family around her; in her return to South Africa she once again places her identity at the disposal of such needs. In this respect, however, the empty individual, like Walter Benjamin's *Unmensch*, is not the most indeterminate, but on the contrary the most *determinate*, subject, constructed only by the objective forces of her historical situation.[42]

Moreover, of this objective construction the convention of the novel's narrative plurality stands as the formal sign. It is not that Rosa Burger has been seen from so many points of view as to become dispersed and indistinct in her commitment. Rather, seeing her from every point of view has merely led to an apparently necessary outcome: that this is the destiny Rosa was born to, that this is the commitment she must undertake. Certainly, her commitment has been seen to have many sides; but then all those sides accumulate towards that commitment. Like a sculpture around which there is circumambience, the novel, in 'walking around' Rosa in its narrative plurality, has increased rather than decreased her final concreteness. Its procedures have set up the narrative 'space' in which Rosa has occurred, defined (if not filled) from both inside and outside, and proceeding towards her historically necessary destiny.

As Green points out, this does not by itself mean that any specific political ideology has been necessarily affirmed in *Burger's Daughter* (in this regard there is an interesting tension in the novel between its post-humanist construction of Rosa, its humanist appropriation of Lionel Burger's tradition and its basic revolutionary alignment). But what has primarily been affirmed is Rosa's sense of historical engagement; in the context of the Soweto Revolt this engagement alone has had final meaning for her. This has been explored not only thematically but, as we have seen, also formally. From every point of view, it seems, this is the step Rosa must take. It is a sense of necessary engagement that has been underwritten by the novel itself.

Here *Burger's Daughter* once again allows us to discern a basic pattern within Gordimer's novels as a whole. For all of Gordimer's novels are geared towards constructing an overdeterminacy in this sense. All of them are designed to find out what is absolutely necessary for their time and situation; to test it from every possible point of view, and by thematic challenge. And all of them, as we have seen, confirm that necessity all the more forcefully when it is discovered. This, fundamentally, is the historic *form* underlying Gordimer's novels, and the basic disposition underlying the historical consciousness of her work.

Rosa Burger finds her own necessity when she decides to return to South Africa, and then becomes involved in the underground struggle. The final vision of the novel, as in Gordimer's others, has a good deal to do with its sense of history; its resolution contains a perfect embodiment not only of Rosa's position, but also of that of the novel itself. Literally Rosa ends up in solitary confinement, but she is solitary in a different way as well. We have seen that 'Burger's daughter' reconnects with the tradition of her father. On the other hand, in the aftermath of Black Consciousness and the Soweto Revolt there can be no special glory attaching to her situation. In contrast to Lionel, whose role as a white leader had been pre-eminent, after the events of 1976 Rosa's can at best be secondary, supportive, peripheral. And so there is a far greater solitude than ever her father knew. In emphasis of this the narrative as a whole begins to withdraw from Rosa towards the end of the novel. Whereas up till now we have had fairly consistent access to her thoughts and feelings (despite the novel's narrative plurality) this domain is now sealed off; even what Rosa has done in the underground remains undisclosed.

It may be suggested that this withdrawal embodies a recognition relating to Gordimer's own position; if the novel cannot speak what Rosa has done, this is because fiction cannot do what Rosa might speak. By this separation, however, Rosa's dignity and heroism are only increased. Both she and the narrative withdraw to their respective solitudes, and perhaps from our point of view 'solitude' is an exact image of the position of the white radical in South Africa in the years immediately following Soweto. There is in addition a slight but distinct note of elegy in the novel's final view of Rosa; here mood is possibly as sure an index of historical consciousness as anything else. But none the less, for Rosa Burger in her way, and for Gordimer's novel in its own, there is the affirmation of an historical synthesis: of the inheritance of Lionel Burger in its post-Soweto form. The revolutionary 'subject' of *Burger's Daughter* has been constructed.

III

July's People

'I live at 6,000 feet,' wrote Nadine Gordimer in 1983, 'in a society whirling, stamping, swaying with the force of revolutionary change.'[43] After what we have seen in *Burger's Daughter*, the image as presented here is perhaps apocalyptic, unsuited to the slow, checked progress of South Africa towards liberation, beset on every side by difficulties, contradictions and reversals. Yet it is not the fact of revolution that engages Gordimer in this vision – the actual revolutionary moment – but a metaphor of deeper patterns of everyday change already at work in her society, and the psychological and cultural tempo of transformation. It is an implicit assertion that revolution is a process, and that in South Africa the process has begun.

The title of the article in which the above statement appears – 'Living in the interregnum' – comes from the Italian Marxist thinker Antonio Gramsci: 'The old is dying and the new cannot be born; in this interregnum there arises a great diversity of morbid symptoms.' The quotation from Gramsci also forms the epigraph to Gordimer's eighth novel, *July's People*, published in 1981;[44] and this is what the work is about. It is a novel that lives 'in the interregnum' between one order and the next; and it is the 'morbid symptoms' of Gramsci's formulation that the text, heightening the revolutionary context, both emerges from and dwells upon. In a subtle interplay of present and future in the novel the 'regime' of the present – cultural, political, semiotic – is exploded, and that of the future addressed. The novel, arrived at a dead-end of history, searches for the only way out.

In a way this fictional development corresponded to Nadine Gordimer's situation in the 1980s. By now the trauma (for whites) of Black Consciousness was passing, though its lessons had been irreversibly learnt. After the climactic year of the Soweto Revolt and its subsidence, a new historical momentum was developing as people sought once again for other terms and methods in which to continue the struggle. This ranged from a new and growing black trade union movement to the plethora of political organizations emerging out of and diverging from the Black Consciousness era. (As the decade progressed the ANC once again reasserted itself with a continuing commitment to what was now called 'non-' and not 'multi-racialism'.)

In a modest way this search for a new beginning applied also to the white writer. For if the image of Rosa Burger in solitary confinement stands as a striking symbol of the alienated condition of a dissident white consciousness in the aftermath of Soweto, then in the years after *Burger's Daughter* was published it seems that Nadine Gordimer too was seeking for some kind of revival and re-engagement. One area in which she again became involved was in the campaign against censorship. Apart from bringing out her booklet laying bare the political motivations behind the banning and unbanning of *Burger's Daughter*, she took every opportunity to castigate the system. Censorship, she declared, was, as a weapon of thought control, as much a part of the armoury of apartheid 'as the hippo cars [heavily armoured police vans] that went through the streets of Soweto in '76'.[45] Elsewhere she dissected the new strategy behind the differential treatment of black and white writers by the censors, especially in terms of their reading publics. Whereas white writing was chiefly 'critical and protestant' in mood, black writing was on the contrary 'inspirational', and therefore much more of a danger to the state. But no amount of preferential treatment would accommodate her to the political and literary scandal of censorship.[46]

But if Gordimer was seeking for a way out of solitude, then she could in the end do this only through her writing, and the signs are that in these years she was once more thinking deeply about the commitments and responsibilities of being a writer in South Africa. The basic problem was this: how could a white writer (or any writer for that matter) authentically become part of a developing or new social order? What would be the terms of that integration? Appropriately, considering her vocation, Gordimer began thinking about the development of a new political culture as a matter of some priority. 'The nature of art in South Africa today is primarily determined by the conflict of material interests in South African society,' she wrote.[47] This was a long way from the view of art informing *The Lying Days*, and a measure of the radicalization Gordimer had undergone in the intervening years.

Given this fact of fracture, the objective for Gordimer – the task of South African writers, both black and white – could only be to make their way towards a single common culture of the future. Such a culture would ultimately be precipitated only by fundamental economic and political change. Equally, however, one of the tests of real social liberation would be whether such a culture had been formed, for only this would ensure that all vestigial forms within the heritage of oppression were eradicated, and that a new social identity could evolve. Black writers, if they remained true to their writing, would inevitably speak with the voice of the people; white writers must find their own more difficult way. But it could only be in terms of this commitment to a future common culture that South African writers could become true 'apprentices of freedom'.[48] Gordimer's view of a 'single common culture' here perhaps needs some refinement; while its attractions as against the fragmenting effects of apartheid are plain, whether a unified national culture as an alternative is either desirable or possible needs questioning. Still this was a central problem on Gordimer's mind, and one that she felt involved certain obligations. In her 'Living in the interregnum' article she pointed out that what passed for reality in South Africa had long been unreality for her. As a writer her work found itself increasingly answerable to the new order 'struggling to be born'.[49]

Such then was the logic whereby Gordimer's fiction was drawn to considerations of the future, as her short stories of this time showed. 'A lion on the freeway' compresses symbolically intimations of liberation. 'A soldier's embrace' deals with the ironies, and betrayal, of a white liberal commitment when liberation comes at last to a southern African country. 'Oral history' examines the same themes in a black village caught up in the bush war.[50] At the time of their writing both these latter stories concerned what was becoming the historical present in Zimbabwe (which gained its independence in 1980), but which still remained in the future for South Africa. But in *July's People* these themes of irony and betrayal – and even the setting in the bush – are transferred to South Africa itself. Not only is *July's People* the first of Gordimer's novels explicitly to be set in the South African future, but it is set at the critical future moment itself: the moment prophesied by *The Conservationist*, heralded by 'A lion

195

on the freeway', and towards which Rosa Burger's vision strains – the moment, at last, of revolution.

The novel can be seen as an act of preparing for the future, and in the cultural sphere it seems to take decisive new steps. All of Gordimer's previous novels deal with the question of culture, but they tend to do so in a large and abstract kind of way, and generally treat it as a question of *absence*; in depicting the alienation of European culture in Africa, its social and environmental identity is indicated essentially as a lack. In *July's People*, however, Gordimer goes a step further, subjecting the features of white bourgeois culture in South Africa to a radical and penetrating analysis.

Maureen Smales, the central character of the novel, suddenly displaced from city to countryside, and from one set of values to another in the revolutionary context, considers how relative all the old absolutes had been. She had always placed ultimate value on the inviolable status and rights of personal relationships. Yet who decided what those rights and status were? 'We,' thinks Maureen,

> understand the sacred power and rights of sexual love as formulated in master bedrooms, and motels with false names in the register. Here, the sacred power and rights of sexual love are as formulated in a wife's hut, and a backyard room in a city. The balance between desire and duty is – has to be – maintained quite differently in accordance with the differences in the lovers' place in the economy. These alter the way of dealing with the experience, and so the experience itself. The *absolute nature* she and her kind were scrupulously just in granting to everybody was no more than the price of the master bedroom and the clandestine hotel tariff.
>
> (p. 65)

Instead of the simple opposition between European and African culture presented in the previous novels, here the problem is more intricate and more disillusioned. What Gordimer gives us is a political economy of culture where 'meaning' is never far from 'means'. And the ambit of this political economy seems to know no existential bounds. As all her abstractions 'harden into the concrete' Maureen realizes that even death is a purchase. One of her husband's business partners could afford his at the price of a private aeroplane in which he crashed. For July's mother, sinking to earth in her poverty-stricken old age, it is an altogether different story.

Equally important in the novel is that if one culture is shown now in its demise, another appears to be taking its place. In *July's People* Gordimer turns to the *details* of culture and shows a new world in the making. Both Maureen and her husband Bam, having fled for safety with their servant July to his rural home while revolution shakes the rest of South Africa, are in a way too old for any immediate transformations in this respect, but it is mainly in their children that the novel's cultural hopes are invested. It is no accident that as Maureen analyses the political economy of white culture she is holding one of the clay oxen her little daughter Gina is learning to make in her new surroundings. And Gina in particular seems to represent a distinct potential for the future; taking immediately to her black friend Nyiko, she learns the latter's language, copies her behaviour and enjoys a mutual world of childish sisterhood and pleasure. As true friends in a wider context of social turmoil the two are shown becoming part of the same sexual, social, political and cultural heritage. Even the young boy, Victor, seems to be learning; foregoing the posture to which his name symbolically seems to entitle him, when July gives him a length of fishing line, he repeats, without parody, the prototypical gesture of black obeisance and gratitude, bobbing at the knees and receiving the handout with cupped palms (p. 157). These are microscopic details, to be sure, but it will perhaps be in the everyday absorption of such changes that transformations in South African culture will, literally, be embodied.

This new culture in the making is contained in the overall engagement of the novel itself. One of the most insistent and assertive practices of *July's People*, along with its devastating analysis of white patronage, is its critique at the same time of the black world. Far from presenting a united front in the moment of revolution, the black world in the novel is shown to be one riven in all directions along both class and sexual lines, and evidently it finds the experience of revolution as complicated, in some ways, as does the white.

Thus July's chief wants Bam to help protect him against the 'Russias' and 'Cubas' if they come, or the other black tribes of South Africa if they are the ones to invade. Consciousness, for this chief, is layered dominantly in terms of much older historical perceptions as well as confused accounts of the present; a thoroughgoing social revolution may be even more of a threat to him and the little power he has than are the structures of apartheid. Seemingly impenetrable divisions are also shown between July and his wife, arising out of their relative gender roles within an overall class structure. July is a migrant domestic worker, and his world is nine-tenths that of the white city, with a brief holiday at home every year or two years. His wife's story, however, is more basic and simple: 'The sun rises, the moon sets; the money must come, the man must go' (p. 83).

As in this case, it is one of the strengths of *July's People* that some of its most significant political moments are also moments of poignancy; and that the poignant (where it exists) is shown to be ineffably political. But of the complications of a black revolutionary response the novel has simply no illusions, not even concerning July's action in 'saving' his white mistress and master. As Maureen puts it: 'What will the freedom fighters think? Did he join the people from Soweto? He took his whites and ran' (p. 128). Here the bare irony of Maureen's recognition suggests how the new political circumstances that have arisen thrust even seemingly innocent humanitarian action into a vast ambiguity. The moment of revolution, for everyone, is also a moment of choice.

In drawing the sheer poverty and *depletion* of black life in the rural areas of South Africa *July's People* has made a powerful contribution to the understanding of what the experience of its current history is like. In order to do so Gordimer has overridden her own observation that in her country the writer's potential has 'unscalable limitations'.[51] Partly these are overcome in this novel by a considerable amount of observation and research. But there are also other limits being scaled here. As the examples that have been given perhaps indicate, in imagining in this fashion the subjective complications of a revolutionary future Gordimer dispels once and for all the misconception that writing fiction in South African conditions is a luxury. On the contrary, in her rigorous construction of the daily meanings of a world turned upside down for everyone – black and white included – she imagines what few others are able, or perhaps willing, to consider. This is possibly the novel's own deepest cultural contribution: by undertaking this critique in a hypothetical revolutionary context, to help make its own way towards defining and constructing a new social and political identity to come. Itself a cultural product, the novel has asserted its right to a place as an 'apprentice' of that future.

It is Maureen who announces the central concern of *July's People*:

> an explosion of roles, that's what the blowing up of the Union Buildings and the burning of master bedrooms is.
>
> (p. 117)

Most directly this explosion in the novel involves relations be
July and his white 'people', the Smaleses. As servant is
overnight into authority, and as master and mistress have to learn
their new parts of dependence, each figure is shown, suddenly
deprived of the social supports of a previous identity, struggling
desperately for a new frame of reference.

Almost as important as the master–servant reversal is that
relations between Bam and Maureen become radically unsettled.
The moment of political revolution is also one of sexual revolution,
and one of the central contributions of *July's People* lies in showing
how [sexual roles are intricately connected with the overall social
structures into which they fit] As a white South African male Bam has
been most in authority; now, displaced socially and politically, his
sexual status also comes unstuck. For one thing the violence of his
prior sexual role is disclosed; dreaming of a wild pig he has shot, Bam
wakes to find blood on his penis. For a confused moment he thinks it
is that of the pig, but it is menstrual blood from Maureen, with whom
he had made love the night before. Symbolically, the point is made
that there is something predatory about Bam's previous sexuality
(this is the last time that he and Maureen engage in physical sexual
relations). When it comes to basic issues to be dealt with – for
instance, who keeps the car keys, the white couple or July – it is
increasingly Maureen who is able and has to take the initiative. As
Bam's sexual and political status degenerates, Maureen's accordingly
grows in strength. These are strongly feminist themes in the novel,
therefore, ones we saw last in a less developed form in the case of
Elizabeth in *The Late Bourgeois World*. Interestingly, at about the
time the novel was being written Gordimer denied that she was in
any sense specifically a feminist writer; women's liberation in South
Africa, as far as she was concerned, was attendant upon, and
secondary to, more fundamental economic and political change.[52]
But here, in the imagined context of that change, we see how
powerfully presentiments of a female liberation emerge.

One of the more telling aspects of this development is that, outside
the usual context of their relations, Bam and Maureen no longer
know who the other one really *is*. For his part Bam decides he no
longer knows how to think of or speak to Maureen. She is by no
means the old 'Maureen' he used to address; nor is she any longer, in
the old sense, 'his wife'. He decides instead that she is simply 'her'
(pp. 104–5). For Maureen, too, Bam becomes simply 'he', and as this

radicalization of sexuality takes place (each of them starkly a representative of their gender) language itself is being radicalized. There can be no more verbal pretence; the words 'wife' and 'husband' no longer exist for each other in the old senses as signs. This revolution of language is also explored between Maureen and July, and indeed is seen as a major component of the social reversal that engulfs them. Whereas Maureen begins the novel in the belief that she and July have a special understanding (a recognizable white South African syndrome), it is a matter of sheer horror to her to learn that the very language she had used as a means of conciliation was for July nothing more than the medium of his everyday oppression:

> How was she to have known, until she came here, that the special consideration she had shown for his dignity as a man, while he was by definition a servant, would become his humiliation itself, the one thing there was to say between them that had any meaning.
>
> (p. 98)

And one of the most mortifying things for Maureen is that in their new circumstances July insists on presenting himself to her as her 'boy' – the derogatory white South African term for a male servant. Maureen had never used this term, but evidently there is a reality to her relationship with July that now subverts its previous mystification in language, and returns with an ironic vengeance.

Throughout the novel it becomes clear that language in this context is a battlefield – as much a battlefield as the realm of private and political relations it helps both constitute and conceal. The climax of this theme occurs when July, in a burst of sheer fury and frustration, gives vent at Maureen in his own language, in terms that by definition she cannot understand. As the machine-gun barrage of his words mows down her emotional defences, July proves something about his own dignity and his way of measuring it, and Maureen's contrary degradation for him.[53]

This presentation in the novel of the revolution of roles, along the lines of culture, class and sex, as well as the destabilization of language accompanying it, is amongst the foremost imaginative feats of *July's People*. In these spheres the novel is a rigorous and sustained exploration of the effects of a future revolutionary moment. But what of the moment itself as it is presented in the novel? What is its status as a vision of what was (or is) to come?

When the novel was written its vision of the future appeared deeply impressionistic. Bombs raining down on Johannesburg; the international airport closed; invasions from foreign territory by South African and other armies: like Gordimer's statement of a year or two later that she was living in a society 'stamping, swaying with the force of revolutionary change', it seemed like an exaggeration. Power, in the early 1980s, appeared to be as much a prerogative of the white state as it had been in 1948 before Gordimer wrote her first novel. Interestingly, however, as the first half of the decade progressed, the degree of exaggeration seemed less marked. An independent trade union movement was growing substantially;[54] strikes became more frequent and more precisely mobilized; mass organizations, such as the United Democratic Front (UDF), began to fill the political vacuum inside the country; as South Africa shifted into recession, police raids and detentions without trial again became the order of the day. Perhaps the most striking feature of all concerned presentiments of insurrection. Twenty-five years to the day after Sharpeville there was another massacre – this time at Uitenhage in the Eastern Cape.[55] As riots broke out in black townships across the country, in many instances the police appeared to have lost control. Where petrol and fire bombings became part of the basic grammar of (sometimes anarchic) social resistance, the South African military moved in, occupying black areas for days or weeks at a time. This by ordinary definitions constituted a state of civil war; and the fact was formally recognized when, just as in that other 'revolutionary' moment of the early 1960s, the Nationalist regime of P. W. Botha declared a State of Emergency in July 1985, with mass detentions again taking place.

The picture presented in *July's People*, then, may have had more of a hold on future reality than it seemed at the time. Apocalyptic though it appeared, its images presented one version of the way in which change in South Africa *might* come about.[56]

None the less, in terms of the method in which its picture of revolution is presented, the novel is still candidly impressionistic. For there may be a way in which the novel is less interested in the future *per se* than in its unfolding in the present. On this issue *July's People* may be the most deceptive, and deceptively simple, of all of Gordimer's novels, and perhaps less genuinely prophetic than, say, *The Conservationist*. What the novel is apparently doing is projecting a vision into the future; but what it may be doing most decisively is in fact the reverse. For what appears to be a projection from the present into the future in the novel is from another point of view *seeing the present through the eyes of the future*; it is after all the present that falls apart in the revolutionary context the novel proposes. Placing the phenomena of the present – its social roles, codes and patterns of behaviour – under the dissecting microscope of the future is nothing less than a brilliant strategical move for analysing the present from a future perspective. The deepest project of the novel is in this sense *semiotic* – decoding the signs and codes of the present in the light of their actual reality – and it is this reality that the projection into the future clarifies. Also, to the extent that this projection is set at the point of revolution, the procedure approximates to a method of revolutionary analysis; Gordimer has viewed the present as it will appear when seen from the vantage point of revolution. This is what 'explodes' social roles in the present, shatters their pretensions and false foundations, and marks out the battlegrounds of sexuality, culture and language. In all of Gordimer's previous novels we have seen how their sense of the present includes a vision of the future. Here we see in extreme – but therefore illuminating – form just how far it is a sense of the future that constructs their vision of the present. Living in the interregnum, *July's People* sees the revolution already going on around it.

IV

In the 1970s and 1980s white writing in South Africa showed increasing signs of turning to the future as a proper subject for imaginative exploration. Karel Schoeman wrote *Promised Land*;[57] J. M. Coetzee's *Waiting for the Barbarians* can in many respects be read as an extraordinary dream-allegory of the future.[58] Nadine Gordimer herself first turned indirectly to the future in *A Guest of Honour*; it is the underlying subject of *The Conservationist*; and it is present explicitly and implicitly in *July's People*. If one trusts the imaginative explorations of fiction as real historical signs, this is perhaps a certain index that the future that has come to obsess these novels is already on the way. White South African fiction is preparing for revolution.[59]

Paradoxically in *July's People*, however, Nadine Gordimer is also revisiting the past. Maureen Smales comes from a mining town background very similar to that of Helen Shaw in *The Lying Days*, and indeed to that of Nadine Gordimer's own biographical past.

Similarly, Gordimer's first socially conscious short stories frequently concerned relations between masters and servants, and in *July's People* she returns to this theme. In this novel, however, she turns the tables on the past and goes a step further; for, crucially, the mere reversal of roles of authority is shown to be not revolutionary enough. Although July rebukes Maureen with a vengeance, the latter's real transformation occurs when she realizes that this too is a circle she must break out of, for the *terms* of the old relationship have been maintained, even if the roles have been reversed; it is a circle that truly leads to nowhere.

Similarly the novel breaks the mould of a liberal myth of reconciliation attendant upon the masters-and-servants theme. There can be no reconciliation between masters and servants, no 'saviours', miracles, moment of mutual recognition and forgiveness, or easy way out. If July has been Maureen's 'man Friday'[60] his island of safety is none the less for both of them one of fantasy, historically isolated and adrift. From her husband, too, Maureen has little worth holding on to. It is not just that Bam has degenerated as a person, but the whole set of relationships and values constructed around his social identity – and therefore Maureen's earlier identity for him – have become obsolete. Maureen is historically entrapped. The old is dead, but nothing new has been born.

In this context at the end of the novel Maureen is running. The circumstances in which this occurs are ambiguous, but their significance surely is not. An unmarked helicopter has flown over near July's village and is coming down to land. No one knows whether it is manned by freedom fighters or by the South African army. But Maureen knows she must run. She is running from old structures and relationships, which have led her to this cul-de-sac; but she is also running towards her revolutionary destiny. She does not know what that destiny may be, whether it will bring death or life. All she knows is that it is the only authentic future awaiting her. Nor does she do this out of weakness. For the first time since leaving Johannesburg – and perhaps for the first time in her life – she has found some personal integration; she runs, says the text, 'with all the suppressed trust of a lifetime' (p. 160). And so we are left at the end of the novel with a runner held moving in flight. In part it is a flight from, but also it is a flight towards: towards what she cannot quite properly see, but which she knows is drawing her on.

It may be that this is a perfect image for Gordimer's own historical consciousness, standing as a fitting culmination of the movement that has lain behind her development so far. There is that inner trust in what she knows she must write. And it is this that is drawing her on, reaching out for the moment she cannot quite properly grasp, but which alone gives definition to her present.

7

Deep History

. . . it was an absence somehow always present.
A Guest of Honour

. . . one is never talking to oneself, always one
is addressed to someone . . . even dreams are
performed before an audience.
Burger's Daughter

I

In drawing an example from geology, Lévi-Strauss suggests that it is through structural oppositions that knowledge becomes available. For it is precisely in the geological 'fault', where two opposed strata come together, that the 'master-meaning' of a landscape, as he puts it, becomes clear. Here the 'space and time' of the past are suddenly juxtaposed and become one; here the entire history of a previous era is laid out for inspection.[1] We may follow up Lévi-Strauss's analogy. If space and time become 'one' in the geological fault, they are also, in a sense, split apart. Were it not for this basic fissure – or contradiction – past history might well be an undifferentiated continuum. The surface patterns of the evidence at hand, through analytic deconstruction and then reconstruction, come to reveal another 'narrative': of the collisions and juxtapositions of the past whose effect has been to produce that ambivalence, opposition, or split.

Viewed in this light the unlikely subject of geology has some relevance for this study. Here too the concepts of structural 'faults' or 'contradictions' have been of central importance; in a sense our whole investigation has developed from such juxtapositions. To begin with, there has been the primary juxtaposition of the subjectivity of Gordimer as a writer and the objective, external world around her; out of the engagement of the former with the latter a 'consciousness of history' itself has been generated,

205

inseparable in this case from its condensation in fictional writing. Contradictions and 'faults' *internal* to Gordimer's work have also been vital, for these have frequently been the key to her historical consciousness, its range and limits and hence perceptible 'shape'. Through the deconstruction of such faults, and their reconstruction in alternative form, by re-enacting the original engagement between subjective and objective that underlies them, the present narrative – a 'history of consciousness' – has been written. In so far as these contradictions in Gordimer's work have been most useful to this study, they have also been of greatest 'value'. This is paradoxical from the point of view of conventional aesthetic theory, since internal fractures are usually held to be a fictional work's greatest 'fault'.

Yet this history so far has been a distinctly localized and linear one; there has been no attempt to survey the overall 'landscape' of Gordimer's situation, as it were. In quantum fashion we have moved from one set of four or five years to the next, tracing the responses of Gordimer's novels to their respective historical moments. Patterns have been traced through these moments, and this is then the diachronic development of Gordimer's consciousness of history. But what we have not really dealt with so far are its *synchronic* features, or what we may think of as the 'deep history' of her writing. It seems this 'deep history' might be considered in two ways. On the one hand, it would refer to those overall circumstances and determinations that affect Gordimer's fiction in general, and the general patterns of her response; in this sense they are the determinations and patterns affecting and characterizing Gordimer's writing as a whole in this period. On the other hand, it appears a 'deep history' may be thought of nearly literally; what we have yet to assess is what goes on at the deeper levels of a consciousness of history itself.

These are, then, the areas of inquiry in this final chapter. First we shall investigate the possibility – perhaps paradoxically for a study of historical consciousness – that there is an 'historical unconscious' in Gordimer's work, underlying its overall responses. Following this, we shall examine the feature with which it is associated, and from which in a sense it proceeds: the degree to which Gordimer writes from a 'split position' in South Africa. This may be the fundamental historical 'fault' of her situation, and certain patterns of her work will be set out in terms of this split.

II

If one is searching for a deep history one cannot go much deeper
than the idea of an 'historical unconscious'.[2] In South Africa this idea
proceeds from the fact of systematic social fracture maintained in the
dual interests of white profit and power. This fragmentation, as
suggested in the Introduction, has to do not only with the basic
division of South African society between black and white along class
and race lines, but also with the numerous subdivisions within these
groups. Its basic effects for writing have been noted time and again,
not least by South African writers. Nadine Gordimer puts it in the
following way:

> living in a society that has been as deeply and calculatedly compart-
> mentalised as South Africa's has been under the colour bar, the
> writer's potential has unscalable limitations.[3]

Others are in broad agreement with her views. Focusing on
questions of characterization and social understanding, Alex La
Guma states:

> The problem is living in one set compartment and knowing only of your
> own life, and then trying to project yourself into the life or the
> environment of another part, of another party.[4]

Ezekiel Mphahlele deals with the problem of social fragmentation
in relation to South African culture as a whole. In conditions that
isolate whole communities and make social intercourse difficult or
impossible, he argues, there can hardly be a healthy common
culture:

> And the problem of a national culture is *per se* the problem of a national
> literature. It must remain sectional and sterile as long as such conditions
> remain.[5]

Nat Nakasa indicates that his cultural identity is intrinsically bound
up with his class and social situation. He is meant to be a Pondo, he
writes, but he doesn't even know the language. He was brought up in
a Zulu-speaking home, but he no longer thinks in Zulu because it
cannot cope with the demands he has to face. He concludes:

> I am just not a tribesman, whether I like it or not. I am, inescapably, a
> part of the city slums, the factory machines and our beloved shebeens.[6]

Elsewhere Nadine Gordimer has suggested a further dimension
of the effects of social fracture in South Africa. At the widest level of

the social formation itself, she writes, external forces enter the very 'breast and brain' of the artist, determining the nature and state of art in South Africa. She carries on to say that as a writer she is fully aware that 'my consciousness inevitably has the same tint as my face'.[7]

Whether it be characterization, culture, class, or consciousness, explicit or implicit in each of these views is a certain aspect of *limitation* for writing in South Africa, consequent on the effects of social fracture. This question was also raised in the Introduction, but there it was suggested that it should not be interpreted too rigorously. Nadine Gordimer, it was anticipated, would not be entirely confined by the general limitations that affect her; and, indeed, the evidence of this study indicates that the writers themselves are perhaps too pessimistic in their assessment of the consequences of social fracture for their work. At different stages we have seen how Gordimer has been closely involved in a black social world; and even at the height of Black Consciousness exclusivism she was at least able to present its tone and tenor with great accuracy. Moreover, in terms of what her novels represent, we have seen that at different times they have crossed boundaries of both colour and class; in both *A World of Strangers* and *The Conservationist* the degree to which these novels respond to an overall historical moment is the same as that to which they escape any strict limitation by their social position – even though that position may none the less be clear. Ideologically Gordimer's work has ranged both within and beyond her 'class' situation.

Nevertheless, at a deep level the fact of limitation still applies. Nadine Gordimer may write about blacks in South Africa; she may mix with them as well as have close black friends. But there is still a crucial sense in which she is divided from the black world, even at those moments of her closest approach. Gordimer, quite simply, is not 'of' the black South African world, nor could she be under present circumstances. This basic social limitation is also, in a deep sense, an historical one; an historical gap stands between Gordimer and the black world. Like Jessie and Gideon in *Occasion for Loving*, or Rosa and Zwelinzima in *Burger's Daughter*, there is a certain history that must pass before they can really stand together on the same ground. And even then it might be problematic, for the question would arise as to which part of the black world Gordimer wished to stand with.

From this deeper, dual aspect of limitation the idea of an historical unconscious develops. In one sense, and perhaps on one level, the idea of an 'unconscious' is already familiar to us here. It is this that has marked out the structural 'silences', 'gaps', or contradictions of Gordimer's work, where it reaches the boundaries of its vision due to an aspect of ideological, social, or historical limitation, or more usually an uneven, superimposed combination of all three. This has been our use of Macherey's concept of the 'not-said', but what it seems to refer to primarily is not so much an unconscious as a 'non-conscious' – it suggests those areas of which Gordimer's work is not or cannot be aware.

Noticeably on occasion Gordimer's work invokes a concept of the unconscious in a classic psychoanalytic sense. In *A World of Strangers* the collective 'nightmare' that the white hunters experience represents, internally at least, an emanation from their subconscious, a projection of their own social and political malevolence rising in the weird surroundings of the blighted hunting landscape to haunt them. In *Burger's Daughter* Gordimer undertakes a psychoanalytic investigation into the deeper compulsions and distortions of a white political response to apartheid. In her latest novella, 'Something out there', she deals again with the political fears and obsessions of a white unconscious, associated analogically in the text with a marauding and threatening wild animal.[8]

The Conservationist is perhaps the most suggestive of Gordimer's works from this point of view. From our discussion of the novel three main features seem relevant. First, as we saw earlier, it is a major theme of *The Conservationist* that the raising of the black body simultaneously represents a 'return of the repressed' on both political and psychological levels; just as the body represents a return of the black world in political terms, equally, internal to Mehring's psyche, it signifies that a site of repression is bound to return to consciousness in threatening and subversive ways. The second point concerns the question of 'address'. Whether consciously or unconsciously, Mehring feels compelled to 'address' himself to the black body as a representative of the oppressed black world; it is precisely as such a representative that the body stands as an ultimate arbiter over the meaning of his own existence. A linked aspect is that this is also address to the future, for it is as an incarnation of a future destiny that the body stands in judgement on Mehring's present. The third point is of basic importance. For the reason there can be this 'return of the repressed' – and the reason there is a compulsion of 'address' for Mehring – is because there is, in the first place, a state of political repression in South Africa. Mehring does not just live in a fractured society. He lives in a state of *oppressive* fracture, or fracture geared to oppression and exploitation. The fundamental political disequilibrium this involves sets up the dynamic of its own reversal in his psyche.

These conjunctions between the political and the psychological, between 'conscious' discourse and subconscious compulsion, seem very suggestive for Gordimer's fiction as a whole. One might normally be wary of leaping from fictional themes to authors as if no difference existed. Nevertheless, it is by no means clear that the themes of a fictional text do not include, whether consciously or unconsciously, the situation of their 'authors'. And the three points that have been isolated in relation to *The Conservationist* can, it appears, be extended to include the situation of Nadine Gordimer herself as a writer, and to some degree to characterize her fictional response to it.

There is one obvious difference between Gordimer and Mehring. Whereas he is a fundamental pillar of the oppressive system in South Africa, she is essentially an opponent. Perhaps we should then not expect anything very similar between the writer and her character, either by way of repression or else by way of 'return'. Yet the two *do* have something in common; both – in Gordimer's case despite herself – are situated in a fractured society and, moreover, one in which fracture and oppression are linked. For Gordimer as well as for her character there is a domain of social repression that objectively applies to her situation whether she desires it subjectively or not. On a deep level, therefore, a whole domain of South African life belongs to the 'unconscious' of her fiction – the repressed black world that her writing cannot really be part *of* and from which (much like the individual unconscious) it cannot directly speak. Indeed, there is good reason to believe that the 'unconscious' as it is apparent here implies more than simply Macherey's definition of the 'non-conscious'. For in Gordimer's work it seems that this state of objective social repression lays the ground for the action of those other two phenomena noted in relation to Mehring: the persistent 'return' of this repressed world in compulsive ways in her fiction; and the way her work repeatedly 'addresses' itself to this world and the future it represents.

One of Gordimer's earliest short stories, already mentioned, again

becomes of relevance. Entitled 'Is there nowhere else we can m[
the story was first published in 1947 when Gordimer was 23. A[
stage, if we remember her first unfinished novel with its incidental
inclusion of racist rhetoric, in ideological terms Gordimer's work
had, at the least, by no means 'settled down' even into the kind of
pre-liberal stance to be found in *The Lying Days*. But because the
story occurs in such an unsettled and formative period, it is perhaps
all the more interesting. Concerning an attack on a young white girl
by a derelict black tramp, 'Is there nowhere else we can meet?' is a
symbolic allegory on numerous levels at once. [Here again the
concept of repression is important, for just as the tramp belongs to a
world of political and economic repression, so too he belongs to a
domain of psychic and sexual repression on the part of the young
girl; again, on all counts the attack is a 'return of the repressed'. Most
disturbing to the young girl is a personal inevitability she feels in
advancing towards the attack; a strong strain of sexual symbolism
indicates her fearful yet irresistible compulsion in this regard.]

This feeling of inescapable necessity lends a mood of destiny to the
encounter, and so the entire episode is raised to the level of an
historical allegory, of an inevitable violent confrontation between
black and white in South Africa. At the same time only an irony
eventuates in the story, for nothing is consummated between the
two figures except the futile theft of a handbag and parcel;
paradoxically, considering her narrow escape, the young girl is left
with a feeling of emptiness and loneliness. Thus the story is at once a
prophecy of a future historic encounter promising an ultimate
release, and an exploration of the agony of its present foreclosure
on the part of the white figure, who at some level desperately needs
that release. But also, it intimates, that release will entail a mauling,
physical or emotional.

As such 'Is there nowhere else we can meet?' seems to have
anticipated the characteristic field explored by much of Gordimer's
later work. The experience and expectation it depicts apply in
varying degrees of intensity to the central characters of all of
Gordimer's novels. Helen Shaw in *The Lying Days*; Toby Hood in *A
World of Strangers*; Elizabeth Van Den Sandt in *The Late Bourgeois
World*; Colonel Bray in *A Guest of Honour*; even, paradoxically,
Mehring in *The Conservationist*; and Rosa Burger in *Burger's
Daughter*: all are confronted by the black world; all at some level
desire some release from their historical impasse; and all are to

varying degrees contained by the ironies of its postponement. The story also anticipates the experience of Maureen Smales in *July's People*, who undergoes her mauling and release at the moment of revolution that the early work projects. This remarkable anticipation in 'Is there nowhere else we can meet?', combined with the facts that it occurs in such condensed and symbolic form, and that it is produced in a work of formative and early youth, might then justify the claim that the short story is a genetic blueprint for all of Gordimer's future historically responsive work.[10]

The story may set up the characteristic field that Gordimer's future work is to investigate, but it does not determine the future forms nor the future implications assumed by that investigation. This, as we have traced, is something that changes from novel to novel. Further, in so far as the story *is* a genetic structure, it is symbolic in a sense beyond which it uses symbolism as a fictional technique. For example, Gordimer may have been able to choose the over-conscious Lawrentian imagery that characterizes the story's sexual symbolism, but what she evidently could *not* choose was the compulsion to represent this theme as part of a fictional complex – a complex which thereby in part becomes symbolic of that compulsion. This is even more significant in that the complex as a whole represents the fictional field to which Gordimer again and again returns. Thus we can say that the story is genetic not in the sense that it *generates* her future work, but only in that it is the first to embody this more deeply generated compulsion. And it is this phenomenon that we are then seeking. For this is, in a general sense, the 'return of the repressed' in Gordimer's fiction: the persistent reappearance in her work of that politically repressed world separated from her at a deep level in the domain of her fictional 'unconscious.' In Gordimer's writing at least, fiction appears to be that 'other place' where oppressive and oppressed worlds can, and perhaps must, meet.

A word of caution: one would not wish to argue in any abstract or deterministic fashion and say that the return of the repressed in Gordimer's fiction is an inevitable and necessary effect of an oppressive social fracture in South Africa. At the very least it might be expected that a certain subjective responsiveness on the part of the writer was a minimal condition for it to take place. Also, it is not entirely clear how far this phenomenon in Gordimer's work should be interpreted in, say, strictly Freudian terms. The Freudian analogy is highly suggestive; in Gordimer's case the 'unconscious' of her world as a writer enters the condensation and displacement not of dreams, but of fiction.[11] On the other hand this 'unconscious' is as much a social as an individual phenomenon; and it might apply to the fiction and the processes of its writing as much as it does to the author.[12]

Nevertheless there *is* a return of the repressed in Gordimer's writing; further, it is a psycho-fictional effect attendant upon a state of oppressive social fracture in South Africa. It is precisely those areas of which Gordimer's work is 'not-conscious', which for her make up a world of objective social repression, that provoke the basic responses of her novels. And this may not be all that unrepresenta-tive, even beyond the domain of her fiction *per se*. Anyone who has lived in South Africa would suspect that the 'return of the repressed', as the psychic equivalent of a political threat, might well affect many white South Africans in the form of dream, wish-fulfilment, or, as in the case of Mehring or Gordimer's hunters, nightmare.

Other writers in other times and places have also been caught up in a situation of intense social and historical division. What common elements, by way of an 'historical unconscious', might apply? In style, mood and subject matter Gordimer's fiction has often been com-pared to that of pre-revolutionary writing in Russia.[13] And in this context one does immediately think of the two 'classic' historical revolutions, the French in 1789 and the Russian in 1917; for in both cases, confronting an impending social upheaval, writers were faced with an 'overwhelming question'.

As far as the French Revolution is concerned, Jean-Paul Sartre has analysed the predicament of its writers in a most interesting way.[14] For the first half of the eighteenth century, he argues, there was in a sense no historical 'problem' for the writer. Typically bourgeois by birth, yet privileged on account of his function, the writer wrote for the readers who commissioned him – royalty and the aristocracy. In these circumstances there was an ideological homogeneity between writer and reader, evinced, says Sartre, as matters of form, content, value and style; writing in this context was, in his words, 'a ceremony of recognition analogous to the bow of salutation'.[15] Yet at about the time of the Revolution the writer experienced a rupture, and it was a rupture in terms of his audience. For now there was an alternative class on the rise, the bourgeoisie itself, and the writer fell into a divided position because he had a foot, as it were, in both class camps. This class became for the writer what Sartre terms a 'virtual public'. By this he does not mean that it was a reading public, or even a *potential* reading public. Rather this class was a kind of *listening* public, a self-projected gallery for the writer, waiting in implicit silent judgement on everything he wrote. It was a hitherto repressed class against whose significance, cause and values the significance, cause and values of all writing now had to be measured. Thus the 'virtual public' makes silent, historic demands on the writer, becoming a presence and a problem he cannot ignore. It becomes a presence and a problem to which he must address himself in his writing.

The example from Sartre, in so far as it gives an 'existential' account of the compulsion of an historical response, reminds us that there may well be a sliding scale in the phenomenon of the writer's 'address', from an 'unconscious' return of the repressed on the one hand to conscious feelings of existential accountability on the other, and probably incorporating aspects of conscience and commitment as well. In addition, with appropriate modifications, Sartre's model would seem to fit Nadine Gordimer perfectly. For the bourgeoisie of eighteenth-century France we need only substitute the oppressed black classes of twentieth-century South Africa as her own 'virtual public'. In her case, however, there is an added intensity to this relationship. For if socially speaking Gordimer is more decisively alienated from her virtual public than the eighteenth-century French writer, then in terms of the cause she supports she is to be located firmly on the side of an oppressed black world. Thus for Gordimer there is a very acute way in which she responds to her virtual public. She must write from her own situation, and of this she is well aware. But if for this reason she cannot write directly *for* her virtual public, she can at least write *towards* it, addressing the question of its oppression, the justice of its cause and the eventuality of its triumph. Implicitly this is also an address to the future, for this represents the moment in which that triumph will be realized.

Here we see just how important for Gordimer's fiction is that phenomenon noted earlier in relation to Mehring: the degree to which there is an 'address' to the black world and to the future. Something else also becomes apparent. The address of Gordimer's work to the black world is at some level a writing *in favour* of that world, for this domain then becomes the arbiter of significance, value and action on Gordimer's side of the social dividing line. Simultaneously the future becomes the arbiter of meaning and action in the present. This dual address, therefore, in part seems to be responsible for the historical commitment of each of Gordimer's novels. In weighing up, against the realities of the present, the implicit demands made by both an oppressed black world and the future, in each given instance for Gordimer the appropriate form of her commitment in fiction is produced.

What we have seen so far bears this out. In the case of virtually every one of Gordimer's novels the question of commitment is highlighted by the fact that there is a central character who has to undertake it. When Toby commits himself to Sam in *A World of Strangers* it is an address to the black world and to the implicit demands of the future that to a large degree underlies it. Similarly, when Jessie attempts some form of solidarity with Gideon in *Occasion for Loving*, in part this dual address engenders the attempt. With slight variation much the same could be said of nearly all the other novels. Mehring does not commit himself either to the black world or to the future – he is not that sort of character. But then his novel in a sense makes his commitment for him. Maureen in *July's People* is not ultimately 'addressed' to the black world. Indeed, in that she undergoes a revolutionary transformation as a matter of necessity and survival for *herself*, the novel seems to mark an important new departure for Gordimer's fiction. But we have also seen just how fundamentally *July's People* is addressed to the future; nothing less than a sense of the future is responsible for the positions it takes up in the present. All in all, then, if we are thinking in terms of a 'deeper history' in Gordimer's fiction, this dual address is an intriguing phenomenon. For, to varying degrees in every case, it seems to be an 'absent' world, considered both socially and temporally, that underlies the response of Gordimer's consciousness of history. The oppressed black world and the absent future together pose a 'deep historic question' to which each novel is an attempted solution. Each attempts to answer the question of where it stands in relation to the oppressed and 'absent' world.

If this 'deep historic question' is a nearly invariable presence underlying the response of Gordimer's novels, then what is not invariable are the kinds of answer that are given. These, we have seen, change markedly from novel to novel, ranging in their ideological implications from the liberal variants of *The Lying Days* and *A World of Strangers*, to the socialist affirmations of *A Guest of Honour*, to the revolutionary alignment of *Burger's Daughter*.

A striking pattern is noticeable in this change: that as a condition of social fracture in South Africa has become more emphatic, and as oppression has intensified, so too has Nadine Gordimer, in response to a black world increasingly divided from her and a future ever more radical in its implications, become ever more radically attuned to the demands that these embody. Thus another layer of significance is added to the fact that in *Occasion for Loving* at the same moment that Gordimer is cut off from the inter-racial world of the 1950s she discovers the failure of liberal humanism – the ideology that had sustained her when she was a part of that world. In *Burger's Daughter*, in a situation of acute social and historical marginality – induced not only by the structures of apartheid, but by the response of the black world itself, in the form of Black Consciousness and the Soweto Revolt – Gordimer turns to the legacy of a revolutionary tradition to negotiate the demands of a now deeply 'absent' world and a problematic future. As for *July's People*, it is set in the 'absent' moment itself: the moment of revolution in South Africa.

Overall, the picture arising from Gordimer's novels is one of inverse proportion on two fronts. The narrower her access to an oppressed black world – in terms of the underlying assumptions that might identify her in any simple fashion with that world – the more radical is her response to its implicit demands. And the less accommodating and simple the prospect of the future becomes, the more insistent is Gordimer's address towards its ultimate resolution. Earlier it was noted that at a deep level Gordimer's objective limits as a writer had two aspects, being both social and historical in nature. Here we see that even *at* a deep level their effects are by no means simple, indeed that they are at least paradoxical and contradictory. For in both social and historical terms these limits seem only to have invited their own transgression in Gordimer's fiction in inverse proportion to their limiting effects. This in perhaps its most dramatic form is the 'return of the repressed' in Gordimer's work. What on one level belongs increasingly to the social and historical 'unconscious' of her fiction, on another returns ever more strongly to her historical consciousness, prompting the deepest engagement and commitments of her work, and the ideological shifts these include.

One last point may be made before leaving the idea of an 'historical unconscious', and this is where we might return to the Russian Revolution. There may be a sense in which what is concealed beneath the surface of Gordimer's work is identical with what lurks in the 'unconscious' of South African history. For the pre-revolutionary Russian writers, too, like those of eighteenth-century France, were active in the shadow of a looming social upheaval. They too could not ignore a new historical presence on their door-step, often falling into a position divided between the class they belonged to materially and that to which they may have been respon-sive in varying degrees ideologically. Turgenev, Chernyshevsky, Dostoevsky, Chekhov, Tolstoy: all fall into this pattern.

There is a sub-text in nineteenth-century Russian writing; it is that sub-text of a coming revolution that, even if it was impossible to foresee exactly, is perhaps the controlling force, the real 'subject', of this fiction in so far as it determines its deepest address, or on the other hand what it tries to avoid. Much like Mehring's unburied body in *The Conservationist* it tells of a repressed world that is 'coming back' inevitably from the future. In the sense that the Russian Revolution did not exist before it occurred, it belonged to the 'unconscious' of history. Yet it was predicated by every moment of what existed, fashioning by the magnetism of its absence all that occurred in the present: an 'unconscious' reality, which so governed a history that it could not but occur.

III

The social and historical limits of Gordimer's situation are para-doxical and contradictory; they nevertheless set up the basic framework within which she writes. If they are in some sense 'transgressed' in her fiction then these limits still determine what it is that has to be transgressed. A basic contradiction then remains for Gordimer's work; the limits that are partially overcome in her novels are yet to be overcome in real life. Gordimer identifies with the disprivileged in South Africa, yet she does so from a position of privilege. She supports the oppressed and exploited classes; yet she does so from a position within the ruling class. There may be a 'return of the repressed' in her work and an 'address' to the black world and the future it represents. But by and large it is an overseas and local white élite that reads Gordimer's novels; and she is ultimately caught up by the confinements of the present. To modify Antonio Gramsci's phrase, Gordimer may be thought of as a 'non-organic intellectual' – linked mentally to the oppressed classes but not physically or materially.[16] If we are thinking of the deep structural determinations of her writing, this is then perhaps the deepest, that Gordimer occupies what can be termed a 'split historical position'. This split has been responsible for the 'historical unconscious' of her work, but it has also generated other broad patterns in her novels, which may be set out in terms of this 'fault'.

Unsurprisingly, given that they are organized around a division, these patterns take the form of oppositions. Thus, one recurrent pairing in Gordimer's work is that between a sense of 'history' on the one hand and a sense of 'existence' on the other. This pairing makes up a basic thematic polarity in *Occasion for Loving* as Jessie – and the novel as a whole – oscillate between one and the other. In *The Late Bourgeois World*, as Elizabeth makes her historical commitment she celebrates it on an existential plane. Bray, in *A Guest of Honour*, finds a way of accepting the conditions of history and of existence in the same instant. There is a definite logic to this pairing if we think of it in terms of Gordimer's split position. The sense of history is understandable enough in South African circumstances, and in terms of Gordimer's basic attitudes. But where feelings of social engagement are counterposed by the reality of social marginality, it is by no means surprising that a sense of solitary 'existence' should vie so strongly with a sense of history. Also, where the effective results of a mental or practical commitment are likely to be all but invisible, it is understandable that a feeling of existential accountability – or even, on occasion, something approaching a sense of the 'absurd' – comes to partner an historical approach and provide the basis for a philosophy of responsibility and endurance.

Gordimer has a personal empathy for existentialism – we remember her fondness for Sartre and Camus; but seen in terms of her split position this empathy takes on an historical intelligibility. This division then explains a further feature of Gordimer's novels: the degree to which they are fundamentally 'meditational'. If we have not asked what her novels 'do', in the sense of what political effect they might have, or might be intended to have, this is because there is really nothing for them *to* do except reflect on the situation from which they emerge and construct essentially meditational hypotheses towards its eventual transformation. For this reason also, in contrast, say, to recent black South African fiction, which tends to present a whole spectrum of black society as a collective resource of historical agency,[17] the ultimate subject of Gordimer's novels is subjectivity itself, and a marginalized white subjectivity at that. In other words, there is something of the soliloquy about Gordimer, and it is an historical effect related to her 'split position'.

One of the central patterns of Gordimer's work has to do with another pair of counterparts: that of romance and realism. Gordimer has described herself as 'a romantic struggling with reality',[18] and something has been made of this by critics, though not from an historical point of view.[19] From this point of view, however, the pairing provides some central insights. For in Gordimer's work romanticism is the mode that overcomes real limitations; romance, for her, begins at the limits of the possible. In *A World of Strangers* we first saw the conjunction between romance and optimism: a romantic mode that carried deep historical truths to Toby. The ending of the novel was, despite its self-probationary procedures, still residually 'romantic'. In *The Late Bourgeois World* it was a vast and transcendent romanticism that overcame the limits of the possible. Most powerfully we saw this function fulfilled in *The Conservationist*, where its prophetic, symbolic mode produced what seemed impossible to achieve realistically. On the other hand, where Gordimer's work has primarily been concerned to estimate what is actually available, historically considered, realism has prevailed over romanticism. We saw this in *Occasion for Loving*, *A Guest of Honour* and *Burger's Daughter*.

There is an implicit dialectic between romanticism and realism in Gordimer's work, therefore, both between the novels and within them, and it clearly corresponds to the basic 'fault' of her split position. Realism represents what is possible within the boundaries of her social and historical limits, romanticism what is desired beyond them. More lately, however, it seems there is a declining romanticism in Gordimer's work, especially in so far as it concerns what may be achieved historically by the white subject. To this degree Gordimer has perhaps internalized the realities of her split position, which is itself a development of some significance.

Romanticism and realism may be examined independently in Gordimer's work as manifestations of a basic contradiction. To take her romanticism first, probably the most important feature we have seen within it is its turn to nature, the land, and an attendant mythology. This, once again, appeared most strongly in *The Conservationist*, but was present in *A World of Strangers* and *A Guest of Honour* as well. In 'Something out there' the wild animal that is linked with the white unconscious is also, by definition, part of an untameable 'nature'. In general this procedure in Gordimer's fiction is itself evidence of a 'split position'. For in her work nature has acted as a locus of symbolic displacement; it represents the world from which she is divided both socially and historically. In *The Conservationist*, as we saw, nature is deeply linked with the people, and vice versa. At the same time it represents the future as it raises its unburied 'child', the black body, to life, and then receives it back into its own. Once again the attractions of this displacement make sense if we consider them from the point of view of Gordimer's position. For the white writer, cut off both from the people and from a desired alternative future, there is a fundamental consolation in nature. As a sign in the very 'nature of things' of eternal revolution and cycle it represents the assurance of a political 'return'. Also, where the limits of the possible seem to be measured out by irony – another recurrent feature of Gordimer's novels – nature represents its overthrow by nothing less than irony itself, in its ever succeeding patterns of succession. In this guise nature easily bears the message of what Terry Eagleton has called the 'ironic wit of history', that oppressors rise only to fall;[20] and this, if we think of Mehring, is exactly how Gordimer has used it. Perhaps most important of all, however, is that where a white political culture has its historical roots in a colonial or *settler* culture, the land 'naturally' becomes a sign of the people. This from the black point of view is the logic of the political slogan 'Afrika! Mayibuye!' – 'Africa! May it come back!' And this too is the logic of Gordimer's use of it in *The Conservationist*.

More generally, Gordimer's symbolic use of nature may have a wider resonance. Stephen Gray has pointed out that, in the original colonial 'romance' hunting novel, the subjection of nature in Africa also came to represent the subjection of its people and the putative 'dark forces' with which they were identified.[21] What we may be witnessing now in one form in southern and South African white fiction is the reverse of this phenomenon, as nature 'romantically' promises to return. It was Doris Lessing's *The Grass is Singing* that first presented a tale of the 'return of the repressed' in political, psychological and environmental terms. André Brink writes of his 'rumours of rain'. There is Gordimer's *The Conservationist*. In J. M. Coetzee's *Waiting for the Barbarians* the demise of the allegoric imperial outpost is connected with natural cycles. To the extent that the return of nature represents the return of the people this fiction

220

seems to be telling us that we are entering the last act – an act of peripeteia or reversal – of a drama that began a long time ago. This does not, however, affect the degree to which it is written from a 'split position'. For the turn to nature in white South African fiction is still an index of a residual alienation as much as it is of a new affiliation; it is a symbolic registration at the same time of identification and distance in social and historical terms.

Finally, there is Gordimer's realism. We have seen realism in her novels as a matter of their 'perspective' – the way in which they link private and social destiny. We have seen it as a question of mode; for instance, in the classical realism of *A World of Strangers*. There is yet another kind of realism in her work, which in one version was understood very well by Bertolt Brecht:

> The demand for a realistic style of writing can . . . no longer be so easily dismissed today . . . The ruling classes use lies oftener than before – and bigger ones. To tell the truth is clearly an ever more urgent task.[22]

This is not exactly Gordimer's realism – it is much more politically motivated. Yet it does capture something of what her writing is about. For at base Gordimer's novels are engaged in 'truth-telling'; hers is a realism of naming and showing, of being witness to the times she has lived through; and a corollary of her realism is that it has undermined many of the 'lies' of apartheid. Yet if to some degree she stands at one with Brecht on this issue, then in the rider he draws to his proposition she must, in a fundamental way, part company. For where the suffering of the masses is so great, remarks Brecht, concern with the difficulties of small groups in society 'has come to be felt as ridiculous, contemptible'.[23] On the contrary, there is only one ally against a growing barbarism, and that is the people. Consequently:

> it is obvious that one must turn to the people, and [it is] now more necessary than ever to speak their language. Thus the terms *popular art* and *realism* become natural allies.[24]

It is the import of virtually everything that has been said in this chapter that such a 'natural' alliance has necessarily been beyond Gordimer. To take only the issue of language mentioned by Brecht: it would be possible for Gordimer to learn a black language, or more than one, and attempt to write directly for a black audience; to the degree that most black readers are literate in English, there is in fact no need to trade languages at all. But to learn to write authentically in the popular codes these languages *speak* – whether in English, Zulu, Xhosa, Sotho, or a new 'workers' language' – this in present circumstances is an issue of a different order altogether. The white South African poet Jeremy Cronin has written of the need 'To learn how to speak/With the voices of this land'.[25] But in a wider dimension, unless he means simply using local or dialect words, Cronin's prescription is altogether more demanding and problematic, for all its real value as an objective. As far as Gordimer is concerned, we have seen that the deep limitations of her situation preclude precisely this. And so direct representation of the people is replaced in her work by an indirect 'address'; as much as her fiction proposes it, it is also subject to a 'return of the repressed'.

This polarity then enables us to make an overall assessment of Gordimer's novels in terms of their fundamental historical 'fault'. We have seen how Gordimer writes from within the overall historical background of a colonial framework; yet also how her work foretells the end of the colonial era. We have seen how Gordimer is contained both socially and historically by the limits of her position within the fractured society of modern apartheid; yet also how the deepest address of her work is towards the people, in a complex attempt to overcome that fracture. There may be problems concealed in too simple an identification of 'realism' with 'popularity'; yet it is also understandable how a perfect realism, in representing truth, totality and justice, might perfectly represent the cause of the people. In this light we may borrow the equation for a moment, for it allows us to appreciate what is perhaps the deepest feature of Gordimer's work, proceeding directly from her 'split position', and to view it, moreover, as a matter of both form and content. In formal terms, measured against the long colonial history of South Africa on the one hand, and the specific class and race structures of modern apartheid on the other, this feature appears as a settler or fractured realism. And measured as a matter of content, it emerges as a settler or fractured populism. The 'populist' feature is itself of some significance. For the writer in Gordimer's position there is, by force of historical circumstances, an address to a largely undifferentiated black world. This in itself is an indication of just how far she is divided from that world, even as she approaches. Still, she is there approaching, across the paths of her own time and place, the broken landscape of her historical environment.

Afterword

History may well end up being harsh to white South African novelists of the twentieth century. It might happen that their work will come to be seen as the final surface flourish – or beneath-the-surface agony – of an oppressive and exploitative political and economic system. There will probably in the end be some truth in such a judgement. Yet it will not be the whole truth. For history also applies to those who are born on its 'bad side', as it were. We have seen here the development of one writer from a position of relative acceptance of the world around her to one in which her work calls an alternative future into being and makes its way towards that future. A great drama unfolds in the novels of Nadine Gordimer, but it is not the expected one of what her work observes in the world it depicts; rather it is the drama of the novels themselves, in their own development from one world to another, one culture to another in the making, from one historical life to the next. It is a fitting irony that whereas Gordimer began her life as an author as apparent mistress of all she surveyed, as she has become more powerful and accomplished as a writer she has had to fight for her historical existence, to justify her place in a new world by the issues she deals with in the present.

The transformations we have seen in her work are perhaps the best evidence of this. Gordimer has moved from political ignorance to a profound politicality, from aspects of a racist mental world to one approaching a revolutionary alignment. She has progressed from an account of growing up as a woman to a politicized feminism adapted to the realities of South Africa.

There have also been formal changes in her writing, embodying some of these shifts. The genre of the *Bildungsroman* has been transformed in its passage from *The Lying Days* to *Burger's Daughter*. Gordimer has gone from the lengthy, prosaic picaresque of her first novel to the pithy poetics of *July's People*; language itself has become a site of historical struggle. In modal terms the transition from *A World of Strangers* to *The Conservationist* reveals the most

223

significant historical change we have seen in the period, through a transformed framework of reality. On this question of form Gordimer's novels prove what Lukács pointed out some time ago: that there is no separable 'historical novel' as a genre.[1] Gordimer's novels, mostly written in the present, establish deep links with broader and more continuous processes because it is here that they find the meaning of the present. And this surely leads us to an important finding: that history can be a mode of existence as well as a temporal locality; it is in history that Gordimer's novels live. From this point of view, perhaps surprisingly, we have seen just how far the future governs an 'historical' consciousness, for this dictates a history that has to be made, one that – for those who take it up – makes few concessions to the present.

Thus it is nothing less than Nadine Gordimer's 'consciousness of history' that defines the special character of her writing and her stature as a novelist. There are no doubt any number of reasons for reading her novels; for many it will be their craftsmanship, or Gordimer's response to the details of her natural environment, that attracts them. This study has suggested another: that if we are searching for an inner pathway to guide us through South African history over the past forty or so years, there are few better places to look for it than in the novels of Nadine Gordimer. Gordimer has not written a history of the whole of her society; this has necessarily been beyond her. On the other hand it is not clear how far it is possible for any novelist anywhere to do so. But Gordimer's work has *responded* to the whole history of her society. With meticulous attention and unremitting clarity she has persistently measured its demands against the circumstances of her world. To this extent her work has been fashioned, even in its marginality, by a much larger totality. And to this degree, in its absences, indirections and contradictions, as well as in those areas of which it is 'conscious', it tells a story much larger than itself.

This has been our history 'from the inside'. We have seen a dramatic ideological shift in Gordimer's writing; we have followed her work into the depths of an historical 'unconscious'. We have seen how broader social and historical codes are embedded in her novels, and how her novels in turn illuminate these codes. Through fiction we have traced major shifts, and shifts of consciousness, in South African history. The focus of this study has deliberately been kept narrow in the belief that much may be learned from a relatively small area of investigation if that area is well enough defined. But it is to be hoped that we have discovered here something of what constitutes an historical consciousness, and how it is implanted in fiction; and that the abiding role of fiction in history as embodying its deeper codes of transformation may again be seen afresh.

Notes

NOTES TO INTRODUCTION

1 Nadine Gordimer, *The Black Interpreters – Notes on African Writing* (Johannesburg: Spro-Cas/Ravan, 1973), p. 7. The original gives the date of the retreat from Moscow as 1815; this has been changed with the permission of Nadine Gordimer.

2 John Bayley points out that Tolstoy originally intended to write a novel about the Decembrist conspiracy of 1825 that would then continue up to, and help explain, his own time. However, driven back to 1812 and even further to understand 1825, this then remained the setting of his novel. See Bayley's *Tolstoy and the Novel* (London: Chatto & Windus, 1966), pp. 120–2.

3 Clive Wake, 'The political and cultural revolution', in C. Pieterse and D. Munro (eds.), *Protest and Conflict in African Literature* (London: Heinemann, 1969), p. 46.

4 'History as the "hero" of the African novel', in Lewis Nkosi, *Tasks and Masks: Themes and Styles of African Literature* (London: Longman, 1981).

5 Chinua Achebe, 'The role of the writer in a new nation', in G. D. Killam (ed.), *African Writers on African Writing* (London: Heinemann, 1973), p. 8. For the view that Achebe's sense of history has itself been less than adequate, however, see Landeg White, 'Power and the praise poem', *Journal of Southern African Studies*, vol. 9, no. 1 (October 1982), p. 13.

6 *Mhudi*, written in about 1917, though published only in 1930, views South African – and particularly black South African – historical life in the 1830s. See Tim Couzens, 'Sol Plaatje's *Mhudi*', in Kenneth Parker (ed.), *The South African Novel in English* (London: Macmillan, 1978), pp. 57–76, where he argues that Plaatje's view of the past had a great deal to do with the present in which he wrote the novel, particularly with the issue of land distribution in the wake of the Natives' Land Act of 1913. Unless quoted, for details of works by other authors mentioned in this section see the Bibliography for a select list of South African fiction.

7 This has been pointed out by Stephen Gray, *Southern African Literature: An Introduction* (Cape Town: Philip; London: Collins; 1979), ch. 6, 'Schreiner and the novel tradition'. What Gray underestimates, however, is how Schreiner's world and the methods she uses to deal with it have been transformed under historical pressure in the century since then.

8 Olive Schreiner (pseud. Ralph Iron), preface to 2nd edn of *The Story of an African Farm* (London: Chapman & Hall, 1887), p. ix.

9 Legislation that came into force at that time included the Industrial Conciliation Act of 1924, which set up machinery for collective bargaining in industry, but excluded blacks from the terms of definition of 'employee',

and the Mines and Works Amendment Act of 1926, which firmly established the principle of the colour bar in key jobs in mining. The Natives (Urban Areas) Act of 1923 set up the modern system of 'influx control' whereby the rights of blacks to move to the cities were strictly curtailed, and the machinery established to enforce this.

10   David Rabkin, 'Race and fiction: *God's Stepchildren* and *Turbott Wolfe*', in Parker (ed.), *The South African Novel*, pp. 77–94.

11   William Plomer, *Turbott Wolfe* (London: Hogarth Press, 1925), p. 122.

12   See, for example, 'The novel and the nation in South Africa' (1961), in Killam (ed.) *African Writers*, p. 48.

13   See his autobiography, *Tell Freedom* (London: Faber, 1954), pp. 257–8.

14   See Kenneth Parker, 'The South African novel in English', in his edn of *The South African Novel,* pp. 18–20; also see Nkosi, 'History as "hero"', pp. 47–51.

15   'True great realism thus depicts man and society as complete entities, instead of showing merely one or the other of their aspects.' Georg Lukács, *Studies in European Realism*, trans. Edith Bone (1950; London: Merlin Press, 1972), p. 6, *et passim.*

16   *The Meaning of Contemporary Realism*, trans. John and Necke Mander (London: Merlin Press, 1963), p. 19.

17   Lukács, *European Realism*, p. 71, and *Contemporary Realism*, pp. 122–3. In this regard Lukács may seem to be having his realist cake and eating it; since for him private and social life must be seen as integral, the most highly individualized characters will by definition engage most deeply with the social forces surrounding them. Yet this seems to have a direct application for Gordimer; the more she delves into the personalities of her characters, the more they come to engage with history.

18   Interview with Alex Tetteh-Lartey, BBC African Service, *Arts and Africa*, no. 283 (transcript, n.d.), p. 4.

19   Suggestions as to the development of Gordimer's views will be made at different places in this study. For basic texts see 'The novel and the nation' and 'English-language literature and politics in South Africa', in Christopher Heywood (ed.), *Aspects of South African Literature* (London: Heinemann, 1976), pp. 99–120.

20   Nadine Gordimer, 'A brilliant bigot', review of *Sarah Gertrude Millin*, by Martin Rubin, *The Times Literary Supplement*, 15 September 1978. This view of Balzac as the 'great realist', who portrayed the objective forces at work in his society despite his own ideological sympathies as a Catholic Legitimist, is the basis of Lukács's approach; in this he is himself following Engels. That Millin should be considered a 'realist' in Balzac's mould is, however, debatable.

21   *The Black Interpreters*, p. 32. In Nadine Gordimer's papers there are 32 pages of detailed, typewritten notes taken directly from *The Meaning of Contemporary Realism*.

22   Personal correspondence from Nadine Gordimer, 27 June 1979.

23   Nadine Gordimer, 'A writer in South Africa', *London Magazine*, May 1965, p. 23.

24   'Leaving school – II', *London Magazine*, May 1963, p. 64.

25 'A writer in South Africa', pp. 21–2.
26 Ibid., p. 22.
27 'South Africa: towards a desk drawer literature', *The Classic*, vol. 2, no. 4 (1968), p. 65.
28 'A writer's freedom', *New Classic*, no. 2 (1975), p. 14.
29 Pat Schwartz, 'Interview – Nadine Gordimer', in *New South African Writing* (Johannesburg: Lorton, 1977), p. 81.
30 'The writing of Realism is far from being neutral; it is on the contrary loaded with the most spectacular signs of fabrication.' Roland Barthes, *Writing Degree Zero*, trans. Annette Lavers and Colin Smith (London: Cape, 1967), pp. 73–4. Barthes is referring here to 'realism' as a convention, but as far as he is concerned he might just as well be referring to it as an intention.
31 Nadine Gordimer, introduction to *No Place Like: Selected Stories* (London: Cape, 1975; Harmondsworth: Penguin, 1978), p. 13.
32 Pierre Macherey, *A Theory of Literary Production*, trans. Geoffrey Wall (London: Routledge & Kegan Paul, 1978). This study, though making use of Macherey's concept of the 'not-said', does so in somewhat different ways. For criticism of a latent idealism in Macherey, see Tony Bennet, *Formalism and Marxism* (London: Methuen, 1979).
33 In 1985 the Mixed Marriages Act and section 16 of the Immorality Act (prohibiting inter-racial sexual relations) were at last repealed. In these and other 'reforms' apartheid may be projecting itself from the class–colour axis to a more deliberately 'class' basis of organization. This will not, however, alter the situation of most of the country's people.
34 M. Wilson and L. M. Thompson (eds.), *The Oxford History of South Africa* (Oxford: Oxford University Press, 1971), Vol. 2, *South Africa 1870–1966*, p. 243.
35 Thus in social, economic and cultural terms one should distinguish migrant labourers, who spend long periods at work in urban areas but are not allowed to live there permanently, from settled black urban workers; similarly, being for the most part males, they should be distinguished from their wives, who are forced to stay behind in the rural areas. In ethnic terms there is the whole South African spectrum, which the apartheid mentality so delights in classifying: blacks, and the various sub-national categories into which they are divided, so-called 'coloureds' and Asians, English, Afrikaners and Jews; and all these identities tend to have class overtones. The South African socio-political structure is extremely complex, and can only be touched on in the most general way here.
36 Robert Green, 'Nadine Gordimer's *A World of Strangers*: strains in South African liberalism', *English Studies in Africa*, vol. 22, no. 1 (March 1979), p. 47.
37 Lucien Goldmann, *The Hidden God*, trans. P. Thody (1964; London: Routledge & Kegan Paul, 1976); see also Goldmann's *Towards a Sociology of the Novel*, trans. A Sheridan (London: Tavistock, 1975).
38 Thus Raymond Williams, in *Marxism and Literature* (Oxford: Oxford University Press, 1977), pp. 104–7, criticizes theories of 'homology' because of their ahistorical implications. Terry Eagleton, *Criticism and Ideology*, (1976; London: Verso, 1978), p. 97, makes a different point: 'not only is it

untrue ... that historically disparate works may "express" the same world-view; it is not necessarily true by any means that the works of the same author will belong to the same ideology'.

39 See, for example, Michael Wade, *Nadine Gordimer* (London: Evans, 1978).

40 Thus Abdul R. JanMohamed, *Manichean Aesthetics: The Politics of Literature in Colonial Africa* (Amherst, Mass.: University of Massachusetts Press, 1983), ch. 4, is able to detect some form of change in Gordimer's work, but is unable to explain why this should occur. Also, an inadequate grasp of the real conditions of Gordimer's development helps produce unlikely readings; for one example see below, Chapter 5, note 39.

41 Eagleton, *Criticism and Ideology*, p. 179.

NOTES TO CHAPTER 1: EARLY WORK AND *THE LYING DAYS*

1 *New Yorker*, 16 October 1954, p. 113.
2 Gordimer quotes four lines from her poem: 'Noble in heart,/ Noble in mind,/ Never deceitful,/ Never unkind'. 'Leaving school – II', p. 61.
3 'The valley legend', *Children's Sunday Express* (Johannesburg), 18 September 1938, p. 1.
4 'Come again tomorrow', *The Forum*, 18 November 1939, p. 14.
5 'Leaving school – II', p. 63.
6 For Gordimer's celebration of the role of the 'small magazine' in promoting South African writing, see 'An unkillable rabbit family', *Contrast*, no. 50 (December 1980), pp. 25–6.
7 'The first circle', in *Six One Act Plays by South African Authors* (Pretoria: Van Schaik, 1949), pp. 43–70.
8 *Face to Face* (Johannesburg: Silver Leaf Books, 1949).
9 *The Soft Voice of the Serpent* (London: Gollancz, 1953). For United States and South African editions of Gordimer's major publications, see Bibliography.
10 For these stories, see 'A commonplace story', in *Face to Face* and *The Soft Voice of the Serpent*; 'The battlefield at no. 29', in *Face to Face*; and 'Sweet dreams selection', *Common Sense*, November 1949, pp. 501–5.
11 This and immediately following information: interview with Nadine Gordimer, Johannesburg, 17 March 1980 (henceforth Gordimer, interview). See also Gordimer, 'A South African childhood'.
12 'A South African childhood', p. 111.
13 'The defeated', in *The Soft Voice of the Serpent*.
14 'Ah, woe is me', *Common Sense*, December 1947, pp. 537–41. Also in *Face to Face* and *The Soft Voice of the Serpent*. 'Monday is better than Sunday', in *The Soft Voice of the Serpent*.
15 'The amateurs', *Common Sense*, December 1948, pp. 540–4.
16 'The train from Rhodesia', *Trek*, September 1947, pp. 18–19.
17 'Is there nowhere else we can meet?', *Common Sense*, September 1947, pp. 387–9. This and the previous two works also in *Face to Face* and *The Soft*

Voice of the Serpent. For discussion of 'Is there nowhere else we can meet?' see Chapter 7, section II.

18 Nadine Gordimer, untitled and unfinished novel (typescript; before 1946), pp. 1–34. All page references to this typescript given hereafter in the text.

19 Sarah Gertrude Millin, *God's Step-Children* (London: Constable, 1924). For an important article analysing various ideological and cultural threads in Millin, see J. M. Coetzee, 'Blood, flaw, taint, degeneration: the case of Sarah Gertrude Millin', *English Studies in Africa*, vol. 23, no. 1 (March 1980), pp. 41–58.

20 Nadine Gordimer, untitled and unfinished novel (typescript; *c.* 1951), pp. 1–84.

21 See again 'A South African childhood'.

22 Ibid., p. 117.

23 Nadine Gordimer, *The Lying Days* (London: Gollancz, 1953), p. 120. Page references to this edn are given hereafter in the text.

24 For analysis and accounts of the 1946 strike, see H. J. Simons and R. E. Simons, *Class and Colour in South Africa 1850–1950* (Harmondsworth: Penguin, 1969), pp. 573–8; Ken Luckhardt and Brenda Wall, *Organize... or Starve!* (London: Lawrence & Wishart, 1980), pp. 65–73; Mary Benson, *South Africa: The Struggle for a Birthright*, rev. edn (Harmondsworth: Penguin, 1966), ch. 8; for personal memories, see Ruth First, *One Hundred and Seventeen Days* (Harmondsworth: Penguin, 1965), pp. 114–16.

25 For the 1922 strike, see Edward Roux, *Time Longer Than Rope* (Madison, Wis.: University of Wisconsin Press, 1972), ch. 14. For an eyewitness account, see Bernard Sachs, 'The 1922 Rand Revolt', in his *South African Personalities and Places* (Johannesburg: Kayor, 1959).

26 Gordimer, interview.

27 Nadine Gordimer, 'What being a South African means to me', *South African Outlook*, June 1977, pp. 87–9, 92.

28 Dan Jacobson, *A Dance in the Sun* (London, 1956; rpt, with *The Trap*, Harmondsworth: Penguin, 1968).

29 Wade, *Nadine Gordimer*. See also his 'Nadine Gordimer and Europe-in-Africa' in Parker (ed.), *The South African Novel*, pp. 131–63.

30 Olive Schreiner (pseud. Ralph Iron), *The Story of an African Farm*, 2 vols. (London: Chapman & Hall, 1883; rpt with an introduction by Dan Jacobson, Harmondsworth: Penguin, 1971).

31 This image of the sun seems to have been in currency at the time. In the issue that broke the news of the election results the Afrikaans daily *Die Vaderland* carried a political cartoon showing a blinding white sun rising over what looks like a previously frozen landscape. The caption is: 'Die son gaan op oor Suid-Afrika!' ('The sun is rising over South Africa!'). *Die Vaderland* (Johannesburg), 28 May 1948. My thanks to Stanley Trapido for remembering the cartoon.

32 For a brief account of the Torch Commando see Janet Robertson, *Liberalism in South Africa 1948–63* (Oxford: Clarendon Press, 1971), pp. 51–61.

33 In the wake of the 1948 election Smuts was able to claim: 'Our policy has been European paramountcy in this country. Our policy has not been equal rights . . . We stand and have always stood for European supremacy in this country.' *Assembly Debates*, vol. 65 (21 September 1948), col. 2905, quoted in Robertson, *Liberalism*, p. 43. For analysis of continuity and change in both structure and ideology before and after 1948, see Martin Legassick, 'Legislation, ideology and economy in post-1948 South Africa', *Journal of Southern African Studies*, vol. 1, no. 1 (October 1974), pp. 5–35, and 'South Africa: capital accumulation and violence', *Economy and Society*, vol. 3, no. 3 (August 1974), pp. 253–91.

34 Because 'coloured' voting rights were entrenched in the constitution, the government required a two-thirds majority at a joint sitting of both Houses of Parliament to effect any change. When it tried to do so by other means it was successfully challenged twice in the Courts of Appeal. Thereafter it achieved its aim by following the expedient of enlarging the Senate, packing it with its own supporters, and gaining the required majority; it also changed the make-up of the Appeal Bench. The whole process lasted from 1951 to 1956.

35 His celebrated phrase, speaking to the Senate in June 1954 as Minister of Native Affairs. Quoted in Baruch Hirson, *Year of Fire, Year of Ash – the Soweto Revolt: Roots of a Revolution?* (London: Zed Press, 1979), p. 45.

36 Photograph of C. R. Swart, later President of South Africa, reproduced in Patrick Duncan, *South Africa's Rule of Violence* (London: Methuen, 1964), between pp. 32–3.

37 *Fighting Talk*, vol. 10, no. 6 (June 1952), p. 1.

38 South African Congress of Democrats, 'Educating for ignorance', pamphlet (Johannesburg, n.d.), p. 12. This pamphlet must have been written some time after *The Lying Days*; clearly the feelings that the novel registered endured.

39 This paragraph and the interpretations that follow based on documents reproduced in T. Karis and G. M. Carter (eds.), *From Protest to Challenge: A Documentary History of African Politics in South Africa 1882–1964*, 4 vols. (Stanford, Calif.: Hoover Institution Press, 1972–7), Vol. 2, *Hope and Challenge 1935–52* (1973), pts 2 and 3; and relevant discussion in Gail M. Gerhart, *Black Power in South Africa: The Evolution of an Ideology* (Berkeley, Calif.: University of California Press, 1978); Peter Walshe, *The Rise of African Nationalism in South Africa* (London: Hurst, 1970); and Simons and Simons, *Class and Colour*, Luckhardt and Wall, *Organize*, and Hirson, *Year of Fire*.

40 Walshe, *African Nationalism*, p. 400.

41 For the memoirs of a trade unionist of this time, see Naboth Mokgatle, *The Autobiography of an Unknown South African* (London: Hurst, 1971), pp. 280–6; see also Simons and Simons, *Class and Colour*, pp. 604–5, and Walshe, *African Nationalism*, pp. 366–7.

42 Simons and Simons, *Class and Colour*, p. 605.

43 G. W. F. Hegel, *Aesthetics*, 2 vols., trans. T. M. Knox (Oxford: Clarendon Press, 1975), Vol. 1, p. 593.

NOTES TO CHAPTER 2: *A WORLD OF STRANGERS*

1 Nadine Gordimer, from 'Which new era would that be?', in *Six Feet of the Country* (London: Gollancz, 1956), p. 83.

2 Nadine Gordimer, *A World of Strangers* (London: Gollancz, 1958; rpt, London: Cape, 1976). All page references, to 1976 edn, are given hereafter in the text.

3 Karis and Carter (eds.), *Protest to Challenge*, Vol. 2, p. 92.

4 The most celebrated multi-racial act of Defiance was the illegal entry into Germiston location (near Johannesburg) of a small group headed by the Mahatma Gandhi's son, Manilal, and Patrick Duncan. Included in the group was one Bettie du Toit, later a very close friend of Gordimer's (see below). Gordimer wrote a short story based on the incident, 'The smell of death and flowers', to be found in *Six Feet of the Country*.

5 In this regard one need only compare the 1949 Programme of Action, with its fundamental principle of 'National Freedom' – Karis and Carter (eds.), *Protest to Challenge*, Vol. 2, p. 337 – with the 1955 Freedom Charter (see below).

6 Gerhart, *Black Power* ch. 4.

7 For a moving account of this event by one of its leading participants, see Helen Joseph, *Tomorrow's Sun* (London: Hutchinson, 1966), pp. 82–5.

8 Freedom Charter, adopted at the Congress of the People, Kliptown, 25–6 June 1955.

9 Quoted in Helen Joseph, *If This Be Treason* (London: Deutsch, 1963), p. 15. For accounts of the Treason Trial, see also Lionel Forman and E. S. Sachs, *The South African Treason Trial* (London: Calder, 1957); and Anthony Sampson, *The Treason Cage: The Opposition on Trial in South Africa* (London: Heinemann, 1958).

10 For the Congress Alliance in the 1950s, see Tom Lodge, *Black Politics in South Africa since 1945* (London: Longman, 1983), ch. 3. On the liberal tradition in the Alliance, see Gerhart, *Black Power*, ch. 4; Robertson, *Liberalism*, p. 145; cf. also Leo Kuper, *Passive Resistance in South Africa* (London: Cape, 1956), who maintains that the immediate aims and assumptions underlying the resistance movement in the 1950s were 'consistent with the spirit of liberalism' (p. 45). As a leading member of the Liberal Party, Kuper would have been well placed (as well as eager) to appreciate such patterns.

11 Two aspects of Liberal policy were anathema to the ANC in the early 1950s: its adherence to parliamentary methods of action alone, and its criterion of 'civilization', proposed as the basis for a qualified extension of the franchise. In 1953 Mandela attacked Liberal policy as a 'crass perversion of elementary tactics of political struggle', while Dr Mji (amongst many others) defined a Liberal as a 'double dealer' (quoted in Robertson, *Liberalism*, pp. 119 and 98 respectively).

12 For the strong anti-communism of a black South African Liberal, see Jordan K. Ngubane, *An African Explains Apartheid* (London: Pall Mall, 1963).

13 For the Liberal Party in relation to the Congress Alliance and the Treason Trial, see Robertson, *Liberalism*, pp. 164–8, 181–3.

14 Albert Luthuli, *Let My People Go* (1962; Glasgow: Fontana, 1963), p. 153. The spelling of Lutuli's name has varied, but without the 'h' seems to be the version he preferred: Karis and Carter (eds.), *Protest to Challenge*, Vol. 3, *Challenge and Violence 1953–64* (1977), p. xviii.

15 Robertson, *Liberalism*, pp. 181–2; on the importance of Johannesburg as a social milieu, see Gerhart, *Black Power*, p. 109.

16 Quoted in Robertson, *Liberalism*, p. 183.

17 Lewis Nkosi, 'The fabulous decade – the fifties', in his *Home and Exile* (London: Longman, 1965).

18 For the celebration of this world by its writers, see Bloke Modisane, *Blame Me on History* (London: Thames & Hudson, 1963); Can Themba, *The Will to Die*, writings selected by Donald Stuart and Roy Holland (London: Heinemann, 1972; rpt, 1976); Nat Nakasa, *The World of Nat Nakasa*, ed. Essop Patel, introduction by Nadine Gordimer (Johannesburg: Ravan/Bateleur, 1975); and Todd Matshikiza, *Chocolates for My Wife* (London: Hodder & Stoughton, 1961). See also Trevor Huddleston, *Naught for Your Comfort* (London: Collins, 1956), ch. 7, by one of the most famous of Sophiatown figures. For a non-fictional account by Gordimer of Sophiatown, see 'Johannesburg', *Holiday*, August 1955, pp. 58–9.

19 Nkosi, 'The fabulous decade', p. 25.

20 Interview with Es'kia Mphahlele, Johannesburg, 1 May 1980; Nkosi, 'The fabulous decade', pp. 23–4.

21 With production by Leon Gluckman, script by Harry Bloom, lyrics by Pat Williams, the score by Todd Matshikiza, a black cast and black musicians, the show was intended to be a true cultural 'mix'. For surrounding complications, however, see D. Coplan, 'The African musician and the development of the Johannesburg entertainment industry, 1900–1960', *Journal of Southern African Studies*, vol. 5, no. 2 (April 1979), pp. 159–61. For Todd Matshikiza on *King Kong*, see his *Chocolates for My Wife*, especially for his fears that he might be done down by his white collaborators.

22 Gordimer, interview.

23 Mphahlele, interview, Johannesburg, 1 May 1980.

24 For the police record of Mphahlele's speech, see Karis and Carter (eds.), *Protest to Challenge*, Vol. 3, pp. 202–3.

25 Gordimer, interview; interview with Bettie du Toit, London, 12 February 1981. See also Gordimer, 'What being a South African means to me', p. 89, col. 1.

26 This and preceding information: Gordimer, interview.

27 Nadine Gordimer, 'Chief Luthuli' (Bulletin Biography no. 1), *Treason Trial Bulletin*, no. 2 (issued by Treason Trials Defence Fund, Johannesburg, May 1958), pp. 4–6 (my thanks to Baruch Hirson for supplying me with this bulletin); and 'Chief Luthuli', *Atlantic Monthly*, April 1959, pp. 34–9.

28 'But Johannesburg sees itself in her book', *Star*, 11 July 1958.

29 Anthony Sampson, *'Drum': A Venture into the New Africa* (London: Collins, 1956) pp. 153–5.

30   Sampson, *'Drum'*, pp. 81–3. Just as Toby might, Sampson relates: 'As I penetrated farther into the world of the Africans, I found myself caught between the two camps of black and white. The contrast, from a cocktail party in the northern white suburbs to a drinking den in the southern black locations, was abrupt' (p. 83).

31   Gordimer, 'Johannesburg'; Sampson, *'Drum'*; and Matshikiza, *Chocolates*.

32   Again, see works by Themba, Nakasa, Modisane and Matshikiza. One of the finest accounts of black township life – though it is set in Marabastad, near Pretoria, and not Sophiatown – is Ezekiel Mphahlele's *Down Second Avenue* (1959; London: Faber, 1971).

33   'Négritude' – a movement begun in the 1930s and 1940s by the Francophone poets Aimé Césaire and Leopold Senghor – attempted to recover a sense of black dignity, in part by celebrating the sensuality of the black body and spirit. Though knowledge of this movement had not reached South Africa by this time, there are some interesting parallels here.

34   This sort of thing may have been endemic at the time. Bloke Modisane remarks that at multi-racial tea-parties hosts would refer to their guests as 'Africans', but talk of their servants as the 'boy' or 'girl'. He relates: 'They tell the delightful story of the African being prompted with a finger in the back by a fashionable woman in mink: "Come on, don't be shy. Tell the gentleman what the police did to you last week." ' *Blame Me on History*, p. 160.

35   For Kenneth Parker, Steven is the real hero of the novel precisely because of his refusal to be beaten, or more importantly, to fit into acknowledged social categories. See 'Nadine Gordimer and the pitfalls of liberalism', in Parker's edn of *The South African Novel*, p. 122. But in the way Steven is classified in death there is a category he cannot escape; and there is surely as much criticism of him in the novel as admiration of his audacity.

36   This is the interpretation given in one of the more useful articles on Gordimer: Robert Green, 'Gordimer's *A World of Strangers*'.

37   Roland Barthes, *Writing Degree Zero*; and *S/Z*, trans. R. Miller (London: Cape, 1975).

38   Something of all these assumptions is perhaps contained in Leo Kuper's definition of 'liberal humanitarianism', which, as he puts it, 'asserts the dignity of the human personality, the belief that all men are born equal, the conviction that the human being is educable, and the assumption that history is the story of the unfolding of freedom'. *Passive Resistance*, p. 109. Interestingly, with regard to the paragraph that follows, Kuper is here discussing the tactics of the Congress movement during the Defiance Campaign.

39   There was one other crucial hope: that an inevitable economic integration in South Africa would involve an inevitable social integration. But while this was perhaps a necessary condition for liberalism, it was not by itself sufficient. Only a liberal morality could guarantee a truly liberal social order.

40   For some of the moral and educative dimensions to Congress methods, which Lodge also mentions, see *Black Politics*, pp. 78, 202.

41   'The breaking up and democratisation of these monopolies will open

234

up fresh fields for the development of a prosperous Non-European bourgeois class.' Nelson Mandela, 'In our lifetime', *Liberation*, June 1956, reproduced in Karis and Carter (eds.), *Protest to Challenge*, Vol. 3, p. 247. Mandela may have had strategic reasons for making this statement; none the less the idea of a 'black bourgeoisie' was not unspeakable to the ANC in the mid-1950s. This specific reference does not appear in the version of Mandela's article reproduced in the collection *No Easy Walk to Freedom*, ed. Ruth First (London: Heinemann, 1965), although the emphasis on a cross-class alliance remains. Lodge, p. 73, has also noted the significance of this passage.

42   This for Barthes is an impossibility. See Introduction, note 30.
43   'Notes of an expropriator', *The Times Literary Supplement*, 4 June 1964.
44   Gerhart, *Black Power*, p. 94.
45   Ibid.
46   'What being a South African means to me', p. 89. 'Only connect . . .' is of course the epigraph to Forster's *Howards End*.
47   Huddleston, *Naught for Your Comfort*, p. 118.
48   Ibid., p. 181.

NOTES TO CHAPTER 3: *OCCASION FOR LOVING*

1   Nadine Gordimer, 'A thing of the past', in *Friday's Footprint* (London: Gollancz, 1960), p. 160.
2   Nadine Gordimer, *Occasion for Loving* (London: Gollancz, 1963); all page references to this edn are given hereafter in the text.
3   For Africanism in the 1950s and the formation of the PAC, see Gerhart, *Black Power*, chs. 5, 6, and Lodge, *Black Politics*, ch. 3.
4   'We aim . . . at government of the Africans by the Africans, for the Africans, with everybody who owes his only loyalty to Afrika and who is prepared to accept the democratic rule of an African majority being regarded as an African. We guarantee no minority rights, because we think in terms of individuals, not groups.' Robert Sobukwe at the Inaugural Convention of the PAC, 4–6 April 1959, in Karis and Carter (eds.), *Protest to Challenge*, Vol. 3, p. 516. 'Afrika' was the PAC – and sometimes the ANC – spelling.
5   Thus it was that Patrick Duncan, a founder member of the Liberal Party, became the only white person to be a member of the PAC, ultimately becoming its official representative in Algeria. For the life of Duncan, a maverick in every respect, see C. J. Driver, *Patrick Duncan: South African and Pan-African* (London: Heinemann, 1980).
6   Gerhart, *Black Power*, p. 213, calculates that by August 1959 formal membership of the PAC, though far short of its set target, may have been more than double that of the ANC.
7   Nkrumah sent a telegram of greeting to the inaugural meeting of the PAC, while the PAC flag showed a star of gold in Ghana, lighting southwards.
8   The PAC adopted the resolutions of Accra *in toto*, while the ANC called it 'a milestone in the forward march of the people of Africa', and listed, among the focal points of its own solidarity, the Belgian Congo, French

Cameroons, Nyasaland, Rhodesia, Tanganyika, Uganda, Kenya, Algeria, Angola, and Mozambique. Report of the NEC of the ANC Annual Conference, 12–13 December 1959, in Karis and Carter (eds.), *Protest to Challenge*, Vol. 3, pp. 463–6.

9   See Lodge, *Black Politics*, ch. 9, pp. 210–23, for a full account.

10   Gordimer, interview.

11   'We will use an iron hand with regard to mixed gatherings aimed at undermining the Government's Apartheid policy.' Quoted in Karis and Carter (eds.), *Protest to Challenge*, Vol. 3, p. 280, from *New Age*, 19 September 1957.

12   Nat Nakasa committed suicide in New York in 1964. Significantly, in relation to the figure of Gideon in *Occasion for Loving*, his passport application had been turned down, and he had left South Africa on an exit permit to take up a Niemann Fellowship at Harvard University. Can Themba died in Swaziland in 1968. Other tragedies in the South African literary world of this time were the suicides of the poets Ingrid Jonker and (slightly later) Arthur Nortje. For the view that these deaths were intrinsically bound up with a social and political anguish, see Lewis Nkosi, 'Obituary', in Can Themba, *The Will to Die*, pp. vii–xi.

13   See Coplan, 'The African musician', pp. 160–1.

14   Nadine Gordimer, 'Where do whites fit in?', *The Twentieth Century*, April 1959, pp. 327–31.

15   Nkosi, 'The fabulous decade', p. 31.

16   Nkosi, 'Obituary', p. ix. On the other hand, for an escape by a (cross-racial) couple that did take place at about this time, see Alfred Hutchinson, *Road to Ghana* (London: Gollancz, 1960).

17   See Nadine Gordimer, 'Egypt revisited', *National and English Review*, January 1959, pp. 47–53.

18   Nadine Gordimer, 'The Congo River', *Holiday*, May 1961, p. 88. This article, by and large, seems to have been composed from two typescripts: 'Towards the heart of darkness', and 'Africa 1960: the great period' (typescripts in Nadine Gordimer's possession; both *c*. 1960–1).

19   For more on this, see the discussion on *A Guest of Honour*, Chapter 4, section III.

20   See, respectively: Plomer, *Turbott Wolfe*; Millin, *God's Step-Children*; Alan Paton, *Too Late the Phalarope* (London: Cape, 1955; Harmondsworth: Penguin, 1971).

21   'The English novel in South Africa', in H. Lewin (ed.), *The Novel and the Nation* (Cape Town: NUSAS, 1959), p. 1; reprinted with slight change in 'The novel and the nation' (1961), p. 41.

22   Paton does not see cross-colour love or sex as sinful, but 'sin' – or the lack of it – nevertheless governs the terms of analysis of *Too Late the Phalarope*. For an alternative view, however, see John Cooke, ' "A hunger of the soul": *Too Late the Phalarope* reconsidered', *English Studies in Africa*, vol. 22, no. 1 (March 1979), pp. 37–44.

23   Respectively: *The Path of Thunder* (London: Faber, 1952); *The Evidence of Love* (London: Weidenfeld & Nicolson, 1960; rev. edn, London: Chatto & Windus, 1970); *Emergency* (London: Faber, 1964).

24 Alan Paton, *Cry, the Beloved Country* (London: Cape, 1948; Harmondsworth: Penguin, 1958), p. 235.

25 On a more personal note, it appears that Gordimer's own mother had kept her out of school at the age of 10 or 11 on the pretext of a heart ailment that Gordimer later realized was false, which she felt free to acknowledge after her mother died. On the one hand the experience was traumatic; Gordimer was passionate about dancing, and had lived a vital and active life up till then, but this was suddenly curtailed. On the other hand the solitude and introspection through which she now lived, as well the only release she could find, in reading voraciously and widely, may well have been contributory factors in turning her into a writer. For details, see 'The art of fiction LXXVII', interview with Nadine Gordimer, by Jannika Hurwitt, *Paris Review*, no. 88 (Summer 1983), pp. 88–90.

26 Such as Simone Weil's *The Need for Roots*, trans. A. F. Wills (London: Routledge & Kegan Paul, 1952), in which the interrelationship between 'identity', 'becoming' and 'community' is put forward very strongly, just as it is in *Occasion for Loving*. Gordimer's other writing of this time reveals similar influences, cf. 'The novel and the nation', where she refers to Niebuhr and Jaspers for her understanding of the concept of 'community'. Information as to this phase in her life: Gordimer, interview; she also mentions reading Weil in 'The art of fiction', p. 115.

27 Cf., for example, Hugh Lewin, *Bandiet* (London: Barrie & Jenkins, 1974), and the reasons he gives for joining the ARM: 'But my efforts seemed puny and hopeless; it seemed that nothing would awaken the whites ... I thought that sabotage might shock the whites into an awareness' (statement from the dock, 1964), pp. 11–13.

NOTES TO CHAPTER 4: *THE LATE BOURGEOIS WORLD AND A GUEST OF HONOUR*

1 Nadine Gordimer, 'Some Monday for sure', in *Not for Publication* (London: Gollancz, 1965), p. 207.

2 Nadine Gordimer, 'No place like', in *Livingstone's Companions* (London: Cape, 1972; Harmondsworth: Penguin, 1975), p. 182.

3 Nadine Gordimer, *The Late Bourgeois World* (London: Gollancz, 1966; rpt London: Cape, 1976). All page references, to 1976 edn, are given hereafter in the text.

4 See Govan Mbeki, *South Africa: The Peasants' Revolt* (Harmondsworth: Penguin, 1964). For an overview of resistance in the Eastern Cape, see William Beinart and Colin Bundy, 'State intervention and rural resistance: the Transkei, 1900–1965', in Martin A. Klein (ed.), *Peasants in Africa* (Beverly Hills, Calif.: Sage, 1980). For the revolt in the Western Transvaal, see Charles Hooper, *Brief Authority* (London: Collins, 1960).

5 This was stressed by Sobukwe as leader of the PAC both in a letter to Major-General Rademeyer, Commissioner of Police, before the anti-Pass campaign started, and in a press release announcing the beginning of the campaign. If arrested, or ordered to disperse, his supporters would comply peacefully. But if the 'other side' so desired, the PAC would provide it with an opportunity to demonstrate to the world 'just how brutal they can be.' Karis and Carter (eds.), *Protest to Challenge*, Vol. 3, pp. 566–7.

6   Ibid., p. 360. Verwoerd used the phrase specifically in relation to the idea of 'coloureds' re-entering Parliament, but it characterized the general attitude of his government perfectly.

7   For *Umkhonto*, sabotage was the most restrained form of violent resistance and would be employed until exhausted as a method. Thereafter, successive phases of action would involve guerrilla warfare, terrorism and finally open revolution. 16 December was a highly significant date in South African history, commemorating the day on which Dingane's Zulu army had been decisively defeated at the battle of Blood River in 1838, and celebrated as such each year by white South Africa. 16 December 1961 was evidently designed to signal the historic reopening of the struggle (though Lodge, *Black Politics*, p. 235, notes that the Durban group acted a day prematurely, on the 15th).

8   On *Poqo*, see Lodge, *Black Politics*, ch. 10.

9   The speech was given on 3 February 1960. The most striking of all the impressions he had formed on his African tour, said Macmillan, was of the strength of African national consciousness: 'In different places it takes on different forms. But it is happening everywhere. The wind of change is blowing throughout the continent.' *Rand Daily Mail*, 4 February 1960.

10   Verwoerd, who had been unusually nonplussed at the time of Macmillan's speech (*Rand Daily Mail*, 4 February 1960), still felt obliged to reply to him over a month later. Using terms only he could, there was, he said now, 'a psychotic preoccupation with the rights, the liberties and the privileges of non-white peoples ... sweeping the world, at the expense of due consideration of the rights and merits of white people.' H. F. Verwoerd, 'The price of appeasement in Africa', pamphlet (n.d.) of his speech in the House of Assembly, 10 March 1960, p. 1.

11   During 1960 and early 1961 there was a capital outflow from South Africa of R12 million per month. Reserves of gold and foreign exchange were reduced to less than a half, falling from R312 million in January 1960 to less than R153 million in May 1961: 'South Africa faced a balance of payments crisis more severe than any experienced since 1932'. This account from D. Hobart Houghton, *The South African Economy*, 3rd edn (Cape Town: Oxford University Press, 1973), p. 184. The crisis did not preclude a massive boom in the remainder of the decade, however, as the state got the political situation under control and the economy recovered due to underlying strengths (see Houghton, ch. 10).

12   See Lodge, *Black Politics*, p. 219.

13   *Rand Daily Mail*, 11 April 1960.

14   Karis and Carter (eds.), *Protest to Challenge*, Vol. 3, p. 343.

15   For an unusual account of the trial by someone who should never have been involved, see James Kantor, *A Healthy Grave* (London: Hamish Hamilton, 1967).

16   This sort of violence was never part of the ARM plan. In the crisis of the arrests, however, John Harris, a man on the fringes of the movement, planted the bomb. See Lewin, *Bandiet*. Harris was later executed.

17 See Gerhart, *Black Power*, pp. 252–3; Lodge, *Black Politics*, p. 247.

18 *A Survey of Race Relations in South Africa 1964*, comp. M. Horrell (Johannesburg: South African Institute of Race Relations), pp. 31–3; hereafter this series will be referred to as *A Survey*, with relevant year and compiler(s); *A Survey 1965*, comp. M. Horrell, p. 62.

19 Legislated respectively under the General Laws Amendment Act ('Sabotage Act') 1962; the General Laws Amendment Act ('90-Day Act') 1963 (designed, according to Minister of Justice B. J. Vorster, to 'break the backs' of *Poqo* and *Umkhonto*); and the Criminal Procedure Amendment Act ('180-Day Act') 1965.

20 The first to die in gaol was Looksmart Solwandle Ngudle. Detained on 19 August 1963, he was found hanged in his cell on the 21 October. On 25 October he was officially banned from attending meetings by the government, presumably so that statements made by him while still living could not be quoted (*A Survey 1963*, comp. M. Horrell and M. Draper, p. 51). Other deaths in detention over the decade were attributed to natural causes, suicide by hanging or jumping out of windows, falling in the shower and slipping on a piece of soap (see *A Survey 1969*, comp. M. Horrell, pp. 68–70).

21 *A Survey 1966*, comp. M. Horrell, p. 66.

22 Thus, under the provisions of the Sabotage Act, 102 people, including journalists and writers, were forbidden to make any public communication, either by way of speech or the written or quoted word; under the terms of the Internal Security Act of 1950, Government Notice R510 of 1966 listed forty-six South Africans in exile whose sayings or writings could no longer be quoted or disseminated in the Republic. The list included nearly all the black writers who have been mentioned in this study, such as Nkosi, Mphahlele, Themba, Modisane, Matshikiza and La Guma, as well as Dennis Brutus and others.

23 This latter tactic was enforced when publications that were banned kept reappearing under new names. Thus the *Guardian*, *Advance*, *New Age* and *Spark* were successive reincarnations of the same publication.

24 *The World That Was Ours* (London: Heinemann, 1967), title to ch. 7. Bernstein, a communist, came from a different ideological background than Elizabeth in the novel, but there are a number of similarities in observation and mood between her memoirs and *The Late Bourgeois World*. Thus, another of her chapter titles that would seem to be of general relevance for the novel is that of 'A world without men', in which the aftermath of the Rivonia arrests is described. Bernstein also describes the same apocalyptic sunsets of this time that appear in the novel and no doubt added to the feel of the period. Another woman caught in the 'net of silence' in these years was Helen Joseph, confined by banning and house arrest, though in her case terror was added to silence in the form of harassment by both police and public. Interview with Helen Joseph, Johannesburg, 23 April 1980.

25 In the paperback edition probably because in this form it might reach a wider audience than in hard covers. Ironically, *Occasion for Loving* was not banned, perhaps because the censors believed it demonstrated the intrinsic futility of a love affair across the colour line. *The Late Bourgeois World* was itself banned upon publication, to have its restriction lifted only in July 1976, a month after *A World of Strangers.*

26 Nadine Gordimer, 'Censored, banned, gagged: letter from Johannesburg', *Encounter*, June 1963, p. 62. This article was written in direct response to the Publications and Entertainments Act 1963 and the Sabotage Act 1962.

27 Apart from the above, see: 'The voices we may not hear', *Rand Daily Mail*, 13 August 1966, reproduced as 'How not to know the African', *Contrast*, no. 15 (March 1967), pp. 44–9; 'South Africa: towards a desk drawer literature' (1968); 'Apartheid and censorship', in J. Paton (ed.), *The Grey Ones* (Johannesburg: Ravan, 1974); 'Catalogue of the ridiculous', *The Times* (London), 2 July 1975; 'South Africa: the way writers live now' (incomplete typescript in Nadine Gordimer's possession). For Gordimer's attack on censorship in the 1980s, see Chapter 6.

28 'Censored, banned, gagged', p. 59.

29 Nadine Gordimer, 'The Fischer case', *London Magazine*, March 1966, pp. 21–30; and 'Why did Bram Fischer choose jail?', *New York Times Magazine*, 14 August 1966, pp. 30–1, 80–1, 84 (in typescript form as 'Profile: Bram Fischer').

30 Gordimer, 'The Fischer case'.

31 See, for example, Arthur Blaxall, *Suspended Sentence* (London: Hodder & Stoughton, 1965). Rev. Blaxall was arrested in April 1963 and charged on four counts, two of them concerning the administration of funds for the PAC and ANC. Over 70 years old, he was sentenced to twenty-eight months' hard labour, twenty-two suspended. In the event he served only one night, being given parole with immediate effect, and left South Africa soon after. It is possible that the figure of Colonel Gaisford in the novel, who precedes Elizabeth in channelling money, relates in some way to people such as Blaxall.

32 'Towards a desk drawer literature', p. 71.

33 A point raised in a slightly different form by M. J. Daymond, *'Burger's Daughter*: a novel's reliance on history', in M. J. Daymond, J. U. Jacobs and M. Lenta (eds.), *Momentum* (Pietermaritzburg: University of Natal Press, 1984), pp. 159–70.

34 For Hugh Lewin's account of the ARM, of which he was a member, see his *Bandiet*.

35 See ibid., p. 70, for details.

36 Here, for example, one thinks of a movement such as the Black Sash, which has been steadfast in its social 'witness' since it was formed in opposition to the removal of the 'coloureds' from the common voters' roll in the 1950s, and of individuals such as Helen Joseph and Helen Suzman. The women's section of the ANC has historically been both very powerful and resilient.

37 C. J. Driver, *Elegy for a Revolutionary* (London: Faber, 1969).

38 Jack Cope, *The Dawn Comes Twice* (London: Heinemann, 1969).

39 Alex La Guma, *The Stone Country* (1967; London: Heinemann, 1974); *In the Fog of the Seasons' End* (London: Heinemann, 1972; rpt, 1977).

40 *A Guest of Honour* (London: Cape, 1971); all page references to this edn are given hereafter in the text.

41 'Nadine Gordimer interviewed', by Stephen Gray and Phil du Plessis, *New Nation*, September 1972, p. 5.

42 'A writer is always writing the same story', interview with Nadine Gordimer, *Rand Daily Mail*, 27 July 1972.

43 'In black and white', interview with Nesta Wyn Ellis, *Harpers and Queen*, November 1978, p. 298.

44 For an amusing account arising out of this time, see 'Hassan in America', *The Forum*, February 1955, pp. 13–19; also see 'Egypt revisited'.

45 'The Congo River', p. 75.

46 Ibid., p. 99.

47 There was no mud hut so isolated, she added, no road so lost in the wilderness, that the basic tenor of this message did not reach it: 'The Congo River', pp. 88, 97. A short story that derives directly from Gordimer's Congo experience, and conveys the quality she evidently felt in both environmental and political terms, is called, appropriately, 'The African magician' (in *Not For Publication*).

48 'In black and white', p. 298. Paradoxically putting the concerns of *A Guest of Honour* into a South African perspective, Gordimer remarked: 'It was a romantic idea. But I discovered I was only a European there, just like any other white person. I took that very hard. At least in South Africa even if I get my throat cut, I'm an African.'

49 Jan Kees Van Donge, 'Nadine Gordimer's *A Guest of Honour*: a failure to understand Zambian society', *Journal of Southern African Studies*, vol. 9, no. 1 (October 1982), pp. 74–92. For Van Donge, who lived in Zambia during the 1960s, *A Guest of Honour* is simply 'about Zambia'; the question being asked in Lusaka circles when the novel came out, he says, was not whether you had read it, but whether you were in it. This is a variation of the 'party game' that the Johannesburg *Star* claimed its readers were playing in relation to *A World of Strangers*. But Van Donge checkmates his own game in three moves. First he asserts that the novel is 'about' Zambia; second, he says it is not 'good enough' in being about Zambia since it persists in getting its details wrong (i.e. it may not be about Zambia); and thirdly, he then blames it for not being about Zambia.

50 *A Survey 1967, 1968* and *1969*, comp. M. Horrell, shows that trials involving both the ANC and PAC continued to take place.

51 This is partly the logic of Gordimer's own reflection on the novel: 'You never know why you choose to write a particular book, why it suddenly impinges upon you, but one thing was I felt I had said all I had to say at that time ... There was nothing pressing in upon me in my own immediate background. I saw how isolated we are *vis-à-vis* Africa ... I myself had moved out of that, and began to think then, what happens after?' Gordimer, interview. Presumably, 'after' apartheid.

52 See Legassick, 'Legislation, ideology and economy' and 'South Africa: capital accumulation'; also F. A. Johnstone, 'White prosperity and white supremacy in South Africa today', *African Affairs*, vol. 69, no. 275 (April 1970), pp. 124–40; Stanley Trapido, 'South Africa in a comparative study of industrialization', *Journal of Development Studies*, vol. 7, no. 3 (April 1971), pp. 309–19; Harold Wolpe, 'Capitalism and cheap labour power in

South Africa: from segregation to apartheid', *Economy and Society*, vol. 1, no. 4 (November 1972), pp. 425–56.

53 *A Survey 1970*, comp. M. Horrell, p. 6. South Africa gave Malawi an R8 million loan and R10 million for contracts (ibid., p. 74), while Vorster and Dr Banda exchanged visits; the 'mad Doctor', as the novel calls him, is mentioned in *A Guest of Honour*. At this time the South African conglomerate, the Anglo-American Corporation, was undertaking 'the exploration of Zambia's agricultural and mineral potential': *A Survey 1971*, comp. M. Horrell, D. Horner, J. Kane-Berman, p. 103.

54 See Legassick, 'Legislation, ideology and economy'.

55 This was an overwhelming impression at the time, though later writing would come to question the ultimate coherency of the apartheid system. It is no surprise that a period of structural elaboration within apartheid should have produced a structural analysis of its working parts. Later, as the system entered successive crises it became possible to 'deconstruct' apartheid, at least analytically. For example, see Doug Hindson, 'The role of the labour bureaux in South Africa: a critique of the Riekert Commission Report', in D. C. Hindson (ed.), *Working Papers in Southern African Studies*, Vol. 3 (Johannesburg: Ravan, 1983), pp. 149–72.

56 Cosmas Desmond, OFM, *The Discarded People*, preface by Lord Caradon, foreword by Nadine Gordimer (Harmondsworth: Penguin, 1971). Desmond quotes General Circular no. 25, 1967, issued by the Secretary for Bantu Administration and Development: 'the Bantus are only temporarily resident in the European areas of the Republic for as long as they offer their labour there. As soon as they become . . . no longer fit for work or superfluous in the labour market, they are expected to return to their country of origin or the territory of their national unit . . . It must be stressed here that no stone is to be left unturned to achieve the settlement in the homelands of non-productive Bantu at present residing in the European areas' (pp. 21–2).

57 Gordimer, interview. Not only African thinkers were important for her at this time, however. In *The Black Interpreters*, p. 9, she cites Albert Camus's definition of the rebel as a man who says 'yes' as well as 'no'; this is clearly significant for the figure of Bray.

58 Frantz Fanon, *The Wretched of the Earth*, preface by Jean-Paul Sartre, trans. Constance Farrington (1965; Harmondsworth: Penguin, 1967), p. 116. The whole of this work is well worth reading in relation to *A Guest of Honour*, but especially ch. 3, 'The pitfalls of national consciousness', for its comments on the leader, the party and the people in the African neo-colonial state.

59 Wade, *Nadine Gordimer*, ch. 5; and 'Nadine Gordimer and Europe-in-Africa'. See also JanMohamed, *Manichean Aesthetics*, pp. 113–14.

60 Van Donge criticizes this in the novel on the grounds that Kenneth Kaunda (as President of Zambia) does not make midnight radio speeches, nor would anyone stay up to hear him if he did. But this is one instance where Van Donge's argument falls down; in setting up this incident Gordimer is concerned with a particular typology of 'the leader' as such and of an incipient tyranny in general; the German and South African analogies make this abundantly clear. Here her thematic concerns override any attempt to write 'about Zambia'.

61 *The Black Interpreters*, p. 5.
62 Ibid., p. 10.
63 Ibid., p. 10.
64 For Gordimer's relationship to Lukács, see relevant discussion in the Introduction. Apart from him and Goldmann, Gordimer was also reading Herbert Marcuse in the late 1960s; see her open letter to André Brink, Johannesburg *Star*, 17 January 1969. For the influence of Lukács on her thought, see also the appendix to 'The novel and the nation in South Africa' (1973), p. 52.
65 *The Black Interpreters*, p. 32.
66 Ibid., pp. 44–5.
67 Nkosi, 'History as "hero" ', p. 46, points out that Gordimer has not taken into account here the work of Ngugi Wa Thiong'o and Sembene Ousmane.
68 *Nadine Gordimer*, p. 180; 'Nadine Gordimer and Europe-in-Africa', pp. 145–6.
69 Ibid., p. 137.
70 Ibid., pp. 161–2.

NOTES TO CHAPTER 5: *THE CONSERVATIONIST*

1 *The Conservationist* (London: Cape, 1974; Harmondsworth: Penguin, 1978), p. 40; all page references, to 1978 edn, are given hereafter in the text.
2 Schreiner, *African Farm* (1883), Vol. 1, p. 229; rpt (1971), p. 130.
3 In *Livingstone's Companions*, p. 222.
4 Nadine Gordimer's own awareness of this aspect of Schreiner's novel has changed dramatically. In 1959–61 she praised *The Story of an African Farm* because it did not attempt to answer the question 'What does man make of life in South Africa?', but the eternal question 'What is the life of man?' 'The English novel in South Africa', p. 21; 'The novel and the nation in South Africa' (1961), p. 49. However, at a conference in 1975 (the date is perhaps significant, coming the year after *The Conservationist*) she wrote of Schreiner's work: 'in the final analysis, this is a book that expresses the wonder and horror of the wilderness, and for the indigenous inhabitant that wilderness is home. The novel exists squarely within the political context of colonialism.' 'English-language literature and politics in South Africa', p. 103. For a suggestive article analysing the discontinuities of Schreiner's text within an historical setting, see Graham Pechey, '*The Story of an African Farm*: colonial history and the discontinuous text', *Critical Arts*, vol. 3, no. 1 (1983), pp. 65–78.
5 *A Survey 1972*, comp. M. Horrell *et al.*, p. 123.
6 In 1972 the Schlebusch Commission was set up to inquire into these organizations, as well as the University Christian Movement (which was later disbanded). As a result of its interim report in 1973, eight NUSAS leaders were banned; at the same time – though not under Schlebusch – eight leaders of the black South African Students Organization (SASO) were

also banned. See *A Survey 1973*, comp. M. Horrell and D. Horner, pp. 24–9.

7 See Legassick, 'South Africa: capital accumulation', pp. 273–4.

8 Trapido, 'South Africa in a comparative study', p. 317.

9 See cited articles by Trapido, Johnstone, Legassick and Wolpe.

10 For the Japanese connection, see Trapido, 'South Africa in a comparative study', p. 317. Christopher Hope has pointed out that it was on account of the pig-iron trade with Japan that Japanese were declared 'honorary whites' for South African purposes; see his 'Out of the picture: the novels of Nadine Gordimer', *London Magazine*, April/May 1975, p. 54. Here Mehring is clearly complicit in the structures of apartheid.

11 Between 13 December 1971 and 20 January 1972 approximately 20,000 migrant workers went on strike against the contract labour system. See Luckhardt and Wall, *Organize*, pp. 447–8; also Hirson, *Year of Fire*, pp. 130–3. In the wake of the strike Gordimer wrote a letter to the Johannesburg *Star* (22 March 1972) berating Peter Becker for claiming that labour recruiters in Namibia symbolized to workers 'everything that is good in that far off land of the white man'.

12 From January to March 1973 some 64,400 workers struck in a total of 160 stoppages: Luckhardt and Wall, *Organize*, p. 449. Hirson, *Year of Fire*, p. 133, estimates that between January 1973 and mid-1976 over 200,000 black workers took strike action in South Africa.

13 See Hirson, *Year of Fire*, for an extended analysis of the political, economic and ideological context of the Soweto Revolt. For the Black Consciousness movement and its political and intellectual antecedents, see Gerhart, *Black Power*.

14 *A Survey 1973*, pp. 86–93.

15 *A Survey 1974*, comp. M. Horrell, D. Horner and J. Hudson, p. 108.

16 A slogan that appeared at Turfloop University at the same time carried the message explicitly:

'Frelimo fought and regained our soil, our dignity.
It is a story. Change the name and the story applies to you.
The dignity of the Black Man has been restored in Mozambique and so shall it be here.
Black must rule.
We shall drive them to the sea. Long live Azania.
Revolution!! Machel will help! Away with Vorster Ban! We are Afro Black Power!!!'

(Quoted in Hirson, *Year of Fire*, pp. 89–90.)

17 'The politics of armed struggle: national liberation in the African colonies of Portugal', in Basil Davidson, Joe Slovo and Anthony R. Wilkinson, *Southern Africa: The New Politics of Revolution* (Harmondsworth: Penguin, 1976), p. 91.

18 Quoted by Anthony R. Wilkinson, 'From Rhodesia to Zimbabwe', ibid., p. 339.

19 Interview with Bernard Zylstra, reproduced in Donald Woods, *Biko* (London: Paddington Press, 1978), p. 95.

20 For his contrast between *The Lying Days* and *The Conservationist* in this regard, see Hope, 'Out of the picture', p. 54.

21 To be found in *Six Feet of the Country*. First appearances in *The Forum*, 25–9 February 1953, and *New Yorker*, 23 May 1953.

22 Cf. Gordimer's own remark on her novel: 'the only "message" is there – for those who know how to read it – on the last page. In fact, the last paragraph.' See 'Gordimer's new book is barred', *Sunday Times* (Johannesburg), 10 November 1974. (The article reports that *The Conservationist* had been embargoed by the South African Department of Customs and Excise, prior to a decision by the censorship board; but the novel was ultimately not banned.)

23 Here one might compare Mehring with Martin Mynhardt, the central character of André Brink's novel *Rumours of Rain* (London: W. H. Allen, 1978). Like Mehring, Mynhardt is an aggressive, jet-setting capitalist with an unproductive attitude to his farm, and whose doom appears to be prophesied in the novel by its 'rumours of rain'. In these respects (as in many others) Brink's novel repeats many of the major themes of *The Conservationist*.

24 'A South African radical exulting in life's chaotic variety', *The Times*, 29 November 1974, p. 21.

25 From the *Sunday Times* (Johannesburg) see 'Alan Paton slams Nadine Gordimer' (1 December 1974); 'Gordimer vs Paton' (22 December 1974; this is Gordimer's reply); 'Paton to Gordimer: express regret' (29 December 1974). For André Brink's views, see 'Author agrees with Gordimer', *Rand Daily Mail*, 23 December 1974. Spread angrily over these pages, with others climbing on the bandwagon, the clash assumed the proportions of an undignified ruckus, and it adds to the feel of the affair to know that it was at least in part based on an ironic confusion. In Ratcliffe's original interview with Gordimer he had, by way of commentary, paraphrased Mehring's statement in the novel in saying that 'liberals are people who make promises they have no power to keep', but this was not said by Gordimer. The Johannesburg *Star*, however, reported the Ratcliffe interview as if it had, suggesting also for good measure that Gordimer had said she 'detested' being called a liberal. ('I'm not a liberal says Gordimer', *Star*, 29 November 1974). It was *this* report to which Paton responded, and the opinion on liberals not keeping promises that in particular raised his ire – an opinion that Gordimer's character had expressed, but she herself had not. None the less, the deeper issues between Paton and Gordimer were real ones, although the dispute was later patched up.

26 Under the threat of the Prohibition of Illegal Interference Act, which made racially mixed political parties illegal.

27 'White racism and Black Consciousness', in Hendrik W. Van Der Merwe and David Welsh (eds.), *Student Perspectives on South Africa* (Cape Town: Philip, 1972), p. 195. In the same volume see Barney Pityana, 'Power and social change in South Africa', pp. 174–89; also see Steve Biko, *I Write What I Like*, ed. Aelred Stubbs, CR (1978; London: Heinemann, 1979).

28 See Nadine Gordimer, 'Speak out: the necessity for protest', the sixth E. G. Malherbe Academic Freedom Lecture, delivered at the University of

Natal, 11 August 1971 (Durban: Academic Freedom Committee, University of Natal, 1971), n. pag.: 'the turning of *their* backs on the white man's back door is necessary for the younger generation of blacks'. Two central themes of this address are the rise (and challenge) of the Black Consciousness movement, and the failure of South African liberalism in terms of any desired historical effect.

29 Northrop Frye sees the farm as one of the major archetypal symbols whereby civilization measures its progress: *Anatomy of Criticism* (Princeton, NJ: Princeton University Press, 1971), p. 113.

30 'Gordimer's *The Conservationist*: "that book of unknown signs" ', *Critique: Studies in Modern Fiction*, vol. 22, no. 3 (April 1981), pp. 31–44.

31 The linkage between the imagination, fiction, the unconscious and intimations of a future destiny is one that Gordimer felt very strongly at this time. As we shall see, it underlies much of what happens in this novel; and for related treatment, see Gordimer's short story of about this time, 'The life of the imagination', in *Livingstone's Companions*.

32 As a number of reviewers considered: see for example 'Kinds of colonialism', *The Times Literary Supplement*, 1 November 1974; and the review by Paul Theroux, *New York Times Book Review*, 13 April 1974, pp. 4–5. In an interview published in 1984 Gordimer commented on people who hadn't read the book 'very carefully', and who thought that Mehring dies: Robert Boyers *et al.*, 'A conversation with Nadine Gordimer', *Salmagundi*, no. 62 (Winter 1984), p. 17. Yet the mistake persists; in the same issue of the same journal the misreading is perpetuated (see Eugene Goodheart, 'The claustral world of Nadine Gordimer', p. 114). And see below, note 39.

33 See the chapter on 'The ideology of modernism' in *The Meaning of Contemporary Realism*. On the other hand Lukács is not entirely formalistic in his approach; he maintains that the interior monologue can be used 'realistically' if its innate subjectivism is indicated within the narrative, as in the depiction of a certain kind of character. In this regard he sees Thomas Mann as diametrically opposed to Joyce, although he made use of the same technique.

34 See commentary by Bloch, Brecht and Adorno in Ernst Bloch *et al.*, *Aesthetics and Politics*, with an afterword by Fredric Jameson (1977; London: Verso, 1980).

35 J. M. Coetzee, *In the Heart of the Country* (Johannesburg: Ravan, 1978).

36 For example, see Michael Vaughan, 'Literature and politics: currents in South African writing in the seventies', *Journal of Southern African Studies*, vol. 9, no. 1 (October 1982), pp. 118–38.

37 Trapido, 'South Africa in a comparative study', p. 310.

38 *Nadine Gordimer*, pp. 195–6.

39 *Manichean Aesthetics*, p. 126. JanMohamed's chapter on Gordimer is a perceptive one in many ways, but the insistence on the 'manichean' theme (together with an apparent Jungian subplot) produces questionable readings. For example, JanMohamed believes not only that Mehring dies at the end of the novel, but that in doing so he 'merges' with the dead body,

becomes one with nature and becomes one of the ancestors of Africa (see pp. 123–4). This is unlikely. Apart from the explicit 'message' mentioned by Gordimer herself (see note 22 above), from what we have seen it does not seem that Gordimer would have been enough of a sentimentalist and idealist at this stage to assume that Mehring, in all he represents, could thus be apocalyptically transformed. It is true that the body represents a site of repression in Mehring's mind (see further discussion in this section) but not one susceptible to some kind of 'organic' reintegration on any terms. It is clear who 'claims the land' at the end of the novel.

40   'Gordimer's *The Conservationist*'.

41   The Rev. Canon Henry Callaway, MD, *The Religious System of the Amazulu* (Springvale, Natal: John A. Blair; Pietermaritzburg: Davis & Sons; Cape Town: J. C. Juta; London: Trübner; 1868). Gordimer used the facsimile edn (Cape Town: Struik, 1970).

42   This may have had a personal relevance for Gordimer; at one time she suffered from fibrositis between the shoulder-blades; and the novelist – perhaps especially in this novel – is a modern *inyanga*.

43   A point made also by John Cooke, 'The novels of Nadine Gordimer', PhD dissertation, Northwestern University, 1976, p. 201; and suggested, without being explored in its own terms, by both Newman, 'Gordimer's *The Conservationist*', p. 43, and Wade, *Nadine Gordimer*, p. 197. Cooke also notes, without much investigation, the 'prophetic' nature of *The Conservationist* (p. 217).

44   But he does on p. 227 where his own internal schism becomes extraordinarily apparent: 'You're there. It seems to you that it is to you that observations are being addressed.' Here, inside Mehring's mind both he and the body are in some way addressor and addressee.

45   See the discussion in Chapter 7, section II.

46   This combination of the political and the symbolic is precisely what is captured by Ben Turok, writing in 1972: 'going underground implies the total rejection of the existing political system. It is wholly subversive in intention and cannot conceal this fact' – 'South Africa: the violent alternative', in R. Miliband and J. Savile (eds.), *The Socialist Register 1972* (London: Merlin, 1972), p. 282.

NOTES TO CHAPTER 6: *BURGER'S DAUGHTER* AND *JULY'S PEOPLE*

1   In *A Soldier's Embrace* (London: Cape, 1980), p. 27.

2   *Burger's Daughter* (London: Cape, 1979); all page references given hereafter in the text; cited where necessary in further footnotes as *BD*.

3   Something that Gordimer herself has not concealed. See 'I know I have not been brave enough', interview with Diana Loercher, *Christian Science Monitor*, 21 January 1980, p. 21.

4   See Chapter 4, pages 95–6.

5   I am indebted for this information to Ruth Eastwood. A pair of more tragic details has also been reversed in the novel; Bram's wife, Molly Fischer, was drowned in a motor-car accident, and their son, Paul, died of cystic

fibrosis of the pancreas in *BD* Rosa's brother drowns in the Burger swimming pool, and her mother, Cathy, dies of multiple sclerosis.

6   Gordimer, interview.

7   Nadine Gordimer *et al.*, *What Happened to 'Burger's Daughter', or How South African Censorship Works* (Johannesburg: Taurus, 1980), p. 18; hereafter referred to as *WHBD*.

8   Z. N., 'The politics of commitment', *African Communist*, 1st Quarter 1980, pp. 100–1. There was perhaps another reason (though unspoken) for the review's objection to *BD* – that Gordimer had dared to 'annex' SACP history in the first place. For details of the review and Gordimer's response, see note 29 below.

9   O. Mannoni, *Prospero and Caliban: the Psychology of Colonization*, trans. Pamela Powesland (London: Methuen, 1956).

10   'Prospero's complex: race and sex in *Burger's Daughter*', *Journal of Commonwealth Literature*, vol. 20, no. 1 (September 1985), pp. 81–99. The only mistake that Newman makes, apart from her assumption that South Africa is simply a 'racist' society, is to imply that Rosa is entirely contained within its framework – which she evidently is not.

11   See Gordimer, 'What being a South African means to me'.

12   Although there is an alarming suggestion that the Security Police knew; see note 41 below.

13   The scene recalls the horse-beating incident in Dostoevsky's *Crime and Punishment*, but is in fact based on an incident that actually occurred while Gordimer was writing the novel: 'I know I have not been brave enough', p. 21.

14   Lodge, *Black Politics*, p. 328.

15   Lodge, ibid., ch. 13, gives a summary of the events of the Revolt as well as a discussion of previous analytical approaches to it. For a full account and analysis, see Hirson, *Year of Fire*; also John Kane-Berman, *South Africa: The Method in the Madness* (London: Pluto, 1979). For a day-to-day account of the Revolt, see *A Survey 1976*, comp. M. Horrell *et al.*, pp. 51–87, and *A Survey 1977*, comp. L. Gordon *et al.*, pp. 55–82.

16   Hirson, *Year of Fire*, is especially critical of the failure of the Black Consciousness organizations to generalize the Revolt more widely in society, especially by linking up with workers. This he sees as following directly from the weaknesses of Black Consciousness as an ideology. Lodge, *Black Politics*, p. 325, suggests that the 'sheer emotional power' of Black Consciousness should not be underestimated as an organizing and political force of its own kind.

17   After twenty members had been detained, in August 1977 the SSRC announced that in future it would be led by a secret executive committee of six members (probably for this exact purpose). *A Survey 1977*, p. 35.

18   For a full description of Biko's detention and death, as well as the eventual decision at the inquest that no one could be held 'criminally responsible' for it (a decision that seemed incredible to most from the evidence), see *A Survey*, 1977, pp. 159–64.

19   Lodge, *Black Politics*, p. 330.

20   'What being a South African means to me', p. 89.

21   Ibid., p. 92.
22   Nadine Gordimer, 'Letter from South Africa', *New York Review of Books*, 9 December 1976, p. 3.
23   'I know I have not been brave enough', p. 21.
24   A suggestion by Stephen Watson set off this line of inquiry.
25   This was one of the reasons for *BD* being banned, since the pamphlet had been declared 'undesirable', and the SSRC had itself been declared an unlawful organization on 19 October 1977. See *WHBD*, p. 11.
26   'Liberation ... is of paramount importance in the concept of Black Consciousness, for we cannot be conscious of ourselves and yet remain in bondage.' Steve Biko, 'The definition of Black Consciousness', in *I Write What I Like*, p. 49. This paper, first given by Biko in 1971, has evidently been an important source for Gordimer. On the other hand, it should not be thought that Gordimer was simply 'plagiarizing'; Biko's sentiments were part and parcel of the common discourse of Black Consciousness, which he helped fashion.
27   Reproduced in Mary Benson (ed.), *The Sun Will Rise*, rev. and enl. edn (London: International Defence and Aid, 1981), p. 41.
28   In Davidson, Slovo and Wilkinson, *Southern Africa*.
29   Gordimer has revealed her sources for *BD* in a most interesting way. The review of the novel that appeared in the *African Communist* (note 8 above) claimed that its politics, 'derived almost entirely from Roux's *Time Longer than Rope* and the gossip that floats about in left-wing circles, is a travesty.' (Edward Roux was a lapsed member of the SACP.) Gordimer wrote a letter of reply (*African Communist*, 3rd Quarter 1980, p. 109) in which she pointed out that her political sources were, on the contrary, 'principally the impeccable ones' of Simons and Simons, *Class and Colour*, Slovo's 'No middle road', and the Black Community Programme publications edited by Mafika Pascal Gwala, B. A. Khoapa and Thoko Mbanjwa (for the Black Consciousness politics). In relation to the SACP her sources could not have been more 'impeccable', since the Simonses, like Slovo, have been long-standing officials and ideologists within the Party.
30   See Slovo, 'No middle road', p. 119.
31   Ibid., p. 161.
32   For example, when Orde Greer asks Duma Dhladhla, without any apparent reference or quotation, whether 'a capitalist society which throws overboard the race factor entirely [could] still evolve here?' (*BD*, p. 157), the question and its phrasing come almost directly from Slovo, 'No middle road', p. 142. Similarly when Dhladhla 'quotes' Biko, no reference marks are given.
33   'World history would indeed be very easy to make if the struggle were taken up only on condition of infallibly favourable chances.' Slovo, 'No middle road', p. 185; *BD*, p. 27, leaves out only the 'indeed'.
34   *WHBD*, p. 30.
35   When the Censorship Committee initially banned *BD*, citing some of the quotations that have just been given as reasons for doing so, this was usually on the grounds of the sentiments expressed, and not on account of the source, which in virtually every case was already banned material, and hence reason enough for banning the novel. That is, when the Committee

cited Slovo, it did not know it was Slovo it was citing. This adds a suitably ironic element to the fact that *BD* was later unbanned (see following discussion). I would have been more reticent about revealing Gordimer's sources had she not done so herself.

36 Gordimer, interview; in *WHBD*, p. 19, Gordimer says that *BD* is 'a novel of ideas'.

37 *WHBD*.

38 Ibid., p. 6.

39 'Nadine Gordimer's *Burger's Daughter*', paper presented at a conference on Literature and Society in Southern Africa, University of York, September 1981.

40 Ibid., p. 21.

41 For example, on p. 177, the Security Police narrative seems to end up partially inside Rosa's own mind: 'But activity within the country suggested by the fact that she should attempt to pass out and in again was what was of concern; there was no hope at all for her that she would get what she had never had, what had been refused her once and for all when she tried to run away from her mother and father after the boy she wanted.'

42 See Terry Eagleton, *Walter Benjamin, or Towards a Revolutionary Criticism* (London: Verso, 1981), p. 150: 'Benjamin's *Unmensch* is a purged space, a deconstructed function of historical forces.' This would apply perfectly to Rosa.

43 'Living in the interregnum', *New York Review of Books*, 20 January 1983, p. 21.

44 *July's People* (London: Cape, 1981); all page references to this edn given hereafter in the text.

45 Nadine Gordimer, address to the C. N. A. Award Dinner, 17 April 1980 (typescript), p. 2. Gordimer won this award, one of South Africa's premier literary prizes, for *Burger's Daughter*. But in South Africa such occasions are evidently not for casual and easily gracious speeches of acceptance.

46 Nadine Gordimer, untitled paper presented at a conference on Censorship, University of Cape Town, April 1980 (typescript), p. 11.

47 'Relevance and commitment', paper presented at a conference on The State of Art in South Africa, Cape Town, July 1979 (typescript), p. 1; also given in slightly different form as the Neil Gunn Fellowship Lecture, Edinburgh 1981, and published as 'Apprentices of freedom', *New Society*, 24–31 December 1981, pp. ii–v.

48 'Relevance and commitment', p. 13; 'Apprentices', p. v. The phrase comes from Mannoni's *Prospero and Caliban*, p. 65 (see note 9 above).

49 'Living in the interregnum', pp. 26–7. For Gordimer's most recent thoughts on the commitments of being a writer, see 'The essential gesture: writers and responsibility', in Sterling M. McMurrin (ed.), *The Tanner Lectures on Human Values*, VI (Salt Lake City, Utah: University of Utah Press; Cambridge: Cambridge University Press, 1985), pp. 1–19; and *Granta*, no. 15 (Spring 1985), pp. 135–51.

50 These three stories in *A Soldier's Embrace*.

51 See Chapter 7, page 207.

52 Gordimer, interview. Also see Hurwitt, 'The art of fiction', p. 120, and

Boyers *et al.*, 'A conversation with Nadine Gordimer', p. 19: '[in South Africa] the white man and the white woman have much more in common than the white woman and the black woman, despite their difference in sex. Similarly, the black man and the black woman have much more in common than the black man and the white man.'

53   On the significance of this incident, see Rowland Smith, 'Masters and servants: Nadine Gordimer's *July's People* and the themes of her fiction', *Salmagundi*, no. 62 (Winter 1984) p. 107: 'The paradox which epitomizes the deadlock of the book's ending is that only when the black man refuses to talk the white woman's language is she able to understand "everything".' All that may be questioned in this formulation is whether the book does end in deadlock, or whether Maureen tries finally to break out of it.

54   In mid-1985 it was estimated that black trade unions had grown from 16,000 members in 1969 to a figure of over 400,000. My thanks to Taffy Adler for these figures.

55   There were twenty officially counted dead and at least twenty-seven injured in police shooting after the latter had cancelled a planned community funeral. The Kannemeyer Commission, which reported on the event, found the police responsible to a significant extent – the first time there had ever been such a finding in South Africa. Reports from Johannesburg *Star*, 12 June 1985, p. 1.

56   Towards the middle of 1985 it was reported that ANC headquarters in Lusaka were calling for an insurrectionary uprising in South Africa as one of the possible paths to revolution. Underground presses inside the country were calling for preparation for 'a long general strike, for small armed bands of youths to turn black townships into "no-go" areas for anything less than a huge police contingent, and for black police and soldiers to quit government service'. David Rabkin, 'ANC urges a popular insurrection', *Guardian Weekly*, 19 May 1985.

57   *Promised Land*, trans. Marion V. Friedmann (London: Julian Friedmann, 1978); first published in Afrikaans in 1972.

58   *Waiting for the Barbarians* (1980; Harmondsworth: Penguin, 1982).

59   I am in part indebted for this point to a conversation with Bernth Lindfors.

60   The comparison is Itala Vivan's.

NOTES TO CHAPTER 7: *DEEP HISTORY*

1   Claude Lévi-Strauss, *Tristes Tropiques*, trans. John and Doreen Weightman (1973; Harmondsworth: Penguin, 1976), pp. 68–9. Lévi-Strauss is discussing here the influences that led towards his becoming an anthropologist. Besides geology, the two other major ones were, perhaps significantly for this chapter, Freud and Marx.

2   This term is an adapted version of that proposed by Fredric Jameson as the 'political unconscious'; see his *The Political Unconscious: Narrative as a Socially Symbolic Act* (London: Methuen, 1981). Jameson has a much broader agenda and a different kind of focus than mine, but I am indebted to him for setting off the central concerns of this section.

3   Appendix (1973) to 'The novel and the nation', p. 52. This is given as a correction to Gordimer's earlier view in the original text of the article that 'there is little reason why a straightforward novel of events in which the protagonists are black men should not be written just as authentically by a white writer as by a black one' (p. 44).

4   Alex La Guma, interviewed by Robert Serumaga in D. Duerden and C. Pieterse (eds.), *African Writers Talking* (London: Heinemann, 1972), p. 92.

5   Ezekiel Mphahlele, quoting from his MA thesis, 'The non-European character in South African English fiction', in *Down Second Avenue*, p. 196.

6   'It's difficult to decide my identity', in Essop Patel (ed.), *The World of Nat Nakasa*, introduction by Nadine Gordimer (Johannesburg: Ravan/Bateleur, 1975), p. 77.

7   'Relevance and commitment', pp. 2, 12.

8   The title piece of *Something Out There* (London: Cape, 1984).

9   See Chapter 1, page 24.

10   It is perhaps significant that 'Is there nowhere else we can meet?' heads the short stories that Gordimer selected for *No Place Like*, although she points out in the introduction to that volume that it could only have come from a very specific time.

11   See Sigmund Freud, *The Interpretation of Dreams*, ed. A. Richards, trans. J. Strachey (Harmondsworth: Penguin, 1976), esp. ch. 6, 'The dream work'.

12   Jameson has stressed the need for the conception of a 'political unconscious' to transcend the categories of individuality in favour of the social or collective. See *The Political Unconscious*, p. 68.

13   See for example both Conor Cruise O'Brien, 'Waiting for revolution', *New York Review of Books*, 25 October 1979, pp. 27–31, and R. W. Johnson, 'Growing up to martyrdom', *New Society*, 14 June 1979, pp. 657–8, on *Burger's Daughter*.

14   Jean-Paul Sartre, *What is Literature?*, trans. Bernard Frechtman, introduction by David Caute (London: Methuen, 1967), ch. 3.

15   Ibid., p. 68.

16   See Gramsci, *Prison Notebooks*, ed. and trans. Quintin Hoare and Geoffrey Nowell Smith (London: Lawrence & Wishart, 1971), pp. 5–14. The notion of what an 'organic intellectual' might be in South Africa is, on the other hand, not entirely unproblematic. As Gramsci's formulation anticipates, with increasing class differentiation in the black world itself, there is, and is bound to be, differentiation amongst its intellectuals.

17   See Miriam Tlali, *Amandla* (Johannesburg: Ravan, 1980); Mongane Serote, *To Every Birth its Blood* (Johannesburg: Ravan, 1981); and Mbulelo Vizikhungo Mzamane, *The Children of Soweto* (London: Longman, 1982).

18   'A writer in South Africa', p. 28.

19   See, for example, Alan Lomberg, 'Withering into the truth: the romantic realism of Nadine Gordimer', *English in Africa*, vol. 3, no. 1 (March 1976), pp. 1–12.

20   *Walter Benjamin*, p. 161. In passing, Eagleton too links this irony with Freudian theory and the possibility of an historical 'unconscious'.

21 Stephen Gray, *Southern African Literature*, ch. 5, 'The rise and fall of the colonial hunter', esp. pp. 108–9.

22 Bertolt Brecht, 'Popularity and realism', in Bloch *et al*, *Aesthetics and Politics*, p. 80.

23 Ibid.

24 Ibid. There are few enough issues on which Brecht and Lukács were agreed, but this it seems was one of them; for Lukács, too, the 'truth-telling' of realism intrinsically favoured the people. On the other hand, the two were not all *that* much agreed; for Lukács this overall realism of effect could be achieved only by a containing realism of mode, or representational realism. For Brecht modal diversity was a basic component of his method in the attempt to construct a 'popular' art.

25 Jeremy Cronin, 'To learn how to speak...', *Inside* (Johannesburg: Ravan, 1983), p. 58. Cronin was a political prisoner for seven years, and his remarkable volume is a rare record of his experiences. Though his voice never deviates from the highly personal, it also speaks through and for many 'inside'.

NOTE TO AFTERWORD

1 See Georg Lukács, *The Historical Novel*, trans. H. and S. Mitchell (1962; Harmondsworth: Penguin, 1969), pp. 286–91.

Bibliography and Sources

(1)   *Work by Nadine Gordimer*

All work in this section is by Nadine Gordimer unless otherwise stated. The material has been divided into categories, and each category has been arranged in chronological order. All typescripts are in Nadine Gordimer's possession; I am grateful to her for allowing me to use these as well as other material.

(a)   FICTION BY NADINE GORDIMER
Including uncollected early works, unpublished material and first publication of some early short stories.

'The valley legend', *Children's Sunday Express* (Johannesburg), 18 September 1938, p. 1.

'Come again tomorrow', *The Forum*, 18 November 1939, p. 14.

'No place like home', *P.S.*, December 1943, pp. 7–8.

'No luck tonight', *South African Opinion*, August 1944, pp. 18–20, 31.

Untitled and unfinished novel (typescript; before 1946), pp. 1–34.

'Is there nowhere else we can meet?', *Common Sense*, September 1947, pp. 387–9.

'The train from Rhodesia', *Trek*, September 1947, pp. 18–19.

'Ah, woe is me', *Common Sense*, December 1947, pp. 537–41.

'The amateurs', *Common Sense*, December 1948, pp. 540–4.

'Poet and peasant', *Hasholom Rosh Hashanah Annual*, September 1949, pp. 26–9, 31, 47.

'Sweet dreams selection', *Common Sense*, November 1949, pp. 501–5.

'The first circle', in *Six One Act Plays by South African Authors* (Pretoria: Van Schaik, 1949), pp. 43–70.

Face to Face (Johannesburg: Silver Leaf Books, 1949).

'A Sunday outing', *Trek*, October 1951, pp. 8–9.

Untitled and unfinished novel (typescript; *c.* 1951), pp. 1–84.

'A story from the top shelf', *Jewish Affairs*, April 1952, pp. 41–4.

The Soft Voice of the Serpent (London: Gollancz; New York: Simon & Schuster; 1953).

Synopsis and plan for *The Lying Days* (typescript, n.d.), pp. 1–12.

The Lying Days (London: Gollancz; New York: Simon & Schuster; 1953).

Six Feet of the Country (London: Gollancz; New York: Simon & Schuster; 1956).

A World of Strangers (London: Gollancz; New York: Simon & Schuster; 1958; rpt, London: Cape, 1976).

Friday's Footprint (London: Gollancz; New York: Viking; 1960).

Occasion for Loving (London: Gollancz; New York: Viking; 1963).

Not for Publication (London: Gollancz; New York: Viking; 1965).

The Late Bourgeois World (London: Cape; New York: Viking; 1966).

Ed. with Lionel Abrahams, *South African Writing Today* (Harmondsworth: Penguin, 1967).

A Guest of Honour (London: Cape; New York: Viking; 1971).

Livingstone's Companions (London: Cape; New York: Viking; 1972; Harmondsworth: Penguin, 1975).

The Conservationist (London: Cape, 1974; New York: Viking, 1975; Harmondsworth: Penguin, 1978).

No Place Like: Selected Stories (London: Cape, 1975; New York: Viking, 1976; Harmondsworth: Penguin, 1978).

Some Monday for Sure (London: Heinemann, 1976).

Burger's Daughter (London: Cape; New York: Viking; 1979).

A Soldier's Embrace (London: Cape; New York: Viking; 1980).

July's People (London: Cape; New York: Viking; Johannesburg: Ravan; 1981).

Something Out There (London: Cape; New York: Viking; Johannesburg: Ravan/Taurus; 1984).

(b) COMMENTARY ON WRITING

'Writing belongs to us all', *The Forum*, September 1954, pp. 9–10.

'The English novel in South Africa', in Hugh Lewin (ed.), *The Novel and the Nation* (Cape Town: NUSAS, University of Cape Town, 1959), pp. 16–21.

'What shall I write about?' (typescript; c. 1961), pp. 1–18.

'Party of one', *Holiday*, July 1963, pp. 12, 14–17.

'Notes of an expropriator', *The Times Literary Supplement*, 4 June 1964.

'A writer in South Africa', *London Magazine*, May 1965, pp. 21–8.

'The dark Venus and the new Desdemona', review of *The Literature and Thought of Modern Africa*, by Claude Wauthier, *London Magazine*, August 1967, pp. 71–6.

'The interpreters: theme as communication in the African novel', paper presented at the 1968 National Arts Winter School, University of the Witwatersrand, Johannesburg (Africana Library, University of the Witwatersrand).

'Some notes on African writing', *South African Outlook*, October 1970, pp. 172–4.

The Black Interpreters – Notes on African Writing (Johannesburg: Spro-Cas/Ravan, 1973).

'The novel and the nation in South Africa' (1961), in G. D. Killam (ed.), *African Writers on African Writing* (London: Heinemann, 1973), pp. 33–52.

'A writer's freedom', *New Classic*, no. 2 (1975), pp. 11–16.

'A writer's freedom' (new version), paper presented at the Durban Indian Teachers' Conference, December 1975 (typescript), pp. 1–10.

'English-language literature and politics in South Africa', in Christopher Heywood (ed.), *Aspects of South African Literature* (London: Heinemann, 1976), pp. 99–120.

'From apartheid to Afrocentrism', *South African Outlook*, December 1977, pp. 181–3.

'A brilliant bigot', review of *Sarah Gertrude Millin*, by Martin Rubin, *The Times Literary Supplement*, 15 September 1978.

'Relevance and commitment', paper presented at a conference on The State of Art in South Africa, Cape Town, July 1979, and in a slightly different version at the Radcliffe Forum, Harvard University, October 1979 (typescript), pp. 1–14. Published as 'Apprentices of freedom', the text of the Neil Gunn Fellowship Lecture, Edinburgh 1981, *New Society*, 24–31 December 1981, pp. ii–v.

'The prison-house of colonialism', review of *Olive Schreiner: A Biography*, by Ruth First and Ann Scott, *The Times Literary Supplement*, 15 August 1980.

'The essential gesture: writers and responsibility', in Sterling M. McMurrin (ed.), *The Tanner Lectures on Human Values*, VI (Salt Lake City, Utah: University of Utah Press; Cambridge: Cambridge University Press, 1985), pp. 1–19 and *Granta*, no. 15 (Spring 1985), pp. 135–51.

(c) POLITICAL AND HISTORICAL COMMENTARY

'Where do whites fit in?', *The Twentieth Century*, April 1959, pp. 326–31.

'Great problems in the street', in Marion Friedmann (ed.), *I Will Still Be Moved* (London: Barker, 1963), pp. 117–22.

'Why must the door be shut in his face?', *Rand Daily Mail* (Johannesburg), 24 September 1964 (on the refusal of a passport to Nat Nakasa).

Foreword to Cosmas Desmond, OFM, *The Discarded People* (Harmondsworth: Penguin, 1971).

'Speak out: the necessity for protest', the sixth E. G. Malherbe Academic Freedom Lecture, delivered at the University of Natal, 11 August 1971 (Durban: Academic Freedom Committee, University of Natal, 1971).

'A letter from Johannesburg' (long version), (typescript), pp. 1–19. Published as 'Letter from South Africa', *New York Review of Books*, 9 December 1976, pp. 3–4, 6, 8–9.

'What being a South African means to me', *South African Outlook*, June 1977, pp. 87–9, 92.

Orientation week address, delivered at the University of the Witwatersrand, 8 February 1982 (typescript), pp. 1–11.

'Living in the interregnum', *New York Review of Books*, 20 January 1983, pp. 21–2, 24–9.

(d) ON CENSORSHIP

'Censored, banned, gagged: letter from Johannesburg', *Encounter*, June 1963, pp. 59–63.

'The voices we may not hear', *Rand Daily Mail* (Johannesburg), 13 August 1966, rpt as 'How not to know the African', *Contrast*, no. 15 (March 1967), pp. 44–9.

'South Africa: towards a desk drawer literature', *The Classic*, vol. 2, no. 4 (1968), pp. 64–74.

'Apartheid and censorship', in Jonathan Paton (ed.), *The Grey Ones* (Johannesburg: Ravan, 1974).

'Catalogue of the ridiculous', *The Times*, 2 July 1975, p. 11.

'South Africa: the way writers live now' (typescript, incomplete; after 1975), pp. 1–6.

With John Dugard, Richard Smith, Director of Publications, Publications Appeal Board, The Press, *What Happened to 'Burger's Daughter', or How South African Censorship Works* (Johannesburg: Taurus, 1980).

Address to the CNA Award Dinner, 17 April 1980 (typescript), pp. 1–7.

Address to a conference on Censorship, University of Cape Town, April 1980 (typescript), pp. 1–14.

(e) LOCAL ENVIRONMENT AND TRAVEL

'Hassan in America', *The Forum*, February 1955, pp. 13–19.

'Johannesburg', *Holiday*, August 1955, pp. 46, 49–50, 57–9.

'South African Riviera', *Holiday*, December 1957, pp. 166, 168, 171.

'Egypt revisited', *National and English Review*, January 1959, pp. 47–53.

'Apartheid', *Holiday*, 25 April 1959, pp. 94–5, 133.

'Africa 1960: the great period' (typescript, incomplete; *c.* 1960–1), pp. 1–21.

'Towards the heart of darkness' (typescript; *c.* 1961), pp. 1–19.

'The Congo River', *Holiday*, May 1961, pp. 74–9, 88, 92, 97–103.

'A time and tailings', *Optima*, March 1968, pp. 22–3, 25–6; rpt as 'The Witwatersrand: a time and tailings', in *On The Mines*, with David Goldblatt (Cape Town: Struik, 1973).

'No place like home: Johannesburg' (typescript), pp. 1–29; *Geo*, August 1979, pp. 116–41.

(f) BIOGRAPHICAL AND AUTOBIOGRAPHICAL

'A South African childhood: allusions in a landscape', *New Yorker*, 16 October 1954, pp. 111–29; in typescript form as 'A South African childhood', pp. 1–19 and additional pp. 1–5.

'Chief Luthuli', Bulletin Biography no. 1, *Treason Trial Bulletin*, no. 2 (issued by Treason Trials Defence Fund, Johannesburg, May 1958), pp. 4–6.

'Chief Luthuli', *Atlantic Monthly*, April 1959, pp. 34–9.

'Leaving school – II', *London Magazine*, May 1963, pp. 58–65.

'One man living through it', *The Classic,* vol. 2, no. 1 (1966), pp. 11–16. On Nat Nakasa.

'The Fischer case', *London Magazine*, March 1966, pp. 21–30.

'Why did Bram Fischer choose jail?', *New York Times Magazine*, 14 August 1966, pp. 30–1, 80–1, 84; in typescript form as 'Profile: Abram Fischer', pp. 1–13.

'Don Mattera' (typescript; *c.* 1973), pp. 1–16.

Foreword to *Ukubamba Amadolo*, by Bettie du Toit (London: Onyx Press, 1978). On Bettie du Toit.

'An unkillable rabbit family', *Contrast*, no. 50 (December 1980), pp. 25–6. On Gordimer's early publications.

(g) LETTERS

'A sestiger for the 70s', open letter to André Brink, *Star* (Johannesburg), 17 January 1969.

'Far-off land of the white man', letter to the *Star* (Johannesburg), 22 March 1972.

'Gordimer vs Paton', *Sunday Times* (Johannesburg), 22 December 1974, including an open letter by Nadine Gordimer to Alan Paton.

Personal correspondence from Nadine Gordimer, 27 June 1979.

'Facts and interpretation', letter to *African Communist*, 3rd Quarter 1980, p. 109.

Personal correspondence from Nadine Gordimer, 23 August 1981.

(2) *Material relating to Nadine Gordimer*

All material in this section and sections following has been arranged alphabetically by author or title, thereafter chronologically.

(a) INTERVIEWS WITH NADINE GORDIMER

Boyers, R., Blaise, C., Diggory, T. and Elgrably, J., 'A conversation with Nadine Gordimer', *Salmagundi*, no. 62 (Winter 1984), pp. 3–31.

Clingman, S., interview with Nadine Gordimer, Johannesburg, 17 March 1980.

Dalglish, C., 'The writers who are hardest hit', *Rand Daily Mail* (Johannesburg), 3 May 1978.

Ellis, N. W., 'In black and white', *Harpers and Queen*, November 1978, pp. 296–8.

Gray, S. and du Plessis, P., 'Nadine Gordimer interviewed', *New Nation*, September 1972, pp. 2–5.

Hurwitt, J., 'The art of fiction LXXVII', *Paris Review*, no. 88 (Summer 1983), pp. 82–127.

Loercher, D., 'South African political novelist Nadine Gordimer: "I know I have not been brave enough" ', *Christian Science Monitor*, 21 January 1980, p. 21.

The Man on the Reef, 'But Johannesburg sees itself in her book', *Star* (Johannesburg), 11 July 1958.

Ratcliffe, M., 'A South African radical exulting in life's chaotic variety', *The Times*, 29 November 1974.

Sachs, B., interview with Nadine Gordimer, in *The Road From Sharpeville* (London: Dobson, 1961), pp. 172–5.

Schwartz, P., 'Interview – Nadine Gordimer', in *New South African Writing* (Johannesburg: Lorton, 1977), pp. 74–81.

Schwartz, P., 'Gordimer still clings to a sense of wonder', *Rand Daily Mail* (Johannesburg), 24 July 1981, p. 11.

Stott, C., 'I must stay and fight', interview with Nadine Gordimer, *Star* (Johannesburg), 13 June 1969.

Tetteh-Larty, A., interview with Nadine Gordimer, BBC African Service, *Arts and Africa*, no. 183 (transcript, n.d.; after 1976), pp. 1–6.

'A writer is always writing the same story', *Rand Daily Mail* (Johannesburg), 27 July 1972.

(b)   BOOKS AND ARTICLES ON NADINE GORDIMER

Abrahams, L., 'Nadine Gordimer: the transparent ego', *English Studies in Africa*, vol. 3, no. 2 (September 1960), pp. 146–51.

Abramovitz, A., 'Nadine Gordimer and the impertinent reader', *Purple Renoster*, no. 1 (September 1960), pp. 13–17.

Daymond, M., *'Burger's Daughter*: a novel's reliance on history', in M. J. Daymond, J. U. Jacobs and M. Lenta (eds.), *Momentum* (Pietermaritzburg: University of Natal Press, 1984).

De Koker, B., 'The short stories and novels of Nadine Gordimer: a critical study', MA thesis, Potchefstroom University, n.d.

Delius, A., 'The next instalment', *Standpunte*, 31 March 1954, pp. 66–71.

Goodheart, E., 'The claustral world of Nadine Gordimer', *Salmagundi*, no. 62 (Winter 1984), pp. 108–17.

Green, R., 'Nadine Gordimer's *A World of Strangers*: strains in South African liberalism', *English Studies in Africa*, vol. 22, no. 1 (March 1979), pp. 45–53.

Green, R., 'Nadine Gordimer's *Burger's Daughter*', paper presented at a conference on Literature and Society in Southern Africa, University of York, September 1981.

Haugh, R. F., *Nadine Gordimer* (New York: Twayne, 1974).

Hope, C., 'Out of the picture: the novels of Nadine Gordimer', *London Magazine*, April/May 1975, pp. 49–55.

JanMohamed, A. R., *Manichean Aesthetics: The Politics of Literature in Colonial Africa* (Amherst, Mass.: University of Massachusetts Press, 1983), chapter 4.

Laredo, U., 'African mosaic: the novels of Nadine Gordimer', *Journal of Commonwealth Literature*, vol. 8, no. 1 (June 1973), pp. 42–53.

Lomberg, A., 'Withering into the truth: the romantic realism of Nadine Gordimer', *English in Africa*, vol. 3, no. 1 (March 1976), pp. 1–12.

Nell, R. J. (comp.), 'Nadine Gordimer: novelist and short story writer', a bibliography of her works and selected literary criticism, University of the Witwatersrand, 1964.

Newman, J., 'Gordimer's *The Conservationist*: "that book of unknown signs" ', *Critique: Studies in Modern Fiction*, vol. 22, no. 3 (April 1981), pp. 31–44.

Newman, J., 'Prospero's complex: race and sex in *Burger's Daughter*', *Journal of Commonwealth Literature*, vol. 20, no. 1 (September 1985), pp. 81–99.

Ogungbesan, K., 'The way out of South Africa: Nadine Gordimer's *The Lying Days*', *Theoria*, vol. 49, no. 49 (October 1977), pp. 45–59.

Ogungbesan, K., 'Nadine Gordimer's *The Late Bourgeois World*: love in prison', *Ariel*, vol. 9, no. 1 (January 1978), pp. 31–49.

Parker, K., 'Nadine Gordimer and the pitfalls of liberalism', in K. Parker (ed.), *The South African Novel in English: Essays in Criticism and Society* (London: Macmillan, 1978), pp. 114–30.

Roloff, B. J., 'Nadine Gordimer: South African novelist and short story writer', MA thesis, University of Texas, 1962.

Smith, R., 'Masters and servants: Nadine Gordimer's *July's People* and the themes of her fiction', *Salmagundi*, no. 62 (Winter 1984), pp. 93–107.

Van Donge, J. K., 'Nadine Gordimer's *A Guest of Honour*: a failure to understand Zambian society', *Journal of Southern African Studies*, vol. 9, no. 1 (October 1982), pp. 74–92.

Wade, M., *Nadine Gordimer* (London: Evans, 1978).

Wade, M., 'Nadine Gordimer and Europe-in-Africa', in K. Parker (ed.), *The South African Novel in English: Essays in Criticism and Society* (London: Macmillan, 1978), pp. 131–63.

Woodward, A., 'Nadine Gordimer', *Theoria* (South Africa), no. 16 (1961), pp. 1–12.

(c) REVIEWS CONSULTED IN:

African Communist
Contrast
Guardian (London/Manchester)
Journal of Commonwealth Literature
Journal of Southern African Studies
London Review of Books
New Society
New Statesman
New York Review of Books
Observer (London)
Quarto
Rand Daily Mail (Johannesburg)
Sunday Times (London)
The Times (London)
The Times Literary Supplement

(d) NEWSPAPERS CONSULTED

Guardian Weekly (London/Manchester)
Rand Daily Mail (Johannesburg)
Star (Johannesburg)
Sunday Express (Johannesburg)
Sunday Times (Johannesburg)
Vaderland (Johannesburg)
Weekly Mail (Johannesburg)

(e) OTHER INTERVIEWS

Abrahams, L., Johannesburg, 25 April 1980.
Bizos, G., Johannesburg, 29 April 1980.
du Toit, B., London, 12 February 1981.
Joseph, H., Johannesburg, 23 April 1980.
Mphahlele, E., Johannesburg, 1 May 1980.
Sampson, A., London, 27 November 1980.

(3) *South African History*

Including social history, memoirs and autobiographies of the period.

Abrahams, P., *Return to Goli* (London: Faber, 1953).

Abrahams, P., *Tell Freedom* (London: Faber, 1954).

Adam, H., *Modernizing Racial Domination* (Berkeley, Calif.: University of California Press, 1971).

Beinart, W. and Bundy, C., 'State intervention and rural resistance: the Transkei, 1900–1965', in Martin A. Klein (ed.), *Peasants in Africa: Historical and Contemporary Perspectives* (Beverly Hills, Calif.: Sage, 1980).

Benson, M., *South Africa: The Struggle for a Birthright* (Harmondsworth: Penguin, 1966).

Benson, M. (ed.), *The Sun Will Rise: Statements from the Dock by Southern African Political Prisoners*, rev. and enl. edn (London: International Defence and Aid Fund for Southern Africa, 1981).

Bernstein, H., *The World That Was Ours* (London: Heinemann, 1967).

Bienefeld, M. and Innes, D., 'Capital accumulation and South Africa', *Review of African Political Economy*, no. 7 (September–December 1976).

Biko, S., 'White racism and Black Consciousness', in H. W. Van Der Merwe and D. Welsh (eds.), *Student Perspectives on South Africa* (Cape Town: Philip, 1972), pp. 190–202.

Biko, S., *I Write What I Like*, ed. A. Stubbs, CR (1978; London: Heinemann, 1979).

Blaxall, A., *Suspended Sentence* (London: Hodder & Stoughton, 1965).

Blumberg, M., *White Madam* (London: Gollancz, 1962).

Bunting, B., *The Rise of the South African Reich* (Harmondsworth: Penguin, 1964).

Callaway, the Rev. Canon H., MD, *The Religious System of the Amazulu* (Springvale, Natal: John A. Blair; Pietermaritzburg: Davis & Sons; Cape Town: J. C. Juta; London: Trübner; 1868).

Carlson, J., *No Neutral Ground* (London: Quartet, 1977).

Coplan, D., 'The African musician and the development of the Johannesburg entertainment industry, 1900–1960', *Journal of Southern African Studies*, vol. 5, no. 2 (April, 1979), pp. 135–64.

Davidson, B., Slovo, J. and Wilkinson, A. R., *Southern Africa: The New Politics of Revolution* (Harmondsworth: Penguin, 1976).

Davis, J. A. and Baker, J. K., *Southern Africa in Transition* (London: Pall Mall, 1966).

Desmond, C., OFM, *The Discarded People: An Account of Resettlement in South Africa*, preface by Lord Caradon, foreword by Nadine Gordimer (Harmondsworth: Penguin, 1971).

Driver, C. J., *Patrick Duncan: South African and Pan-African* (London: Heinemann, 1980).

Duncan, P., *South Africa's Rule of Violence* (London: Methuen, 1964).

du Toit, B., *Ukubamba Amadolo*, foreword by Nadine Gordimer (London: Onyx, 1978).

Feit, E., *Urban Revolt in South Africa 1960–1964* (Evanston, IL: Northwestern University Press, 1971).

Fighting Talk, available issues September 1943 to February 1963.

First, R., *One Hundred and Seventeen Days* (Harmondsworth: Penguin, 1965).

Forman, L. and Sachs, E. S., *The South African Treason Trial* (London: Calder, 1957).

Bibliography

Bibliography

Friedmann, M. (ed.), *I Will Still Be Moved* (London: Barker, 1963).

Gerhart, G. M., *Black Power in South Africa: The Evolution of an Ideology* (Berkeley, Calif.: University of California Press, 1978).

Hindson, D., 'The role of the labour bureaux in South Africa: a critique of the Riekert Commission report', in D. C. Hindson (ed.), *Working Papers in Southern African Studies*, Vol. 3 (Johannesburg: Ravan, 1983).

Hirson, B., *Year of Fire, Year of Ash – the Soweto Revolt: Roots of a Revolution?* (London: Zed Press, 1979).

Hooper, C., *Brief Authority* (London: Collins, 1960).

Hopkinson, T., *In the Fiery Continent* (London: Gollancz, 1962).

Houghton, D. H., *The South African Economy*, 3rd edn (Cape Town: Oxford University Press, 1973).

Huddleston, Fr T., CR, *Naught for Your Comfort* (London: Collins, 1956).

Hutchinson, A., *Road to Ghana* (London: Gollancz, 1960).

Innes, D. and O'Meara, D., 'Class formation and ideology: the Transkei region', *Review of African Political Economy*, no. 7 (September–December 1976).

Johnstone, F. A., 'White prosperity and white supremacy in South Africa today', *African Affairs*, vol. 69, no. 275 (April 1970), pp. 124–40.

Joseph, H., *If This Be Treason* (London: Deutsch, 1963).

Joseph, H., *Tomorrow's Sun* (London: Hutchinson, 1966).

Kane-Berman, J., *South Africa: The Method in the Madness* (London: Pluto, 1979).

Kantor, J., *A Healthy Grave* (London: Hamish Hamilton, 1967).

Karis, T. and Carter, G. M. (eds.), *From Protest to Challenge: A Documentary History of African Politics in South Africa 1882–1964*, 4 vols. (Stanford, Calif.: Hoover Institution Press, 1972–7), Vol. 2, *Hope and Challenge 1935–52* (1973), Vol. 3, *Challenge and Violence 1953–64* (1977).

Kuper, L., *Passive Resistance in South Africa* (London: Cape, 1956).

Legassick, M., 'South Africa: capital accumulation and violence', *Economy and Society*, vol. 3, no. 3 (August 1974), pp. 253–91.

Legassick, M., 'Legislation, ideology and economy in post-1948 South Africa', *Journal of Southern African Studies*, vol. 1, no. 1 (October 1974), pp. 5–35.

Legassick, M. and Wolpe, H., 'The Bantustans and capital accumulation in South Africa', *Review of African Political Economy*, no. 7 (September–December 1976).

Lewin, H., *Bandiet* (London: Barrie & Jenkins, 1974).

Lodge, T., *Black Politics in South Africa Since 1945* (London: Longman, 1983).

Luckhardt, K. and Wall, B., *Organize ... or Starve! The History of the South African Congress of Trade Unions* (London: Lawrence & Wishart, 1980).

Luthuli, A., *Let My People Go* (1962; Glasgow: Fontana, 1963).

Mandela, N., *No Easy Walk to Freedom*, ed. with a new foreword by Ruth First (1965; London: Heinemann, 1973).

Matshikiza, T., *Chocolates for My Wife* (London: Hodder & Stoughton, 1961).

Mbeki, G., *South Africa: The Peasants' Revolt* (Harmondsworth: Penguin, 1964).

Modisane, B., *Blame Me on History* (London: Thames & Hudson, 1963).

Mokgatle, N., *The Autobiography of an Unknown South African* (London: Hurst, 1971).

Mphahlele, E., *Down Second Avenue* (1959; London: Faber, 1971).

Ngubane, J. K., *An African Explains Apartheid* (London: Pall Mall, 1963).

Nkosi, L., *Home and Exile* (London: Longman, 1965).

Nkosi, L., 'Obituary', in Can Themba, *The Will to Die*, writings selected by Donald Stuart and Roy Holland (London: Heinemann, 1972; rpt, 1976), pp. vii–xi.

Pityana, B., 'Power and social change in South Africa', in H. W. Van Der Merwe and D. Welsh (eds.), *Student Perspectives on South Africa* (Cape Town: Philip, 1972), pp 174–89.

Reeves, A., *Shooting at Sharpeville* (London: Gollancz, 1960).

Robertson, J., *Liberalism in South Africa 1948–63* (Oxford: Clarendon Press, 1971).

Roux, E., *Time Longer Than Rope* (Madison, Wis.: University of Wisconsin Press, 1972).

Roux, E. and Roux, W., *Rebel Pity: The Life of Eddie Roux* (London: Collings, 1970).

Sachs, B., *South African Personalities and Places* (Johannesburg: Kayor, 1959).

Sachs, B., *The Road From Sharpeville* (London: Dobson, 1961).

Sampson, A., *'Drum': A Venture into the New Africa* (London: Collins, 1956).

Sampson, A., *The Treason Cage: The Opposition on Trial in South Africa* (London: Heinemann, 1958).

Segal, R., *Into Exile* (London: Cape, 1963).

Simons, H. J. and Simons, R. E., *Class and Colour in South Africa 1850–1950* (Harmondsworth: Penguin, 1969).

South African Congress of Democrats, 'Educating for ignorance', pamphlet (Johannesburg, n.d.), pp. 1–12.

Stanton, H., *Go Well, Stay Well* (London: Hodder & Stoughton, 1961).

A Survey of Race Relations in South Africa, 1951–1977 (Johannesburg: South African Institute of Race Relations), compiled annually by M. Horrell, except:

1963 comp. M. Horrell and M. Draper;
1971 comp. M. Horrell, D. Horner and J. Kane-Berman;
1972 comp. M. Horrell, D. Horner, J. Kane-Berman and R. Margo;
1973 comp. M. Horrell and D. Horner;
1974 comp. M. Horrell, D. Horner and J. Hudson;
1975 comp. M. Horrell and T. Hodgson;
1976 comp. M. Horrell, T. Hodgson, S. Blignaut and S. Moroney;
1977 comp. L. Gordon, S. Blignaut, S. Moroney and C. Cooper;
also: *1983* comp. C. Cooper, S. Motala, J. Shindler, C. McCaul and T. Ratsomo.

Tatz, C. M., *Shadow and Substance in South Africa* (Pietermaritzburg: University of Natal Press, 1962).

Trapido, S., 'South Africa in a comparative study of industrialization', *Journal of Development Studies*, vol. 7, no. 3 (April 1971), pp. 309–19.

Turok, B., 'South Africa: the violent alternative' in R. Milliband and J. Savile (eds.), *The Socialist Register 1972* (London: Merlin Press, 1972).

Verwoerd, H. F., 'The price of appeasement in Africa', pamphlet of speech in the House of Assembly, 10 March 1960, pp. 1–8.

Walshe, P., *The Rise of African Nationalism in South Africa* (London: Hurst, 1970).

Wilson, M. and Thompson, L. M. (eds.), *The Oxford History of South Africa*, 2 vols. (Oxford: Oxford University Press, 1969–71), Vol. 2, *South Africa 1870–1966*.

Wolpe, H., 'Capitalism and cheap labour power in South Africa: from segregation to apartheid', *Economy and Society*, vol. 1, no. 4 (November 1972), pp. 425–56.

Woods, D., *Biko* (London: Paddington Press, 1978).

(4)   *Select South African Fiction and Criticism*

Abrahams, P., *Dark Testament* (London: Allen & Unwin, 1942).

Abrahams, P., *Song of the City* (London: Dorothy Crisp, 1944).

Abrahams, P., *Mine Boy* (1946; London: Heinemann, 1976).

Abrahams, P., *Wild Conquest* (London: Faber, 1951).

Abrahams, P., *The Path of Thunder* (London: Faber, 1952).

Benson, M., *At the Still Point* (London: Chatto & Windus, 1971).

Bloom, H., *Episode* (London: Collins, 1956).

Bloom, H. and Williams, P., *King Kong* (London: Collins, 1961).

Bosman, H. C., *Bosman at his Best* – a choice of stories and sketches culled by Lionel Abrahams (Cape Town and Pretoria: Human & Rousseau, 1969).

Brink, A., *Looking on Darkness* (London: W. H. Allen, 1974).

Brink, A., *Rumours of Rain* (London: W. H. Allen, 1978).

Brink, A., *A Dry White Season* (London: W. H. Allen, 1979).

Coetzee, J. M., *Dusklands* (Johannesburg: Ravan, 1974).

Coetzee, J. M., *In the Heart of the Country* (Johannesburg: Ravan, 1978).

Coetzee, J. M., 'Blood, flaw, taint, degeneration: the case of Sarah Gertrude Millin', *English Studies in Africa*, vol. 23, no. 1 (March 1980), pp. 41–58.

Coetzee, J. M., *Waiting for the Barbarians* (1980; Harmondsworth: Penguin, 1982).

Cooke, J., 'The novels of Nadine Gordimer', PhD dissertation, Northwestern University, 1976.

Cooke, J., ' "A hunger of the soul": *Too Late the Phalarope* reconsidered', *English Studies in Africa*, vol. 22, no. 1 (March 1979), pp. 37–44.

Cope, J., *The Dawn Comes Twice* (London: Heinemann, 1969).

Driver, C. J., *Elegy for a Revolutionary* (London: Faber, 1969).

First, R. and Scott, A., *Olive Schreiner* (London: Deutsch, 1980).

Gray, S., *Southern African Literature: An Introduction* (Cape Town: Philip; London: Collings; 1979).

Heywood, C. (ed.), *Aspects of South African Literature* (London: Heinemann, 1976).

Jacobson, D., *The Trap* and *A Dance in the Sun* (1955, 1956; Harmondsworth: Penguin, 1968).

Jacobson, D., *The Evidence of Love* (London: Weidenfeld & Nicolson, 1960; rev. edn, London: Chatto & Windus, 1970).

Klima, V., *South African Prose Writing in English* (Prague: Czechoslovak Academy of Sciences, 1971).

La Guma, A., *A Walk in the Night and Other Stories* (1962, 1967; London: Heinemann, 1968).

La Guma, A., *And a Threefold Cord*, introduction by Brian Bunting (Berlin: Seven Seas, 1964).

La Guma, A., *The Stone Country* (1967; London: Heinemann, 1974).

La Guma, A., *In the Fog of the Seasons' End* (London: Heinemann, 1972; rpt, 1977).

La Guma, A., *Time of the Butcherbird* (London: Heinemann, 1979).

Millin, S. G., *God's Step-Children* (London: Constable, 1924).

Mphahlele, E., *The African Image* (1962; rev. edn, London: Faber, 1974).

Mphahlele, E., *In Corner B* (Nairobi: East African Publishing House, 1967).

Mphahlele, E., *Voices in the Whirlwind* (London: Macmillan, 1973).

Bibliography

Mphahlele, E., *Chirundu* (Johannesburg: Ravan, 1979).

Mzamane, M. V., *The Children of Soweto* (London: Longman, 1982).

Nakasa, N., *The World of Nat Nakasa*, ed. Essop Patel, introduction by Nadine Gordimer (Johannesburg: Ravan/Bateleur, 1975).

Nkosi, L., *The Rhythm of Violence* (London: Oxford University Press, 1964).

Nkosi, L., 'South Africa: literature of protest', in H. Kitchen (ed.), *A Handbook of African Affairs* (London: Pall Mall, 1964).

Parker, K. (ed.), *The South African Novel in English: Essays in Criticism and Society* (London: Macmillan, 1978).

Paton, A., *Cry, the Beloved Country* (London: Cape, 1948; Harmondsworth: Penguin, 1958).

Paton, A., *Too Late the Phalarope* (London: Cape, 1955; Harmondsworth: Penguin, 1971).

Paton, J. (ed.), *The Grey Ones* (Johannesburg: Ravan, 1974).

Pechey, G., '*The Story of an African Farm*: colonial history and the discontinuous text', *Critical Arts*, vol. 3, no. 1 (1983), pp. 65–78.

Plaatje, S. T., *Mhudi: An Epic of South African Native Life a Hundred Years Ago* (1930; rpt, with introduction by Tim Couzens, London: Heinemann, 1978).

Plomer, W., *Turbott Wolfe* (London: Hogarth Press, 1925).

Rabkin, D., 'La Guma and reality in South Africa', *Journal of Commonwealth Literature*, vol. 8, no. 1 (June 1973), pp. 54–61.

Rabkin, D., 'Ways of looking: origins of the novel in South Africa', *Journal of Commonwealth Literature*, vol. 13, no. 1 (August 1978), pp. 27–44.

Rive, R., *Emergency* (London: Faber, 1964).

Rive, R., La Guma, A., Matthews, J. and Wannenburgh, A., *Quartet*, ed. R. Rive (1963; London: Heinemann, 1965).

Schoeman, K., *Promised Land*, trans. Marion V. Friedmann (London: Julian Friedmann, 1978).

Schreiner, O. (pseud. Ralph Iron), *The Story of an African Farm*, 2 vols. (London: Chapman & Hall, 1883); 2nd edn, with preface by author (London: Chapman & Hall, 1887); rpt, with introduction by Dan Jacobson (Harmondsworth: Penguin, 1971).

Serote, M., *To Every Birth its Blood* (Johannesburg: Ravan, 1981).

Smith, P., *The Beadle* (1926; rpt, Cape Town: Balkema, 1979).

Snyman, J. P. L., *The South African Novel in English, 1880–1930* (Potchefstroom: University of Potchefstroom, 1952).

Themba, C., *The Will to Die*, writings selected by Donald Stuart and Roy Holland (London: Heinemann, 1972; rpt, 1976).

Tlali, M., *Amandla* (Johannesburg: Ravan, 1980).

van der Post, L., *In a Province* (London: Hogarth Press, 1934).

Vaughan, M., 'Literature and politics: currents in South African writing in the seventies', *Journal of Southern African Studies*, vol. 9, no. 1 (October 1982), pp. 118–38.

Zwelonke, D. M., *Robben Island* (London: Heinemann, 1973).

(5) *African Literary Criticism; General Literary Theory and Criticism; Other Works*

Barthes, R., *Writing Degree Zero*, trans. A. Lavers and C. Smith (London: Cape, 1967).

Barthes, R., *S/Z*, trans. R. Miller (London: Cape, 1975).

Bayley, J., *Tolstoy and the Novel* (London: Chatto & Windus, 1966).

Benjamin, W., *Illuminations*, ed. with introduction by H. Arendt, trans. H. Zohn (London: Cape, 1970; Glasgow: Fontana, 1973).

Bennett, T., *Formalism and Marxism* (London: Methuen, 1979).

Bloch, E., Lukács, G., Brecht, B., Benjamin, W. and Adorno, T., *Aesthetics and Politics*, afterword by F. Jameson (1977; London: Verso, 1980).

Duerden, D. and Pieterse, C. (eds.), *African Writers Talking* (London: Heinemann, 1972).

Eagleton, T., *Marxism and Literary Criticism* (London: Methuen, 1976).

Eagleton, T., *Criticism and Ideology* (1976; London: Verso, 1978).

Eagleton, T., *Walter Benjamin, or Towards a Revolutionary Criticism* (London: Verso, 1981).

Fanon, F., *The Wretched of the Earth*, preface by J.-P. Sartre, trans. C. Farrington (1965; Harmondsworth: Penguin, 1967).

Fanon, F., *Toward the African Revolution*, trans. H. Chevalier (New York: Grove, 1967).

Fanon, F., *Black Skin White Masks*, trans. C. L. Markmann (1968; London: Paladin, 1970).

Freud, S., *The Interpretation of Dreams*, Pelican Freud Library, Vol. 4, ed. A. Richards, trans. J. Strachey (Harmondsworth: Penguin, 1976).

Goldmann, L., *The Hidden God*, trans. P. Thody (1964; London: Routledge & Kegan Paul, 1976).

Goldmann, L., 'Structure: human reality and methodological concept', in R. Macksey and E. Donato (eds.), *The Languages of Criticism and the Sciences of Man* (Baltimore: Johns Hopkins Press, 1970).

Goldmann, L., *Towards a Sociology of the Novel*, trans. A. Sheridan (London: Tavistock, 1975).

Gramsci, A., *Prison Notebooks*, ed. and trans. Q. Hoare and G. Nowell Smith (London: Lawrence & Wishart, 1971).

Hegel, G. W. F., *Aesthetics: Lectures on Fine Art*, 2 vols., trans. T. M. Knox (Oxford: Clarendon Press, 1975).

Heywood, C. (ed.), *Perspectives on African Literature* (London: Heinemann, 1971).

Jahn, J., *A History of Neo-African Literature* (London: Faber, 1966).

Jameson, F., *Marxism and Form: Twentieth-Century Dialectical Theories of Literature* (Princeton, NJ: Princeton University Press, 1971).

Jameson, F., *The Political Unconscious: Narrative as a Socially Symbolic Act* (London: Methuen, 1981).

Killam, G. D. (ed.), *African Writers on African Writing* (London: Heinemann, 1973).

Lévi-Strauss, C., *Tristes Tropiques*, trans. J. and D. Weightman (1973; Harmondsworth: Penguin, 1976).

Lukács, G., *Studies in European Realism*, trans. E. Bone (1950; London: Merlin Press, 1972).

Lukács, G., *The Historical Novel*, trans. H. and S. Mitchell (1962; Harmondsworth: Penguin, 1969).

Lukács, G., *The Meaning of Contemporary Realism*, trans. J. and N. Mander (London: Merlin Press, 1963).

Macherey, P., *A Theory of Literary Production*, trans. G. Wall (1966; London: Routledge & Kegan Paul, 1978).

Maes-Jelinek, H. (ed.), *Commonwealth Literature and the Modern World* (Brussels: Didier, 1975).

Mahood, M., *The Colonial Encounter* (London: Collings, 1977).

Mannoni, O., *Prospero and Caliban: The Psychology of Colonization*, trans. Pamela Powesland (London: Methuen, 1956).

Marx, K., and Engels, F., *On Literature and Art* (Moscow: Progress Publishers, 1976).

Nkosi, L., *Tasks and Masks: Themes and Styles of African Literature* (London: Longman, 1981).

Pieterse, C. and Munro, D. (eds.), *Protest and Conflict in African Literature* (London: Heinemann, 1969).

Sartre, J.-P., *What is Literature?*, trans. B. Frechtman, introduction by D. Caute (London: Methuen, 1967).

Wästberg, P. (ed.), *The Writer in Modern Africa* (Uppsala: Nordiska Afrikainstitutet, 1968).

Watt, I., *The Rise of the Novel* (1957; Harmondsworth: Penguin, 1972).

Weil, S., *The Need for Roots: Prelude to a Declaration of Duties Towards Mankind*, trans. A. F. Wills (London: Routledge & Kegan Paul, 1952).

White, L., 'Power and the praise poem', *Journal of Southern African Studies*, vol. 9, no. 1 (October 1982), pp. 8–32.

Williams, R., *Marxism and Literature* (Oxford: Oxford University Press, 1977).

Wright, E. (ed.), *The Critical Evaluation of African Literature* (London: Heinemann, 1973).

Index

Index